Love and Loss

Loving and grieving are two sides of the same coin: we cannot have one without risking the other. Only by understanding the nature and pattern of loving can we begin to understand the problems of grieving. Conversely, the loss of a loved person can teach us much about the nature of love.

Love and Loss, the result of a lifetime's work, has important implications for the study of attachment and bereavement. In this volume, Colin Murray Parkes reports his innovative research that enables us to bring together knowledge of childhood attachments and problems of bereavement, resulting in a new way of thinking about love, bereavement and other losses. Areas covered include:

- Patterns of attachment and patterns of grief
- Loss of a parent, child or spouse in adult life
- Social isolation and support

The book concludes by looking at disorders of attachment and considering bereavement in terms of its implications on love, loss, and change in a wider context.

Illuminating the structure and focus of thinking about love and loss, this book sheds light on a wide range of psychological issues. It will be essential reading for all those working with bereavement, as well as graduate students of psychology, psychiatry, and sociology.

Colin Murray Parkes is a psychiatrist, researcher and author. He has contributed to and edited numerous books and articles on the nature of human attachments and loss. His *Bereavement: Studies of Grief in Adult Life*, first published in 1972 and now in its third edition, remains a classic. He has been a consultant psychiatrist at St Christopher's Hospice since 1966, and is Life President of Cruse Bereavement Care. In 1996 he was awarded an OBE for services to bereaved people.

Love and Loss

The Roots of Grief and its Complications

Colin Murray Parkes

Routledge
Taylor & Francis Group

LONDON AND NEW YORK

First published 2006 by Routledge
27 Church Road, Hove, East Sussex BN3 2FA

Simultaneously published in the USA and Canada
by Taylor and Francis Inc
270 Madison Avenue, New York, NY 10016

Reprinted 2006

Routledge is an imprint of the Taylor and Francis Group, an informa business

Typeset in Garamond Three by
RefineCatch Limited, Bungay, Suffolk
Printed and bound in Great Britain by
TJ International Ltd, Padstow, Cornwall

British Library Cataloguing in Publication Data
A catalogue record for this book is available from the British Library

Library of Congress Cataloging-in-Publication Data
Parkes, Colin Murray.
  Love and loss : the roots of grief and its complications / Colin
Murray Parkes.
    p. ; cm.
  Includes bibliographical references and index.
  ISBN 0–415–39041–9
1. Bereavement – Psychological aspects. 2. Grief. 3. Loss
(Psychology) 4. Attachment behavior. 5. Love.
  [DNLM: 1. Object Attachment. 2. Bereavement. 3. Love.
WM460.5.O2 P245L 2006] I. Title.
  BF575.G7P374 2006
  155.9′37 – dc22
                                    2005024406

ISBN 13: 978–0–415–39041–5

ISBN 10: 0–415–39041–9

To Patricia Margaret Parkes, the sole object of my romantic attachment and main source of my security.

Contents

Figures

Tables

Acknowledgements

Bereavements are sad and those that cause people to seek for psychiatric help more so. Many of the people who helped with this research were facing the worst crisis in their lives, yet they agreed to fill in a long and disturbing questionnaire and trusted us not to misuse it. I suspect that they did this in the hope that others would learn from their suffering and by doing so reduce the suffering of others. We owe them a debt of gratitude.

Sue Knott carried much of the graft of typing, sending out and retrieving the questionnaires. She and her colleagues at St Clement's Hospital also spent many hours retrieving case notes from the dusty record stores, even after I had retired from clinical practice. Duncan Cramer and Julian Holmes gave invaluable help with the statistics.

In my experience some of the most important findings in any research are the ones that fail to meet one's expectations. My friend Margaret Stroebe sent me detailed criticisms of the first draft of this book and recommended, quite rightly, that I seek a control group to test the validity of some of my assumptions. Consequently I was delighted when Anne Ward kindly allowed me to make use of the data from her control group. This analysis suggested that some of my assumptions were wrong and caused me to rethink and rewrite part of the book. Others who helped me to revise both the book and my own assumptive world include Dorothy Blythe, Holly Prigerson, Bob Weiss, Selby Jacobs, Christoph Holting, Linda Machin, John McLeod and Len Doyal. I am indebted to them all.

Thanks are also due to the Society of Authors who granted permission on behalf of the Bernard Shaw Estate for me to use the quote at the head of Chapter 4; to A M Heath and Co. Ltd for permission to quote Thomas Szasz at the head of Chapter 5; to the estate of James McGibbon for permission to quote from Stevie Smith at the head of Chapter 7; and to Dr John Rae for permitting me to quote from *The Custard Boys* at the head of Chapter 11.

Introduction

There will not be wanting, I presume, one or other that will much discommend some part of this Treatise of Love Melancholy, and object . . . that it is too light for a Divine, too Comicall a subject to speake of Love Symptomes, too phantasticall, fit alone for a wanton Poet, a feeling young love-sicke gallant, an effeminate Courtier, or some such idle person.

Robert Burton *The Anatomy of Melancholy* (1621–51) pt 3

The heart has its reasons, which the head knows not.

Pascal *Pensees* (1670) 4, 277

For most people love is the most profound source of pleasure in our lives while the loss of those whom we love is the most profound source of pain. Hence, love and loss are two sides of the same coin. We cannot have one without risking the other. Knowing this, some people choose not to invest in love, the risk is too great; others deny the equation, they fool themselves into thinking that they, and the ones they love, are immortal and inseparable. They take love for granted and are outraged if it is threatened or lost.

It is the very transience of life that enhances love. The greater the risk, the stronger grows the attachment. For most of us, the fact that one day we shall lose the ones we love, and they us, draws us closer to them but remains a silent bell that wakes us in the night.

Our intelligence often enables us to predict when we and those whom we love will die; to some degree we can grieve for the loss before it happens and much has been written about the value of anticipatory grief as a preparation for the losses to come (see, for instance, Rando's 1986 review of this literature). Yet there is an important difference between the grief that comes before and that which follows loss. Whereas the grief that follows loss eventually declines as we learn to live without the living presence of the one we love, the grief that precedes loss leads to an intensification of the attachment and a greater preoccupation with the other person. Mothers will sacrifice themselves and neglect the needs of their healthy children in order to cherish one who is sick; family and friends of a person who is close to death often maintain their vigil long after the dying one has lost all awareness of their presence.

Observations of this kind, which stem from common experience as well as psychological research, suggest that there is a set of rules that governs love and loss, some kind of dynamic force that can be assessed and, to a degree, measured. We hesitate to express these measurements in mathematical terms, partly because no simple equation can measure anything as complex as love, but also out of a sense of reverence for the very subject of our equation. It seems too calculating for the head to measure the heart. Yet we already make use of such calculations when, for instance, an unattached single person chooses whether or not to make a date with a much older person or when parents who have lost a baby decide whether or not to try for another.

Scientists, whose lack of such scruples allow them to dissect the 'sacred temple' of the human body, have, in recent years, begun to measure aspects of love and grief and to unravel some of its mysteries. Their first attempts can already be seen as simplistic, yet they were a necessary step towards a science of human relationships.

The work to be considered here may be another step along the way and will, in its turn, be superseded by others. It is offered, not out of arrogance or lese-majesty, but in the hope that an increase in our understanding of the building blocks which explain our joys and our suffering will help us to enhance the former and minimise the latter.

What is this thing called love? Love has many aspects but an essential component without which it cannot be said to be present is commitment. Love is the psychological tie that binds one person to another over a lasting period of time. Once established it is not easily severed and some argue that it can never be entirely broken (Klass *et al.* 1996: 14–23). Be that as it may, it is the nature of a tie that it resists severance. In physical terms love resembles an elastic band rather than any other type of tether, that is to say it grows stronger the further apart the lovers are located. By contrast, lovers who are never separated are inclined to take each other for granted. A consequence of this is that love is easier to measure when the parties are separated than it is when they are together.

Infants separated from their mothers behave in ways that teach us a great deal about their relationship with this particular mother and about the way they view the world and themselves within it. Likewise adults who lose a loved partner behave in ways that teach us not only about their relationship with the partner but about much else beside. Love may not make the world go round but it is an important source of security, self-esteem and trust. Without these essential supplies we feel and are endangered.

In the environment in which mankind evolved these were dangers to survival. A child who became separated from its parents would not live long and even adults were at risk if they got lost or separated from those who kept them safe in a dangerous world. Even today there is evidence that separations and losses of the people we love can have significant effects on our health and even increase the risk of mortality. These harsh facts may account for the special intensity of the emotions evoked by love and loss, but most of the current dangers are more psychological than physical. These psychological dangers include frank mental illnesses as well as lesser psychological difficulties (Parkes 1996). It is the purpose of this book to unravel the causal sequences that explain these dangers and to suggest ways in which they can be reduced. Along the way we may gain new perspectives on the nature of love.

Another important component of love is its 'monotropy' (Bowlby 1958); love is a tie to one particular person only. There can be no substitute for the parent, child or loved partner who has been lost. True, some of the pain of grief may be mitigated by making a new attachment. A bereaved parent may have another child or a divorced person may marry again, but people are not interchangeable and each new relationship will be unique in its own right. For this reason alone, each person we love is priceless. We cannot count their value alongside other objects which are replaceable and utilitarian. We may criticise the people we love for not being useful or meeting a particular criterion of beauty, but the very things we criticise are part of the uniqueness of the individual and we love them 'warts and all'.

These qualities – vital importance, uniqueness and persistence – account for the very special quality of love relationships. Not without reason are they the stuff of prose and poetry, the major preoccupation of the media and the source of endless delights in song from grand opera to pop. Love disturbs the even tenor of our ways, complicates our plans and upsets political machines. It is worshipped and deplored, longed for and dreaded. We take great risks when we embark upon love relationships and greater risks if we abjure them. One way and another we need to find a way of living with love.

Because of the emotional connotations and ambiguities of the word 'love' scientists have preferred to use other words to study it and to separate out its various forms. There are few today who continue to use Freud's ambiguous term 'libido' and the more recent term 'object relations' seems too impersonal; people are not 'objects'. The most widely used term is 'attachment', which was used by John Bowlby (1969) to indicate the child's tie to its mother. Because he was observing the child's behaviour his preferred term was 'attachment behaviour'. By contrast the mother's behaviour towards her child he referred to as 'maternal caretaking behaviour'. Subsequent workers have preferred to use the term 'nurturance' for this type of mother love and the term 'romantic attachment' has been proposed for love between adult peers, although this love, as we shall see, is often very unromantic.

Most researchers now use the term 'attachment' for all bonds of love and qualify this by adding parent–child or child–parent, etc. when a more specific connotation is needed. This certainly makes for scientific objectivity but the very neutrality of the term 'attachment' may mislead us into thinking of love as cognitive and instrumental when, in fact, it is experienced as a complex of feelings and emotions. In this book I shall attempt to move back and forth between the objective and the subjective view and will try to attain a balanced overall view.

A recurrent finding in the research into attachments, which will be described henceforth, is their lasting influence. Relationships formed in infancy colour all future relationships.

The work to be reported here set out to investigate a proposal that, at first sight, may seem unlikely. Are the problems which cause bereaved adults to seek help from a psychiatrist attributable, in some degree, to the particular kinds of attachment, the patterns of loving, which these bereaved people made to their parents in their childhood?

In attempting to answer this question and to understand the chain of causation, I have had to take into account a number of likely causes and to figure out how they influence each other. This study has taken up a large part of my working life as a psychiatrist with a special interest in bereavement. It is rather like trying to solve a very large jigsaw puzzle. I have moved slowly from speculation to clinical judgements and finally to a systematic attempt to test the fit between theory and data. Sometimes the pieces of the jigsaw have fallen neatly into place while at other times they have not and it has been necessary to take another look at the evidence and revise my theories. Little by little, what has emerged is very much more than a treatise on the psychiatric problems of the bereaved. The issues are important, not only to the minority of bereaved people who need psychiatric help but also, I suggest, to a much wider range of people in many life situations.

Steve Grand, in a recent article, writes:

> The fundamental problem is that science is dull. It really is tremendously dreary and boring most of the time . . . But so what? Science is just a methodology, not a body of knowledge. We don't describe the graphic arts as 'mixing paint'. What really matters – what is deeply and tremendously exciting – is the universe in which we live, and science is merely the means by which this is revealed to us. Unfortunately, the luminous beauty of one is tarnished by the dull sheen of the other . . . Scientific research has uncovered much of the elegance and rational splendour of the world around us, and this is what matters, not science itself.
>
> (Grand 2004: 7)

Boring old science has enabled us to probe the limits of space and the minutiae of the microscopic world, but I would suggest that its greatest challenge is not the world about us but the world within. It is inner space that now requires our urgent attention and this is of sufficient moment to justify the hard slog which may be necessary to reach our goals. In this volume the reader will have to be prepared for a certain amount of tedious spelling out of methodology and critical review of the work of other researchers. Hopefully the light that this will shed on the 'luminous beauty' of love will justify the effort.

My interest in bereavement as a topic of psychological research stemmed from a realisation that losses of one sort or another are very common. Bereavement by death is only one of the host of major life change events which we all face from time to time. It is, perhaps, one of the most severe and potentially harmful of stresses and this makes it an appropriate topic for clinical research, but the problems which cause people to seek psychiatric help after a bereavement are not unique to bereavement and the lessons which we can learn from studying them penetrate, as we shall see, to the roots of human psychology.

This work has not been carried out in a vacuum. Much has been learned in the last 50 years about the psychology of the attachments that people make to each other and about the consequences that arise when these attachments are interrupted by death. It has been my privilege to know and to work with many of the pioneers in this field whose studies will be reviewed in Chapters 1 and 2 and reconsidered in other places in this volume.

This corpus forms the background to the major research project by which I have attempted to link together the field of Attachment and the separate, but related, fields of Loss and Trauma. The rationale for this research and the way in which the various interacting factors were measured and turned into 'variables' is described in Chapter 3. Because the issues are complex, this chapter contains a great deal of information. Although I have tried to make the argument accessible, by avoiding jargon terms and confining much technical detail to appendices, readers may find it necessary to dodge back to this chapter later in the book in order to understand better the meaning and the limitations of the data.

This introduction and the three first chapters make up Part I of the book. Part II reports the main findings of the study and reveals the powerful influence which patterns of childhood attachment, as recalled in adult life, were found to have on the reaction to bereavements arising much later in life.

Part III looks at the other influences that contribute to the reaction to bereavement and attempts to disentangle the interaction between these various elements. We examine how each chapter of life is reflected in a new pattern of loving and how one pattern leads to another. Only when all are taken into consideration can we hope to obtain a balanced view of the part played by early attachments in the later lives, loves and losses that follow.

In Part IV we examine the wider context of a study that has up to now focused on bereavement. The pattern of attachments is found to have played a significant part in contributing to many of the other problems which people brought to this psychiatrist, even when no bereavement by death had taken place. Indeed some of the problems that followed bereavement have more to do with the wider context than they have with the bereavement. However, bereavement remains important in providing us with an opportunity to understand better the interweaving of love, loss and change. The wheel has come full circle and my original expectation, that the study of bereavement would throw light on the meaning and consequences of other stresses, has been confirmed.

The question arises whether some of the more extreme variants of the problematic attachment patterns should be regarded as psychiatric disorders in their own right. Can there be disorders of loving? The existence of attachment disorders in childhood has already been widely accepted and the data presented in Chapter 17 enables us to examine the evidence for the existence of attachment disorders in adult life. Whether or not this categorisation is accepted, it seems that attachment issues contribute to a wide range of problems throughout life and Chapter 18 examines the implications of these for the care given by others, be they medical professionals, volunteers, friends or relatives.

Finally, we attempt to take a broader view of the world in which these problems have arisen and draw some conclusions about the priorities which cause many of us to place our commitments to the large social units to which we belong (particularly the occupational niches to which our education has led us), above our commitments to our children, families and homes. Our attachments, it seems, remain our most important source of security, serenity and support at times of trouble. We neglect them at our peril.

Part I

Attachment and loss

1 Review I: Attachment and love

Happy he
With such a mother! Faith in womankind
Beats with his blood, and trust in all things high
Comes easy to him, and tho' he trip and fall
He shall not blind his soul with clay.
                                    Alfred, Lord Tennyson
                              The Princess (1847) pt 7, song l.308

Science and love

In recent years a large amount of research has been carried out into the
patterns of attachment made between parents and children in childhood and
these, as we shall see, have been found to influence the patterns of attachment,
not only to parents but to others in later childhood and adult life. They also
profoundly influence the ways in which people view themselves and the world
at large.

In this chapter theories about the nature of human attachments will be
considered in the light of recent scientific research. In Chapter 2 we go on to
examine the relevance of this work for understanding the reaction to the loss
of a loved person. The rest of the book draws on the experience of people with
problematic reactions to bereavement to fill in the intervening links in the
chain of causation between patterns of love and patterns of grief. What
emerges is a new understanding of the anatomy of love.

Ever since Breuer and Freud developed the 'talking cure' (1893) the influence of events occurring in a person's early childhood has been recognised as
likely to contribute to psychiatric problems in later life. In fact the whole
field of psychoanalysis takes this assumption as its basis. During the first half
of the twentieth century numerous theories were formulated to explain how
parents could damage their children. Freud, Jung and Klein led the way but
many others followed in their train and the field was rived with disagreement.

Freud's theory of repression, which claimed that painful memories and
ideas were 'forgotten' and transferred to 'the unconscious', ruled out ordinary
introspection as a valid method of research. Each school of psychoanalysis

relied on the interpretations that its proponents made of the memories, dreams and free associations made by psychiatric patients. But these claims proved controversial and nobody came up with a satisfactory way of finding out who was right and who wrong.

To this day, within the main stream of psychiatry, psychoanalysis is highly suspect, but this does not prevent most psychiatrists from acknowledging that childhood influences are important, if only because of the significance attached to them by our patients. The 'eclectic' view held by most psychiatrists since the mid-twentieth century is that psychiatric disorders can only be explained by taking into account many factors which each contribute to decide why this person, at this moment in their lives, is suffering this particular combination of symptoms and problems. Genetic influences, childhood influences and the later problems and traumas to which we are exposed throughout our lives, all need to be taken into account. This psychobiological approach, of which Adolf Meyer was the most influential exponent (Muncie 1948), laid emphasis on the importance of taking a detailed life history from each patient at the end of which the concatenation of problems would be summarised as a 'psychiatric formulation' and a treatment plan proposed.

Though less speculative than the psychoanalytic method, this approach also suffered from the lack of any satisfactory way of deciding which of the many circumstances and events that patients recalled were contributing significantly to their current difficulties and what should be done about them. Again the door was open to numerous theories and prejudices.

Not that there was any shortage of research. Great strides had been made in genetics, neuro-anatomy, neuro-physiology, psychology, psychiatry, ethology, sociology and neuro-pharmacology and each of these disciplines has something important to contribute. But, as is usually the case with scientists, workers in each discipline tend to act in isolation from the rest and to develop their own language and frame of reference rather than to make links with other disciplines. Few people attempt to cross the boundaries in order to produce an integrated theory.

More recently the information explosion has made it more difficult than ever to keep up to date with all the literature. Renaissance Man is dead and we are all afraid of being labelled dilettantes. Yet the pay-off when people take the time and trouble to cross the boundaries between fields of study is very great and modern techniques of multivariate analysis do enable us to study more than one variable at a time.

One who succeeded in bridging the gaps between disciplines was John Bowlby, the originator and pioneer of attachment theory. Having obtained a first-class honours degree at Trinity College, Cambridge in natural sciences and psychology he went on to study medicine and psychoanalysis. His scientific training made him critical of many of the theories of his fellow analysts and caused him to look beyond the confines of that discipline in his attempts to understand the problems that he met.

After the Second World War, when many children had been evacuated from danger zones and separated from one or both of their parents, Bowlby was invited to carry out a review, for the World Health Organisation, of empirical studies of the effects of maternal deprivation. This was published in 1953 as *Child Care and the Growth of Love* and it established, beyond reasonable doubt, the damage that could be done to small children by the absence of or rejection by a mother or mother-substitute in early childhood. It also established Bowlby's reputation as someone who could draw together and integrate the findings of research from many sources.

During 1951 Bowlby was looking for a theoretical explanation for these empirical findings. The answer came to him 'in a flash' after he read a draft of Konrad Lorenz's *King Solomon's Ring* (published in 1952). Lorenz was the founder of ethology, the study of animal behaviour, and his seminal book enabled Bowlby to explain, in evolutionary terms, the mechanisms by which mothers become attached to their children, and the consequences which arise when they are separated. These ideas were worked out in more detail during a fruitful year (1958) at the Center for Advanced Studies in Stanford, California. They formed the basis of his major work, the three volumes on *Attachment and Loss*, which took him another 22 years to complete (Vol. I *Attachment* 1969; Vol. II *Separation* 1973a; Vol. III *Loss* 1980). Between them these provide a body of well-argued scientific evidence in support of a new understanding of parent–child relationships and much else beside.

In *Attachment* (1969), and in an earlier paper which appeared in 1958, Bowlby addressed the problem of the nature of the child's tie to its mother. He had, by this time, recognised that the primary attachment was not always to the child's biological mother and he used the term 'mother-figure' for this person. He saw this tie as rooted in instinct and much of the book consists of a detailed scrutiny of the complex interaction between instinct and learning which underlies all human behaviour and emotion. He described the 'internal working models' of the world, which each child builds up and which are then used as a means of orientation and planning.

Bowlby reviewed the attachments of infants and mothers of non-human animal species, including the fascinating and important concept of 'imprinting'. This term was coined by Heinroth from observation of greylag geese who, when hatching from the egg, become attached to the first large moving object that they see. In the wild this is likely to be the mother, but in a laboratory situation it may be a man in a white coat. Konrad Lorenz was fond of walking into a lecture theatre followed by a line of goslings. He would then hand his coat to his assistant who would lead the goslings from the room. This attachment, once formed, was difficult to change and gave rise to the concept of 'fixed action patterns', which could only be learned during 'critical learning periods'. Many other examples of imprinting have now been discovered in a variety of species and are most likely to arise shortly after birth (McFarland 1981: 303–305).

Bowlby then turned his attention to human infants and described the sequence of behaviours by which the attachment to the mother-figure is developed and expressed during the first two years of life. These 'attachment behaviours' include sucking, crying, smiling, clinging and following. Each of these is modified, from the time of its inception, by the behaviour of the mother-figure so that, by the end of the second year, large differences are already evident between the patterns of attachment exhibited by different infants. These differences, in turn, influence the internal models of the world as seen by each child.

An explanation for many of the important differences was given in Bowlby's second volume, *Separation: Anxiety and Anger* (1973a). In this he showed how temporary separations from mother-figures can evoke a distinctive type of anxiety, 'separation anxiety', and anger, both of which can give rise to a second level of problems such that lasting difficulties in relationships and personality development may persist even after the return of the mother-figure. He referred to the intense but anxious attachments made by children whose mothers have stayed away too long and showed how clinging may itself evoke the very behaviour that it is intended to prevent, rejection.

During this very productive period Bowlby attracted to him, at the Tavistock Institute of Human Relations, a team of researchers whose work enabled him to flesh out the bones of the theory that he was developing. James Robertson made films of children in institutional care with and without their mothers (Robertson and Bowlby 1952) and later, with his wife Joyce, was able to demonstrate that many of the damaging effects of separation from mother could be prevented by the provision of sensitive foster care (Robertson and Robertson 1967–73). Tony Ambrose carried out systematic studies of the smiling responses of young babies and showed how easily they could be augmented or extinguished by interaction with smiling or non-responsive adults (1961).

Attachment patterns in early childhood

Another of Bowlby's trainees was the American psychologist, Mary Ainsworth, who, after a brief spell at the Tavistock, applied Bowlby's theories to studying mother–child interaction in native Ghanaians. She it was who made the important distinction between strength of attachment and security of attachment. She asked 'Is the child who clings to his mother – who is afraid of the world and the people in it, and who will not move off to explore other things or other people – more strongly attached or merely more insecure?' (1963).

Ainsworth deduced that a way of studying love would be to observe the effects of separation. Returning to the USA she achieved considerable distinction by developing a systematic method of observing and classifying the patterns of attachment between infants and mothers, her Strange Situation Test (SST). It was this test which, more than anything else, placed the study of parent–infant love on a firm scientific footing and showed how the particular ways in which mothers love their babies can have a profound effect on the ways those babies come to view themselves and their world.

In the classic SST mothers and infants, in the second year of life, are observed through a one-way mirror before, during, and after a brief period of separation in a strange room. Ainsworth described one pattern of secure attachment and two patterns of insecure attachment (Ainsworth *et al.* 1978). Her colleague Mary Main subsequently added a third insecure pattern following further research (Main and Goldwyn 1984; Main and Hesse 1990; Main and Solomon 1990) and Ainsworth accepted the validity of this modification, which will be included in the version that follows. Their research also showed that each pattern of attachment is associated with a particular pattern of parenting. Their categories of attachment, as observed in the SST, together with the pattern of parenting that has been found by George and Solomon (1989, 1996) to be associated with each of them, can be summarised:

1   Secure
2   Insecure
   - Anxious/Ambivalent
   - Avoidant
   - Disorganised/Disoriented

Secure (Ainsworth's Category B)

Parents whose sensitivity and responsiveness to their infant's needs for security and a safe base from which to explore their world are adequate, or 'good enough', have children who tolerate brief separations without great distress and respond rapidly and warmly to their mothers' comforting behaviour when she returns. Subsequent research shows that, although some of these mothers may have experienced problems with their own parents, they are aware how their past has influenced the present and can describe and accept their parents in a realistic and credible way. In other words they have overcome any attachment problems of their own. It comes as no surprise to find that their marriages are also less likely to be conflicted than those of the parents of insecurely attached children (Simpson and Rholes 1994).

Insecure

Anxious/ambivalent (Ainsworth's Category C)

Mothers who are over-anxious, insensitive to their infants and discourage exploration, have children who, in the SST, show great distress during the period of separation and who both cling and cry angrily when she returns. Their distress continues after reunion for much longer than that of the securely attached infants.

Avoidant (Ainsworth's Category A)

The children of mothers who do not show feelings, cannot tolerate closeness and/or punish the child's attachment behaviour, learn to inhibit their tendencies to cling and to cry. When, in the SST, mother leaves the room they appear indifferent and uncaring. When she returns they often continue playing, ignore or turn away from her.

In the early stages of her research Ainsworth saw these children as 'detached', but further investigation showed that, however uncaring they may appear to be, they are in fact physiologically aroused, as reflected in a rapid heart rate, during the period of separation and for long afterwards; their indifference is more apparent than real (Sroufe and Waters 1977).

A more recent study by Belsky *et al.* (1984) showed that many mothers of avoidant infants are responsive to their child at low levels of stress but become less responsive if the stress level rises. This reversal of the usual pattern would seem to defeat the object of the care which is, presumably, to provide protection and security when it is most needed and to encourage autonomy when it is not.

Disorganised/disoriented (Main and Ainsworth's Category D)

This group of children exhibit disorganised and contradictory activity. They may cry during separation but avoid the mother when she returns, or they may approach the mother, then 'freeze' or fall on the floor; some show stereotyped behaviour, rocking to and fro or repeatedly hitting themselves. To a greater extent than other infants the disorganised group have an increase in the stress hormone cortisol, as measured in their saliva 20 to 30 minutes after the SST (Spangler and Grossmann 1993; Hertsgaard *et al.* 1995).

Main and Hesse found that most of the mothers of these children had suffered major losses or other trauma shortly before or after the birth of the infant and had reacted by becoming severely depressed. No less than 56 per cent of mothers who had lost a parent by death before they completed high school went on to have children who had disorganised attachments (Main and Hesse 1990).

Main refers to the mother's grief as 'unresolved' and Schuengel *et al.* (1999) have shown that problems in grieving are associated with disorganised attachments *only* when the mother is otherwise insecure. What is it about the mother's grief and depression that produces disorganised behaviour in the child? One answer comes from a recent study by Gunning *et al.* (2004) which shows that mothers who become depressed after the birth of a baby are measurably less sensitive and responsive to their child's behaviour. The infants are helpless to influence their mothers.

The 'disorganised' pattern may also be associated with parental abuse (Carlson *et al.* 1989), alcoholism (el-Guebaly *et al.* 1993) and drug abuse (Rodning *et al.* 1991). Such mothers are often helpless, frightened of their own children and lacking confidence in their ability to care for and control them. They may see their infants as more powerful than themselves. Consequently, their behaviour is both 'frightened' and 'frightening' and the child's 'haven of safety is at once the source of alarm'.

Although Ainsworth's categories appear clear-cut, one of the deficiencies of the SST is its failure to measure the strength of the attachment patterns it describes. Infants are forced into all-or-nothing categories according to defined cut-off points. Common sense suggests that there must be degrees of security/insecurity of attachment and that the use of graded measures would give more subtlety to the results.

In addition, the fact that stressed parents often have insecure children should not blind us to the possibility that some stress can be a valuable learning experience for parents and children. Simpson and Rholes (1994) cite evidence from several studies that support the idea that stress of mild to moderate degree can foster attachment security rather than undermine it.

Although it is tempting to think of the insecure attachment patterns as dysfunctional, each of them has a function: 'the heart has its reasons'. The anxious/ambivalent child learns to cope by clinging, staying close to the parent and protesting vigorously when she or he departs. This strategy persists because it enables this child to relate to this parent. The avoidant infant is forced to stand on its own feet from an early age and learns to inhibit attachment behaviour (cuddling, crying, etc.). This strategy too is successful to a degree within the context of the relationship in which it arose and is therefore likely to become perpetuated. The strategies for coping of the disorganised infant are less obvious but it too may learn to withdraw from potential conflicts and become inconspicuous, the human equivalent of 'freezing' in the face of danger. Indeed, Main and Hesse use the word 'frozen' to describe a characteristic behaviour pattern sometimes observed in this group. We shall see below that other strategies become available to these children as they mature.

Note that fear *per se* is not a psychological problem. It may, indeed, be an appropriate and even life-saving adaptation to situations of danger. The child who cries out in alarm is more likely to survive than one who stays silent. By the same token those children who, as a consequence of insecure attachments, are prone to distress should not be assumed to be poorly adapted to their environment. Within the family in which they are growing up their distress may be quite appropriate. Indeed Radke-Yarrow *et al.* (1995) have suggested that children who make a secure attachment to a deviant parent may sometimes be at risk as a result.

Attachments in later childhood

These patterns, having become established in the first two years of life, remain remarkably stable thereafter and predict the quality of relationships to others during later childhood. The experience of sensitive and secure love makes for a child who can be sensitive and secure in their relations with others. Thus, children who had been classified as secure using the SST at 18 months have been found, six months later, to be more sociable in a playgroup towards playmates; anxious/ambivalent children tend to stay close to mother and look towards her; avoidant children look towards objects rather than playmates or mother (Pastor 1981).

When they reach school age, anxious/ambivalent children seem to lack the assertiveness and confidence necessary for effective interaction with peers (Erickson *et al.* 1985), avoidant children show more aggression towards other children and their teachers rate them as more hostile, impulsive, lacking in persistence and withdrawn (Egeland and Sroufe 1981; Erickson *et al.* 1985). It is worth noting, however, that although avoidant children are more aggressive and fear being too close, they still try to find a safe enough proximity to teachers. Thus, Sroufe (1983) found that avoidant schoolchildren, as well as anxious/ambivalent children, sat closer to their teacher than securely attached children and were judged to be more dependent overall.

Followed up to the age of 10, significant differences between secure and insecure children are still found with secure children rated as more self-assured and competent. Children who have experienced the anxious/ambivalent pattern of attachment are prone to anxiety disorders (Warren *et al.* 1997). Avoidant children show lower levels of understanding of others and of sensitivity (Elicker *et al.* 1992). Follow-up studies of children assigned to the disorganised pattern indicate that it is this group that may be at greatest risk of psychiatric problems, particularly dissociative symptoms,[1] in later childhood (Lewis *et al.* 1984; Carlson 1998). Liotti (1992) sees trance-like states (a kind of dissociative symptom) in people with a history of disorganised attachment as a defence against fear of caregivers.

It is a tempting to attribute these problems to persisting helplessness and inability to cope but follow-up studies also show that alternative strategies for coping are adopted by most of these children as time goes by. Thus two studies (Main and Cassidy 1988; Wartner *et al.* 1994) found that disorganised attachment predicted controlling behaviour, of either a caregiving or punitive type, at aged 6 in 84 per cent cases. Indeed, these researchers take controlling behaviour in later childhood as a measure of disorganised attachment, which they then term 'controlling attachment'. It seems that these children find a way of dealing with their own feelings of helplessness by themselves taking control of their parents and others.

Although these older children may no longer be subjected to the more

---

1   Dissociation is the capacity to split off areas of mental activity from consciousness. It occurs quite normally in emergencies when people may continue to rescue others without awareness of their own personal injuries. Dissociation becomes a symptom if it interferes with normal functioning, for instance, when amnesia for an accident prevents someone from giving evidence.

intense parenting that they received in early childhood, their basic assumptions about the world (or assumptive world) often include an internal model in which current authorities are expected to think and behave in the same way as did their parents.

Trust in self and others

At the risk of oversimplification I derived from these data a classification of the basic assumptions that influence relationships (Parkes 1991). This resembles a similar classification of attachments between adults, which was proposed independently by Bartholomew and Horowitz (1991; this is described on pages 22–3). My classification brings together Erikson's concept of 'basic trust' (1950) and Bowlby's observation that secure attachments to parents leave a child with trust in itself and others (1973b). It rests on the assumption that the principle function of parenting is to provide a secure base from which developing children will learn the extent to which they can rely on themselves and the extent to which they can rely on others. These two dimensions I have termed 'self-trust' and 'other trust'.

Four combinations of these measures of trust are likely to result from the four patterns of attachment (shown in Table 1.1). Secure attachments, I suggest, give rise to high levels of trust in self and others. Anxious/ambivalent attachments lead to lack of trust in self but not others. Avoidant attachments lead to lack of trust in others but not self. Disorganised attachments lead to lack of trust in both self and others.

Problems can arise from lack of trust, but we should not assume that trust in self and others is always and necessarily a good thing. Nobody is completely trustworthy and none of us can completely trust ourselves or others. It follows that secure children with high levels of trust in self and/or others may feel more secure than others but they may not be well able to recognise the degree to which doubts about ourselves and others are reasonable. Nobody is perfect and one of the lessons we all need to learn is the appropriate limit of trust.

It may be that the self-doubts of anxious/ambivalent children will make them more willing to seek help when help is needed, whereas the distrust of others, which characterises avoidant children, will make them more

Table 1.1 Categories of basic trust

	Self-trust	Other trust
Secure attachment	High	High
Insecure		
Anxious/Ambivalent	Low	High
Avoidant	High	Low
Disorganised	Low	Low

wary. Sometimes the strategy of help seeking is successful, but it may also lead to exploitation. Sometimes the strategy of self-reliance is successful, but it may also lead to failure and isolation. Distrust in self and others in disorganised children may lead them to attempt to remain inconspicuous or to adopt controlling strategies with varying degrees of success. Thus the basic assumptions of insecurely attached children, and the strategies which result from them, are likely to lead to anxiety, but they may also be appropriate and effective ways of coping in some situations but inappropriate in others.

While most of the initial studies of attachment focused on mother/infant dyads, subsequent studies of father/infant dyads have shown that secure parenting from either parent can, to a degree, modify the effects of insecure parenting by the other (Easterbrooks and Goldberg 1984; Cox *et al.* 1992; Belsky 1996). They have also shown a weak but significant degree of concordance across parents, that is to say secure attachment to one parent is often, but not always, associated with secure attachment to the other (Fox *et al.* 1991).

In a sample of children followed up to 11 years, Steele *et al.* (1996) showed that mothers are more likely than fathers to teach the child coping strategies and emotional lessons (including the ability to acknowledge distress in others and other complex feelings). Fathers, on the other hand, teach outer world social lessons including peer relationships. Behavioural problems in adolescence are more closely associated with insecure attachments to fathers than to mothers.

Other influences on attachments

Could these attachment patterns be attributed to the child's genetic inheritance? Two observations suggest that, if there is a genetic factor, it is not large. First, children who are assigned to one attachment pattern when observed with their mothers are not necessarily assigned to the same pattern when with their fathers (Steele *et al.* 1996). Second, in two studies, identical twins, who share precisely the same genes, were no more likely to share the same attachment patterns than ordinary siblings or non-identical twins (Ricciuti 1992; O'Connor and Croft 2001).

This said, it would be very surprising if genetic factors played no part in determining how infants react to their parents and this may account for the finding that some children who are seriously abused subsequently make secure attachments. Indeed, one genetic study showed that infants who had been assigned to the disorganised attachment category were much more likely than others to carry a gene with the abbreviated label DRD4 (Lakatos *et al.* 2000). This does not necessarily mean that the gene is a direct cause of the disorganised attachment; it may, for instance, influence the parent's sensitivity to danger which, in turn, can be expected to affect the child's pattern of attachment. If the genetic influence is on the child, we would expect there to be other effects on temperament, but in a meta-analysis of 12 samples involving 1877 participants, van Ijzendoorn and Bakermans-Kranenberg (1996) reported absence of an association between disorganised attachments and 'constitutional and temperamental variables'.

Are there *cultural influences* on attachments in childhood? When the Strange Situation test has been carried out with parent–child dyads from various cultures, the same attachment patterns have been found as those described in the USA by Ainsworth and Main. Cultural factors have been shown to influence the relative frequency though not the types of pattern found (Grossmann and Grossmann 1991; Van Ijzendoorn *et al.* 1991).

Studies in adult life of childhood attachment patterns

The patterns of attachment and their consequences become much more complicated by the time we reach adult life and both the instruments we use to measure them and the interpretation of the data that result may leave the reader confused. Nevertheless it is important to examine this data if we are to draw valid conclusions from the research that follows.

Few researchers have had the opportunity to follow into adult life infants whose attachment patterns were identified by means of the SST in their infancy. Those that have have come up with inconsistent findings (see below). Several studies of adults have attempted to assess their remembered relationship with their parents. Gerlsma and Lutejin (2000) have reviewed these and found only one that has been adequately researched, Parker's Parental Bonding Instrument (PBI, Parker *et al.* 1979). This enables parents to be assessed as high or low on 'care' and 'protection' (by which Parker means overprotection). These measures have not been closely tied into particular patterns of attachment.

Parker suggests that uncaring parents undermine their child's self-esteem. In adult life those who as children received 'affectionless control' have been found, in several studies, to be prone to minor but not to major depression. Those who recall their parents as 'protective' are found in later life to have low self-esteem in social situations, although it may be reasonably high at home (Parker 1994).

Feeney summarises the findings of this and other research: 'secure individuals tend to remember their parents as warm and affectionate, avoidant individuals to remember their mothers as cold and rejecting, and ambivalent individuals to remember their fathers as unfair' (Feeney 1999: 363).

The Adult Attachment Interview

Main's Adult Attachment Interview (AAI) is commonly regarded as the most reliable measure, in adult life, of the lasting influence of childhood attachments. It classifies adults as 'autonomous-secure' (50–60 per cent), 'insecure-preoccupied or entangled' (10–15 per cent), 'insecure-dismissing' (25–30 per cent), or 'unresolved' (Main and Goldwyn 1984). These correspond, more or less, to Ainsworth and Main's 'secure', 'anxious-ambivalent', 'avoidant' and 'disorganised' categories.

Is Main's AAI a reflection of childhood attachment patterns? It relies not so much on the accuracy of memories of parents, but on the way in which these memories are reported in adult life. The questions focus on separations rather than on the particular styles of parenting adopted by the parents and weight is given to the extent to which the reports are coherent and organised. Thus, an individual providing a coherent narrative, even though it includes descriptions of physical or sexual abuse by parents, will, following Main's scoring system, be judged autonomous/secure.

We might expect that, in people who completed both tests, the results of Parker's PBI would correlate highly with Main's AAI, but this is not the case. Manassis *et al.* (1999) who compared the results of these two tests in 130 disturbed adolescents, concluded that the PBI and the AAI were not comparable 'in participants showing idealisation or anger towards their mothers'. We must conclude that Parker's retrospective measure of parenting is not a predictor of whatever it is that Main's AAI is measuring. Main claims that insecure adults, particularly those in the avoidant group, distort or forget memories of the way their parents treated them and this throws doubt on Parker's instrument.

Three studies enable the results of the SST carried out during a person's infancy to be compared with the AAI in later life, but the results conflict with each other. Thus Waters *et al.* 2000) found an impressive agreement between the attachment patterns derived from the two tests on middle-class adults who were followed from infancy to young adult life while Weinfeld *et al.* (2004) found little concordance in poorer families with a high incidence of negative life experiences. The exception was children rated as having disorganised attachments by the SST who were most often classed as 'insecure' or 'unresolved' on the AAI at age 19. Zimmermann and Grossmann (1996) also found that SST in infancy did not correlate[2] with the attachment classification by the AAI at age 16. It did, however, correlate with the mother's AAI when the child was aged 6, but only after families troubled by divorce, separation or life-threatening illness had been eliminated. It seems reasonable to conclude that traumatic experiences destabilised the subsequent pattern measured by the AAI.

To make confusion worse confused, neither of these measures correlates highly with the measures of attachments between adults which will be considered below (Hickie *et al.* 1990a; Hickie *et al.* 1990b; Feeney and Noller 1990; Kobak 1993).

---

2   Throughout this book the terms correlate and correlation will be used to refer to the extent to which one score varies with another. Thus, throughout childhood, age and height tend to be highly correlated, they both tend to increase together. Age and gender, however, are uncorrelated.

It seems that the AAI is not a retrospective measure of the parenting received in infancy nor is it a measure of current attachments. What does the AAI measure? The most convincing evidence for the meaning of the instrument, and the main justification for giving it serious consideration here, comes from its ability to predict the patterns of nurturant attachment (as measured by the SST) that many of these women will have with their own infants (Fonagy *et al.* 1997). Apart from the 'preoccupied' (or 'anxious/ ambivalent') women, the other maternal attachment categories are found to predict the child's attachment category in about 77 per cent of cases. Followed over three generations Benoit and Parker (1993) found that the AAI categories of grandmothers correctly predicted 75 per cent of the AAI categories of mothers; these, in turn, predicted 77 per cent of the SST categories of the infants. It would seem, from these findings, that the AAI is a reasonably good indicator of a person's propensity to make a particular caregiving or nurturant bond.

Adults, it seems carry within them a set of assumptions about their parents and about themselves which influence how they will behave towards their own children. These stem from their experiences throughout childhood and are not confined to infancy. They have learned about parenting from their parents, but we should not assume that this means that they will treat their partners in the same way in which they treat their children. The AAI does not predict the bonds which adults will make with other adults (see p. 23–4).

AAI attachment scores have not been found to be strongly predictive of psychiatric problems and Allen *et al.* (1996) found that former psychiatric inpatients reported no more insecurity of attachment than controls. Only when patient groups are compared with each other do differences emerge. Thus suicidal adolescent psychiatric patients were more likely to fall into 'unresolved' or 'preoccupied' categories than non-suicidal patients (Adam *et al.* 1996). Adam's findings are so striking that he claims that 'the acute suicidal crisis can be better conceptualised as an acute attachment crisis'. He goes on:

> Those who have experienced their caregivers as insensitive and unavailable, or whose childhood experience has been intruded upon by parental needs are more likely to have poor regard for themselves and pessimistic and hostile expectations of others, both of which are likely to contribute to difficulties in forming and maintaining relationships. Extensive evidence shows just these characteristics to be present in patients making suicidal attempts.
>
> (Adam 1994: 260)

In another study of adolescent psychiatric patients, depression was more common in 'dismissive' patients than others (Ivarsson *et al.* 1998) but in adult patients depression was more closely related to the 'preoccupied' category (Rosenstein and Horowitz 1991). 'Unresolved' categories have been found to be associated with borderline personality disorder (Hobson and Patrick 1998; Barone 2003).

The link with borderline personality disorder and other aspects of personality will be explored in Chapter 17, as will the notion that there are specific disorders of attachment in childhood and adult life. Suffice it to say that the research into childhood attachments suggests that the persisting effects of childhood attachments do not predicate mental disorders in adult life, but may influence the form that they take. If we regard attachment patterns as strategies for survival, it would seem that each strategy has its advantages and disadvantages. Although these ordinarily balance out, the minority in whom the disadvantages predominate may well need help.

Other studies of attachments in adult life

Studies of close relationships in adult life have enabled patterns of attachment to peers and partners to be identified. The field is a large and complex one; it has been reviewed in two multicontributor volumes (Bartholomew and Pearlman 1984; Sperling and Berman 1994). To cut a long story short, Hazan and Shaver (1987) developed a self-report questionnaire to measure attachment patterns similar to those described by Ainsworth but for use in studying 'romantic attachments' during adult life. Main's discovery of a fourth attachment pattern led to modifications and others developed several derivatives to the point where the sheer number of variants and extensions produced confusion.

Perhaps the best of these measures is Brennan *et al.*'s Experiences in Close Relationships (ECL) questionnaire (1998). They scanned the literature and identified 323 items in 60 subscales. The statistical technique of factor analysis revealed that these fell into four clusters, which could be subsumed under two dimensions. A similar review was also carried out by Bartholomew and Horowitz (1991). They too reached the conclusion that all measures could be reduced to two similar dimensions, which they termed 'sociability' and 'self-esteem'. They subsequently chose a combination of questions that best capture these dimensions (Griffin and Bartholomew 1994). The result was their Relationships Scale Questionnaire (RSQ). The dimensions are shown, along with the attachment patterns to which they are assumed to give rise, in Table 1.2. People who scored highly on both 'sociability' and 'self-esteem' were classed as 'secure'; those high on 'sociability' but low on 'self-esteem' were 'preoccupied with their relationship(s)' (cf the anxious/ambivalent attachments of childhood); those low on 'sociability' but high on 'self-esteem' were 'dismissing of relationships' (cf avoidant attachments), while those who had low scores on both dimensions were 'fearful of intimacy' (cf disorganised attachments).

Bartholomew's measure of 'sociability' equates with my concept of 'other trust' and Bartholomew's measure of 'self-esteem' with my concept of 'self-trust'. With Bartholomew, I see those high on both trust in self and others as

Table 1.2 Dimensions of attachment in adult life (Bartholomew and Horowitz 1991)

Self-Esteem	Sociability	
	High	*Low*
High	Secure	Dismissing
Low	Preoccupied with relationship	Fearful of intimacy

'secure'; those low on self-trust and high on other trust are 'dependent' (or 'anxious/ambivalent'). Conversely those with low scores on other trust and relatively high scores on self-trust are 'compulsively self-reliant' (or 'avoidant'). Finally the combination of low trust in both self and others leaves the individual very insecure indeed and with a high propensity for anxiety and depression. Evidence to support this view and further discussion of its implications for our understanding of bereavement are one of the themes of this book.

Although cut-off points are used to separate the various categories by means of these measures, they can also be used to measure the strength of the two underlying dimensions.

'Dismissing' adults are less likely to support their romantic partner (Hazan and Shaver 1987), score lower on expressiveness, kindness and awareness of others (Collins and Read 1990) and are less likely to offer their partner reassurance and support in an anxiety-provoking situation (Simpson *et al.* 1992). 'Preoccupied' are more emotional and self-critical (Mikulincer *et al.* 1993), they idealise their romantic partners and depend too much upon them (Feeney and Noller 1990). Reviewing the field Feeney concludes that individuals with high anxiety about relationships tend to have conflicted marriages because their distrust and coercive clinging bring about the very rejection that they most fear. But they are not doomed, like AAI categories, the patterns of romantic attachment may not persist over time, 'particularly when significant events in the social environment disconfirm [*sic*] existing expectations. For example, becoming involved in a stable, satisfying relationship may lead to change for those whose models of self and others have led to scepticism' (Feeney 1999).

Several studies have shown that these self-assessments predict how people will react under stress. Like the avoidant infants who seemed indifferent to the Strange Situation but had rapid heart rates (see p. 14), 'dismissing' college students act as if not bothered by a stressful situation, but they have high levels of skin conductance, a sensitive measure of sweating (Dozier and Kobak 1992).

Main's AAI only correlates weakly with these measures of romantic attachment (Crowell *et al.* 2000; Shaver *et al.* 2000). Why should this be? Probable explanations are:

1   Although infants are responsive to the expectations of their parents, the conditions which perpetuated the attachment pattern in childhood may no longer be present in adult life. Peers and lovers may react to attachment behaviour in ways which are very different from those of parents.

2   Social stereotypes and other social pressures may push individuals to inhibit nurturant behaviour towards partners.

3   It takes two to make a romantic attachment; partners may themselves exert similar pressures, perhaps because of their own attachment needs.

For example, the relationship which results when a formerly anxious/ambivalent adult becomes attached to an avoidant partner may be very different from the relationship which results if the partner is similarly anxious/ambivalent. Some people may choose a partner whose own attachment pattern complements their own or one which resembles their own; others may have little opportunity to pick and choose. By comparison, the needs of infants for nurturance are relatively unambiguous and none can choose their own parents.

It seems that neither the effects of childhood attachment patterns nor those arising in adult life are written in stone. The AAI emerges as probably the best measure of the attachment style which predicts child/parent attachments but even this gives little indication of the pattern of adult/adult attachment. Love relationships, it seems, are difficult to pin down. They are likely to be influenced by particular partners and situations and we must beware of oversimplification.

Sexuality, attachment and nurturance

While these measures have proved valuable in studying certain aspects of attachments between adults, they make no distinction between the three basic components which contribute to adult ties, sexuality, attachment (here taken to reflect the need to be cared for) and nurturance (the need to care for another).

Most people would agree that sexual attraction is at its most intense in the early 'attraction phase' of a relationship. Hazan and Zeifman (1994) refer to it as the bond which ties adults together for long enough for attachment to take place. Freud conflated sexuality with all other ties and, in so doing, brought about a large amount of muddled thinking. Bowlby's view, which separates sexuality from attachment and downgrades the importance of sexuality, is less 'exciting'. As Jeremy Holmes puts it: 'In comparison with Freud's and Klein's passionate world of infantile sexuality, Attachment Theory appears almost bland, banal even' (1993: 6). This may make attachment theory less popular but it does not make it any less true or important.

Attachment patterns do seem to influence sexual behaviour. Thus, Hazan and Zeifman (1994) found that avoidant individuals are more inclined to value sex without love and to engage in 'one-night stands' but this was not associated with increased frequency of intercourse. Feeney *et al.* (1993) showed that avoidant women and anxious/ambivalent men reported less intercourse than others. In both sexes cuddling without sex seems to be favoured by anxious or dependent people (Hazan and Zeifman 1994).

Liebowitz (1983) suggests that, in attachments between adults, the 'attraction phase' usually peters out after about two years and the strength of the relationship thereafter depends on the strength of the attachment that has been established. This does not, of course, mean that sex ceases to be pleasurable and there are some relationships that continue to rely on little else, but they are the exception. For most people the excitement of the period of intense sexual stimulation is followed by a more peaceful, gradual and reassuring contentment, which derives less from the arousal of sexuality and more on the security of a shared mutual attachment. A partner may complain that 'he (or she) takes me for granted', but it is this very assumption that I know what my partner is thinking, where he or she will be, and that I can trust him or her to be available if needed, that constitutes the 'secure base' which, sooner or later, most of us come to rely on.

Sexual attraction is not the only explanation for the common experience of 'falling in love'. Other factors include the assuaging of fear and insecurity, the excitement of expanding horizons, the realisation of long-standing dreams and the fulfilment of the expectations and hopes of parents and peers. All of these get things 'off the ground' and help to minimise the fears of disappointment and rejection which cause some to hold back from 'taking the plunge' into a committed attachment.

Both attachment and nurturance play a part in lasting adult relationships with a great deal of variation in the extent to which partners seek to care or be cared for. Even in societies in which men are still expected to look after and nurture the 'little woman' this sex linkage is often more apparent than real. So intertwined are these two components of lasting bonds, that few studies have attempted to disentangle them. For most purposes, therefore, the term 'attachment' is taken to include elements of both.

Conclusion

Love, it seems, is a very much more complex thing than we may have thought. The love that permeates our household when young may leave us warmly confident of our place in a secure world, sure of ourselves and trusting of others, but relatively unprepared for failure or betrayal. Alternatively it may leave us aware of our weakness and ready to seek help, but inclined to rely over much on those whom we expect to protect us from a dangerous world. Others of us may be wary of closeness and determinedly self-reliant, but reluctant to seek help when it is needed. Yet others may lack confidence both in other people and themselves, but survive by keeping their heads down or exerting indirect control. How these assumptions and strategies continue in later life will depend on what happens next; the experience of trauma and deprivation may confirm or disconfirm them. So too may the love relationships of adult life which are both influenced by and influence how we now experience and cope with the world. Once again it is love that determines how we see the world and ourselves within it. The deep love for our children that arises in most adults upon their birth is profoundly influenced by the pattern of loving that we experienced in our own childhood. And so the wheel comes full circle and, for good or ill, our young are moulded by the power of love.

2 Review II: Loss and change

Time turns old days to derision,
Our loves into corpses or wives;
And marriage and death and division
Make barren our lives.
                    Swinburne 'Dolores' (1866)

Thus far we have focused on the formation and development of attachments and the consequences of separations from parents in childhood. But loss is the common consequence of love and grief, the price that must be paid. How do the patterns of loving influence the patterns of grieving? We now turn to a consideration of the lasting dissolution of relationships in adult life. This is always painful but varies greatly from one person to another and it is reasonable to ask what influences the response.

Determinants of outcome after bereavement

Much empirical research has been conducted to identify the factors that decide who will do well and who badly after bereavement. One of the earliest attempts was the Harvard Bereavement Project in which 59 young Boston widows and widowers were followed up for two to four years after bereavement (Parkes and Weiss 1983). Subsequent studies have confirmed and expanded the findings of the Harvard study and included a wider range of kinship and age groups (see Stroebe and Schut 2001b for a recent review). Four types of risk factor have been identified,

- the personal vulnerability of the bereaved person
- the kinship to the deceased person
- the events and circumstances leading up to and including the death
- the social supports and other circumstances obtaining after the death.

The first, the issue of personal vulnerability, is most relevant to attachment research and is discussed below. The second, the kinship factor, is covered in

Chapters 11 to 13. The third implies that some deaths are more traumatic than others and is discussed in Chapter 9 and the last, the social and other influences, in Chapters 14 and 15.

The Harvard Study showed that a powerful determinant of problematic reactions to bereavement was the attachment to the lost person. Two types of attachment were found to give rise to two distinct types of problematic reaction:

- a dependent relationship was found to predict chronic grief
- an ambivalent relationship was found to predict conflicted grief.

By 'chronic grief' we implied a form of grief that is intense from the outset and continues for an undue length of time. This differs from the 'conflicted' type of reaction in that the latter is often delayed; it reaches a peak some time after the death and is complicated by feelings of anger and/or guilt.

Further evidence for the influence of attachment patterns on grief comes from Pistole who used Bartholomew and Horowitz's RSQ (see p. 22) to study the influence of romantic attachments on the ways in which college students coped with the ending of such a relationship (Pistole 1994). He concluded that securely attached individuals grieved less than those who were insecurely attached.

Finally there is a recent study by Waskowic and Chartier (2003) of 65 widows and 11 widowers who completed the RSQ at varying periods after their bereavement. Secure attachments to the lost person were associated with less anger, social isolation, guilt, death anxiety, somatic symptoms, despair, depersonalisation and rumination after bereavement. They also found that the securely attached reported more 'interchange' with and reminiscence about the dead person than the insecurely attached. Interacting with these inter-personal factors is more general vulnerability to stress and a wide range of variables have been deduced to explain these.

All in all the empirical studies show that a variety of factors influence the expression of grief but they do not explain why. To find the answers we need to look at the main theories that have been proposed to explain the phenomenon of grief. These are best understood in historical perspective.

Grief and attachment theory

As we have seen, one of the functions of attachment is to prevent lasting loss. Crying and searching, which are innate in babies but are soon affected by learning, remain part of the reaction to later losses. One of the first to recognise this was Charles Darwin whose book *The Expression of the Emotions in Man and Animals* (1872) points to the similarity in the expression of sorrow not only between children and adults but also across other species of social animal.

John Bowlby, who was much influenced by Darwin and later wrote a biography (1990), saw the relevance of this thinking and developed it further in the third volume of his trilogy, *Loss, Sadness and Depression* (1980). In collaboration with James Robertson he described the phases of grief through which small children pass when separated for more than a short length of time from their mothers. These they characterised as 'protest', 'despair' and 'detachment'.

My own work in the field of bereavement started at the Institute of Psychiatry, London, where I delineated the problems of bereaved psychiatric patients (Parkes 1964a, 1964b). This research showed that many kinds of psychiatric disorder can be triggered by bereavement. 'Affective disorders' (notably anxiety states and clinical depression) are the most common but some bereaved people suffer from other disorders including chronic grief and delayed/inhibited grief. (These are variously referred to as pathological, traumatic or complicated grief.)

A problem which became apparent during the course of these studies was the lack of any standard of comparison. I joined Bowlby's research unit in 1962 in order to undertake one of the first systematic studies of 'normal' or uncomplicated grief in unselected London widows. The first fruit of our collaboration was a joint paper (Bowlby and Parkes 1970) in which we pointed out the similarities between the response of adults to the loss of a partner or spouse and the response of young children to separation from their mothers. We modified Robertson and Bowlby's 'phases of grief' to include an initial phase of numbness or blunting of emotions which was often reported by London widows, particularly after unexpected deaths.

The paper was important in recognising that grief is a process of change through which people pass and suggesting one way in which it could be construed, but it presented a model of grief which made it appear simpler than it really was and was rather too easily associated with psychoanalytic phases such as Freud's phases of infantile sexuality. Before long the 'phases of grief' were being used as a prescription for normal grieving, a use which had never been our intention.

Part of the difficulty lay in the lack of an accepted definition of grief, a problem that still exists today. Most people define grief as the reaction to bereavement and a number of instruments have been developed which purport to measure this. The most widely used are Faschingbauer's 'Texas Inventory of Grief' (Faschingbauer *et al.* 1977) and Sanders *et al.*'s 'Grief Experience Inventory' (1991). They include such things as anger, self-reproaches and depression, which can occur following a wide variety of stressful life events and are certainly not peculiar to grief.

The reaction to bereavement includes much more than grief alone. In addition to grief for the loss of a loved person, bereavement usually faces us with:

- threats to our security
- major changes in our lives
- major changes in our family.

It may or may not also be associated with:

- horrific memories of terrifying events
- blame towards others for the death
- shame and/or guilt for our own complicity or neglect.

None of these is a part of grief though they may complicate grief and cause lasting problems.

A satisfactory definition of grief should distinguish it from these other psychological phenomena. In my view its essential components are the experience of a loss and a reaction of intense pining or yearning for the object lost (separation anxiety). Without these a person cannot truly be said to be grieving.

What then of the so-called *'complicated grief reactions'*? These too require definition if they are to be distinguished from the many other psychiatric problems which can complicate bereavement. Although severe grief has many of the features that characterise psychiatric disorders, it is only when it is unusually prolonged and gives rise to impairment of normal life functions that it can be regarded as 'pathological'. With this in mind, Jacobs (1999) and Prigerson *et al.* (1995a, 1995b) have put the diagnosis of 'complicated grief' on a scientific footing. They have developed diagnostic criteria that are confined to the grief that follows loss of a person and include intrusive and distressing core symptoms of separation anxiety (including preoccupation with thoughts of the dead person). Their criteria are sufficiently broad to include both chronic and delayed forms of grief.

Prigerson and Jacobs have also developed their own systematic measure of 'complicated grief', which is much more focused than the imprecise measures of bereavement outcome described above. They have demonstrated, beyond doubt, that 'complicated grief' is quite distinct from major depression although it is often accompanied by that condition. We look more closely at complicated grief in Chapter 17.

Psycho-social transition theory

Clearly no single theory is going to cover all of the consequences of bereavement let alone the other losses that we suffer. In order to clarify the similarities and differences between the reaction to loss of a person and the reaction to other losses I moved on from bereavement to study reactions to loss of a limb (Parkes 1972, 1976). There were striking similarities in the response. Most amputees, like bereaved people, found it hard to believe what had happened. They were preoccupied with and pining for all that they had lost and, most striking of all, they had a strong sense of the presence of the lost part.

Even so this response requires a different explanation to attachment theory, which only explains the reaction to separation from people. I do not love my left leg in the same way that I love my wife; the two types of attachment are very different. My research led me to formulate a theory of psycho-social transitions (Parkes 1971).

Human beings are distinguished from other species by the complexity and magnitude of the mental models of the world that we create. We have already explored some of the ways in which the child's internal models include assumptions about parents and others that colour the way in which they come to view the world. In 1971 I coined the term 'the assumptive world' for that aspect of the internal model that is assumed to be true (Parkes 1971). Other internal models include dreaded or hoped-for worlds; these can be used for the purposes of planning and they have a provisional quality. They merge into the fantasies that are the stuff of dreams and fiction.

While the assumptive world contains assumptions about objects such as tables, chairs, doors and windows, which enable us to recognise these things when we meet them and plan our behaviour accordingly, it also contains much else. Everything that we take for granted is part of our assumptive world. This includes assumptions about our parents and ourselves, our ability to cope with danger, the protection which we can expect from others, including the police, the legal system and the people around us and the countless cognitions which make up the complex structures on which our sense of meaning and purpose in life depends.

Like computer programmes these assumptions are built one upon another. Most of the modifications take place at a surface level; they do not require us to modify our basic assumptions. Basic assumptions are the operating systems that run and give meaning to the other programmes. We saw above how the attachments that infants make to their parents enable them gradually to build up assumptions about their parents, themselves and the world at large. These constitute the templates against which subsequent events are compared and through which they are comprehended.

Our assumptive world is our most valuable piece of mental equipment; without it we are literally lost. But it is not fixed, it is constantly being modified by new information that adds to or negates particular assumptions. In fact, one of the pleasures of life is to visit new places, do new things and meet new people who will add to and enrich our assumptive world.

This theory of mind fits well with current *constructivist theory*, which is based on the assumption that our view of the world is essentially subjective. Thus, Arvay (2001: 215–216) states: 'The nature of reality is formulated in both individual and collective constructions', each person's view of reality is unique and 'there is no "single truth" or "reality" that can be known'. He goes on: 'Constructivists maintain that knowledge and truth are not discovered but are created or invented.' In the end every person's world is unique to them even when it reflects a shared environment.

Neimeyer (2001) has written extensively about the 'narratives' by which people explain and 'construct' themselves and their world. He sees it as the role of the 'therapist' to help people to review these 'narratives' in much the same way in which a psychiatrist takes a life history. This is an important development in our ways of thinking about grief and is currently receiving the attention which it deserves.

In pointing up the subjective nature of the internal world the constructivists blur the distinction between the assumptive world and the fantasy world; this, in my view, is a mistake. I hold that the belief that a particular view of the world is true and real places it in a mental category which is quite different from the other types of construction. It is this belief that enables us, most of the time, to approach the world around us with confidence and to feel secure.

My studies of amputees showed how people faced with a major change in their lives regularly find that the models of the world which, until that moment, they had taken for granted, must now be modified. The amputee who springs out of bed in the morning and finds himself sprawling on the floor is operating an obsolete model. Likewise the widow who lays the table for two, reaches for her husband in bed at night, or thinks to herself 'I must ask my husband about that', is continuing, out of habit, to live in an assumptive world that no longer exists.

All events that cause major changes in our lives, particularly those that had not been anticipated, challenge our assumptive world and bring about a crisis during which we are likely to remain restless, tense, anxious and unsettled until the necessary modifications have been made. This is hardly surprising since our assumptive world is all we have; it is our only resource for orienting ourselves and fulfilling our aims. Much of the work of relearning which follows a major loss and which, in the past, has been termed 'grief work', is better seen as part of the work of transition. The issues involved are particularly clear and relevant following traumatic life events.

Current thinking about trauma and bereavement

A 'trauma' is a blow and a 'bereavement' is a loss. Over the years two very different fields of service, each with its own theories and practices, have grown up around these related concepts. On the one hand we have psychologists working with war veterans, victims of abuse and other people faced with stress, violence and/or threats to life; on the other we have bereavement and divorce counsellors, social workers and others who have focused on understanding the needs of separated or bereaved people. Although each group has tended to ignore the others and to develop their own approaches, there is too much overlap between the fields for this isolation to benefit anyone. This is most obvious when bereavement is accompanied by violence or other trauma.

If, in fact, there are important differences between the psychological reactions to the two types of experience, then it should be possible to elucidate these by comparing the reactions to bereavement with and without trauma, and trauma with and without bereavement.

Most studies of the psychological consequences of bereavement have demonstrated that deaths that are sudden, unexpected and untimely are more

likely to give rise to problems than those that have been
prepared for. Other factors that contribute to bereaveme
witnessing violence or mutilation, deaths for which some
(including murders and suicides) and deaths when no intact
(see Rando 1986 and Parkes 1996 for reviews). It is these
have been termed traumatic losses.

If, in western societies, traumatic loss can increase the risk, is this a general
stress or is there a particular type of response that characterises traumatic
losses? In the Harvard Study we found that unexpected and untimely
bereavements in young widows and widowers were associated, in the short
term, with more disbelief and avoidance of confrontation with the loss. As
time passed, there was a persisting sense of the presence of the lost person, a
feeling of continued obligation to them and social withdrawal along with
lasting anxiety, depression, loneliness and, often, self-reproaches. All of these
features were less common in those who had anticipated the loss (Parkes and
Weiss 1983).

Horowitz (1986) suggests that numbing, disbelief and failure to integrate
a traumatic death into a bereaved person's assumptive world are defences
against overwhelming feelings of helplessness and insecurity which threaten
to erupt. Despite these attempts at avoidance, however, traumatised individuals commonly experience intense anxiety, hypervigilance and startle
reactions, which can be triggered by any reminder of the loss. Horowitz
developed his 'Impact of Events' scale as a means of measuring these twin
aspects of avoidance and intrusive recall (Horowitz *et al.* 1979).

Horowitz's observations were not confined to bereavement. Similar reactions are found to many life situations in which, over a short space of time,
people are confronted with *intense fear, helplessness or horror.* A large literature
has now grown up around the whole topic of 'traumatic stress' and it is not
possible here to do justice to this growing field. The combination of avoidance and intrusive images has given rise to the psychiatric diagnosis of
'post-traumatic stress disorder' (PTSD) and so much research has focused on
this syndrome that one gets the (false) impression that it is the commonest
psychological consequence of trauma.

The focus on 'fear, helplessness and horror' has led many investigators to
assume that it is the magnitude of the danger that is the cause of the problems that follow, yet human beings, in common with other species, are well
adapted to danger. We have an entire autonomic nervous system to help us to
deal with it and there is no evidence of an increased risk to mental health at
times of war or other danger; something more is needed. Recent work by
Janoff-Bulman has postulated that, if a traumatic situation is to cause lasting
problems it must, in a short space of time, shatter certain basic assumptions
about the world (Janoff-Bulman 1992).

There are some life events whose consequences are so profound that they
invalidate entire sections of our assumptive world. Quite suddenly we can
take nothing for granted any more, like the person with inverting spectacles

ε feel as if the world has turned upside down. It is these situations that Janoff-Bulman terms *'shattered assumptions'*. The changes which must follow are much more difficult to make than those which follow minor changes but they too can be achieved if we have the opportunity and the time to anticipate and adjust to the change. Unfortunately this is not always the case.

No matter how unsatisfactory the world may be, the possession of a reasonably accurate assumptive world enables us to know where we stand and, most of the time, we can get by. The assumptive world is, therefore, a major source of security. By the same token, anything that undermines the assumptive world or renders it obsolete will undermine our security. It follows that a major bereavement faces us with both the need to grieve for the person we have lost and the need to revise our assumptive world.

Major revision of the assumptive world is a cognitive task but it takes time and, particularly if it is suddenly thrust upon us, it evokes powerful emotions (e.g. fear, helplessness and/or horror), which may themselves interfere with the cognitive task. It follows that both cognitions and emotions need to be taken into account in any attempt to give help to traumatised people.

Although our assumptive world is based on our perception of a real world it should not be confused with the real world and is subject to error. As we saw in the last chapter, errors may arise because our experience of the world is limited, our interpretation of events incorrect or the information that we receive from others fallacious. Again, such errors can be corrected but those that require changes in basic assumptions are more difficult to change than others.

What are these basic assumptions and how do they come about? Basic assumptions are the guiding principles, the root systems, which underlie and direct our attention and judgement. They include the assumptions about the world and ourselves that arise out of our experiences of early childhood. We take them for granted but, because they are abstractions from reality and at one remove from direct experience, they are more prone to error, so much so, that Janoff-Bulman refers to them as 'illusions'. She suggests that the function of basic assumptions is to protect us from distressing emotions but this is not their primary function, although it may be a secondary effect. Their primary function is to protect us from threats to our survival in the infant environment.

Can attachment theory and psycho-social transition theory be integrated?

If attachment theory explains the urge to cry and to search for someone who is lost and psycho-social transition theory explains the need to rethink and replan one's life in the face of a major change, how are these two alternatives worked out in the moment-to-moment life of bereaved people? The answer to this question is to be found in the Dual Process Model of grieving, which has been postulated by Stroebe and Schut (2001a). They have shown that, in the normal course of grieving, bereaved people tend to oscillate between what they term 'loss orientation' and 'restoration orientation'. By 'loss orientation' they mean the painful search for the lost person which, as we have seen, is the *sine qua non* of grief. By 'restoration orientation' they mean the struggle to reorient oneself in a world that seems to have lost its meaning. This, as we have seen, is the essence of the psycho-social transition. Problems arise if either focus becomes exclusive. Thus, people who become preoccupied with the search and are unable or unwilling to look forward become chronic grievers, while those who avoid grieving and devote themselves to a future orientation tend to suffer delayed or inhibited grief.

The normal outcome of this process of oscillation is that, eventually, the bereaved person discovers that there is much in their past relationship which continues to have relevance in planning for the future. In the early stages of bereavement the sufferer often feels as if they have lost every good thing that came with the lost person; only with time do they discover that this is not true. Just as adolescent children can separate from their parents because they now carry their parent's assumptive world within them, so when a widow says, 'He lives on in my memory' this is literally true. The recognition of this continuing bond with the dead (Klass *et al.* 1996) is one of the things which makes it possible to let go of the person 'out there' simply because we realise that we never lost them 'in here'.

Thus, the aspect of grieving which arises out of our infantile need to search for a lost parent and which is the essence of attachment theory, comes, in the course of maturation, to be complemented by the discovery that, thanks in part to the assumptive world which the parents helped us to develop, we can survive the transition to a world without them. By loving her child well a mother teaches the child to separate from her. Viewed in this light the acid test of a love relationship may well reside in the success with which it can survive the death of one of the lovers.

Coping

The idea that the expression of emotion is helpful goes back to psychoanalytic researchers such as Deutsch (1937) and Lindemann (1944) who recognised that both cultural and other factors might lead to the inhibition of the expression of grief. In accordance with the psychoanalytic theory of repression this was seen as a potent cause of later psychiatric problems. It also suggested a solution to the problems in the form of therapies that would facilitate the expression of grief. Some psychotherapists and bereavement counsellors still see this as their primary aim, although the proportion of people who benefit from this approach is not large. We return to examine this and other therapies in more detail in Chapter 18.

More recently it has been recognised that emotional expression is only one of several ways of coping with loss. Lazarus and Folkman (1984) have specified the repertoire of strategies with which we habitually cope with new or problematic situations. These include instrumental (or cognitive) strategies, such as problem solving, and more emotive approaches such as crying, which may be a way of seeking help. Each of these strategies is likely to be more appropriate in some situations than others. Thus, problem solving is valuable when a problem is soluble but less appropriate when it is not. Help seeking is valuable when help is needed and available but less appropriate when others are equally helpless or unavailable. On the face of it, it seems unlikely that instrumental methods of problem solving will bring back a dead person, nor will emotional expression solve the problem. This said, the process of oscillation that was described above could be said to involve both cognitive attempts to recover and develop those memories of, and beliefs about, the lost person that mitigate the loss, and recognition that many of the old assumptions about the world, that relied upon the lost person's presence for their veracity must be relinquished. Since this is inevitably painful, the process of relearning cannot be carried out rapidly or without experiencing the emotions that go with it.

Bowlby (1973a) maintained that the function of attachments is to provide the security that arises from having a parent-figure who is known to be available and responsive when needed. This function continues throughout childhood and is complemented by the increasing number of individuals to whom the child is attached. This network of attachments is another factor which makes it easier for parents to leave their child and, eventually, for the child to leave home. In adult life reciprocal attachments to family and friends continue to provide security. Indeed, one way of coping with possible future losses is to become attached to other people. Even those who have lost the person to whom they are most closely attached will find some of their distress assuaged if they have others to whom they are attached and whom they see as 'supportive' (Raphael 1977). People who have an expectation that others can be trusted will be more likely to seek help when they become aware of danger.

We have seen how Ainsworth's attachment patterns are themselves ways of coping and may influence subsequent coping strategies. Thus, anxious/ambivalent (or dependent) attachments are ways of coping with parents who pay attention and reward emotional demands. They are likely to give rise to emotion-focused strategies. Avoidant attachments are ways of coping with parents who discourage emotional demands, consequently they are more likely to evoke control of emotions and cognitive attempts at problem solving. Disorganised attachments may reflect situations of helplessness in which high levels of anxiety and depression are likely to arise.

Secure attachments teach the developing child to trust itself and others, and are generally regarded as the most desirable pattern; but they may limit the child's ability to cope, later in life, with people who cannot be trusted and with situations which lie beyond their control. On balance the advantages of secure attachments are thought to outweigh the disadvantages. Thus, several studies have been made of the influence of attachment patterns, as measured by the AAI, on people's ability to cope with trauma. Steele and Steele (1994), reviewing this research, conclude: 'Given two victims of a similar trauma, the AAI has the potential to identify which victim is likely to be prone to develop severe and ongoing post-traumatic difficulties.' This said the experience of secure attachment in childhood is no guarantee of later success and in the end it is the fit between a particular situation and a particular worldview that determines who will cope well and who badly.

Conclusions

In the last chapter we saw that by studying how children react when separated from their mothers in the strange situation, patterns of loving have been identified which influence the way we come to view the world. We have seen here that by studying how adults react following the death of a loved person, grief too has its patterns, which influence long-term adjustment to life.

We move on now to consider a research project the results of which will, I hope, help us to discover how these patterns influence each other. We shall see how love in its various forms can enrich or impoverish, strengthen or undermine, cure or even kill us.

3   The research project

Life is the art of drawing sufficient conclusions from insufficient premises.
Samuel Butler *Notebooks: Life* (1912) ix

Bereavement, as we have seen, is not only one of the most painful stresses faced by most people, and a cause of lasting problems in some, but it is also the prime example of the common life experiences which we call losses. If we can understand bereavement we may find ourselves better able to understand these other losses and to help those who suffer them.

Over the years psychiatrists have developed their own theories about such problems and make use of these theories in their attempts to help their patients. However, it is easy for doctors to find 'evidence' for their pet theories and to ignore anything that contradicts them. As a result, there are rather too many theories of the causes of psychiatric problems, but little agreement about which theory is best. Psychiatric problems have in the past been attributed to masturbation, constipation, high protein diet and hidden infections on no more basis than the fact that they sometimes co-exist with these common phenomena. More recently, methods of research and statistical analysis have been developed which enable us to estimate the chances of a particular association occurring by chance alone.

It follows that any study that attempts to go beyond mere speculation has to be systematic and rigorous. It requires careful planning and analysis, with safeguards to ensure the reliability and validity of the data and the conclusions reached. Questions and answers need to be recorded in such a way that they can be replicated and confirmed by others.

The study to be described here was carried out with the help of 278 people who attended my psychiatric outpatients clinic at the Royal London Hospital. It was set up to test my clinical impression, and evidence from the studies described in Chapters 1 and 2, that love and loss are intertwined, that childhood attachment patterns, separations from parents and relationships in later life all influence how we cope with stress and loss and predict the kinds of problem which cause people to seek help after bereavement in adult life. I hoped to explain any patterns that were found, to understand the chains of causation and to clarify the reasons why some people come through the pain of bereavement and emerge stronger and wiser than before, while others suffer lasting damage to their physical and/or mental health.

Psychiatrists are only called upon when things go wrong, and we tend to get a blinkered view of the world. For this reason it was important to include in my studies people who had not been referred for psychiatric help. Fortunately, through the good offices of Dr Anne Ward, I was able to obtain the same information from a comparison group of 78 young women who had assisted her with her own research and had not sought psychiatric help. Thirty-five of them had suffered bereavement in the past five years. They provide us with an opportunity to identify the factors influencing the reaction to bereavement in a less disturbed population.

While much of the technical detail has been assigned to the appendices, it is important for the reader to understand how the research was carried out and the logical basis of the various scores that will be referred to elsewhere in this book. In this chapter and elsewhere I shall not assume that my reader is trained in statistics and will explain, in footnotes and in non-technical language, those statistical tests and technical terms which are important to an understanding of the research. Readers who are already familiar with these terms and tests can skip the footnotes and read the appendices.

Is it ethical to study bereaved people?

Research of this kind, involving as it does the statistical comparison of replies to a battery of questions (157 in all) about a wide range of events and circumstances in the lives of 278 respondents, many of them bereaved, is beset with ethical problems.

Grief is one of the most distressing experiences that we can undergo and all research in this field must be carried out with sensitivity and tact. This said, most bereaved people are glad to share with others their thoughts about this important experience in their lives and *bona fide* researchers, who are open about their intentions and respect the bereaved person's wishes, will usually find them quite willing to help us. A more detailed consideration of ethical issues together with guidelines for carrying out ethical research in bereavement is given in Parkes (1995).

In the research to be described here the bereaved psychiatric patients were already asking for help and expecting to answer questions about their lives. The object of the research was to help us to understand the life circumstances and events which had contributed to their present problems; as such it was likely to be a useful addition to my psychiatric assessment of their problems and this may explain why very few people declined to co-operate. I made use of a questionnaire the front page of which explained this objective and requested permission to make use of the information for research purposes. Each participant signed a form indicating that they gave this permission. It was, of course, important for the participants to know that my research would not compromise the confidentiality which they had a right to expect of me as a doctor and the form went on to make it clear that the person's name would not be disclosed and that no other information which would enable them to be identified would be revealed in any publications arising out of the research. I have kept this promise and the names used in this book together with any other identifying information have been changed.

The final version of the questionnaire is given in full in Appendix 3.1 and the information and permission form in Appendix 3.2.

Background to the research

Eighty-three men and 195 women who had been referred to me, a consultant psychiatrist at the Royal London Hospital, completed the questionnaires. Because I am known to have a special interest in problems of bereavement and to have written widely on this topic, they included 181 bereaved people. But not all of my patients were bereaved; I am also a general psychiatrist and was able to obtain the help of 97 non-bereaved psychiatric patients. Most were referred from the vicinity of the hospital, which is a large teaching hospital located in the East End of London. The non-bereaved people are considered in Chapter 16 but are not included in the analyses given elsewhere in this book.

To obtain the help of a psychiatrist in Britain through the National Health Service, most people need first to convince their general practitioner (GP) of their need for such help. The GP then writes a referral letter to the psychiatrist requesting an outpatient appointment (in urgent cases the contact may be made by telephone). Because the Royal London Hospital is a large general hospital I also receive referrals from consultants in other departments of the hospital.

This means that these patients had been seen first by one or more other doctors most of whom had tried other approaches before asking for psychiatric help and many had received an antidepressant or other form of medication. Support from trained bereavement volunteers is widely and freely available in London and is often the first option to be considered by bereaved people who need help from outside their own families. In these circumstances it is not altogether surprising that 74 per cent of the bereaved people referred to my outpatient clinic had been bereaved for over a year before they saw me. You could say that I was at the end of the line.

Ward's comparison group, on the other hand, were recruited either through advertisements in a local paper which asked for volunteers to help with a study of how women cope with life events (25 cases), or by direct contact at a university and research institute (57 cases). While they cannot be taken as a random sample of the UK population, they do provide some comparison with the young women in the psychiatric sample.

The rationale of the questionnaire

In order to place my investigation on a systematic footing, to avoid any suspicion that I may have biased the patient's replies or that I might have recorded evidence to fit my theories and ignored conflicting data, I asked people to fill in a questionnaire before they attended for their first appointment with me. The questionnaire included a large number of questions about attachments in the past so I have termed it the Retrospective Attachment Questionnaire and will refer to it throughout this book as the RAQ.

Most people seem to have found it interesting and useful to think about the issues raised by the questionnaire and one remarked that it was 'the most valuable questionnaire I have ever completed'. For him, the opportunity to take another look at the experiences that had contributed to his current problems was therapeutic. Despite this comment I do not pretend that the questionnaire is ideal and there are undoubtedly better ways of measuring many of the variables that have been included. Some of these measures were not available when the RAQ was initiated; others are too time consuming to be included in the questionnaire, which already requires a major commitment on the part of the respondents. Time and again it was necessary to balance the competing demands of keeping the questionnaire as simple and concise as possible, and using longer and more complex instruments that have been tried and tested by others. I was interested in five interrelated sets of circumstances:

1 *Parenting*: the person's view of their parents (including adoptive or foster parents).
2 *Childhood vulnerability*: their view of themselves as children.
3 *Events and circumstances of adult life*: including adult relationships and bereavements.
4 *Coping*: how they usually deal with stress.
5 *Current symptoms and emotions* at the time when the form was completed.

Thanks to the research into attachments, which was described in Chapter 1, I started this study with expectations about the ways in which particular patterns of parenting would be associated with particular patterns of childhood vulnerability. These influenced my choice of questions to ask but it was for the research to tell me if these expectations would be fulfilled. The questions will be described and explained below and we shall see how the analysis of these questions confirmed my expectation that the patterns of parenting do indeed relate to the patterns of childhood behaviour as recalled by my patients. It is the combination of the two, the parent-related and child-related variables, which turn out to resemble the dyadic patterns of attachment found by Ainsworth and Main and justifies us in using these patterns of attachment as our starting point for examining the influence of childhood attachments on later life.

The next section explores the nature of any attachment to spouse or partner in adult life together with several major life events that are likely to contribute to cause or aggravate problems. Finally the respondents were asked to assess their ways of coping with stress and the symptoms and emotional distresses that now trouble them. Let us look in more detail at each of the above categories.

Section I: Questions about parents

For each one of us our parents are the only parents we have, our family is the norm for us and we have few opportunities to obtain a standard of comparison. While most people are reluctant to judge their parents, this does not mean that they are not able to describe them and such descriptions usually ring true. In other words, a case history that encourages people to reflect in a non-judgemental way about the events and circumstances of their early life, and whose aim is to explore important experiences, is seen by the client as very worthwhile. In these circumstances I have seldom found evidence for distortion of the story.

Obtaining such information in a questionnaire is rather more problematic and I have tried to couch the questions in as unthreatening and impartial a way as possible. Even so it is important to bear in mind the fact that the reliability of people's recollections of their parents and their childhood may have been coloured by their current feelings and by their desire to give 'correct' answers to my questions. This is one of the inevitable weaknesses of retrospective data but, as we shall see below, it is not without remedy.

The parts of the questionnaire dealing with parenting (questions I/1–I/30 and II/1–II/4) were developed with three things in mind:

- accurate recording of factual information about parents
- circumstances and events that my clinical experience had indicated might be important
- the types of parenting that had proved to be associated with insecure attachments in the studies reviewed in Chapter 1 (see pp. 13–15).

There were 30 questions asked separately about mother and father (making 60 in all) and an additional three general questions about boarding school or orphanage (question II/1), being an only child (II/2) and the family being subjected for a long time to serious danger or persecution (II/4).

Questions about parenting include several about separation from parents, which as we have seen (p. 12) has been counted one of the major detrimental influences on young children. These are followed by questions about the parent's temperament (nervous, depressed, aggressive) and any history of psychiatric disorder or threats of suicide, violence or alcoholism. Aspects of parenting that received special attention were inconsistency, overprotection, dependence, unusual closeness, inability to show warmth, teasing, rejection and physical or sexual abuse. All of these have been found, in other studies, to influence attachment patterns and children's views of themselves and others.

The reliability of the questions was checked by asking 45 of the bereaved people to repeat the questionnaire after the end of therapy. It was assumed that questions which people found difficult to answer would be less consistently answered on the second occasion. Two questions that were not answered consistently were dropped from the questionnaire. The details of this analysis are described in Appendix 3.3. Appendix 3.1 gives the final version of the RAQ after the elimination of these unreliable questions.

Replies to two other questions were found to be unreliable: question I/2b 'How old were you when your mother died?' and the same question applied to fathers. When these figures were subtracted from the patient's age about 10 per cent gave a negative result implying that in these cases the parent's age at death had been recorded rather than the patient's age when the parent died.

Section II: Questions about childhood

Children, as we have seen, are very sensitive to separation from their parents and to the security of the parenting they receive. The research reviewed in Chapter 1 indicates that this sensitivity is likely to be reflected in their trust in themselves and others, their ability to learn and their overall feelings of security. This section (questions II/5–II/35) seeks for early evidence of insecurity and problems in trusting oneself and others. It includes questions about the child's feeling states (insecure, unhappy, anxious, timid, tearful, etc.), trust or distrust, performance at school relative to their potential, periods of illness, dependence on others, preferences for closeness or distance, affection, irritability, temper and controlling behaviour. As in the preceding section, replies to these questions were tested for reliability by repeating the questionnaire. As a result, a further four questions were dropped leaving 31 in this section (see Appendix 3.3 for details). The final list of questions about childhood will be found in Section II of the questionnaire (in Appendix 3.1).

Section III: Questions about adult life

Adult life brings its own stresses some of which are likely to result from and/ or aggravate insecurity. These include physical illnesses, experience of migration, lack of social support and the presence or absence of children of one's own. Questions about these are included in section III along with an assessment of the person's relationship with any spouse or partner (III/7). This section does not attempt to explore the relationship in detail and none of the established but lengthy relationship scales which have been developed in recent years have been employed. Rather the RAQ focuses on attachment issues, particularly, closeness and dependency on either side and ambivalence, as reflected in a check list of nine common areas of disagreement (III/7d).

Particular attention is paid to bereavements. The number of deaths during the last five years of any person close to the respondent is recorded and further details obtained about the most important of these bereavements (III/8). Questions cover the factors which other research has shown to place bereaved people at special risk – unexpected deaths, deaths for which the bereaved blame themselves or others, suicide, homicide and the loss of people with whom one has a dependent or ambivalent relationship.

In this section, only those questions whose replies are unlikely to change following bereavement and the passage of time could be tested for reliability by repeating the questionnaire. This led to the elimination of one further question (see Appendix 3.3).

Section IV: About you now

Two types of question are included in section IV which is headed 'About You Now'. These assess how this person copes with stress and their current symptoms and distress.

Questions about coping

The concept of 'coping' is widely used in psychology and several scales and questionnaires have been developed to measure instrumental and emotive strategies. As we saw on p. 36, neither of these approaches provides an adequate solution to the problems of bereavement.

The aspects of coping which are included in the RAQ focus on the issues of trust and interaction which influence our reaction to stress in adult life. It was anticipated that a person's ways of coping with bereavement will be intimately bound up with the assumptions and strategies that have arisen out of the attachments made in childhood. Thus, our trust in ourselves and others and our ability to show feelings of affection and grief can be regarded as ways of coping that will influence the reaction to bereavement. Even childlike or 'immature' behaviour, which tends to be seen as dysfunctional, may be a way of evoking the nurturance of others. Alternatively, those who lack confidence in their ability to evoke nurture may, even so, find that they can control others by assertive or aggressive behaviour. Several questions to elicit these strategies were included in the RAQ.

The term 'stress' is usually taken to refer to any situation that arises when our accustomed ways of dealing with serious problems are no longer adequate. This is what most people mean by 'getting to the end of my tether'. A question (IV/17) which attempted to get to the root of the person's habitual ways of handling stress consisted of replies to a hypothetical situation: 'If you got to the end of your tether would you', followed by nine possible responses – 'seek help from a friend', 'seek help from your family', 'seek help from a doctor', 'seek help from some other person', shut yourself away from people, 'drown your sorrows with alcohol', 'take an overdose or otherwise harm yourself', 'become irritable or bad tempered with others', or 'turn your frustration inwards, feeling guilty or self-reproachful?'

These 'end of tether' questions get to the heart of the attachments that, as we saw in the first chapter, developed to provide us with survival strategies at times of danger. Other questions relevant to coping include taking medication for nerves (IV/7), behaving in childish or immature ways (IV/12) and becoming aggressive or challenging (IV/22). It was anticipated that these too are likely to influence and be influenced by attachments.

While we have no means of knowing whether or not people react in the way they say they would when 'at the end of their tether', the fact that 75 per cent of bereaved respondents said that they had indeed got to the end of their tether (IV/18) increases the probability that they do, and may account for the fact that most respondents had no difficulty in answering this question.

Questions about symptoms and distress

While coping can be seen as having a function, 'symptoms and distress' are more obviously evidence of dysfunction. Questions covered anxiety, depression, tension, tearfulness, distrust, panic or fear, loneliness, 'pining for someone or something you have lost', shyness, wishing to be looked after and regrets.

Although 'coping' as defined seems different from 'symptoms and distress', there is in fact some overlap between these categories arising out of the fact that our feelings both determine and reflect the ways we cope. For example, aggressiveness can be regarded both as a way of coping with threat and a measure of anger, a reaction to stress. Likewise, positive answers to question IV/17f in which the respondent agrees that at the end of their tether they would 'drown your sorrows with alcohol' and IV/8 'Do you use alcohol to control anxiety and depression, if so do you take rather more than you should?' could be seen as a way of coping but are here regarded as dysfunctional and an indicator of alcohol problems. Similarly, 'Do you sometimes rely on others more than you should?' (IV/15) sounds like a way of coping but was found to correlate highly with a positive response to the question 'Have you recently got to the end of your tether?'(IV/18) which seems more to do with 'symptoms and distress'. Again, both of these questions were included in the 'symptoms and distress' category.

To sum up, after the removal of unreliable questions we were left with a questionnaire which asked a number of questions as shown in Table 3.1.

Missing data

In all research using questionnaires some questions are likely to remain unanswered and there are accepted ways of dealing with small amounts of missing data. Details of these are given in Appendix 3.3 and the rules of thumb that result are included in the instructions for scoring the questionnaire (Appendix 3.7).

Table 3.1 Number of questions in each section of the RAQ

Parenting	↔	Childhood	→	Adult Life	↔	Coping	→	Current state
30 questions re Mother 30 re Father 3 re Family		31 questions		35 questions		15 questions		15 questions

The only questions for which appreciable amounts of data were missing (in about a third of the sample) were those concerning the former relationship with the person now dead. Replies to questions about previous disagreements, dependence and unusual closeness to the person now deceased were included in the analysis of data, but their reliability and validity is in doubt, perhaps because of the difficulty experienced by bereaved people in giving an objective account of those now dead.

Facilitating scoring the questionnaire

A large amount of information was obtained and it was necessary to organise it into 'bite-sized chunks' in order to facilitate analysis. As we saw on p. 38, a major problem in psychiatry has been that of weighing up the relative importance of competing variables. If we are to make any sense of the complex interactions between the replies to the 157 questions in the RAQ we need to find some way of reducing their number without oversimplifying them.

In some cases this is quite easy. Thus, the question on physical disability in adult life (III/3) has five subquestions, which can easily be added together to give a score of *Disability*. Similarly the checklist of nine areas of disagreement with spouse or partner (III/7d) can be summed to make a *Marital Disagreement* score. When this is added to the other three questions in this section (III/7 a, b, c), which cover aspects of dependency, a *Marital Disharmony* score can be obtained. A *Social Support* score is obtained by adding the number of Yes replies of questions IV/17a and b). These indicate that at the end of their tether the person would turn to family or friends. These were then added to Yes replies to question III/6 'Do you have anyone in whom you can confide your inmost thoughts and feelings?'

Although replies to most of the symptoms and distress questions carry no implication of psychiatric disorder, being common responses to the problems of life, there were a few which imply that the person is unable to function effectively in their day-to-day life. Such dysfunction is regarded by psychiatrists as one of the prime justifications for a psychiatric diagnosis (see p. 226 for details). These questions include four about drug and alcohol consumption (IV/7a–8b), one reflecting inability to cope with responsibilities (IV/9) and one acknowledging that the person has recently got to the end of their tether (IV/18). These were summed together to give a *Dysfunction* score.

The remaining questions posed a rather more difficult problem. Although many of the questions had been chosen in the expectation that they would reflect the patterns of attachment described by Ainsworth and Main and other questions were expected to reflect particular ways of coping or particular patterns of reaction to bereavement, it remained to be seen whether or not these patterns would be found in this data.[1] The first step was to analyse how the replies cluster, or vary, together by means of factor analysis. This is a test of the extent to which particular replies to one question are associated with particular replies to others (details are given in Appendix 3.4).

This analysis enabled scores of various aspects of parenting to be obtained. With few exceptions, replies to questions about attachments to fathers clustered together in much the same way as questions about attachments to mothers and it has been possible to use scores derived from the same clusters for each parent. This also makes it possible, when appropriate, to add together scores for mother and scores for father to give combined scores of 'parenting'. The following names have been assigned because they seem to reflect the meaning of each cluster of variables which, when added together, can be used as a score. (The questions which make them up are given in Appendix 3.4 along with the statistical justification.)

Parenting scores

- *1/40 Distant control.* People who saw their parents as distant and controlling also saw them as lacking in warmth and strict; they were also said to have discouraged their child from playing with other children. By adding together the replies to questions about each of these issues a single score, which has been labelled 'Distant control', was obtained. In like manner, the headings of the sections below are the names that I have chosen to reflect the meaning of scores derived from questions about the succeeding issues.

- *1/41 Overprotection.* Those who saw their parents as overprotective also said

---

1   By a pattern we mean a clustering of replies to the questions such that a particular answer to one question will repeatedly be associated with a particular answer to another. For example, Ainsworth found that mothers who are over-anxious, insensitive to their infants and discourage exploration have children who, in the Strange Situation Test, show great distress during the period of separation and who both cling and cry angrily when mother returns. If this pattern is reflected in our data we would expect that replies to questions indicating overprotectiveness and insensitivity in the mother will be associated with each other and with intolerance of separation and clinging in the child. This is what statisticians mean by correlation and there are well-established mathematical tests to measure the extent to which answers to several questions go together.

   The situation is made more complicated by the fact that the RAQ contains several questions about overprotectiveness, several about insensitivity and several about childhood clinging. To sort out which replies correlate together seems like an enormous task. Fortunately, statistical tests now enable this task to be performed quite easily. The test most often used for this purpose is factor analysis.

that the parents worried about their health and safety and saw the world as a dangerous place in which it is important for children to stay close. Together, these make up a score termed 'Overprotection'.

- *I/42 Depression/Psychiatric Problems.* Parents subject to depression were also seen as worriers and more likely to have threatened suicide and required psychiatric care.
- *I/43 Separations.* Both the frequency and duration of separations from parents during childhood were taken into account (see pp. 42–3).
- *I/44 Unusual Closeness.* People who rated their parents as unusually close were also more likely to fear that they would die or be killed.
- *I/45 Rejection/Violence.* Parents who were said to have been violent towards their partner were also likely to drink more alcohol than was good for them, and to tease or beat their child.

A *Problematic Parenting* score (I/46) was obtained by adding together each of these scores.

Childhood vulnerability scores

- *II/40 Timidity.* Those who said that they had been timid children also tended to see themselves as insecure, lacking in confidence, under-achievers, passive and loners, unable to ask for help.
- *II/41 Aggressiveness/Distrust.* People seeing themselves as aggressive were also more likely to say that they were stubborn, bad tempered, suspicious and distrustful.
- *II/42 Dresden Vase (Precious Child).* People who said that as children they had been sweet and appealing were also more likely to see themselves as delicate and fragile, anxious, fearful of separation from their parents, helpless and unable to cope.
- *II/43 Unhappiness.* Those who reported being unhappy children were also more likely to say that they cried 'often' and wished themselves dead.
- *II/44 Compulsive Caregiving.* Those who were always looking after others also said that they were seen by others as tougher and more capable than they really were.

A *Childhood Overall Vulnerability* score (II/45) was obtained by adding together each of these scores.

Current coping and personality

- *IV/40 Emotional Inhibition/Distrust.* People who found it hard to show feelings of affection also said that they found it hard to show grief and to cry. They wished they could cry more than they did. They were also more likely to distrust others. At first glance emotional inhibition and distrust may not appear to go together but in fact high scores on one went along with high scores on the other. On reflection this may arise both because people who distrust others tend to conceal their feelings from them and because people who appear inhibited do not attract friends.

- *IV/41 Aggressive/Assertive.* Those who described themselves as aggressive or challenging also said that, at the end of their tether, they would become irritable or bad tempered. They also accused themselves of behaving in childish or immature ways.
- *IV/42 End of Tether – Seek Help.* These were the group who, at the end of their tether, would seek help from family, friends, doctors or others.
- *IV/43 End of Tether – Turn Inward.* Others who, at the end of their tether, said that they would turn inward and feel guilty, also said that they would shut themselves away from people.

An overall score of *Problematic Coping* was derived from these scores by adding together the IV/40, 41 and 43 and subtracting IV/42. Seeking help when at the end of one's tether seems to be a more satisfactory way of coping than those reflected in the other scores.

Current symptoms and distress

- *IV/44 Anxiety/Panic.* People who said they were very anxious were also likely to panic, lack confidence and find it hard to cope.
- *IV/45 Grief/Loneliness.* People who said that they were very lonely, spent much time pining and many were filled with regrets. In theory grief, loneliness and regrets are three different phenomena. In practice people who scored high on measures of grief also scored high on self-assessments of loneliness and had more regrets.
- *IV/46 Depression/Medication.* People who said that they were very depressed were also tense and more likely to be taking medicines for their nerves. The most frequent medication to be prescribed for bereaved people in this study were antidepressants and this probably accounts for the correlation between self-ratings of depression and reports of medication consumption.
- *IV/47 Clinging.* People who said they relied too much on others also said that they had recently got to the end of their tether and wished that someone would look after them.
- *IV/48 Alcohol Consumption.* People who admitted to using alcohol to control feelings also said that they tend to drink more than is good for them and that, at the end of their tether, they would drown their sorrows with alcohol.

An *Overall Distress* score (IV/49) was derived by adding together these five scores.

Are these scores reliable?

As with the individual questions, the reliability of the parenting and child-hood vulnerability scores was tested by repeating the questionnaire in the follow-up study and analysing to what extent the scores had changed. Results are shown in Appendix 3.5. These findings confirm the reliability of all save the scores of 'Unusual Closeness' to both mother and father. These inconsistent replies may arise because, while 'closeness' is usually taken as a sign of love and highly value laden, 'unusual closeness' is more ambiguous. Respondents may have found themselves torn between the desire to give an answer that would be approved, a 'right' answer, and a strict regard for truth. This problem should be taken into account in any analysis that makes use of these scores.

The scores of coping and current symptoms and distress were likely to change as a consequence of therapy and the passage of time and test/retest was not an appropriate way of assessing their reliability.

Do the patterns of attachment found here resemble Ainsworth and Main's patterns?

It will not have escaped the reader's notice that many of the clusters of questions which make up the scores of childhood vulnerability and parenting resemble the components of Ainsworth and Main's patterns of attachment (pp. 12–15). In the section that follows we shall examine whether or not scores reflect particular childhood patterns of attachment and can be combined to give us scores for each pattern. Sometimes no score has been found to reflect a particular pattern; in this case individual questions which did reflect the pattern will be used instead of scores. Either way we end up with a separate score, which can be used as a pointer to each pattern. This said, it is important to remember that we are not directly measuring the patterns themselves, only the extent to which the bereaved person now recalls a pattern that resembles Ainsworth's patterns. Nor are we measuring current attachment patterns. It is to remind us of this that the word 'retrospective' has been included in the title of the questionnaire.

Some of the questions and scores derived from parts III and IV of the questionnaire reflect current ways of viewing the world and the correlations between these and the childhood patterns will be found to support the theory that childhood attachment patterns do continue to influence the lives of adults. In the end, however, only longitudinal studies that follow people from infancy to adult life will provide us with conclusive evidence of the causal sequence. For the time being we have to be content to ask ourselves whether or not the data, with all its inadequacies, does hang together, does make sense.

Secure attachments

As we saw in Chapter 1, Ainsworth found that parents who were sensitive and responsive to their infant's needs for security and a safe base from which to explore the world have children who tolerate brief separations without great distress and respond rapidly and warmly to their parent's comforting behaviour when they return. On follow-up these children are found to have an adequate trust in themselves and others. This leads us to predict that people who assign to their parents low scores on overall problematic parenting (I/46) will assign to themselves, as children, low scores on overall childhood vulnerability (II/45). A high correlation between these scores would support this prediction.

Figure 3.1 shows the Overall Problematic Parenting score plotted against the Childhood Vulnerability score; as the level of Problematic Parenting rises so does the level of Childhood Vulnerability. This constitutes strong presumptive evidence to suggest that the two are connected and justifies us in creating a score of *Security of Attachment* by adding together the scores of Problematic Parenting and Childhood Vulnerability. The average score for this in the bereaved sample is 17. The lowest third of scores (less than 11 in our sample) can be taken as indicating Secure and the highest third of scores (more than 21) indicates Insecure Attachment, with intermediate values from 11 to 21.

Our data also enables us to identify subdivisions of *insecure attachment patterns* which resemble those described by Ainsworth and Main.

Anxious/ambivalent attachments

As we have seen, Ainsworth and Main found that mothers who are over-anxious, insensitive to their infants and discourage exploration, have children

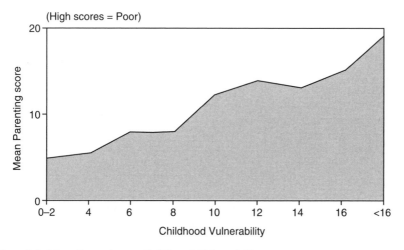

Figure 3.1 Mean Parenting × Childhood Vulnerability scores.

who, in the SST, show great distress during the period of separation and who both cling and cry angrily when she returns. In follow-up studies they are found to lack confidence and to depend too much on others. This is the pattern of anxious/ambivalent attachment.

This suggests that, in the current study, those people who assign to their parents high scores on Overprotectiveness will assess themselves as children as high on Unusual Closeness, Childhood Timidity and/or Dresden Vase (Precious Child). In fact, this prediction was indeed correct; each of these scores correlated with the others justifying us in adding them together to make a single score of *Anxious/Ambivalent Attachment*. The average score is 7.0 and a high score is reflected in a score of 10 or more.

Avoidant attachments

Ainsworth found that mothers who do not show distress, who cannot tolerate closeness and who punish attachment behaviour have children who learn to inhibit their tendencies to cling and to cry. Follow-up studies indicate that these children become intolerant of closeness and distrustful of others. This leads us to expect that, in the current study, avoidant attachments will be reflected in positive replies to questions indicating intolerance of closeness and strict control in parents and high scores on childhood distrust of others and agreement with the statement 'Did you find it hard to accept cuddles and other demonstrations of affection?'

Again, each of these questions was found to correlate with the others enabling us to create a measure of *Avoidant Attachment* by adding the replies to individual questions regarding parental avoidance of closeness, similar avoidance in the child and the Childhood Aggressiveness/Distrust score. In this case the average score is 3.8 and a score of over 6 can be taken as a high score.

Disorganised attachments

In Main's studies, parental losses and other stress at the time of the child's birth and infancy were associated with depression in the mother and Carlson *et al.* (1989) found that the pattern was also associated with violence and abuse in the home. The children of these mothers reacted to the Ainsworth's Strange Situation by becoming unpredictable and disorganised. Follow-up studies found these children prone to distress. They lacked trust in themselves and others. It was this pattern of attachment that she termed disorganised/disoriented. Follow-up studies showed that some of these children subsequently develop ways of coping, which enable them to control others without necessarily trusting them. They might do this either by coercion or by the more subtle strategy of caring for them, thereby incurring a debt which increases the chance that if the need arises the other will in turn care for them.

As predicted, in the current study, a significant proportion of those children who said that their families had been exposed to danger or persecution also obtain higher scores on Parental Rejection/Violence and Depression/Psychiatric Problems. The only childhood score that approximated to the helplessness of the disorganised behaviour pattern was the Childhood Unhappiness score which included agreement with statements that the child had often cried and often wished him or herself dead. In the event, significant correlations were found between all of these scores. Three of them also correlated with the Compulsive Caregiving score, the exception being the question about family danger.

This enables us to obtain a measure of *Disorganised Attachment* by adding together replies to the question about family danger and persecution and the scores of Parental Rejection/Violence, Depression/Psych. Problem, Childhood Unhappiness and Compulsive Caregiving. The average score was 4.5 and a third scored 6.0 or over, which can be taken as a high score.

Coercion is a strategy likely to be associated with aggressiveness and, as we have seen, is a likely consequence of avoidant attachments. In fact, it takes a fair degree of confidence in one's own strength to attempt to dominate others. It does not fit comfortably with the concept of low self-trust, which I take to be part of both anxious/ambivalent and disorganised attachments. In the current study, people who saw themselves as having been 'controlling, bossy or dominant' have been included in the Avoidant rather than the Disorganised category. These findings can be summarised as shown in Table 3.2. This shows the Ainsworth/Main categories on the left and on the right the equivalent RAQ scores, which are added together to give four attachment scores. For the sake of simplicity, I have used Ainsworth and Main's titles for

Table 3.2 Attachment pattern and RAQ equivalent

Attachment pattern	RAQ equivalent
Secure	Low score Overall Problematic Parenting (I/46)
	Low score Overall Childhood Vulnerability (II/45)
Insecure	
Anxious/Ambivalent	High score Parental Unusual Closeness (I/44)
	High score Parental Overprotectiveness (I/42)
	High score Childhood Timidity (II/40)
	High score Dresden Vase (II/41)
Avoidant	Parents Intolerant of Closeness (I/28)
	Child Intolerant of Closeness (II/26)
	High score Child Aggressiveness/Distrust (II/41)
Disorganised	Family experienced danger or persecution (II/4)
	High score Parental Rejection/Violence (I/45)
	High score Parental Depression/Psych. (I/42)
	High score Childhood Unhappiness (II/43)
	High score Compulsive Caregiving (II/44)

these scores, but it is important to remember that the relationship between my retrospective scores and scores derived from the SST is conjectural, the RAQ is not a direct measure of childhood attachment patterns.

The correlations between the components of the various attachment patterns are shown in Appendix 3.6. This shows that all of them correlated as predicted and that almost all of the correlations were statistically significant.[2]

Scoring the questionnaire

Drawing together these various findings it is possible to derive a set of instructions by which the RAQ can be scored and the scores used for the purposes of research and as an aid to problem assessment and management. These instructions are given in Appendix 3.7.

Do adults accurately remember the parenting they received as children?

Common sense suggests that adults' recollections of their relationship with their parents in childhood can only approximate to evidence obtained by direct observation of parent–child interaction and Main claims that insecurely attached adults are unable to recall details of their relationship with their parents (Main *et al.* 1985). On the other hand, the findings reported above do confirm predictions based on Ainsworth and Main's categories and suggest that such categories can be identified by retrospective analysis. Main's claim assumes the following:

- People are unlikely to recall events and circumstances that obtained during the first two years of life. This may well be the case, but the research reviewed in Chapter 1 also showed how the patterns of attachment established during those first two years persist and it may well be the later relationship that is remembered by these respondents.
- Painful experiences are more likely to become dissociated and repressed from memory. Again this may sometimes be true but it is certainly not always the case and the questions in the RAQ were not about specific events so much as ongoing tendencies.
- It has been suggested that the value judgements which children make about their parents are coloured by the parents' own evaluations. Thus, a

---

2 Levels of statistical significance of a correlation indicate the probability that this degree of correlation could have been reached by chance alone. Only those correlations that have less than a 1 in 20 probability of occurring by chance will be reported as 'significant'. These are shown in the appendix by an asterix* indicating significance levels (labelled as 'p') of less than 0.05. More satisfactory is a 'p' of less than 0.01, which reflects a 1 in 100 chance of a correlation occurring by chance alone, indicated by **.

child may learn that father 'loves you' because one or both parents repeat that assertion despite evidence to the contrary. In the questionnaire I have tried to avoid value judgements of this kind and the questions are so phrased as to permit the adult to make retrospective assessments that are not necessarily criticisms of the parent. It may also be the case that the distortions of perception that are common during childhood are, to some degree, corrected during adult life.

The findings of this study confirm the notion that attachment patterns are dyadic; that is to say, they reside essentially in the interaction between two people rather than in either one of them. For this reason it is appropriate to amalgamate the scores derived from our measures of childhood vulnerability with those of parenting.

Are these measures of attachment patterns reliable?

One way of testing reliability is to see whether or not a similar consistent pattern is found in different samples of people. In this study it was possible to compare the RAQ results in the bereaved group with two other samples: (A) 97 psychiatric patients who had not been bereaved; (B) Ward's sample of 77 young women who had not sought psychiatric help. Space does not permit the publication of all the details of this analysis here but these can be obtained from the author.

Group A

As we shall see in Chapter 16, the attachment patterns reported by the non-bereaved psychiatric patients were much the same as those reported by the bereaved. The overall measure of Insecure Parenting correlated highly with Childhood Vulnerability confirming that these two variables could reasonably be combined in both samples as an overall measure of Insecure Attachment. Similarly the correlations between Unusual Closeness, Parental Overprotection, Childhood Timidity and Childhood Dresden Vase scores were all highly significant and justify us in combining them in the Anxious/ Ambivalent Attachment score. Parental inability to tolerate closeness was found to predict similar inability in the child and both were significantly correlated with the Childhood Aggressiveness/Distrust score. This confirms the decision to combine these as our score of Avoidant Attachment.

Minor problems arose in connection with two of the constituents of the Disorganised Attachment score. Only six non-bereaved people answered 'Yes' to the question 'Was your family subjected for a long time to serious danger or persecution?' and this number is too small to justify statistical analysis of correlations with the other scores. Also the Childhood Unhappiness score was only weakly correlated with the Parental Depression/Psychiatric score. This said, as in the bereaved group, the Parental Rejection/Violence score did

correlate at a highly significant level with both the Parental Depression/
Psychiatric score and the Childhood Unhappiness score. All in all it seems
justifiable to regard the attachment patterns in the two samples as similar
and to continue to combine these measures to make up the Disorganised
Attachment score when analysing the non-bereaved sample. The influence
of attachment patterns on these non-bereaved psychiatric patients will be
examined in Chapter 16.

Group B

In Ward's full sample of 77 young women who had not sought psychiatric
help, as in the psychiatric patients, the score of Problematic Parenting
correlated highly with the score of Childhood Overall Vulnerability. Three
of the four components of the Anxious/Ambivalent score, Parental Overprotection, Childhood Timidity and the Dresden Vase (Precious Child)
score correlated well together but the Unusual Closeness score did not. The
components of the Avoidant Attachment score (Parental Distant Control,
distrust and affirmative replies to the question 'Did you find it hard to accept
cuddles and other demonstrations of affection?') were significantly associated.
Finally, two of the three components of the Disorganised Attachment score,
Parental Depression/Medication and Parental Rejection/Violence, correlated
with Childhood Unhappiness, but replies to the single question 'Was your
family subjected for a long time to serious danger or persecution?' did not.

By and large the results of this analysis confirm the findings in the larger
psychiatric sample and those that did not all showed a trend in the same
direction. They do not throw serious doubt on those findings.

Retrospective distortion as a possible source of error

Thus far the current research justifies us in concluding that parental influences
affect childhood vulnerability in ways that reflect the attachment patterns
found in the SST. If we are to rely on these patterns after bereavement we need
to eliminate another possible source of error: that the subjective assessments
which bereaved people make of their parents are coloured by their present
state of mind. Thus, it is not unreasonable to guess that people who are
anxious or depressed may see their parents in a more negative light than
they do when they are not anxious or depressed. If this is the case it will cast
doubt and might, for some purposes, invalidate the retrospective measures.

The follow-up study enabled these influences to be assessed. It was
anticipated that, if these doubts about the data are justified, any change in
the level of anxiety or depression over time would be reflected in a change of
similar magnitude in the attributions which people made about their parents.
This was tested in the group who completed the questionnaire a second time
by calculating the changes in anxiety, depression and overall distress scores
which had taken place between the completion of the RAQ on the first and

second occasions and correlating these scores of change in mood with changes in each of the parenting scores. Results of this comparison are shown in Appendix 3.8. Contrary to expectation, change in the Depression/Medication score was associated with only one significant change in a parenting score. There was a small, but significant association between improvement in Depression/Medication and the tendency to see parents as overprotective (as reflected in the Parental Overprotection score). Changes in Depression/Medication did not correlate, to a significant degree, with any of the Childhood Vulnerability scores or with the Disability score in adult life.

Changes in the Anxiety/Panic score were associated with small but significant changes in the Parental Insensitivity and Rejection/Violence scores and with a somewhat larger change in the Parental Overprotection score. Although changes in Anxiety/Panic did have a small but significant influence on the Childhood Overall Vulnerability score, this was not reflected to a significant degree in any of the individual scores that made it up, nor did it affect the Disability score.

The overall conclusion from this section is that mood does indeed have some influence on the assessments of parents and childhood but that this influence is relatively small. It should be taken into account when we come to examine the other findings of the research, particularly those that rely on the Parental Overprotection score.

Information from case notes

Additional information was obtained from the case notes. This included data about age, sex, marital status and dates of attendance. Note that these items were not included in the questionnaire and additional questions should be added to cover them by anyone planning to use the RAQ elsewhere.

Information was also recorded of the psychiatric diagnosis, physical health, medication, duration and outcome of treatment and reasons for ending therapy. Salient details were kept separately in the form of case summaries. The summaries do not contribute to the statistical analysis but proved to be a valuable source of illustrative case material.

Whenever a person had been referred for treatment of a bereavement-related problem, details of the relationship to the person who died, the cause of death and the time that had elapsed since the death were recorded. This information was not recorded for the 30 people who were not referred for treatment of a bereavement-related problem but who subsequently answered 'Yes' to the RAQ question 'Has any person close to you died in the last five years?'

Validity of the questionnaire data?

This was examined in two ways, by comparing the questionnaire scores with the clinical assessments and by comparing them with Ward's group of non-psychiatric respondents.

Comparison with clinical data

The clinical data provided some opportunities for verifying the validity of the questionnaire (see Appendix 3.9 for details). There was a highly significant association between a clinical diagnosis of depression and the RAQ Depression/Medication score but the overlap between the two was not so high that one can be taken as a measure of the other. More consistent is the relationship between the diagnosis of alcohol or drug-related illness and the RAQ Alcohol Consumption score with which it was highly correlated.

The association between clinical diagnosis of anxiety state and the RAQ Anxiety/Panic score just misses statistical significance. The difficulty here arose from the sheer frequency with which this mood was reported. Anxiety was so common in the bereaved people who sought my help that it could not easily be distinguished from the grief that accompanied it.

A significant correlation between a clinical diagnosis of chronic grief and the Grief/Loneliness score was found in those who had been bereaved for more than a year. Even so the correlation is not high and future research will be needed to determine whether Prigerson's more rigorous definition of 'complicated (or traumatic) grief' is more closely correlated to persisting Grief/Loneliness than my own, imprecise clinical diagnosis (Prigerson *et al.* 1995a, 1995b, 1996; Jacobs 1999).

Comparison with non-psychiatric sample

A further test of the validity of the scores of Symptoms/Distress was obtained by comparing these in the non-psychiatric and psychiatric samples. If the scores are valid measures of psychiatric symptoms, we would expect the psychiatric patients to have the higher scores. Ward had recruited her control group of volunteers to match a group of patients with eating disorders; these are most common in young women. For this reason her sample differed in age and gender from most of my own.

To correct for this difference 35 of the bereaved women in my psychiatric study were matched by age with 35 women in Ward's group. The matching is not perfect; no account could be made of social class and education and Ward collected the data for her study about eight years after I collected mine.

Appendix 3.10 gives the results of this comparison. As expected, the psychiatric patients reported many more symptoms and more emotional distress than the non-psychiatric comparison group. All of the Symptoms and Distress scores were higher in the psychiatric group and only the measure of alcohol problems, which were few in these young women, failed to reach statistical significance. Coping strategies are less likely to distinguish the non-psychiatric from the psychiatric groups. There was only one significant difference between them. Ward's group were rather more likely to say that when at the end of their tether they would seek help from family, friends, doctors or others.

Characteristics of the bereaved psychiatric patients

The questionnaire was completed by 278 psychiatric patients. All had been referred to me for psychiatric help during the period 1987 to 1993: 151 (54 per cent) were referred for treatment of a bereavement-related problem and there were another 30 (11 per cent) who, although referred for other reasons, answered 'Yes' to the question 'Has any person close to you died in the course of the last five years?' Since they resembled the first group in most respects they are included with them to make up the total sample of 181 bereaved people. The 97 people who had not been bereaved have been excluded from most of the analysis that follows. We shall look more closely at this group in Chapter 16.

Of the bereaved people 138 (76 per cent) were women and 43 (24 per cent) men. This sex distribution is typical of referrals for psychiatric help after bereavement and will be discussed in Chapter 10. The average age of the bereaved respondents was 41 years with only 8 per cent over the age of 65. Although this is a young age group for bereavement this may result from the fact that elderly patients are normally referred to the psycho-geriatric service of this hospital.

The relationship of the dead person to the survivor is shown in Table 3.3. From this it is clear that loss of a spouse (23 per cent), loss of a parent (21 per cent) and multiple losses (22 per cent) are the three commonest types of loss to be reported, with loss of a child next in frequency (17 per cent, or 19 per cent if stillbirths, miscarriages and termination of pregnancy are included). Only two (1 per cent) had lost a grandparent. There were no major differences between the sexes in the frequency of different types of loss.

Comparison with non-psychiatric sample

Among those who had lost 'someone close to you' in the last five years in Ward's non-psychiatric comparison group multiple losses were not found, none had lost a spouse or child, a half had lost a grandparent and only five

Table 3.3 Relationship of the dead person to the respondent

	n.	*Per cent*
Spouse or partner	34	23
Mother	31	15
Father	9	6
Child	25	17
Stillbirth	1	0.7
Miscarriage or termination	3	2.0
Sibling	12	8
Other	12	8
Multiple	33	22

This table does not include the 30 people who were not referred as bereaved.

(9 per cent) a parent. It would seem that loss of a child, loss of a spouse and multiple losses are over-represented among the psychiatric patients while loss of a grandparent is under-represented. This conforms to the general impression that multiple losses and losses of children and spouses are more traumatic and more likely to give rise to psychiatric referral than the death of an elderly parent or grandparent. These findings will be discussed in later chapters.

Gender influences in parents and children

Although Ainsworth's original Strange Situation research was limited to mothers and children, others (p. 60) have examined the father/child dyad. In general these studies show similar attachment patterns to fathers as were found in the earlier studies of attachments to mothers, although it is usually true to say that the influence of mothers is greater than that of fathers. Major differences have not been found between male and female children in their responses to the SST.

Statistical details of the influence of parental gender in the current study are shown in Appendix 3.11. Although there are no appreciable differences between the overall quality of parenting (as shown by the Overall Parenting score) between mothers and fathers and between male and female respondents, some interesting findings are apparent when each of the attachment scores is examined separately. Thus mothers are seen as having been more close and overprotective than fathers, particularly if the child was male. They were also more likely to be rated as depressed. Fathers, on the other hand, were more often separated from the child and seen as rejecting and/or violent. Female respondents did not differ appreciably from males on any of their scores of Childhood Vulnerability, nor did their mean Attachment scores differ. Other differences between male and female respondents will be considered in Chapter 10.

Conclusions

We have seen here that in a sample of men and women who had all sought psychiatric help the replies which they gave to a series of questions about their parents, childhood, adult life and current psychological state do seem to be reasonably reliable and consistent. Nor do the replies to the retrospective questions seem to have been influenced to a great degree by the prevailing mood of the respondent.

The reliability studies reveal some possible sources of bias but these are not so large as to seriously undermine the value of the questionnaire. Although the clinical data only provided partial confirmation of the validity of the statistical measures, the large differences between the scores of symptoms and distress in psychiatric and control respondents do confirm the validity of these measures.

The replies to individual questions cluster together in meaningful ways, which enable us to give names to the clusters. The clusters of questions about parents correlate with each other and with the clusters of questions about childhood in patterns that confirm and correspond to Ainsworth and Main's categories of secure and insecure attachment. These patterns of attachment were found independently in bereaved and non-bereaved psychiatric patients and in Ward's comparison group of young women who had not sought psychiatric help.

These findings confirm both the validity of my scores and of Ainsworth and Main's patterns. I suspect that it is the first two parts of the RAQ, those which enable patterns of parenting and patterns of childhood vulnerability to be distinguished, which will be of the greatest use to future researchers.

The sample of bereaved psychiatric patients contains a preponderance of women in middle life who have lost close relatives: spouses, parents or children. By contrast the non-bereaved group were much more likely to have lost grandparents and other more distant relatives.

Men did not differ from women on any of the main attachment variables. It follows that it is reasonable to simplify much of the analysis that follows by analysing both sexes together.

When the influence of the gender of the parents is considered some differences emerged. Fathers were more often absent from the home than mothers and were more often seen as rejecting and/or violent. Mothers, on the other hand, were more often rated as depressed, overprotective and/or unusually close to their child. Even so, when the Problematic Parenting scores are considered, neither parent is shown to have had a greater influence than the other on the Childhood Vulnerability or on the Overall Attachment score.

By this time some readers may be feeling impatient. Is all this agonising about the reliability and validity of the data strictly necessary? The more scientifically inclined, on the other hand, are unlikely to have been reassured about the weaknesses of retrospective data whose meaning will always be uncertain. All I can say is that in our attempts to make sense of a complex world and to help people through the turning points in their lives we are often forced to make use of data that is less than perfect. If, in the end, the conclusions we draw make logical sense, then it is reasonable to act upon them, at least until someone else comes up with something better.

We now examine the ways in which a new set of predictions is fulfilled. These show how each of the four attachment patterns is associated with particular types of adult relationship, particular ways of coping with stress and particular reactions when people suffer bereavements in adult life. The fascinating picture that emerges begins to make sense of the pervasive influence of love on loss.

Part II

Patterns of attachment and patterns of grief

4 Secure and insecure attachments

Parentage is a very important profession; but no test of fitness for it is ever imposed in the interest of the children.
George Bernard Shaw *Everybody's Political What's What* (1944) ch. 9

Ainsworth's prime contribution to our understanding of parent–child relationships was her recognition of the importance of secure attachments. By distinguishing clearly between strength of attachment and security of attachment she demolished the naive view that lack of love is the only kind of parenting which is likely to do harm. Her work demonstrated, beyond reasonable doubt, that a child may love his or her mother very strongly but in an insecure way, which may well sow the seeds of later difficulties. This seminal concept has changed the way in which psychologists think about the influence of parenting on the developing child but its influence in later life is only now beginning to be understood.

This said, it would be unwise to assume that 'insecure' attachments are always and necessarily harmful. Wilkinson (2003) dislikes the distinction between 'secure' and 'insecure' attachments on the grounds that all patterns of attachment between parents and children involve coping strategies that enable the children to become as secure as they can be in the context of their particular family. Only later is it likely that a strategy which fosters security in one setting may be found to create insecurity in another. It may be that the same strategies and assumptions that create problems in some bereaved people and cause them to seek psychiatric help may have no such consequences in others. Indeed, if Rando (2002) is to be believed, the experience of stressful circumstances in childhood sometimes leaves the child better prepared for stressful circumstances later in life than the experience of 'perfect' parenting.

Secure attachment and the RAQ

In analysing responses to the RAQ, low scores of Overall Problematic Parenting and Childhood Vulnerability (which, as we saw on p. 51, correlate highly together) have been taken as indicators of secure attachment during childhood. It is not assumed that they measure current security of attachment or that they correspond precisely to Ainsworth and Main's direct measure of security of attachment in childhood. It is, however, assumed, on the basis of the evidence presented in Chapter 3, that they are sufficiently indicative of this childhood pattern to act as an approximate indicator.

At the start of the project I formulated a series of predictions[1] about the probable influence of secure attachments on the relationships which these people would be found to make in adult life, on the ways they would cope with stress and, finally, on their reactions to bereavement. The questions and scores to be used as indicators of these relationships, coping strategies and reactions were then identified and the predictions tested by examining the extent to which the predictive variables correlate with those derived from adult life. Thus I was able either to confirm the predictions or to negate them.

Predicted concomitants of secure attachment

It was predicted that people who have low scores on insecurity of attachment in childhood (the securely attached) will make similarly secure attachments in adult life as reflected in low scores of problematic relationships. It was also expected that the securely attached would, in adult life, have low scores on our measures of poor coping, aggressiveness and distrust of others. These findings of less problematic relationships, better coping, less aggressiveness and less distrust would, in turn, predict lower levels of overall distress after bereavement. As a consequence, low scores of insecure attachment in childhood would also be found to predict low levels of overall distress after bereavement.

Results of testing these predictions

Appendix 4 (pp. 321–6) gives the results of the correlations. All of them did confirm the predictions and at a high level of statistical significance. Perhaps

---

1   The reader may ask why it was necessary to make these predictions. Why not simply set the computer to examine whether or not each question about parenting and childhood predicts or is correlated with each of the feelings and symptoms which were reported after bereavement? The answer is quite simple, given the fact that the RAQ includes 89 questions about parenting and childhood and 15 questions about symptoms and feelings this gives rise to $89 \times 15 = 1335$ possible correlations. With this number it is likely that many misleading results will occur by chance. Thus, even if we limit our measures of likely error to 1 in 100, we would expect 13 or 14 misleading results. The risk could be reduced by confining the tests to the 11 combined scores of Parenting and Childhood Vulnerability and the 5 scores of Symptoms and Feelings but even this would result in 55 results, one of which would probably be erroneous. By making predictions before the analysis the risk of error is greatly reduced. These predictions are not made with hindsight unless stated otherwise; all of the predictions reported in this book were formulated before the analysis was carried out.

the most striking finding is the high correlation between low scores on Insecure Attachment in Childhood and low scores of Overall Distress at the time when the person completed the RAQ many years later. These are clearly seen in Figure 4.1, which shows how the Overall Distress score rises steadily with the score of Insecure Attachment in the bereaved psychiatric patients. In other words, the more secure the reported security of attachment, the less severe the distress reported by these people after bereavement in adult life.

A further test of the theory that secure parenting influences childhood vulnerability, which in turn influences the intensity of distress, comes from the statistical techniques of path analysis and structural equation modelling details of which are given in Appendix 4. These take account of errors of measurement and confirm that the influence of our measure of Parenting on Overall Distress in later life is best accounted for by its influence on the developing child as measured by the Childhood Vulnerability score.

Assuming then, that these scores of Problematic Parenting and Childhood Vulnerability are valid measures of secure attachment in childhood, this supports the theory that securely attached persons will be less distressed by bereavement than those who have, in their childhood, been insecurely attached.

Figure 4.2 summarises the results of the analysis of the intervening variables. The relationship with the person now dead has been omitted for the sake of simplicity and because it is often the spouse who has died. Many of the scores that have been expected to influence each other are listed here, with continuous lines showing the links between those which are statistically significant. The magnitude of the influence is reflected in the figures (correlation coefficients) on each line.

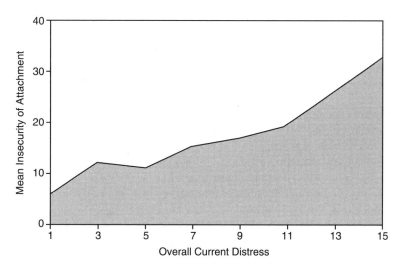

Figure 4.1 Insecure Attachment × Overall Current Distress scores.

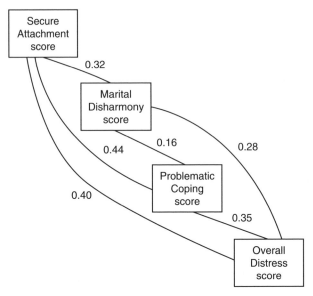

Continuous lines indicate significant correlations

Figure 4.2 Secure Attachments: links with other variables. Figures are correlations between variables in 181 bereaved psychiatric patients.

The hypothesis that the correlation between Insecurity of Attachment and Overall Distress after bereavement occurs because secure attachments in childhood predispose to secure attachments in adult life and that the dissolution of these attachments by death will be less distressing than would be the dissolution of less secure attachments is supported. Low scores of Insecurity of Attachment correlated with low scores of Marital Disharmony and Disharmony with the person who died. Marital Disharmony and Disharmony with the deceased person, in turn, correlate with levels of Overall Distress at the time when the questionnaire was completed.

Despite this confirmation of the hypotheses it is worth noting that the correlation between Secure Attachment and Low Overall Distress after bereavement (rho = 0.40) is higher than either of the correlations with the intermediate relationship variables. This suggests that, although the relationship between childhood attachments and adult distress may be mediated by the quality of the relationships in adult life, these are not the only factors contributing to this correlation.

More striking was the finding that low scores on Insecure Attachment are highly correlated with low scores on Problematic Coping. (This reflects low Inhibition/Distrust, low Aggressiveness/Assertiveness and less tendency for people to say that they would turn in on themselves when at the end of their tether.) Low scores on Problematic Coping are, in turn, correlated with low Overall Distress scores.

Further analysis

In the analysis thus far it seems that problematic parenting influences childhood vulnerability, which in turn influences both relationships in adult life and the assumptions and attitudes that decide how people will cope with stress. These then influence the level of distress and other problems that follow bereavement. While this chain of causation makes logical sense, it is worth asking if the sequence can be established from the quantitative data. The statistical technique of hierarchical regression was developed in order to answer questions of this kind.

The results of such an analysis are given in Appendix 4. The following scores were entered in sequence: Problematic Parenting by Mother, Problematic Parenting by Father, Childhood Vulnerability, Marital Dysfunction, Dysfunctional Relationship with the Deceased person and Problematic Coping. Their influence on our main measure of outcome, the Overall Distress score, was then calculated.

Considered on its own, the influence of the Mother's Parenting on the Overall Distress score was powerful and highly significant but this influence dropped considerably when Father's Parenting was added. The explanation for this is probably that both of these measures correlated with each other, that is to say, when mothering was poor so too was fathering. It was their joint influence which had the greatest effect on the Overall Distress score.

When Childhood Vulnerability was added to the equation this too was found to have a highly significant influence and the influence of both mother and father dropped below significant levels. This confirms our assumption that the problematic effects of parenting arise through its influence on childhood vulnerability.

Contrary to my expectation, the next two variables, Marital Disharmony and Disharmony with the person now dead had very little influence on Overall Outcome and only diminished the effects of Childhood Vulnerability to a small degree. It follows that it is most unlikely that the distress reported by people with childhood vulnerability was mainly caused by the influence of childhood vulnerability on these later relationships. On the other hand, the inclusion of Problematic Coping produced a drop in the influence of all other variables suggesting that the main influence of childhood vulnerability is through its effect on adult coping.

In conclusion, the main links would seem to be from Problematic Parenting → Childhood Vulnerability → Problematic Coping → Overall Distress after bereavement. This does not imply that other factors may not also have contributed to the distress and, in fact, the statistics confirm this. The variables included in this analysis only explained a third of the variation ('variance') in Overall Distress.

From this it is clear that the chains linking parental influences to the reaction to bereavement pass through two distinct strands. There is the chain from secure parent–child relationships to harmonious adult relationships to lower distress after bereavement; and there is a second, more important, strand from secure parent–child relationships to effective coping to lower distress after bereavement. It would seem that both of these strands contribute to the final outcome but with the influence on coping the more important.

This evidence is suggestive but not conclusive. Correlations do not prove causation, though they may suggest it. For example, people who drink wine may be more likely to vote Conservative than people who prefer beer but this does not mean that the wine consumption causes the Conservatism. Nevertheless, in the absence of a more likely explanation, the sequence of causation postulated above does make sense.

Security of attachments in other non-psychiatric settings

As in the psychiatric sample the respondents' assessments of their childhood insecurity of attachment in Ward's comparison group were found to be highly predictive of their Overall Distress after bereavement in adult life. Figure 4.3 shows this and also shows that Overall Distress is lower in Ward's group at all levels of insecure attachment and seldom rises above the score of 8 which is

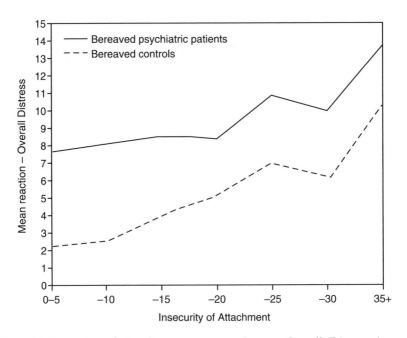

Figure 4.3 Insecurity of Attachment scores × Current Overall Distress in age-matched psychiatric and control groups.

the threshold above which lie most of the psychiatric patients, including those with Secure Attachment scores. It would seem that the influence of insecure attachments on distress after bereavement in adult life is not confined to people who seek psychiatric help after bereavement even though the overall level of distress is lower.

To examine the extent to which each of the scores of childhood insecure attachment were found in both psychiatric and Ward's non-psychiatric controls the average scores were compared in age-matched groups. Detailed results are given in Appendix 4 (pp. 324–6). Contrary to my expectations, the average score of Overall Insecurity of Attachment was as high in the non-psychiatric as in the psychiatric sample. Figure 4.4 shows that all of the links (correlations) shown in Figure 4.2 are also found in Ward's non-psychiatric sample.

I had expected that my psychiatric sample would report more instances of insecure attachments than the non-psychiatric but there were no significant differences between the two groups. This finding seems to contradict my expectation that insecure attachments contribute to the problems that caused people to seek help after bereavement. Before dismissing this hypothesis, however, we need to consider two other possibilities:

- that the members of Ward's comparison group may themselves have

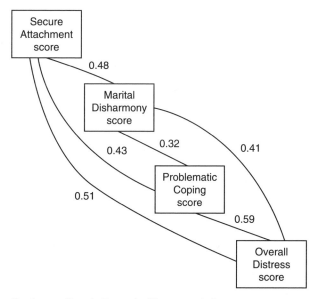

Continuous lines indicate significant correlations

Figure 4.4 Security of Attachment and other links with Overall Distress in bereaved non-psychiatric sample. Figures are correlations between variables in 35 bereaved non-psychiatric patients.

psychological problems and may not be representative of the population at large

• that the coping strategies which characterise insecure patterns of attachment may have several effects, some of which may increase the risk of people later seeking psychiatric help after bereavement while others reduce it.

Ward's comparison group

Are Ward's 'controls' a group with many problems? This group, as we have seen, was made up of volunteers, 46 per cent of whom had suffered bereavement. We do not know why they volunteered to help with the research and it may be that they hoped to resolve problems of their own. We can get some idea of this from their replies to the questions. Thus, 38 per cent said they have recently got to the end of their tether (IV/18), 44 per cent were 'very anxious' (IV/1), and 49 per cent said that they lack confidence in themselves (IV/4). These replies certainly seem to suggest that the group is rather more anxious and insecure than one might expect of a random sample of young women.

Since the average age of Ward's bereaved sample was 26 years most of them would have been born around 1970. My matched sample had the same average age but would have been born around 1962–3. Given the changes in child rearing which have taken place during the 1960s and 1970s, partly as a result of a steady rise in the proportion of women who work outside the home, this may have led to an increase in insecure attachment patterns in Ward's group.

Regardless of the validity of this speculation it remains true that the Symptoms and Emotions scores indicate that Ward's group are much less distressed than the psychiatric group and this implies that other factors must be playing a part in causing added distress in the psychiatric group.

Insecure attachments may have multiple effects

We now discuss the possibility that insecure attachments may have multiple effects, some of which may increase and others reduce the probability of people seeking help from a psychiatrist. We have seen in Chapter 1 that each pattern of attachment enables the individual to develop strategies for coping with particular parents. These strategies are accompanied by assumptions about the world and about oneself that may persist into adult life. It is not unreasonable to guess that the strategies may be beneficial in some situations and problematic in others. If that is the case then it is less the attachment that is the problem than the fit between the attachment and the current situation.

There are some circumstances in which confidence in oneself and trust in others may be misplaced. This is particularly likely in circumstances in which neither self-help nor the help of others is likely to be of any use. The loss by death of a loved person may be one such situation. This would certainly fit Rando's (2002) claim that a childhood that is too perfect may leave children unprepared for the sorrows to come (her work is considered more closely on pp. 145–6).

It would be premature to draw firm conclusions at this point and we should continue to bear these questions in mind as we examine the problems that brought some securely attached persons into psychiatric help.

Problems of the securely attached

Why did the minority of people in my psychiatric sample, whose RAQ scores suggest that they had experienced secure attachments in childhood and who suffered relatively low levels of distress seek psychiatric help after bereavement in adult life? In all samples of bereaved people there will be a range of scores of Overall Distress. The fact that people with insecure attachments had higher scores than the rest does not necessarily mean that those with secure attachments were not distressed, simply that they were less distressed than the rest. This is borne out by the findings in Figure 4.3, which show that psychiatric patients with low scores of Insecure Attachment reported Symptom/Distress scores that were still considerably higher than those in Ward's matched control group.

The case notes recorded a variety of symptoms in the bereaved psychiatric patients with secure attachments. These included bodily symptoms of various kinds, obsessional symptoms, sleep disorders and symptoms of post-traumatic stress. There were six patients who had been referred for complaints of depression or anxiety that did not show up on the RAQ, perhaps because they had not been so recognised by the patient or because they had improved by the time the form was completed.

Perusal of the case notes points to a number of causes for these symptoms including unusually traumatic deaths (6 of the 15 people who reported low scores on Insecurity of Attachment and low Overall Distress had suffered unexpected and untimely, multiple or violent bereavements); five cases fitted the picture of 'ideal' childhoods which left the person unprepared for subsequent traumas such as the death of a parent in childhood; in four other cases major stresses coincided with the bereavement or resulted from it (four cases) and social circumstances, including lack of social support, which added to the trauma (three cases). In two cases the bereavement had triggered off a recurrence of a longstanding mental disorder which preceded the bereavement and was only incidentally related to it.

In a few cases there was evidence in the case histories that conflicted with secure attachment scores in the RAQ. For instance, one man had been born with a harelip, which had required a long series of operations during his childhood and led to a very close attachment to his mother whom he described in ideal terms. Another had accepted his parents' evaluation of himself as 'the black sheep of the family' and felt unable to criticise them. On the whole, these findings seem to support the view that secure attachments in childhood sometimes leave people unprepared for subsequent traumatic life events.

> Sarah Green was the youngest of three children in a middle-class Jewish family. Her RAQ showed her to have been securely attached. She described her parents in ideal terms and was 'spoilt' by both of them. The exalted image of herself and others, which resulted from this relationship, was shattered when she went to school and came face to face with racial prejudice. She was teased by the cockney boys and responded by becoming bad tempered, babyish and easily moved to tears.
>
> Leaving school she took a clerical job and remained at home until the age of 35 when she met a fellow clerk, Sidney, with whom she had much in common, despite his being a Christian. They shared interests in dancing, music and opera. Both had a strong persisting attachment to their parents and to each other. Asked why they never had children Sarah replied, 'We were far too bound up with each other to consider it.' Over the next few years, thanks to her close relationship with Sidney, she coped well with the death of both her parents, but the unexpected death of her older sister, when she was 43 years of age, upset her a great deal. She took two weeks off work and her GP prescribed an antidepressant. Sidney was very supportive and this helped to get her through her grief. Five years later she developed back pain and was found to have degenerative changes in her spine and spondylolisthesis. Back pain became a chronic problem thereafter and limited her mobility, but not to the extent that surgery was thought justified.
>
> All of these factors seem to have contributed to the chronic grief and loneliness that she suffered after Sidney's death from cancer. Although his death had been expected Sarah reacted very strongly. When I met her two years later, she was still in a state of chronic grief, lonely, anxious, depressed and missing him a great deal. She said she was finding it very difficult to cope with life.
>
> She was already receiving regular appointments from a bereavement counsellor and we worked together to try to build up her confidence and help her to move forward. When it became apparent that she was making little progress a course of anti-depressant medication was given, but again without benefit. I saw her six times and she then continued to receive counselling. When

followed up a year later there had been no improvement in her symptoms.

Sarah had low scores on the attachment questionnaire and this seems to have reflected an idealised memory of her parents. The effects on her sense of security of the persecution which she suffered at school may have reflected racial prejudice, but may also have been aggravated by the devotion of her parents, which left her quite unprepared for the rough and tumble of school life and lacking in any strategy for coping with it.

When she married, it appears that the intense, mutually dependent relationship which she developed with her partner echoed and eventually superseded the similarly intense relationships which she had had with both her parents. She found in Sidney a man like her father by whom she felt loved and protected. The old assumptive world, which had been so rudely overturned when she went to school, could now be re-established, and with it the feeling of security which had permeated that world. Sarah's felt need for closeness was offset by Sidney's similar wish and as long as they were together a balance was maintained. But Sarah could never forget that she had once lost her security and this made her reluctant to rock the boat by having children. It also made her vulnerable to any separation from her husband.

Sidney's death provoked severe, chronic grief and alarm in Sarah, but neither her counsellor nor I was able convince her that her felt need to be nurtured by him and her belief that she could not cope without him were unjustified, and her symptoms persisted despite our attempts to help her. Her case reminds us that a need that is experienced as essential to survival in early life is an imperative, however irrational it may seem to others.

General conclusions

The findings reported here confirm my clinical impression, obtained over many years, that people who grow up in secure relationships with their parents experience less intense distress after bereavement in adult life than those from insecure relationships. The evidence from both psychiatric and non-psychiatric samples suggests that this is a reflection of a more positive view of self and of other people with more harmonious marriages and a greater willingness to turn to others for support at times of stress.

This supports Bowlby's claim that the main function of a loving family is to provide a secure base in which children can discover their own potential and can also learn that other people can be trusted to provide support and guidance when it is needed. As the children reach maturity their increasing knowledge, self-confidence and trust enable them to achieve a reasonable degree of autonomy.

However, we also found that the incidence of insecure attachment, which was reported by young women in my psychiatric sample, was reported with similar frequency in the young bereaved women who had not sought psychiatric help. While the matching between the samples was not perfect, this finding suggests either that insecure attachments played little part in causing the psychiatric problems or that insecurity of attachment can have mixed effects, some of which reduce while others increase the tendency to seek psychiatric help after bereavement. The insecurely attached who do well are unlikely to be found in a sample of psychiatric patients but may well have been present in Ward's sample. Those of Ward's young women who reported insecure attachments in their childhood were more distressed than those who reported secure attachments, but they seem to have learned to live with their distress without seeking help or equating distress with pathology. As Irving Berlin put it, 'You're not sick, you're just in love' (*Call me Madam*).

Looking more closely at the attachment patterns that we have been studying, as we have seen these are strategies which children develop to enable them to cope with particular parents. It seems that the strategies which we have been referring to as 'insecure attachments' sometimes remain useful ways of coping with the imperfect world of adult life. Indeed, securely attached children may have certain disadvantages. Those whose parents protect them from all dangers may not learn to cope with the dangers that they meet later in life. Parents who are utterly reliable and sensitively responsive to their children may not leave them prepared for a world in which many people cannot be trusted and some are dangerous. Self-trust and other trust will always be relative, for nobody can be so competent that they can always rely on their own powers; neither can other people be so trustworthy that they will always protect and help us. We shall seek for further clarification of these issues in the chapters that follow.

5 Anxious/ambivalent attachments

The proverb warns that, 'You should not bite the hand that feeds you.' But maybe you should, if it prevents you from feeding yourself.

© Thomas Szasz *The Second Sin: Control and Self Control* (1973)

Helen Bond was an attractive and intelligent young woman. She was married, had two children and enjoyed working as a barmaid in a local pub. When she was 35 years of age her father died. Following that event she became intensely distressed, suffered a series of panic attacks while in the street and began to fear that she too would die. Her symptoms persisted and 14 months later she was referred to me for psychiatric assessment.

In this chapter we shall hope to understand better why Helen found it so hard to cope with a loss that, however sad, would not normally give rise to disabling fears which necessitated psychiatric referral. We shall find that the love of caring but anxious parents can sometimes sow the seeds that lead to dysfunctional reactions to bereavement in later life.

The first of Ainsworth's categories of insecure attachment she termed the anxious/ambivalent group. These, as we have seen, are children who in the Strange Situation react to separation with distress and when their mother returns cling to her and continue to cry in an angry manner. Their mothers are characterised as over-anxious and controlling, concerned for their children's safety but insensitive to their needs for autonomy and discouraging exploration. The picture emerges of children who have learned that the world is a dangerous place in which they will not survive unless they stay close to mother. They are likely to grow up with little confidence in themselves and to be preoccupied with anxious, clinging but ambivalent relationships with others who are seen as more powerful than them. In the current study they correspond to the group who have high scores on Parental Unusual Closeness and/or Overprotection along with Childhood Timidity and/or high 'Dresden Vase' scores.

The tendency to cling is usually termed 'dependency'. This term has become so value laden that it is almost a crime to be 'dependent' and people so labelled are regularly made to feel that they are to blame. In a society that values independence above obedience and conformity, people who lack confidence in themselves and turn to others for support in times of trouble are told 'You must not be dependent.' This injunction may only serve to further undermine their self-confidence and make them cling all the harder.

Warren *et al.* (1997) followed children assessed by SST to 17.50 years. At this age those who had experienced anxious/ambivalent attachments (which they refer to as 'resistant') were significantly more likely to experience anxiety disorders of adolescence (as measured by a modified form of the Present State Inventory). This remained true even when controlled for neo-natal nurse's ratings of 'reactivity'. Given this anxious tendency we may expect that a similar anxious reaction will follow bereavements in adult life, particularly if the bereaved people were unusually dependent on the person who died.

We saw in the Harvard Study (p. 28) that having a dependent relationship in adult life was one of the most powerful predictors of problematic reactions to bereavement. Close and dependent relationships have also been found by Stroebe (personal communication) to predict high scores of 'complicated grief' in a prospective study of 59 spouses of people with terminal illness who were studied before and after bereavement. At first glance some of their results seem confusing. People who rated their marriages as secure suffered more 'complicated grief' than others, but the study also included a measure of insecure 'attachment style' which also predicts 'complicated grief' though less powerfully than the relationship score. The two measures did not correlate with each other; that is to say, people who rated their marriages as 'secure' were no more or less likely than others to rate their 'attachment style' as 'insecure'. This suggests that 'attachment style' and actual attachment are two different things. It is possible for someone to have an insecure attachment style and to see their relationships as secure. We return to consider this insight below.

Evidence for a link between clinging to parents in childhood and problems in bereavement in adult life comes from the Yale Bereavement Study and was reported in a recent paper by Vanderwerker *et al.* (2006) of which I was a co-author. We used a retrospective questionnaire to identify bereaved people whose replies indicated that they had refused to go to school and/or experienced other symptoms of separation anxiety during their childhood. Among the 283 recently bereaved people, high scores of Childhood Separation Anxiety were found to be significantly more frequent among those who suffered complicated grief than those whose grief was uncomplicated. Our measure of separation anxiety included questions similar to some in the Anxious/Ambivalent Attachment score used in the current study, to which we can now return.

Predicted concomitants of anxious/ambivalent attachments

As in the preceding chapter my expectations based on clinical experience and theory led me to make a series of predictions about the relationships, coping strategies and reactions to bereavement in adult life of those identified as having had anxious/ambivalent attachments in childhood. It was predicted that anxious/ambivalent attachments in childhood would give rise to a view of the world as a dangerous place in which it is necessary to stay close to those to whom we are attached, to cling and to protest vigorously when separated, thus:

- Higher scores of anxious/ambivalent attachment in childhood were expected to be associated with dependence on both the spouse and the person who subsequently died.
- In turn, this dependency was expected to predict the intensity of grief, as indicated by the Grief/Loneliness score, and our measure of Clinging and a clinical diagnosis of chronic grief.
- To complete the circle, the measure of Anxious/Ambivalence was also expected to predict these measures of grieving and clinging.

Results of testing these predictions

Appendix 5 shows the results of the analysis. It is clear from these findings that people with high scores on Anxious/Ambivalent Attachments in childhood were indeed significantly more likely to receive high scores on Grief/Loneliness and Clinging after bereavement in adult life than were those with low scores.

Given that most of the bereaved people in the sample had been bereaved for several years this confirms the association of Anxious/Ambivalent Attachment with severe protracted grief after bereavement and a persisting tendency to cling. The correlations are of moderate size, implying that although this attachment type is an important determinant of the intensity of grief and clinging it is not the only cause.

> Helen, whose reaction to the death of her father was described above, was the youngest of four children. She describes both of her parents as having been anxious and overprotective. Her mother was a quick-tempered worrier with a tendency to agoraphobia. Her father had also been a worrier. He attributed his fears of thunderstorms and other things to the experience of being blown up by a bomb during World War II, an event which subsequently led to his receiving psychiatric treatment. They had both regarded Helen as a 'delicate' child who needed protection.

Given this background it is easy to see why Helen describes herself in childhood as insecure, anxious and with a tendency to cling to her parents. She made few friends and was haunted by the fear that her parents would die; a fear that mirrored their fear that *she* would die. Her RAQ showed her to have a high score on Anxious/Ambivalent Attachment (20), above average Disorganised Attachment (6) and below average Avoidant Attachment (1) scores.

Clearly Helen's RAQ scores confirm the clinical picture of an anxious/ambivalent attachment to her parents. The question remains whether the link between clinging in childhood and problematic grief is mediated by dependent relationships in adult life.

People who said in the RAQ that they had been dependent on their spouse and/or the deceased person showed significantly higher levels of Grief/Loneliness after bereavement than those who were independent, and those dependent on the deceased (but not the spouse) were also inclined to report high scores of Clinging. This confirms Prediction 2 and the results of previous research.

It was expected that the dependence on the partner or deceased resulted from the lasting effects of anxious/ambivalent attachment in childhood, but the Anxious/Ambivalent Attachment score, which was a retrospective measure of this childhood attachment, did not correlate with adult dependence on the spouse/partner or dependence on the deceased person. These findings suggest that, contrary to Prediction 1, the correlation between anxious/ambivalent attachments in childhood and severe, lasting grief after bereavement was not explained by the effect of anxious/ambivalence on dependence on the lost person.

Scrutiny of the case summaries led me to consider the possibility that anxious/ambivalent clinging to others in adult life, instead of leading to dependency more often has a very different consequence, anger and rejection. This led to a supplementary prediction of a correlation between the Anxious/Ambivalent Attachment score and the scores of Disagreements with the Spouse and the Deceased Person. The result of this prediction, which is shown in Appendix 5, confirms this hypothesis. People with high scores of childhood Anxious/Ambivalence tend to report more disagreements with their spouse and with the person now dead than those with lower scores.

Do these disagreements explain the correlation between the Anxious/Ambivalent Attachment score and the high score of Grief/Loneliness? Common sense suggests that people who had numerous areas of disagreement with a person will grieve them less than those who had an unconflicted relationship. On the other hand, the Harvard Bereavement Study showed that high levels of marital conflict are more often followed by severe grief and continued yearning for the dead person than are less stormy relationships (Parkes and Weiss 1983). Summarising our findings we wrote: 'As time went on [those with high levels of conflict with their spouse] seemed more often to be stuck in the grieving process, still unaccepting of their loss, self-reproachful and yearning for the return of the spouse.'

Our examination of the case histories of our subjects led us to suggest a possible explanation for this finding: 'Some among those who form and remain in troubled marriages are individuals who, because of earlier experiences in their lives, have difficulty establishing more satisfactory attachments and . . . these same earlier experiences make them less capable than others of successfully recovering from loss.' We were referring to the lack of self-confidence that we found in this group and the ways in which this undermined both the selection of a marital partner and the person's ability to cope with the stress of bereavement.

To check this out one more supplementary hypothesis was formulated, that our measures of disagreements in adult life would be associated with our scores of Grief/Loneliness and Clinging after bereavement. In the event, high levels of disagreement with spouse and/or deceased, in turn, were found to be associated with intense Grief/Loneliness and Clinging after bereavement.

We are now in a position to sum up the results of this analysis. Figure 5.1 shows the links between each of the relevant variables. The score of Anxious/Ambivalent Attachment is significantly correlated with Marital Disagreements, Disagreements with the Person now Deceased, Clinging and Grief/Loneliness. All of these variables are linked with each other and all reach significant levels. The moderate magnitude of the influence of the Anxious/Ambivalent Attachment Pattern (as reflected in the size of the correlations) on the other scores suggests that other factors also contribute to this influence.

Although the variables have been ranked in temporal sequence this should not be taken to mean that the childhood influences act only through their effects on the later relationships, which in turn explain the reaction to bereavement. Other variables, which include social influences, will then be taken into account in later chapters.

We can now return to our case study for a more detailed example of these problems.

It was in her role as barmaid that Helen had met and, at the age of 24, married Jim, an electrical engineer. At the time of her marriage Helen knew that Jim had a drink problem, but after their marriage he was able to reduce and, eventually, stop drinking.

In due course Helen gave birth to two sons. Her attitude to her children resembled that of her own parents towards her. She cared for and about them but found them a constant source of anxiety. Her eldest suffered a congenital dislocation of the hip,

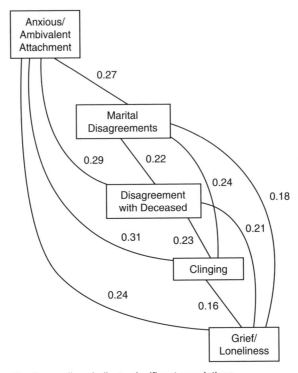

Continuous lines indicate significant correlations

Figure 5.1 Anxious/Ambivalent Attachments: links with other variables. Figures are correlations between variables in 181 bereaved psychiatric patients.

which necessitated several operations during his childhood, and the younger son Helen describes as an insecure boy with a speech defect.

Despite the improvement in Jim's drinking habit, the couple's marital relationship remained troubled. Jim saw Helen as intrusive and expecting too much of him. Helen, on the other hand, never felt that he gave her the support that she needed in caring for the children or taking responsibility for financial matters. She accused him of being too uncommunicative. This failure to find a mutually comfortable distance which would satisfy Helen's need for closeness and Jim's need for distance may also have contributed to their failure to achieve a satisfying sex life.

Throughout her marriage Helen remained in close touch with her parents and this sometimes conflicted with her commitments at home. Jim complained that he was taking second place to Helen's parents and Helen complained when he returned to the company of his friends in the local pub.

When Helen's father died suddenly and unexpectedly from a myocardial infarction at the age of 75, her longstanding fear that he would die had been realised. To make matters worse, her mother, to whom she normally turned at times of trouble, was herself grieving so deeply that she needed to lean on Helen. The world seemed to have become very dangerous indeed and Helen was waiting for the next disaster. Panic attacks in the street led to a vicious circle. Fearing a recurrence of these attacks she stayed at home and tried to cling to her husband.

Jim, while sympathetic, had no idea how to respond to her clinging. He tried to persuade her to pull herself together and distanced himself from her in the expectation that in time she would 'get over' her grief. Spending more and more time at the pub he gradually slipped back into his former way of dealing with his problems.

It is clear that Helen's relationships in adult life, to her husband, her parents and her children, had been influenced by the problems arising from her childhood attachment insecurity. Her low self-esteem may have contributed to her choice of a man whom she knew to have problems of his own. Her continued closeness to her parents caused conflicts with her husband, who may himself have needed support that she was unable to give. When at last her mother's own grief made her turn to her husband for support he was at first unable to respond.

In this case, as in others, it seems that there are two main reasons why the marital relationships that follow anxious/ambivalent attachments in childhood are at risk. Those who, in adult life, continue to cling to their parents may be seen, by the partner, as rejecting the partner; while those who cling to their partner often find that the partner cannot tolerate their clinging.

Is Anxious/Ambivalent Attachment linked to Clinging and Grief/Loneliness after bereavement in non-psychiatric settings?

Most of the links, which were shown in Figure 5.1, can be examined on the data from Ward's study of young women who had not sought psychiatric help. Because they include a measure of Grief/Loneliness this analysis has been limited to the 35 young women who had been bereaved. Since only three of these reported many disagreements with the person now dead and this is too few for statistical analysis, responses to this question have been omitted from Figure 5.2.

All of the correlations are similar to or greater than those found in the

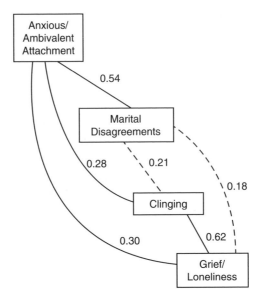

Continuous lines indicate significant correlations
Interrupted lines indicate non-significant trends

Figure 5.2 Bereaved non-psychiatric sample. Anxious/Ambivalent Attachments: links with other variables. Figures are correlations between variables in 35 bereaved non-psychiatric controls.

psychiatric sample, suggesting that a similar pattern of response to this attachment pattern is to be found in this sample. Several of them, shown by a dotted line, now miss statistical significance, probably because the sample size is so small. It seems that the influence of anxious/ambivalent attachments on later relationships and reactions to bereavement is not limited to the minority who seek psychiatric help.

The correlation between Anxious/Ambivalent Attachment and the number of Marital Disagreements is much higher in the non-psychiatric group than it was in the psychiatric. A possible explanation is that some of those anxious/ambivalent people who are most prone to psychiatric problems are too insecure to dare to disagree with their partners.

In Chapter 4 (p. 71) attention was drawn to the fact that, on average, the members of Ward's group, none of whom had sought psychiatric help, obtained scores of Insecure Attachment which were just as high as those of the psychiatric group. Table A4.3 on page 326 indicates that in Ward's group the later development of the anxious/ambivalent group did not lead to requests for psychiatric help despite the increase in distress that followed bereavement. Anxious/ambivalent attachments may even have had some beneficial consequences.

In theory, anxious/ambivalent persons who as children learned to place more reliance on the support and advice of others than on their own strength, initiative and judgement may, even so, develop special skills in relating effectively with others; they may become 'people persons'. To test this theory I looked more closely at the 35 women in Ward's comparison group who had high scores (8+) on Anxious/Ambivalent Attachment. Twelve of them had low scores (0–3) on Overall Distress and these 12 can be compared with (a) the 23 who reported higher Overall Distress and (b) with the people in my psychiatric sample (most of whom had high Overall Distress scores). Although the numbers are too small for adequate statistical analysis the results are interesting.

Eleven out of Ward's 12 with high Anxious/Ambivalent but low Distress scores (93 per cent) said that, at the end of their tether, they would turn to family, friends or others. (This was so in only half of the members of the other two groups, 56 per cent and 53 per cent.) All had partners or spouses and two-thirds acknowledged their dependence on them but the same proportion also accepted that they 'find it necessary to get away from this person from time to time in order to reduce tension' (III/7i).

This seems to indicate that these people have developed strategies that enabled them to preserve their relationships despite their continuing wish to depend on others. A factor in this may be their insight into their own wish to depend and their awareness that this wish needs to be resisted from time to time. Clearly a wish and a need are not one and the same thing.

Further considerations

Although, as we have seen, high scores on childhood Timidity and Dresden Vase do interrelate, it is not unreasonable to expect that the child who is valued as precious will have some advantages over other children. Should such children be regarded as a separate category of anxious/ambivalent attachments, as Crittenden and Clausen (2000) have suggested? In fact no such advantages were found. Comparing people in the psychiatric sample who had high Dresden Vase scores with those who had high scores of Childhood Timidity, no significant differences were found in their ways of Coping in adult life or their Symptoms and Feelings; both were equally vulnerable.

We are now in a position to consider the crucial question: How do patterns of anxious/ambivalent attachment established in childhood continue to influence adult life? Are we doomed by our childhood experiences or is it possible for older children and adults to change their assumptions about the world and to discover reasonable degrees of trust in themselves and ways of coping with persisting insecurity? The case reports provide rich data which may lack the rigour of the quantitative data but which enable us to go beyond pure speculation in bringing it to life.

The implicit aim of the anxious/ambivalent pattern is to enable the child to survive by staying close to parent(s) and home. The child learns that it is not safe to wander or explore, and the mother learns that the child, with expressions of extreme anger and anguish, will punish her if she does not stay close. Both are caught in a trap from which they see no escape. Adolescence, when both maturation and social pressures push towards independence, is likely to be a difficult time for both child and parent who by now are likely to be in conflict with each other and with themselves. Case records indicate that the outcome of the struggle will depend on circumstances. Some children remain permanently attached to one or both parents and their other attachments to spouses and children may take second place. Others find a partner who fits the mould of the protective parent and perpetuates the pattern. Yet others find themselves repeatedly at odds with partners who resent the clinging but give way in the long run, either because they cannot stand the anger which their bids for freedom evoke or because they are seduced by sexual or nurturant enticements (some partners find 'babies' irresistible).

Other anxiously ambivalent persons move from one relationship to another as successive partners back away. Eventually they may learn to mitigate their clinging but at the cost of persistent anxiety. I suspect that the anxiety persists because it is rooted in the basic assumption that survival depends on maintaining a pattern of clinging behaviour that by now feels 'natural'.

All of these problems reflect the negative influences, in later life, of anxious/ambivalent attachments that arose in childhood. What of the positive influences? The psychiatric data teach us little about these, but it is not unreasonable to suppose that those who have experienced the influence of parents who are fearful of separation will learn to cope with closeness. They may become sensitively responsive to the moods of others, giving priority to the other's needs much of the time but also punishing them for any neglect of their own needs, perhaps by evoking feelings of guilt. They may be better at seduction than domination, at evoking and rewarding the nurturant needs of others, and at applauding their superior strength and powers, which they believe that they lack. They will become good at making and retaining friends, show interest in their points of view and trust their judgements. Their lack of self-confidence may be balanced by their ability to bolster the confidence of others who can then bask in the glory of their adulation.

Implications for therapy

If, as Ward's data suggest, it is possible for people with a history of anxious/ambivalent attachment to learn to cope effectively with the stress of bereavement, it may be that an understanding of attachment and its consequences would enable therapists to assist with this process. Although this will be the main theme of Chapter 18, we conclude this chapter with a brief account of the short-term psychotherapy that was undertaken with Helen and Jim Bond.

Both attended my clinic and, from the outset, found it valuable to review their life situation and get into perspective the powerful feelings that Helen had feared would overwhelm her. She soon came to see that her tendency to cling, far from enabling her to achieve the closeness that she craved, was threatening her marriage. At the same time her husband realised that his attempts to distance himself from Helen had aggravated her fears and only caused her to cling all the tighter.

By the time of our second interview a change was already taking place. Each partner seemed to have lost their fear of the other and to be enjoying a more mature form of closeness than they had previously experienced. Recognising that he had an important role to play at home, Jim no longer felt the need to escape to the pub. Helen was already much less anxious, she had had no more panic attacks and readily agreed that 'I had nothing to fear but my fear'. Her grief for her father was still present but no longer dominated her life, nor did she feel intimidated by her mother's demands for support. This change in the dynamics of the family was such that she decided that there was no need to continue therapy beyond our third meeting.

It would be unwise to assume that this abrupt ending of therapy necessarily meant that Helen's problems were solved and, as we shall see in Chapter 18, the overall results of therapy with this group of patients do not give cause for optimism.

Helen illustrates well the way in which anxious/ambivalent attachments, persisting into adult life, can impair relationships with partners. Both the continuing relationship with parents and the tendency to cling can drive a wedge between partners who then feel that they are unable to support each other. Helen's reaction to bereavement, which would meet diagnostic criteria for complicated grief, can be seen as one manifestation of a disorder of attachment, which long preceded her bereavement. We shall examine this issue in more detail in Chapter 17.

Case histories of this kind can give only a superficial account of the complexity and depth of a real person. They do little to capture the feeling tone of the interviews and the rapport between patient and therapist. People with anxious/ambivalent attachments may at times seem childlike. They have long experience of maintaining their security by staying close, perhaps too close, to those whom they see as protective. At the same time, other people have often told them that they must not become dependent so they are constantly at war with themselves. While, in our society, 'love' is good, 'dependence' is decidedly bad. People get the message that they should not feel that way. Yet feelings are not things we can choose to have, and the feelings that evoke dependent behaviour are only aggravated by rejection.

Freud (1914) claimed that love given to another reduces self-love (narcissism), yet there is something narcissistic about the love of the anxious/ambivalent person whose clinging reflects their intense fear of being abandoned. To them, love is not given but demanded, and when love is lost their fear and rage complicate and magnify their grief. At the same time they are only too aware that this is not the way things should be.

People with a tendency to cling are in a state of conflict between their wish to cling and their need to hold back from clinging. The outcome is a spectrum of behaviours, some affiliative others rejecting, which reflect that struggle and which are carried out in a state of high anxiety. Rather than judging them, we should recognise that, given the intensity of their fear, their struggle may be a heroic battle which deserves our respect. We must show that we care, but that does not mean that we should give the client what they most want from us, a promise of perpetual protection and proximity. Our value to the potentially dependent person arises from our respect for their true value and strength, not our pity for their weakness. We hold back from intervening in the struggle, not because we do not care, but because we know that they need our respect more than our protection.

Conclusions

This research confirmed the expectation that people who experienced anxious/ambivalent attachments in childhood and people who make dependent attachments in adult life are both likely to suffer severe and lasting grief and loneliness after bereavement. What it did not show was that one led to the other. Instead, we found that people who make anxious/ambivalent attachments in childhood tend to have very conflicted relationships in adult life and this contributes to the lasting grief and loneliness that follows bereavement. Their tendency to cling remains a problem and has important implications for those who set out to help this group of people.

6 Avoidant attachments

Then fly betimes, for only they
Conquer Love who run away.

Thomas Carew (c.1595–1640) 'Conquest by Flight'

Florence Harmony was 35 years of age when referred to me. Both she and her husband had been on a waiting list for marital counselling when he was killed in a road traffic accident. Her immediate reaction was to exert a rigid self-control, which masked feelings of intense anxiety and a fear that she would panic. She became extremely anxious for the welfare of her children, overcontrolling them and constantly vigilant for fear of another disaster.

During the months that followed Florence was tense, anxious and at times depressed, but found it hard to grieve. Although she sometimes wept a little this was never sufficient to assuage her distress and she wished she could cry more. She blamed herself for the failure of her marriage and had many other bitter regrets. Eventually she could stand the situation no longer and asked to be referred to a psychiatrist.

Any young woman who loses her husband in circumstances such as these is likely to experience intense distress and Florence's reaction is not unexpected. Even so there are hints, both in her marital problem and her difficulty in expressing grief, that the consequences of avoidant attachment may need to be considered. We might think that avoidant attachments would be easier to sever than close attachments, but this is not necessarily the case, and in this chapter we shall find out why.

At first sight the behaviour of infants who avoid their parent in the Strange Situation would seem to contradict the fundamental tenet of attachment theory: that the infant's chances of survival are increased by maintaining proximity to parents – staying close to them, rewarding nurturance with smiles, hugs and cuddles and, when threatened or separated, crying and clinging. However, there is no doubt that all instinctual behavioural tendencies are modified by learning from the moment of their first inception. Main's finding that infants who avoid their mothers have mothers who are themselves intolerant of closeness suggests that this is the most likely explanation for the behaviour (Main 1977). Infants faced with a parent who consistently fails to respond to their bids for attention, or who punishes such behaviour, soon learn to inhibit this behaviour when in the presence of that parent and may even generalise the inhibition to include other people. This does not mean that the wish to stay close will disappear but simply that the child discovers that it is safer to keep their distance. Main and Weston (1982) observe:

> Some infants [in the SST] respond to reunion with alternating move-ments of approach and avoidance. Thus we have seen a number of infants start for the parent and, without looking into the parent's face, veer away immediately and continue to move away at least a short distance. This behaviour seems strange. The change from approach to avoidance does not seem to be related to any changes in the environment but only to the infant's having reached a certain proximity to the parent. It is our impression that this is usually a distance of about three feet, which is to say, just out of the parent's reach.
>
> (Main and Weston 1982: 35)

These observations are consistent with the findings reported in Chapter 3 (p. 52) that respondents who answered 'Yes' to the question 'Was your parent unable to show warmth or to hug or cuddle you?' were also likely to reply 'Yes' to the question 'Did you find it hard to accept cuddles or other demon-strations of affection?'

The children of mothers who cannot tolerate closeness and punish attach-ment behaviour seem to learn that the expression of affection is dangerous. They may distrust others and as they grow older and meet their peers they may keep their distance but learn to control them by non-affiliative means such as dominance, assertion and aggression. As we saw in the current study (pp. 53–4, there was a highly significant association between parental intoler-ance of closeness and self-assessments of aggressiveness towards and distrust of other children. These findings justify the use of a measure of Avoidant Attachment made by adding the replies to questions regarding parental avoidance of closeness, similar avoidance in the child and the Childhood Aggressiveness/Distrust score.

Predicted concomitants of avoidant attachments

Again, three hypotheses will be tested:

1   If, as seems likely, these avoidant attachments, and the assumptions

about the world which accompany them, persist into adult life, they can be expected to be associated with inability to express affection, with difficulties in making and maintaining relationships and with reluctance to turn to others at times of trouble.

2 These in turn will predict delayed or inhibited grief after bereavement. Since some psychosomatic disorders have also been postulated to result from the repression of emotional reactions, a supplementary prediction was that these too may be more common following avoidant attachments and inhibition of grief.

3 It follows that avoidant attachments are also expected to predict delayed or inhibited grief and psychosomatic disorders after bereavement.

Results of testing these predictions

Appendix 6 shows each of these predictions along with the predicted correlations. Hypothesis 1 is confirmed, with reported avoidant attachments in childhood highly correlated in adult life with difficulty in showing affection and with high scores of Emotional Inhibition/Distrust and Aggression/ Assertiveness. In the light of these findings it is hardly surprising that the score of Avoidant Attachment is also highly significantly associated with Marital Disagreements. One of the commoner complaints of married couples in discordant marriages is that the other will not communicate or show feelings.

At a lower level of significance, avoidant attachment in childhood is also associated, in adult life, with disagreements with the person now deceased and with the assertion that the bereaved person 'never' cries. It seems that the inhibition of attachment behaviour and distrust of others, which was found in childhood, is persisting into adult life. In the light of this it is also interesting to find that, far from being proud of their independence and control, avoidant persons, particularly those who never cry, are also more likely than others to say 'Yes' to the question 'Do you wish you could cry more than you do?' (IV/20, see pp. 334–5).

Bereaved people who are emotionally inhibited and find it hard to express affection for people close to them were also likely to say that they never cry and find it difficult to express grief; this confirms Hypothesis 2. Five out of the ten adults who said they never cry were diagnosed as having psychosomatic disorders (compared with a quarter of the rest), but my prediction that those who reported other indicators of Emotional Inhibition, and/or high levels of Aggression/Assertiveness, would be diagnosed as suffering delayed grief and psychosomatic disorders was not confirmed. Possible explanations will be considered below.

Those who scored high on Aggressiveness/Assertion, also had many Marital Disagreements but they were no more likely than others to say that they had difficulties in expressing grief. It would seem that the influence of avoidant attachments on the expression of grief in adult life is mediated by its influence on emotional inhibition rather than these other factors.

Hypothesis 3 was supported by an association between Avoidant Attachment and difficulty in expressing grief. This is clearly seen in Figure 6.1, which shows the average Avoidant Attachment scores in people who answered 'Yes' and 'No' to the question 'Do you find it hard to express feelings of sadness or grief?'

Because the full score of Emotional Inhibition includes replies to question IV/23 'Do you find it hard to express feelings of sadness or grief?', this question has not been included in the measure of Emotional Inhibition used in this chapter.

There was a trend for people with a clinical diagnosis of Delayed Grief to have higher scores of Avoidant Attachment but this did not reach statistical significance, nor was there any association between Avoidant Attachment scores and a diagnosis of psychosomatic disorder. Clearly we shall have to look elsewhere for an explanation of these problems.

Looking first at those with a clinical diagnosis of delayed grief, perusal of the case summaries revealed a number of other causes for delay in the 22 people who were accorded this diagnosis. The commonest was a need to remain in control. Sometimes this resulted from a conscious need to hold one's own grief in check in order to look after a parent or child (four cases); sometimes it was a reflection of a lifelong obsessional tendency (three cases). In three cases the person had been overwhelmed with tearless depression and two, though not depressed, were fearful that crying might bring about a recurrence of depression that they had suffered in the past. Two had suffered massive losses which had overwhelmed them and one of these had clear-cut post-traumatic stress disorder (see p. 33). Two more seem to have been so intoxicated with alcohol that they were unable to grieve. Other factors that may have contributed to the delay were longstanding personality disorders (two cases) and social isolation (two cases). There were only three cases in which an avoidant attachment pattern seemed to be the prime cause of the delayed grief. In these circumstances it is not surprising that the link

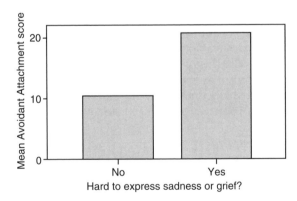

Figure 6.1 'Do you find it hard to express feelings of sadness or grief?' × Mean Avoidant Attachment score.

between avoidant attachment and delayed grief did not reach statistical significance.

People with psychosomatic disorders had higher Disability scores than those without but on most other variables they did not differ from the rest of the bereaved people. It is my impression, from studying the case histories, that their symptoms had several causes. Thus, in some the psychosomatic symptoms were a reflection of the physical symptoms caused by anxiety and tension; in others anxiety about a minor physical disorder seemed to have escalated into a hypochondriacal symptom. All in all, these effects balance out in a statistical study and they are not attributable to any predominant attachment pattern.

Despite the lack of a correlation between Avoidant Attachment and psychosomatic disorder, a significant correlation was found between Avoidant Attachment and the Disability score. This is a measure of life-threatening and/or disabling illness, which usually preceded the bereavement under consideration here. Statistical details and possible explanations for this correlation will be considered in Chapter 15 (p. 376).

Further considerations

The influence of Avoidant Attachments on the Grief/Loneliness score was hard to predict. Since Avoidant Attachment was associated with difficulty in expressing grief in childhood and adult life, it seemed likely that the Grief/ Loneliness score would be low. On the other hand, if grief that is repressed persists for longer than the normal course of grief and then appears in delayed form, the Grief/Loneliness score, as measured long after the bereavement, might be increased.

In the event, the latter proved to be the case. The scores of both Avoidant Attachment in childhood and Emotional Inhibition/Distrust in adult life were correlated at a low but significant level with the Grief/Loneliness score indicating that by the time they sought treatment some of the people who reported avoidant attachments in childhood and inhibition of feelings in adult life also reported more intense and lasting grief and loneliness than those who acknowledged less difficulty in expressing their feelings.

Given the difficulties that these people had in expressing feelings, it seemed likely that they would also have problems in their relationships with their partners. This is confirmed by the finding that Avoidant Attachments are associated with Disagreements with the spouse and with the person who has died.

A further prediction, which was not included in the original list, was that people with high scores on Avoidant Attachment would choose partners whom they saw as dependent on them rather than themselves being dependent on their partners. Appendix 6, Table A.6.8, shows that in 19 per cent of cases partners of people who scored high on Avoidant Attachment in childhood saw their partner as dependent and themselves as independent (the proportion in the low Avoidant Attachment group was 8 per cent), but it also shows that a greater proportion of the high Avoidant Attachment group saw themselves as the more dependent partner (34 per cent compared with 23 per cent). This surprising finding seems to suggest that a need for distance is not the same thing as independence. It may well be the case that people with this kind of insecure attachment depend on their partners without getting close to them.

I had expected that on the whole people would rate their partner's dependence as different from their own, but in those with low Avoidant Attachment scores there was a high level of mutual concordance between dependence on self and partner. Either both partners were seen as depending on each other or neither was. By contrast the relationship between those with high Avoidant Attachment scores was more likely to be discordant, with one depending on the other.

While it is easy to see how people who are intolerant of closeness may choose a partner whom they feel they can control, that is, who is dependent on them, it is less easy to explain the situation when it is the 'avoidant' one who is more dependent. It is my impression that in such cases there has been a strict allocation of roles within the marriage. Thus, an 'avoidant' husband may depend on his wife for child rearing and housekeeping. If she should die he may be forced to acknowledge his reliance on her and may see himself as the dependent partner.

Figure 6.2 summarises the significant findings associated with Avoidant Attachments. The findings confirm the overall assumption that the children of parents who discourage the expression of attachment will find it difficult to acknowledge and express both affection and grief. This is likely to persist into adult life, to increase the risk of interpersonal conflicts and to inhibit the expression of grief. These influences are evident in the case of Florence Harmony whose reaction to the death of her husband was described above:

> She was the only child of a business executive who was often away from home. She describes her father as an anxious man who was never able to show affection and who would tease her if she failed to meet his high standards. Her mother was similarly fearful and inhibited. Florence has mixed feelings towards them both.
>
> She grew up an insecure child who lacked trust in others and would never cry or ask for help. She reports that, like her parents, she was unable to hug or cuddle. Although of above-average intelligence, Florence was an under-achiever at school. Both parents discouraged her from playing with other children and she developed a tough, irritable, bossy manner. This caused people to think that she was stronger than she felt. The RAQ showed her to have a high score on Avoidant Attachment (12), average on Disorganised Attachment (4) and below average on Anxious/Ambivalent Attachment (6).

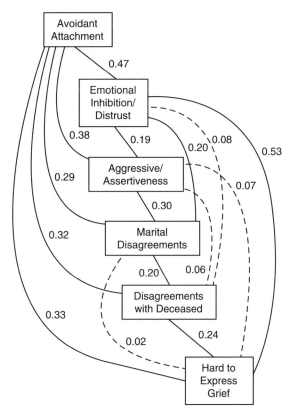

Continuous lines indicate significant correlations
Interrupted lines indicate non-significant trends

Figure 6.2 Avoidant Attachment: links with other variables. Figures are correlations between variables in 181 bereaved psychiatric patients.

Clearly Florence meets criteria for avoidant attachment. How this affected her relationships in adult life also becomes clear:

> In later years she developed a talent for music and subsequently made a career as an organist and choral director. She married to Dick, an intelligent academic, by whom she had two children.
>   Their marriage was conflicted. She found it hard to get close to Dick and to express affection. Sex was unsatisfactory and she acknowledged that her aggressive and assertive manner was driving a wedge between them. She describes Dick as unreliable and inclined to use alcohol as an escape and she blamed him for spending too much money on drink. It was these problems which,

at the time of his death, had caused them to request marital counselling.

It seems that both Florence's need to control Dick and her difficulty in getting close to him contributed to their marital problems and left her with a load of guilt and unresolved issues after his death.

Correlates of avoidant attachment in the non-psychiatric sample

Once again we can examine the extent to which our findings can be applied to a non-psychiatric population by repeating the above analysis in Ward's control group of young women. Difficulty in expressing grief was assessed from replies to question IV/23 ('Do you find it hard to express feelings of sadness or grief?'), which was answered by non-bereaved as well as bereaved women. For this reason I was able to include the full sample of 77 in this analysis. The relevant correlations are shown in Figure 6.3. Again it has been necessary to omit the score of Disagreements with the Deceased because only

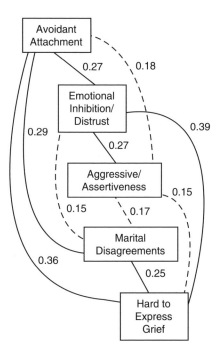

Continuous lines indicate significant correlations
Interrupted lines indicate non-significant trends

Figure 6.3 Bereaved non-psychiatric sample (n = 35). Avoidant Attachments: links with other variables.

three of Ward's respondents reported such disagreements and this is too few for statistical analysis.

Comparing these findings with those shown in Figure 6.2 we can see that the levels of correlation are very similar. In both psychiatric and non-psychiatric samples the Avoidant Attachment score is correlated with difficulty in expressing grief, with Emotional Inhibition/Distrust and with Marital Disagreements. It seems that the consequences of avoidant attachments are not confined to psychiatric populations.

We saw in Appendix 4 that the women in Ward's non-psychiatric sample had scores of Avoidant Attachment which were just as high as those found in my psychiatric sample. Could it be that some people who experienced avoidant attachments in childhood learn strategies which reduce the risk of psychiatric complications following bereavement in adult life?

Although not included in the Avoidant Attachment score a positive answer to the question 'Did you learn to be independent, to stand on your own two feet, at an early age?' (II/22) also correlated with the Avoidant Attachment score to a small but significant degree. These people may have distinct advantages in a world in which independence is highly valued.

We saw how this group tend to avoid closeness and to control others by aggression and assertiveness (see p. 53). These traits may be quite compatible with occupations in which control is more important than affection. It is also distinctly possible that some of those who experienced avoidant attachments avoid commitment and when bereaved have less cause for grief than their more committed peers. They may have learned that it is safer not to fall too deeply in love. Unfortunately these issues could not be measured by means of the RAQ so we are not able to confirm them in Ward's control group.

Coping strategies

We have seen that avoidant attachments in childhood are associated with higher scores of both Emotional Inhibition/Distrust and Aggressive/Assertive coping. It is reasonable to ask if these are alternatives or do they occur together; can people both inhibit their emotions and be aggressive? In fact there was only a small correlation between the two coping strategies and this barely reached statistical significance. It seems that people seldom adopt both inhibitory and aggressive strategies.

What, then are the consequences of each strategy? In fact *Emotional Inhibition/Distrust* was associated with more Overall Distress and increased scores on all the Symptoms/Emotions categories than Aggressive/Assertive coping (except Alcohol Problems which were not correlated with either strategy).

Aggressive/Assertive coping, on the other hand, was associated with higher Marital Disagreements and, to my surprise, an increased Clinging score. This last finding may be linked to the elevated scores of dependency on partners that was reported above (pp. 93–4) and supports the theory that this sometimes reflects a controlling type of relationship.

Therapeutic implications

These considerations have implications for therapy. Therapists may find it hard to sympathise with people who keep us at arm's length, yet if they get as far as our consulting room this means that they are trying to reach us. It takes bravery to set aside the strategies that, from the child's point of view, enabled them to survive, but this is what they must do if they are to overcome their difficulties in the world of adults. Like the anxious/ambivalent clients who seek our help, they deserve our admiration and respect and we may well be the only people in the world who recognise the magnitude of the struggle that they are undertaking:

> Seen in my clinic Florence impressed me as a clever woman who was quite capable of fighting her corner. She obtained great insight and benefit from reviewing her life and her fears of losing control rapidly diminished. I made no attempt to force her to express feelings but improvement in her confidence was accompanied by a general relaxation of tension and she seemed to become more 'at home' with herself. After only four sessions she decided that there was no need for me to continue seeing her but she recognised that she still had much unfinished business and accepted my suggestion that she seek further help from a psychotherapist.

Although the manner of her husband's death contributed to the severity of Florence's reaction, the essential picture is typical of avoidant attachments rather than post-traumatic reactions (see Chapter 9 for discussion of the problems of trauma). She illustrates well how children who learn to keep their distance from their parents then repeat the pattern with their teachers and peers. Lacking confidence in their ability to attract or cope with affection they may instead attempt to dominate and control others.

We should not assume that 'avoiders' avoid all problematic situations or settle for short-term gains; their need to remain independent and in control prevents this. They are, for instance, no more likely to turn to alcohol or drugs as a solution to their problems than are others. Florence's avoidance was confined to maintaining a safe distance from people and she seemed to compensate by becoming very good at handling things. She learned to 'stand on her own two feet' and tried to become independent of others. Insofar as she had to relate to people this was in a controlling or masterful way; thus she adopted a challenging and aggressive attitude. Other people tend to assume that people like Florence are as strong and secure as they seem, but those who avoid attachments are less not more secure than others and their masterful front conceals much inner turmoil.

Most of the time avoiders learn to cope effectively with the world that they meet. Their controlling style may be seen as quite appropriate in a society that values independence and control above affection and sentiment. Problems arise when avoiders reach the limits of their ability to cope (e.g. as a result of physical illness) or when those attachments that they have made are disrupted (hence Florence's vulnerability to bereavement). At the same time their compulsive independence may make it hard for them to ask for help when they most need it.

Although, on the face of it, people with avoidant attachments seem to be the opposite of those with anxious/ambivalent attachments, in reality they are not so different. While the anxiously ambivalent try hard not to cling, so the avoidant may struggle to find ways to get close to people despite their fears. Both are dimly aware of the effects on others of their distorted perception of the world and of their ways of coping with it.

Do avoiders care?

Avoidant people are often perceived as uncaring but attachment theory suggests that in fact they care but are afraid to show it. They are blamed for failing to communicate and ridiculed for the 'macho' attitudes with which they strive to cover up their insecurity. Of course the criticisms do not only come from other people. Florence bitterly regretted the way she had treated her husband and her feeling of guilt contributed to her problems after bereavement. It is hard to make restitution to someone once they are dead.

Clinical experience suggests that regrets are common following this type of loss and, although it was not included in the original set of predictions about Avoidant Attachments, a subsidiary analysis of the psychiatric sample confirms that feelings of guilt are a common problem. Figure 6.4 shows the statistically significant links between Avoidant Attachment and other relevant variables in the 181 bereaved psychiatric patients (further details are given in Appendix 6).

The question that revealed feelings of guilt most clearly was IV/24 'Are you filled with regret about something which you did or said, but cannot now put right?' Over a half of the bereaved people agreed with this statement. They were significantly more likely to have high scores on Emotional Inhibition/Distrust, Aggressive/Assertiveness and Marital Disagreements than those from other groups. Surprisingly there was no significant association with disagreements with the person who died suggesting that the regrets relate to surviving others (who are in a position to give support at this time) more often that to the person who has died.

Because question IV/24 is a component of the Grief/Loneliness score, it is not appropriate to examine the influence of 'regret' on this score. However,

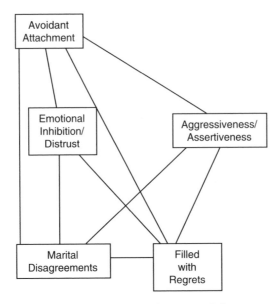

Continuous lines indicate significant association

Figure 6.4 'Filled with regrets about something, which I said or did, but cannot now put right' (IV/24): links with Avoidant Attachment and other variables. Figures are correlations between variables in 181 bereaved psychiatric patients (see Appendix A.6, pp. 334–5).

among 118 people who answered 'Yes' to question IV/14 'Do you spend a lot of time pining or longing for someone or something you have lost?', no less than two-thirds (67 per cent) also said that they are 'Filled with regret'. Further support for this finding comes from research by Bauer and Bonanno (2001) who found that avoidant coping is often associated with feelings of self-blame. They believe that it is this guilt that adversely affects long-term adjustment.

The higher the score of Avoidant Attachments, the more marital conflicts and regrets were reported (see Appendix 6). Thus, among 39 people with high scores on Avoidance there were only two (5 per cent) who were not 'filled with regret' and had few disagreements with their partner, whereas 19 (49 per cent) reported both regrets and many disagreements. Thus the main reason that avoidant attachments are associated with regrets is because of their effect on relationships with partners.

Avoidant people, it seems, blame themselves for their inability to express love and other feelings, as well as for the harm done to others by their behaviour. Following bereavement, when they are most in need of the affection and support of others, they are likely to regret their inability to seek for or accept it.

Self-reproach and avoidant attachment – a case study

Another person for whom feelings of guilt were a major problem was Jane Constable, aged 38. She was driving the car in which her mother was a passenger when it was struck by a lorry on the passenger's side. Her mother was killed outright and Jane was seriously injured.

Although she recovered from her injuries Jane remained distressed and preoccupied with feelings of guilt. She was afraid to leave the house for fear that people in the street would accuse her of killing her mother. She avoided her sister whom she was sure would never forgive her and spent most of her time lying in bed. She persisted in blaming herself despite the fact that, after a thorough police investigation, the coroner decided that nobody was to blame.

To fully understand her reaction it is necessary to look at her attachment history. Jane was the older of two daughters of a publican and his wife. She describes her father as a distant man who was unable to show affection and was inconsistent, sometimes ignoring her needs for attention or affection. Asked 'Was your parent often away or not available?' she wrote on the RAQ form 'Being there is not always the same as being available'. This applied to both her parents.

During Jane's childhood her mother suffered from clinical depression. As a result, she had threatened suicide and been admitted for psychiatric treatment on several occasions. From an early age Jane felt that she was duty bound to look after her mother, but despite this her mother made it clear that she preferred Jane's younger sister.

Jane was older and stronger and, by comparison, her little sister was 'weak'. Since it was clear that neither could rely on their mother to look after them, Jane felt that she must be in control at all times. She grew up an 'independent' girl who was always looking after others and would never ask for help for herself. Like Florence, she found it difficult to accept cuddles or other demonstrations of affection and was inclined to dominate her friends. People tended to think of her as tougher than she felt herself to be and she described herself as stubborn, rebellious and aggressive.

In other words, she had all the characteristics of the pattern of Avoidant Attachment and her RAQ score (9) confirmed this. Her score on Anxious/Ambivalence (4) was low and Disorganised Attachment (6) slightly above average. Leaving school she went to a teacher training college where she met Ian and, against her father's wishes, cohabited with him. Despite this they were never very close. Ian resented Jane's continued closeness to her parents and spent more and more of his time away from home.

Six years before her referral to me Jane's father died unexpectedly of a myocardial infarction. Following that event her mother again became clinically depressed and Jane felt that she had to contain her grief in order to look after her. During the following year Jane gave birth to a son and he too helped to drive from her mind any other demands on her attention. Ian felt excluded and started drinking. After a series of rows he left home and Jane was left to care for her small son at home and her mother nearby. Another five years passed before the accident took place in which her mother died.

In the light of this history it is not unreasonable to suppose that there was an element of ambivalence in Jane's relationship with her mother. Freud, in his classical paper 'Mourning and Melancholia' (1917) wrote:

> The loss of a love-object constitutes an excellent opportunity for the ambivalence in the love relationship to make itself felt and come to the fore. Consequently, when there is a disposition to obsessional neurosis, the conflict of ambivalence casts a pathological shade on the grief, forcing it to express itself in the form of self-reproaches, to the effect that the mourner himself is to blame for the loss of the loved one, *i.e.* desired it.

When we wish people dead and they then die, it is only to easy for us to blame ourselves.

Jane's total withdrawal had already come to an end before we met. She described how she had been referred to a psychotherapist who had incensed her by saying that she was 'not yet ready to get better'. She immediately terminated the therapy and returned to work. Even so she remained preoccupied with distressing feelings of guilt, anxiety, depression and worthlessness and she eventually accepted referral to me.

Seen at the hospital I was impressed by her intelligence, courage and sensitivity. She already had a fair amount of insight but could find no solution to her predicament. I did not blame or excuse her, rather I faced her with the challenge – 'If guilt is what you feel, what are you going to do about it?' It seemed important to indicate that there are things that one *can* do about such feelings. After careful thought she decided to do something which would bring good out of the bad thing that had happened, she undertook voluntary work caring for destitute people.

Her next step was to face her sister. This took courage as she was quite convinced that her sister would blame her for killing her mother. In the event her sister did no such thing and their reunion was deeply moving for both of them. She then organised a formal ritual of blessing at the graveside of her parents. Her sister was at first reluctant to come, but later relented and described the occasion as 'very healing'.

All of these activities took place in the course of 13 sessions of psychotherapy, which enabled Jane to take stock of her life. She came to see how her 'rebellious' behaviour had been the natural reaction of a young girl to the deep hurts that she had received. She realised that some of the guilt that she now felt reflected the guilt that she already felt for resenting her parents, as if by wishing her mother dead she had made herself into a murderer. In the end she was able to go some way towards forgiving herself and her parents and to recognise that they too had feelings for which they should not be blamed.

She was followed up six months after the end of therapy at which point she again completed the RAQ. By now she no longer saw herself as very anxious and depressed although she still felt tense, lacked confidence and found it hard to trust people. She was still 'filled with regret', found it hard to express grief and wished that she could cry more. The improvement in her depression had not made her any less critical of her parents, in fact she now disclosed that her mother had beaten her 'more than most parents' and admitted to feelings of ambivalence toward both parents.

Jane's problems were improved but not 'resolved' and it is doubtful if the attitudes and strategies which enable us to survive the vulnerable years of childhood can ever be completely given up.

Why do patterns of avoidant attachment established in childhood continue into adult life?

At times of loss and stress it is natural to slip back into the habits of thought that were ingrained in childhood because they enabled us to survive. I use the word 'survive' advisedly for we are speaking of matters of life and death. Adults may realise that children's lives are seldom in serious danger, but to the child it feels literally vital to find a way of living with this mother and this father. If that means suppressing natural tendencies to cuddle, to cling and to cry then so be it. We should not expect them to find it easy to unlearn such strategies or to believe that they do not deserve punishment if they should take the risk of getting closer to the object of their love or complaining when the loved one leaves.

Avoidant attachments only seem to make children independent of their parents. From the child's point of view they survive not because they have learned to keep away but because they have found the safest proximity to parents who continue to feed and protect them. Having been rewarded from an early age for behaviour that is seen as evidence of 'independence', such people may grow up with a very good 'front'. They may even come to believe in their apparent strength and wisdom and may choose as a partner someone who is happy to perpetuate that myth. Yet in this world nobody can be truly independent of others and any situation that brings this home will create considerable anxiety. At these times the willingness of the partner to give support, without challenging the myth, only serves to perpetuate the myth. Gant's sheep, having learned to avoid an electric shock by walking on three legs, continued to walk on three legs even when the electrical apparatus had been disconnected. So the effects of avoidant attachments tend to persist because the avoidant person has no means of finding out whether or not avoidance of closeness is still necessary.

It will not have escaped the reader's attention that the characteristics of avoidant attachment are part of the masculine stereotype in contemporary western society. Men, more than women, are expected to keep a rein on their feelings, to remain in control at all times and to adopt more aggressive attitudes to others. Just how this interacts with the influence of avoidant attachment will be examined in Chapter 10.

Further evidence, derived from multivariate analysis, about the sequence of circumstances connecting Avoidant Attachment in childhood with Grief/ Loneliness after bereavement in adult life is presented on pp. 371–3; other variables, to be discussed elsewhere, will then also be taken into account.

Conclusion

This research has identified avoidant attachment as a strategy developed in childhood in order to enable the child to cope with parents who cannot tolerate the expression of needs for attachment. In time these strategies are associated with and can reasonably be assumed to give rise to similar strategies when the child enters adult life. They reflect attitudes and assumptions that may complicate love relationships and give cause for deep regrets.

While this pattern may sometimes cause people to seek psychiatric help, it is found with similar frequency in those who have not sought help and may enable some people to develop a type of independence and assertiveness which is of value in a world that appreciates and rewards these strategies. Major bereavements leave most of us in need of the love and support of others, but those whose patterns of attachment are avoidant find it difficult to accept the love or seek the support. We shall look more closely at this issue in Chapter 14 (p. 187). Perhaps the most important task for the avoidant person is to discover that the basis for their avoidance is no longer valid. It is usually safer and more rewarding to get close to the people you love than it is to maintain an unnecessarily 'safe' distance.

7 Disorganised attachments

I was much too far out all my life
And not waving but drowning.

Stevie Smith, Not Waving but Drowning (1957)

Mollie McKay was 19 when her mother and, five months later, her father died. These events undermined a sense of security, which had never been strong. She was surprised to find herself pining for the parents she had lost and felt that she was experiencing the disaster that she had dreaded through most of her childhood, that her parents would die and leave her unprotected from the dangers of the world. She became extremely apprehensive and inclined to panic. She attempted to relieve the tension and anxiety with alcohol, but although this gave some immediate relief she found herself becoming increasingly dependent on this drug.

When I first saw her, three years later, she was filled with regret, seeing herself as childish and a failure. She was drinking heavily and had nobody in whom she could confide, perhaps because she found it so hard to trust anyone. Although she was desperate for help and longed for someone to look after her, she found it equally hard to accept the help that was available to her and had, ominously from my point of view, failed to turn up for an appointment with a psychologist. Asked in the RAQ what she would do if she got to the end of her tether she replied that she would not seek help from her friends or family but would seek it from a doctor. She also said that she would turn her frustrations inward, feeling guilty and self-reproachful, shut herself away from people, drown her sorrows in alcohol and might take an overdose or otherwise harm herself. Asked 'Have you recently got to the end of your tether?' she replied 'Yes.' Her GP had prescribed an antidepressant but she had taken the whole bottle in an overdose. He now refused to give her any more.

In some adults the death of parents is associated with an increase in maturity as they face up to the fact that they no longer need to maintain their child-hood dependence. In Mollie's case the death of her parents seems to have had the opposite effect. Why should this be?

As we saw in Chapter 1 (pp. 13–14), Main's modification of Ainsworth's patterns of attachment included a third category of insecure attachments that is here termed 'disorganised attachment'. Children in this category behave in the Strange Situation in an unpredictable and inconsistent way, both to sep-aration and reunion with their mothers. Sometimes they oscillate between approaching and avoiding their mother, at others they freeze suddenly in the middle of a movement or rock back and forth. They seem indecisive as if they had no effective way of coping with the situation.

We saw how this pattern often occurs when parents have suffered severe traumatic stresses before or shortly after the birth of this baby and have reacted with feelings of helplessness and despair. Sometimes this is associated with abuse and/or neglect of the child. Such parents are unable to provide consistent parenting to their children. Sometimes they are so preoccupied with their own emotional needs that they are unresponsive to their child, at other times they are overconcerned about the child. In either case the child has very little influence on the parent's behaviour.

The parents of infants with disorganised attachments are unpredictable and uncontrollable by the child and the child is both drawn toward and frightened by its primary caregiver(s), the people to whom it naturally turns in times of trouble. It seems likely that the reaction to this situation is one of helplessness and hopelessness.

Seligman has shown that assumptions of helplessness and hopelessness lie at the root of much depression in both childhood and adult life (1975). His seminal studies involved humans and other species in a variety of life situations that were found to evoke these assumptions. They explain the origin of the 'negative cognitions' that lie at the root of Beck's cognitive theory of depression (1967). This forms the basis of Cognitive Behaviour Therapy, which has revolutionised the psychological treatment of clinical depression (see p. 253 for further discussion of this therapy).

If the assumption of helplessness lies at the root of the disorganised attachment pattern and if this persists into adult life, it may well explain some of the anxiety states, panic disorders and depression that can bring people into psychiatric care following bereavement. This said, children with disorganised attachments may not be entirely helpless. They may not be able to resolve their predicament but they can cope with it to an extent by adopt-ing a low profile, 'freezing' or remaining inconspicuous. With the passage of time they may even learn to exert a measure of control over their parent and others by inverting the caring role so that it is they who are caring for the parent. Some may even develop sufficient confidence (self-trust) to control parents and others by coercion, although I have argued (p. 53) that this group belongs more appropriately in the avoidant pattern.

In the current study (as we saw in Chapter 3, p. 53 and Appendices 3–6) people who obtained high scores on Parental Depression/Psychiatric Problems and Parental Rejection/Violence to their parents also obtained high scores on Childhood Unhappiness and Compulsive Caregiving. People who reported that their families had been exposed to danger or persecution also obtained high scores of Childhood Unhappiness. It is the sum of these five items that constitutes our measure of Disorganised Attachment.

> Mollie was the youngest of four children born in Scotland. Shortly before her birth her maternal grandmother had died and this event had precipitated a serious depressive illness in her mother who was subsequently admitted to a mental hospital and treated with electro-convulsive therapy. Thereafter her mother remained liable to episodes of depression in the course of which she sometimes threatened to kill herself. At such times she was often violent towards her husband.
>
> Neither parent was able to show warmth and Mollie describes them as laid back and inconsistent in their care of her. She admits to having ambivalent feelings about them both. Mother was suspicious of other children and discouraged Mollie from playing with them. Consequently she grew up a loner and distrustful of her peers.
>
> She was an insecure and unhappy child who lacked confidence in herself and often wished she was dead. She suffered from a stammer, which was always at its worst when she was at home. At school she was an under-achiever and now thinks she suffered from dyslexia. Her teachers and peers, however, saw her as 'stupid'. The fact that she was also left-handed added to her feeling that she was not as good as other children.
>
> At times she showed signs of both of the other types of insecure attachment: thus, she was fearful of separation from her parents and afraid that they would die if she stayed away (suggesting an anxious/ambivalent attachment), she was unable to accept or express affection, could not ask for help and was suspicious and distrustful of others (all evidence of avoidant attachment). Her RAQ confirmed high scores on Disorganised (11), Anxious/Ambivalent (15) and Avoidant (8) Attachments.

Just as the disorganised child in the Strange Situation shows elements of both anxious/ambivalent and avoidant behaviour, so people in this study who scored highly on Disorganised Attachment commonly had elevated scores on other insecure attachment patterns. We shall return to examine the overlap and its significance below.

It is this mixture of unsatisfactory attachment strategies that distinguishes the disorganised pattern. Lacking both confidence in herself and trust in others Mollie became socially isolated and trapped in an insecure world from which there was no escape.

Predicted concomitants of disorganised attachments

Based on the foregoing considerations, it was predicted:

1   Those who report Disorganised Attachments in childhood will show evidence of helplessness as reflected in the tendency to turn in on themselves at times of stress.
2   Following bereavement, people who turn inward will react with high levels of depression, anxiety and a tendency to panic.
3   This sequence will explain a correlation between Disorganised Attachment and depression, anxiety and the tendency to panic.

Results of testing these predictions

Appendix 7 reports the results of testing all these predictions. There were highly significant correlations of moderate size between Disorganised Attachment scores and the current scores of Anxiety/Panic and Alcohol Problems with trends in favour of an association with Depression/Medication and a tendency to respond to question IV/17 (If you got to the end of your tether would you . . .) by selecting g. (Take an overdose or otherwise harm yourself?) Thus Prediction 3 is substantially confirmed.

The prediction that Disorganised Attachment will correlate with passive coping is also confirmed. Disorganised Attachment correlated, at a highly significant level, with the Turn In score, suggesting that people with these attachments are more likely to turn in on themselves when at the end of their tether than are others. Furthermore the Turn In score was highly predictive of the current Depression/Medication score, the Anxiety/Panic score, and agreement with the statement that, at the end of their tether, the person would 'overdose or otherwise harm yourself'.

Further confirmation of this sequence came from two path analyses. These are sophisticated statistical tests which included a correction for measurement error. These confirmed that the correlation between Disorganised Attachment and Anxiety/Panic is best explained by its influence on the Turn In score. Rather to my surprise, the Disorganised Attachment score was not associated with a lower End of Tether Seek Help score. Possible explanations for this are:

1   People who report disorganised attachments may lie about their preferences to seek help, perhaps because they recognise the social expectation that they ought to seek for help.
2   They do seek for help but not from their friends or family.

Examining the association between Disorganised Attachment scores and replies to the individual End of Tether questions tested the second of these hunches. Many people with disorganised attachments said that, under stress, they would not seek help from friends and family although they would seek help from doctors or other sources. Indeed, the people in this sample had done just that and had all sought help from their GP and from a psychiatrist (myself). The finding is statistically significant, though not at the high level of the association between Disorganised Attachment and the Turn In score (see Appendix 7, p. 339).

Since the function of family and friends is to provide mutual support and security at times of trouble, this represents a serious disturbance of attachment. In this sample of bereaved people, all of whom had sought psychiatric help, it seems that those whose attachments were disorganised may turn to outsiders such as doctors and counsellors rather than to their own family and friends when they were in trouble. We return now to consider how, in Mollie's case, disorganised patterns of attachment continued to influence her relationships and ability to cope in later life:

> Mollie's trust had been undermined when, at the age of 6, she was sexually abused, at first by a friend of her older brother and later by her brother himself. The insecurity and tensions of her teenage years further aggravated her problems and at the age of 15 her distress became so great that she took an overdose.
>
> She is unsure now why she did this. She was not happy at home and, like many youngsters of her age, wanted to leave, yet she was unsure that she could survive the upheaval that would result. Eventually she broke away from her home and went to live with siblings; over the next four years she began to achieve some kind of independence. Life was still not easy. Mollie's siblings had grown up in the same environment and under the same influences as Mollie and all of them had problems of their own. It was in this situation that the death of her parents took place. Her reaction of severe anxiety, depression and alcohol abuse have been described above.

By the time she was referred to me Mollie had already sought an alternative source of help, with temporary improvement:

> Six months after her father's death a friend took her to a Pentecostal church and before long she underwent a conversion experience. Despite her stammer she found herself with the ability to 'speak in tongues', a direct line of communication with God who she hoped would protect her and keep her safe. This experience was

associated with another surge in confidence. She stopped drinking and even found that her reading ability improved.

We shall look more closely at the part which attachment to a divine being can play in fostering security (pp. 184–5) Sadly, Mollie's trust in God, like her other relationships, did not stand the test of time:

> Tensions between her and her brother had been building up and after a major quarrel which led to him beating her up she left home to live on her own. She had been living alone for three years when she was referred to me. During that time her feelings of insecurity, anxiety and tension had again built up.
>
> Seen in the clinic it was clear to me that she was not stupid. She told her story in an articulate manner and there was little evidence of her stammer. She showed little of the fear which she undoubtedly felt and was inclined to play down the seriousness of her problems. Nevertheless, I found myself in a cleft stick. If I reassured her of her strength and value, she took this as confirmation of her assumption that she must stand on her own and that I did not wish to help her. If, on the other hand, I acknowledged the seriousness of her position and her need for support, she found in this attitude confirmation of her worst fears, that she was weak and helpless.
>
> By our second interview the very empathy that had begun to spring up between us had become a threat. She now knew that I had no magical solution to her problems and in sharing her life history she had begun to realise the magnitude of the problems that she faced. At the same time, she had little reason to trust that I would be able to cope with her need to depend on me and her past experience led her to expect that, in the long run, I would let her down.
>
> In these circumstances I was disappointed, though not altogether surprised, when she failed to arrive for our third interview or to respond to my offer of further appointments.

Mollie's case illustrates well the problems that can result from disorganised attachment, distrust in its deepest and most personal sense in oneself and in other people. While ambivalence may be present in all three patterns of insecure attachment it is most destructive in this one. Anxious/ambivalent children may resent the need to cling and may do so in an aggressive, punitive manner, but they still have sufficient confidence in the strength and goodwill of others to turn to them. Avoidant children have learned to keep their distance from others and to trust their own strength and independence. Their ambivalence may be channelled into dominance of others, which may enable them to achieve a great deal. By contrast disorganised children need to inhibit their ambivalence if they are to adopt the passive, compliant or caregiving strategies which will enable them to 'fit in'.

If they fail to do this, their lack of trust in themselves and others leaves them anxious and helpless in the face of adversity and they may give up too easily when obstacles and dangers are put in their path. In adult life, faced with such circumstances they panic, plummet into depression or take easy ways out by drinking or otherwise running away. Sadly their distrust makes it hard for them to ask for help from others and, if they do ask, to persist with therapy when the going gets tough.

The inclination to suicide or self-harm

Overdosing, and other forms of self-harm are often dismissed as 'attention-seeking behaviour'. Despite this, in the current study, even those who said that at the end of their tether they would turn to doctors and others, were significantly less inclined to self-harm than those who said that they would not seek for help (see Appendix 7, p. 339). It seems that other explanations are needed for this inclination.

An alternative is to see the impulse to self-harm as a form of self-punishment and, in fact, three-quarters of those who were so disposed were 'filled with regret about something which you did or said, but cannot now put right' (IV/24). The combination of depression and alcohol abuse, along with feelings of restless anxiety, are well recognised by psychiatrists as increasing the risk of suicide. While suicide cannot be regarded as an 'easy' way to escape, the urge to self-punishment may push people towards adopting this desperate strategy or 'solution' to their problems. If the suicidal attempt should fail, it may provide dramatic evidence of the sufferer's desperate need for help and persuade others to acknowledge that need.

Summary of significant statistical findings in psychiatric patients

These findings are summarised in Figure 7.1. They suggest that the influence of disorganised attachments on psychological problems is not limited to the years of childhood. Although none of the correlations is high, Disorganised Attachments are linked at a significant level with Anxiety/Panic and Alcohol Problems, and with a tendency to respond to stress by turning in on oneself and taking an overdose or otherwise harming oneself. If help is sought it will be from outside the family or circle of friends.

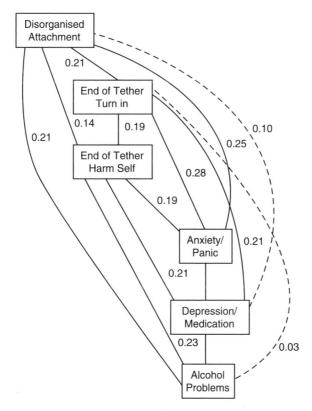

Continuous lines indicate significant correlations
Interrupted lines indicate non-significant trends

Figure 7.1 Disorganised Attachment: links with other variables, n = 181 bereaved
 psychiatric patients.

Is disorganised attachment linked to similar problems in non-psychiatric settings?

Again we can examine the same correlations in Ward's sample of young
women who did not seek psychiatric help. Although there is not space to give
details, the results are summarised in Figure 7.2. This shows that most of the
links found in the psychiatric patients were also found in the non-psychiatric.
It appears that the influence of disorganised attachment is present in both
populations although the overall level of anxiety is less in the non-psychiatric
group.

In addition the Disorganised Attachment score is significantly correlated
with the Depression/Medication score in the non-psychiatric group. (It just
missed statistical significance in the psychiatric.) This suggests that other
factors may be playing a part in causing depression in the psychiatric group
(see Appendix 7, pp. 341–2 for details).

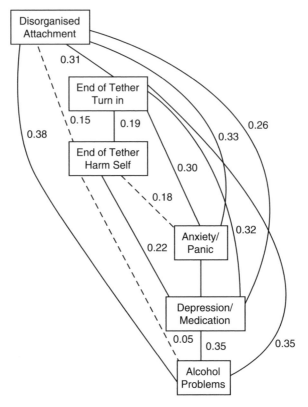

Continuous lines indicate significant correlations
Interrupted lines indicate non-significant trends

Figure 7.2 Non-psychiatric control group – Disorganised Attachment: links with other variables, n = 35 non-psychiatric bereaved controls.

Disorganised attachments in the non-psychiatric sample

Once again we must ask if, alongside the problems that are apparent in both the psychiatric and Ward's non-psychiatric group, there may also be benefits to result from the experience of disorganised attachment in childhood? If so, this may account for the finding that disorganised attachments are just as common in the non-psychiatric as in the psychiatric groups (see p. 326).

It has been suggested that disorganised attachments may tend to passivity. Lacking confidence in themselves and wary of others, some may keep a low profile and may even develop skills at remaining unnoticed and merging into the background; others may get credit for their selfless care of others. If modern life rewards those who take initiatives and leadership, those who lack these qualities may also find their niche as friends, followers and supporters who will fit in unobtrusively, caring for others and challenging nobody. It may be that the control group had learned to make and maintain peer relationships despite their experiences with parents while the psychiatric group had not.

To test this theory we can take a closer look (see Appendix 7, pp. 341–2) at the 27 members of Ward's control group who reported high levels of Disorganised Attachment (4+) in their childhood and compare them with the 28 similarly high-scoring members of the psychiatric group. Of the controls 88 per cent had someone 'in whom you can confide your inmost thoughts and feelings'. By contrast nearly a half of the psychiatric group said that they had nobody in whom they could confide. Despite the influence of the disorganised attachment the control group were also less likely than the psychiatric patients to say that they would turn in on themselves when at the end of their tether. This seems to indicate that the controls had not given up on relationships as a source of security. On the other hand, their marriages were no less conflicted, nor did they see themselves as less aggressive/assertive than the psychiatric group. They do not seem to have found it any easier to make and maintain adult attachments as opposed to friendships.

This suggests that although the 'disorganised' members of the control group are able to confide in friends, their closer 'romantic attachments' are not without conflict, nor are they as submissive as we might expect. Indeed, it may be that their success at maintaining a balance between asserting themselves, confiding in others and avoiding too close an emotional involvement accounts both for their lack of psychiatric difficulties and their conflicts. It is only the members of the group who fail to achieve this balance who are likely to become distressed and seek psychiatric help.

Why do patterns of disorganised attachment established in childhood sometimes continue into adult life? Disorganised attachments provide few benefits to children or their parents. At best, such children may discover that they can survive by forming confiding friendships with their peers; at worst life may become a long succession of crises as children and parents strive to persuade each other to give them what they cannot give – security.

Several theories have been proposed to explain the biological function of depression. One is that it is the human equivalent of the 'freezing' adopted by many animals in situations from which they see no escape. This would seem to be in keeping with the above observation. Another explanation is that depression represents, in human beings, the passivity behaviour exhibited by those who see themselves as weak when faced with challenge from a stronger adversary (Price 1967). All social animals are in status hierarchies, 'peck orders' which determine their place in society. These are relatively fixed and seldom challenged. When they are challenged a fight may ensue which will continue until one or other of the combatants 'loses heart'. At this point, confronting behaviour is replaced by passivity. This 'switches off' aggression in the opponent and the conflict immediately ends (for a clear exposition of the biological roots of aggression and passivity see Lorenz's classic *On Aggression* 1963).

Children, both human and non-human, often play at conflict and may appear to be challenging their own parents. Some parents are very tolerant of this and know that it is 'just a game', but all parents have their limits and the children need to 'know their place'. Some insecure parents are less tolerant and come down heavily on any child whom they see as challenging them. This may well be the case with parents in disorganised attachments with their children. But in social animals passivity behaviour seldom persists for long once the conflict is at an end. While conflicts with parents may trigger reactions of passivity, neither this nor the freezing behaviour alluded to above will persist once the danger is past. Only if the danger is seen to be ever-present is it likely that these behaviours will last.

Returning now to the issue of the reason why people who suffered disorganised attachments in childhood remain at risk of psychological problems in later life, two types of problem need to be considered. On the one hand there are some who, like Mollie, remain trapped by self-defeating assumptions about themselves and others. On the other hand, there are people who, despite negative influences in childhood, do make a fair adjustment to adult life, but their new-found confidence may not stand the test of time and they may revert to earlier and less appropriate ways of coping when faced with more than ordinary stress.

The self-defeating assumptions that entrap people include ideas which prevent them from doing the very things that would enable them to escape the trap. These include the ideas that Bateson termed 'double binds' (Bateson *et al.* 1956). Although originally introduced to explain aspects of schizophrenia, these have much wider relevance. For instance, small children may be blamed by parents for their lack of speech, but ridiculed whenever they attempt to use words. Treatment of this kind may well account for Mollie's stammer. Similarly, children may be accused of being uncaring if they do not show affection, but be sexually abused and/or accused of being a slut if they do. Again Mollie's experience of sexual abuse may well reflect this kind of problem. Binds such as these can only lead to confusion, to a stunting of learning and action.

The loss of confidence and the social stigma that follows make it hard for children to do the very things that would enable them to learn new ways of coping. As they grow older their lack of confidence may cause them to sell themselves short in many ways, taking poor jobs and choosing for their partners people who are themselves too insecure to meet the other's needs for support and encouragement. When people who have experienced disorganised attachments have children of their own their insecurity may be perpetuated and a cycle of deprivation passed from generation to generation.

However pessimistic these observations, it is reassuring to find from Ward's group that people with disorganised attachments in childhood may do well. Many of those who report having been brought up in an unpredictable and at times hostile world developed skills that enabled them to maintain confiding friendships, which stood them in good stead. They may not meet the stereotype of independence, assertiveness and control that seem to be the desired objectives of our educational system, or to become skilled romantic lovers, but those who learn to cope with loss without withdrawing from friendships are enabled thereby to achieve a measure of equanimity. They may value their friendships all the more because of their recollection of hard times and those attachment relationships they do make may blossom for the same reason.

From the point of view of the therapist it is important for us to discover how we can help those with problems arising from disorganised attachments to achieve a similar peace of mind. The existence of the second category of problems which were described above, the people who find a contented niche but relapse when faced with setbacks, suggests that people who have adjusted successfully to life may continue to be at risk. Thus a woman who has been abused as a child may seem to have made a good adjustment; she may have a good marriage and be a caring and solicitous mother to her children. But then things go wrong, her husband is on a business trip, her elder daughter has the measles and the younger one wakes her up in the middle of the night. Suddenly she finds herself shouting at the child and shaking her. She is horrified to realise that she is treating the child in just the way that she was treated when young.

Social workers recognise the risks of this kind of impulsive child abuse and try to provide support systems that both prevent the mother from reaching the end of her tether and teach her alternative ways of coping if she does. The situation is far from hopeless and well worth the expenditure of time and effort that is necessary if it is to succeed.

Case study: Disorganised attachment, improvement, relapse and reorganisation

Among the patients who were referred to me with problems after bereavement were several who fit into this second relapsing category of disorganised attachments.

> Esther Kleinman, now 74 years of age, was the eldest child in a Jewish family of nine children. She describes her father as a strict, cruel man who physically abused his wife and his children. She saw both parents as anxious people who were mutually dependent on each other. Neither expressed affection and both made it clear that she was an unwanted child. Throughout her childhood she was controlled by her parents with blows and with threats that they would leave unless she behaved. They were inconsistent in their care, sometimes overprotecting her and worrying about her health and at other times making her feel that she had to look after them and her younger siblings.

In these circumstances it is not surprising that Esther grew up an unhappy child who cried a great deal and often wished she were dead. She lacked confidence in herself and felt that she was dependent on others, but at the same time she could not ask for help and was seen as strong, bossy and inclined to dominate and bully her friends. Her RAQ showed her to have high scores on all three patterns of attachment, Disorganised (13), Avoidant (14) and Anxious/Ambivalent (18).

In her teens she solved her problems of insecurity by marrying a tailor 13 years older than herself. We can speculate that he resembled the good father whom she had never had and their relationship seems to have been based on mutual trust rather than sexual attraction. It is not altogether surprising that they had no children; instead they devoted their lives to each other. Esther sees them as having been mutually dependent but in fact she gradually grew in confidence and trust over the years and they were very happy.

He died at the age of 88 from pneumonia as a complication of cancer of the prostate gland. Although she says that his death was unexpected she had always known that he would be the first to go. Her immediate reaction was to panic. She could not believe that she could survive without her husband and persuaded her GP to refer her to me within three weeks of his death. At that time it seemed that she had reverted to her childhood assumptions about the world. When she filled in the RAQ she described herself as very anxious and depressed, lacking in confidence, pining for her husband and very lonely. Her GP had prescribed a tranquilliser and she admitted taking rather more of this than she should.

When I saw her in my outpatients clinic a week later things were already improving. She was still sleeping badly and had lost weight, but her grief seemed very normal and she certainly did not give me the impression that she was the insecure person whom she had been as a child. In fact she had achieved a great deal and her warmth and composure were very evident.

She told me how in the week after his death she felt that she had lost every good thing that had come with her husband. She feared that she would revert to being the broken reed that she had been before she ever met him. But this feeling had not lasted and by the end of the first month she had realised that the lessons that she had learned in the course of her marriage still held true. She could now treasure the memory of her husband and go on without him because she carried him within her.

I agreed that she was not in need of psychiatric treatment but suggested that she report back if there were further problems. She was happy with this advice and did not contact me again.

Esther demonstrates the fact that the children of disorganised attachments can make stable relationships. They can learn to trust and their relationships are all the more appreciated because they were not expected. Negative assumptions can gradually change and even if people return to their former assumptive world in the immediate aftermath of a disaster this will not necessarily last.

Other ways in which people from disorganised attachments can be helped by appropriate counselling or psychotherapy will be discussed in Chapter 18.

Mixed pictures

As we have seen, people who score highly on Disorganised Attachment are likely also to have elevated scores of both Anxious/Ambivalent and Avoidant Attachment. This was certainly the case in both of the case examples described above. In fact there was a great deal of overlap between the different patterns of insecure attachment. Each of them can co-exist with either or both of the other two. The amount of overlap can be seen in Appendix 7 (pp. 342–3), which shows the intercorrelations between the three insecure patterns of attachment. The highest are the correlations between Disorganised and Avoidant Attachment scores and between Disorganised and Anxious/Ambivalent Attachment scores. This suggests that many people who report disorganised attachments also had parents to whom they either clung or from whom they kept their distance. Further scrutiny indicates that, among 27 people who had high scores of Disorganised Attachment (i.e. scores of seven or more) only two did not also report high scores on one or both of the other Attachment Patterns.

More surprising is the finding that there was also a correlation between Anxious/Ambivalent and Avoidant Attachment scores. Although lower than either of the other correlations, this was still highly significant and implies that it is possible both to cling and avoid. This finding confirms a similar observation by Feeney (1991). At first sight this seems to be contradictory: how can a person both cling to and avoid a parent? On reflection several explanations are possible. Thus, there were 12 (7 per cent) respondents who said that they had changed from being passively obedient (II/16) to rebelling against authority (II/30). This often occurred during the teenage years when sexual and peer group pressures came into conflict with parental attachments. Alternatively, children might oscillate between clinging and avoiding or they might cling to one parent but avoid the other. There were

28 respondents (15 per cent) who said that they were 'unusually close' to their mother (I/24) but ambivalent towards their father (I/30) and 20 (11 per cent) who were unusually close to their father and ambivalent towards their mother.

If, as has been suggested, the disorganised pattern reflects a conflicted state in which the child feels drawn towards parents who are unpredictably reject-ing or overconcerned, then it is not surprising to find both clinging and avoidant behaviour in one and the same person. This viewpoint is supported by Belsky (1996) who has pointed out that, although traditional attachment theory suggests that in most children one internal working model of their parents predominates and gives rise to stable attachment patterns over time, it is quite possible for a child to hold more than one working model and to switch between them as the occasion demands. He suggests that a hierarchy may exist, with the primary model serving as the default option and the second model coming 'on line' only when the primary model fails.

It is arguable that disorganised attachment in the form described by Main and Ainsworth is part of a wider category, which includes all of those who in this study obtained high scores on both Anxious/Ambivalent and Avoidant Attachment. The justification for this claim comes from recognising that whenever these two attachment patterns co-exist people are likely to lack trust in themselves and others. This is the double jeopardy that, I have suggested, explains the particular vulnerability of people with disorganised attachments and it fits the data obtained from both bereaved and non-bereaved respondents (we shall consider this further on p. 243).

Conclusions

Disorganised attachments contain elements of anxious/ambivalent and avoid-ant attachments and can be seen as reflecting lack of trust in oneself and others. Without effective ways of coping people feel helplessness and tend to turn in on themselves in the face of stress. While these problems are not necessarily intractable, they often persist into adult life, or improve but then relapse when disaster strikes.

Love relationships, though difficult, provide what little security these people can attain. When these relationships are severed by bereavement, they more than others are likely to become very anxious and inclined to panic. They may also become depressed and/or rely on alcohol to calm their nerves. The combination of feelings of helplessness, fear, shame, depression and the disinhibiting effects of alcohol increase the risk that they will both punish themselves and solve their problems by suicide.

Yet these feelings are rooted in a life situation that no longer obtains. Clearly it is important for the disorganised person and for those who care for them to discover that the self-doubts and distrust of others which underlie these problems are not justified. They reflect a view of the world that is now obsolete.

Conclusions from Part II

In the preceding chapters evidence has been presented of the ways in which patterns of attachment, developed in childhood, can influence, for good or ill, the subsequent security, self-confidence, trust and worldview of the adult. These in turn influence our relationships to others, be they friends, family or partners and the way we react when these relationships are impacted by bereavement.

In Chapter 4 we examined the influence of people's recollection of secure attachments in childhood on the security of their attachments in adult life and their subsequent reaction to bereavement. We concluded that those who recall being securely attached made more secure relationships in adult life and were less distressed by bereavement than the insecurely attached. Some of the psychiatric problems that follow bereavement may be expressions of ongoing problems of attachment. On the other hand the evidence from the comparison group suggests that the strategies which people adopt in order to cope with insecure attachments are not uniformly harmful and may, indeed, prepare some people for insecurity, stress and loss in later life.

Chapter 5 demonstrated how those who recollect anxious/ambivalent attachments in childhood are predisposed to cling and to react with severe and lasting grief to losses in adult life. These are partially explained by the influence of these childhood attachments on later attachments; these tend to be conflicted, rather than dependent. Clinging and lasting grief are also explained by the anxious/ambivalent person's lack of confidence in their ability to cope alone.

In Chapter 6 we saw how those who report avoidant attachments in childhood seem to have learned that attachments that are too close can be dangerous. This assumption complicates relationships later in life and fosters distrust of others and compulsive self-reliance. It also gives rise to the inhibition of the expression of both love and grief.

While those who have experienced anxious/ambivalent attachments in childhood grow up lacking confidence in themselves and those with avoidant attachments lack trust in others, we saw in Chapter 7 how people who report disorganised attachments in childhood lack trust in both themselves and others. Faced with bereavement and other disasters in adult life, they turn in on themselves, become highly anxious and may use alcohol or other drugs to escape. These are the group at most danger of self-harm.

Although evidence from psychiatric sources tends to highlight the negative consequences of insecure attachments, possible positive consequences have also been considered and evidence from the comparison group suggests that a crucial factor which determines whether or not someone with a history of insecure attachment in childhood seeks psychiatric help after bereavement is their ability to confide in others and not to turn in on themselves when faced with a loss.

Although the evidence is not conclusive, it seems likely that many of those with a history of anxious/ambivalent attachments succeed in making relationships with friends and family members. These stand them in good stead despite or even because of the continuing influence of a tendency to cling. People with a history of avoidant attachment may be well prepared for a world in which independence and self-reliance are esteemed. In both cases the strategies that were learned in childhood may continue to meet the needs of the adult. Finally, we speculated that the experience of disorganised attachment, with its consequent wariness of others and awareness of one's own weakness, leaves some people more sensitive than others to emotional issues and able to make confiding friendships.

Since it takes at least two to make a relationship, it is not unreasonable to suppose that those people who find partners whose attachment strategies fit their own will be glad of the feeling of familiarity and mastery which this brings. Others may find that they are attracted to people whose attachment strategies provide what theirs lack. The fit may be less snug but in time the relationship may provide a greater depth of security.

Attachment patterns have emerged as important influences on later reactions to bereavement, but they are not the only such factors. In Part III we examine some other influences to see how they interact with attachments.

Part III

Other influences on attachment and loss

8 Separation from parents

When my mother died I was very young,
And my father sold me while yet my tongue
Could scarcely cry, 'weep! weep! weep! weep!'
William Blake *Songs of Innocence*, 'The Chimney Sweeper' (1789)

In every parting there is an image of death.
George Eliot *Scenes of Clerical Life* (1858)

Marie Waida, aged 31, was referred to me after she had lost both her father and, two years later, her mother. She missed her parents intensely and wished she could find someone else to look after her. She was 'comfort eating' and was overweight. In addition to severe grief she also felt depressed and became frightened that this might mean that she was following in her depressive father's footsteps.

Here we shall try to understand how a history of separations from parents during childhood contributes to the intensity and persistence of the grief and depression from which Marie, and other similarly bereaved people, sometimes suffer. As we saw in Chapter 1, current interest in attachment stems from the seminal work of John Bowlby who demonstrated, beyond doubt, the potentially damaging effects of separating children from their parents. His interest in this topic grew out of his study of 'forty-four juvenile thieves' who had been referred to the London Child Guidance Clinic and whom he compared with a group of non-delinquents. This revealed the part which separation from their mothers played in the problems of these delinquents and enabled him to described a subgroup who were unable to make permanent satisfying relationships with other people (Bowlby 1944). Subsequently he drew on the growing number of studies by others who were attracted to this important field of research. A recent review (Mireault *et al.* 2002) reports seven studies in which separation from parents were associated with later maladjustment. These included depression, anxiety, aggression and separation disorders. (We shall look more closely at separation disorders in Chapter 17.)

Much of Bowlby's initial work was focused on the effects of 'maternal deprivation' and it was only in later years that he began to stress the importance of fathers and of types of parental influence other than separations. The damaging effects of separating children from their parents has since been confirmed by others including Harris and Bifulco (1991).

Initially Bowlby (1960) had attributed the harmful effects of maternal deprivation to the trauma of separation. This salience was challenged by Rutter (1972) who pointed out that separations do not occur in a vacuum. Often they are the consequence of conflicted relationships which themselves may cause the problems that Bowlby had attributed to the separation experience. Also the loss of a parent may seriously disrupt the quality of the care that the child continues to experience thereafter. Many of the problems associated with separation do not become apparent until some years later.

In responding to these criticisms Bowlby accepted Rutter's arguments and concluded that all three types of influence, the quality of parenting before and after the separation and the traumatic effects of the separation, need to be taken into account (Bowlby 1980: 298).

Do separation experiences contribute to the effects of insecure attachments? Mireault *et al.* (2002) examined the relationship between the loss of a mother in childhood and attachment patterns in adult life. They used Brennan *et al.*'s 'Experience in Close Relationships' scale to measure the attachment patterns in adult life of young mothers whose own mothers had died. Higher levels of both 'avoidance' and 'attachment anxiety' were found in this bereaved group than in a group of mothers whose own mothers were still alive. In a similar study Feeney and Noller (1990) showed that undergraduates rated as 'avoidant' reported more experiences of lengthy separation from their mothers than did others.

Evidence that losing a parent can influence the reaction to bereavement in adult life comes from a study by Silverman *et al.* (2001). They interviewed 85 women four months after the death of their husbands. Both the death of a parent or sibling during childhood and a history of childhood abuse were more frequent among those who suffered complicated grief than among those whose grief was uncomplicated. Both separations and abuse are likely to contribute to insecure attachments and are included in the RAQ.

Separations in the current study

This study enables us to look more closely at the relationship between separations and attachments. The RAQ includes five questions about separations from each parent (see p. 308). When added together these comprise our overall measure of parental separation (the Separation score). This means that added weight is given to numerous or long separations by comparison with few or brief episodes.

From the studies reported above it seemed likely that people who experienced the most frequent and/or protracted separations from their parents will be found to have higher scores on insecure attachments, more problematic relationships in later life, poorer coping skills and more distress after bereavement than others. It was also expected that, in view of the fact that the mothers of these respondents played a larger part in parenting than did the fathers, the influence of separation from mothers would be greater than the effects of separation from fathers.

These predictions were not included on my original list of predictions because they were not concerned with my hypotheses about the particular styles of parenting and their influence on the patterns of insecure attachments. I made no attempt to predict the effect of separations on particular styles of parenting, subsequent relationships in childhood or adult life, coping strategies or particular responses to bereavement. However, it did seem likely that separation scores would both influence and be influenced by problematic parenting and that this would then be reflected in the subsequent responses.

The bereaved psychiatric patients in this study frequently reported separations. Nearly two-thirds had been separated from their father for more than a month at some time during their childhood years and nearly a half had experienced similar separations from their mother.

Separations and insecure attachment patterns

Appendix 8 shows that separations from parents were significantly associated with all three of our insecure attachment patterns. The highest correlations were with the Disorganised and the Avoidant patterns. The correlation with Anxious/Ambivalence was relatively low. It is not possible, from these figures, to know whether it was parental problems that caused both the insecure attachment and the separation or the separation that undermined security and contributed to the insecure attachment. Common sense suggests that both explanations play a part. Thus, as we have seen, disorganised attachments were associated with rejection and violence between parents and avoidant attachments with intolerance of closeness. Both of these patterns were likely to have increased the risk of parents separating; so too is the clinging associated with anxious/ambivalent attachments. On the other hand separations constitute the very traumata to which Main attributed disorganised attachments (see p. 14) and the insecurity caused by separation may give rise to or aggravate clinging and/or avoidance.

When separation from father and mother are analysed separately it is clear that separations from mother are more highly correlated with all three insecure attachment patterns than are separations from father. Once again, the highest correlation is with Disorganised Attachment. Separations from father were found to correlate, at a low but significant level, with Disorganised and Avoidant patterns though not with Anxious/Ambivalence.

Separations and childhood vulnerability

Appendix 8 shows that the Separation score is significantly correlated with the overall score of Childhood Vulnerability. This applies to separations from father as well as mother but the correlations are rather stronger following separations from mother. Although it is tempting to assume that it is the separations which cause the childhood vulnerability, it may also be the case that both result from problematic relationships between the parents. If it is the separation that does the damage we would expect that separations occurring early in childhood would be associated with more vulnerability than those occurring later. In fact the RAQ findings show that this holds true of those who lose a mother in early childhood. Loss of father is, if anything, more closely related to childhood vulnerability when it occurs during the teenage years than at earlier periods. It seems that the presence of mothers is more important than fathers during early childhood, whereas fathers come into prominence in later childhood.

> Marie Waida had been born in England, the eldest of six children of a Polish shopkeeper who was subject to episodes of depression. Times were hard and on several occasions the family was evicted from their home for non-payment of rent.
>
> Marie's father had left his legal wife to live with Marie's mother after she became pregnant with Marie; they never married. Although he worried excessively about her, Marie also saw him as insensitive to her needs.
>
> Her mother always maintained a close relationship with her much-loved sister, Julia, who died on the day on which Marie was born. Marie was seen as replacing her. She responded by attempting to emulate this aunt, whom she had never met ('I wanted to be Julia not Marie').
>
> Unsurprisingly she was unable to live up to her mother's expectations. Mother seldom showed warmth towards her and Marie admits to feeling closer to her father. She showed me a snapshot of her mother with her arm round Bill, Marie's husband, but added bitterly, 'I can never remember her cuddling *me*.'
>
> Her RAQ showed that she had a moderate Anxious/Ambivalent Attachment score (8) and average score on Avoidant (4) and Disorganised Attachment (4).
>
> Experiences of separation fed into and aggravated Marie's insecure attachment to her parents and distrust of other children. Her mother had another baby each year for the first five years of Marie's life. As the birth approached Marie would be sent to a children's home until it was over, an experience that she dreaded.

During this time she suffered nightmares and walked in her sleep. Another separation took place when Marie was aged 9 and her mother was sick. She was 14 years of age when her mother had another 'love affair' and, shortly thereafter, developed a deep-vein thrombosis and was admitted to hospital. Marie was terrified that mother would die and leave her, the eldest daughter, to bring up her siblings.

She grew up an anxious youngster who lacked self-confidence and was afraid to be left alone. She was 'bossy' towards other children, found it difficult to ask them for help and was seen as independent and tougher than she felt. She got into trouble for pulling out her hair and for hiding; this behaviour was dismissed as 'attention seeking'.

In this case Marie's anxious/ambivalent attachment seems to have predated the separations from her parents but to have been aggravated by them. Hiding behaviour seems paradoxical in this context, but because hiding evokes seeking may indeed have been a form of 'attention seeking'. Her fear of mother dying, of being left alone and her 'attention seeking' are evidence of separation anxiety, the feature of anxious/ambivalent attachments most likely to be aggravated by separations.

Separations and relationships in adult life

Appendix 8 shows the association between separation scores and relationship problems in adult life with the partner or spouse and with the now deceased person. Although the correlation between the Separation score and Marital Disagreement score does reach statistical significance the level is not high.

There was also a trend for Separation to be associated with a history of disagreements with the person now dead but none of the correlations between the parental Separation score and the relationship with the person who died reached significance. It seems that the influence of separation from parents on relationships in adult life is evident but not strong.

Despite her childhood difficulties Marie did quite well at school and left at 18 to take a series of clerical jobs. In her twenties she met and cohabited with Bill. This was an insecure attachment in which she saw him as unusually close and dependent on her. Neither seems to have been able to meet the other's need for support and they had numerous quarrels. Marie is aware of the fact that she held back from getting close to Bill or to the two children whom she bore. 'I'm afraid of letting them love me too much,' she said.

Marie's first experience of childbirth was traumatic. Labour

continued for 23 hours and 'I felt I was going to die'. She was much
helped by her mother at this time. Subsequently she was able to
redress the balance when her mother became ill.

It appears that by now Marie's earlier tendency to anxious/ambivalent
attachment had given place to avoidance. She avoided getting close to her
husband and children for fear that she would lose them too. But any
independence that she achieved was undermined by a stressful pregnancy and
she then turned not to her 'dependent' husband but to her mother for
support.

Separation and coping

Having made no particular predictions about this category it was interesting
to find a highly significant correlation between the Separation score and the
End of Tether Turn In score; the latter seems, on the basis of the foregoing
analysis, to be a measure of helplessness (Appendix 8). Confirmation of this
assumption comes from the ominous finding that there was also a small
but significant tendency for people who thought that at the end of their
tether they might take an overdose or otherwise harm themselves to report
more separations than those who had no such suicidal tendencies. There
were also trends linking the Separation score with the scores of Coping by
Aggressive/Assertiveness and Emotional Inhibition/Distrust. These did not
reach statistical significance.

Bearing in mind the correlation of Separation scores with Marital Disagreements reported above it seems reasonable to conclude that people who
have experienced much separation from their parents in childhood are likely
to have rather more difficulty in trusting others than those who have not. The
underlying assumption here seems to be that people cannot be trusted to stay.

When the scores for separation from mother and from father were examined
separately the overall pattern is confirmed, along with a slight tendency for
separation from father to be associated with aggression/assertion, while separation from mother is more closely associated with a tendency to become
inhibited and turn in. Possible explanations for this will be considered below.

Separation and current distress

Although none of the correlations was high, the Parental Separation score did
predict the Overall Distress score at the time of referral to a significant
degree. When the individual scores that make up the Overall Distress score
were examined separately, the only two to show a significant correlation with
Separation were the Clinging score and the Anxiety/Panic score. People who
reported the most separation from parents were more likely to become
anxious and to cling to others following bereavement than those who report

less separation. As in most of the preceding analyses, separations from mother were marginally more highly correlated with current Emotion/Distress scores than separation from father.

Shortly after her father died Marie's mother was found to have a pancreatic cancer. Despite her grief, Marie was able to repay her mother for her support during her pregnancy by looking after her. But she was apprehensive when, four years after her first pregnancy, she became pregnant again. Her anxiety increased greatly when, in the course of her pregnancy, her mother died. Just as Marie's aunt's death during her mother's pregnancy had caused her mother to identify Marie with the aunt, so during the course of this pregnancy Marie became convinced that she would have a girl. She intended to name the child after her mother.

The birth itself was uncomplicated but she felt numb 'as if part of me had died'. Contrary to expectation she had a boy, but this did not prevent her from identifying him with her mother. Her ambivalence is reflected in the way she subsequently described her 16-month-old son as 'stronger than me . . . a tyrant, wins all the time'. She alternated between angry quarrels with the boy and inability to set limits to his demands.

Of particular importance and interest is the repetition with her son of a way of dealing with grief that she had learned in her own infancy. Marie's experience as a child seems to have caused her to strive to become like the aunt whom she was supposed to replace. In later life she attempted to maintain a bond with her dead mother by identifying her with the new baby. The consequences for the child of this kind of misidentification can be profound.

Summary of findings from the statistical analysis

In Figure 8.1, for the sake of simplicity, only the links with the Parental Separations score (which includes separations from either or both parents) are shown. Most of the intermediate links have been described above.

All of our expectations about the variables that correlate with separation from parents have proved correct. The Separation score is significantly associated with lack of trust and aggression towards others in adult life, with marital conflict and with anxiety and clinging after bereavement. Even so the modest levels of correlation do not lead us to conclude that separation from parents in childhood is a very powerful determinant of the reaction to bereavement. The evidence supports the assumption that separation from mother is usually more damaging than separation from father, although both have similar effects.

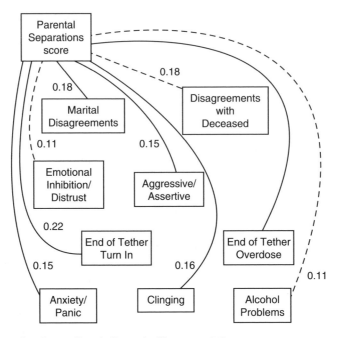

Continuous lines indicate significant correlations
Interrupted lines indicate non-significant trends

Figure 8.1 Separation from parents: links with other variables, n = 181 bereaved
psychiatric patients.

Separations are more likely to arise in families who are insecurely attached. In adult life they are associated with an increased risk of marital disagreements and a tendency to turn inward and even to overdose or otherwise harm oneself when under stress. It is reasonable to conclude that they aggravate the later influence of insecure attachment patterns and relationships on coping and the anxiety and clinging which may then follow bereavement.

Separations in the non-psychiatric sample

Although Ward's non-psychiatric respondents reported fewer separations from their parents than the psychiatric patients, this difference did not quite reach statistical significance in the matched samples. As in the psychiatric patients, separations from mother and father were each associated with Insecure Attachments, particularly Disorganised Attachment scores (see Appendix 8).

In adult life highly significant correlations were found between the Separation score and the End of Tether Turn In score (Spearman's rho 0.36) and between Separation and Marital Disagreements (Spearman's rho 0.33).

These are higher than in the psychiatric sample and confirm the findings that separations in childhood increase the tendency for adults to turn inward under stress and to report high levels of marital disagreement.

Although several of the correlations between the Separation score and scores of Symptoms/Distress were similar to those found in the psychiatric sample, the smaller sample size means that they did not reach statistical significance. For this reason no firm conclusions can be drawn about the influence of separations on current psychological state.

When the Separation scores in the matched psychiatric and non-psychiatric samples were compared there was no significant difference between them. This raises the possibility that, rather than being uniformly harmful, the experience of separation from parents in childhood may sometimes confer benefits. Perhaps some children who have experienced separations from parents learn from this experience to cope well with loss, to become more independent and/or develop skills at persuading others to relate to them on a mutually protective basis.

To examine these possibilities we can take a closer look at the 32 women in Ward's control group who had high scores (2+) of Separation from parents. Sixteen of these 32 had low scores (0–3) on Overall Distress and these can be compared with the remaining 16 who reported high Overall Distress; they can also be compared with the people in my psychiatric sample most of whom had high scores of Overall Distress. Some of the figures are too small to justify statistical analysis but the findings are of interest nonetheless.

Looking first at the possibility that the separated group who do well will have become more independent than the rest (Appendix 8, pp. 346–7), this is supported by the finding that only a third of the controls with low levels of distress (despite much separation from parents) described themselves as dependent on their partner, compared with two-thirds of the more highly distressed controls and of the psychiatric group. Although this suggests that the more independent respondents were coping better, it does not imply that they lacked support and the low distress group were less likely than the distressed to turn in on themselves when under stress.

These figures suggest that people who have experienced separations from parents may learn to become independent and not helpless in the face of stress. By contrast, those whose experience of separation leads them to become dependent on their partners will be helpless in the face of stress and suffer more distress after bereavement.

This leads us to the final question: Why did some become dependent and helpless while others did not? The answer is found in the lower scores of Insecure Attachment which were found in the controls who had less distress after bereavement despite high separation scores. The most likely explanation for these findings then is that it is the combination of insecure attachment and separation that leads to later distress after bereavement. Conversely those who are securely attached can not only tolerate separations from their parents but may even learn from them to become independent of others without the need to turn in on themselves at times of stress. This enables them to cope well with subsequent losses. Indeed, such separations may prepare secure people for the losses to come. Again, this supports the idea that the experience of stress in childhood can promote psychological toughness provided it does not exceed tolerable limits. It may also suggest that therapeutic efforts to restore security may improve tolerance of loss. This was the aim of therapy in the case of Marie Waida.

> Within three sessions of psychotherapy, focused on her attachment problems, Marie began to feel much better. She said that she was now able to accept her mother's death instead of relocating her inside her son. She had become much less aggressive towards him and found that she could smile at him. She told me, 'I'm a terrific Mum.' When last seen she was undertaking a sponsored diet in aid of her local hospice.
>
> She missed an appointment during the Christmas holiday and subsequently decided that she did not need to come again. However, when followed up some months later she reported that she had recently got to the end of her tether and was again depressed and anxious. Despite this she decided that she did not need another appointment.

A key factor in therapy was the focus on her ambivalence to her own child. This may well have been a reflection of her ambivalence to her mother. It was only when in therapy she was able to make this link that she was able to see her son in his own right. The change in their relationship that resulted was impressive and we can only hope that it lasted.

Final conclusions

This case example illustrates the findings of the statistical study and shows how the effects of separation from parents and insecure attachments are entwined. Separation from and loss of parents is a cause for grief which in people who are already insecure in their attachment to the parent may easily give rise to fear of making further attachments and a 'double bind'; a situation similar to that of the avoidant child who both desperately needs comfort and simultaneously fears the closeness and commitment that would make it possible. To repeat Marie's declaration, 'I'm frightened of letting them love me too much.'

This conclusion is supported by Mireault *et al.* (2002) who found that young adults who lost a parent in childhood now think themselves more vulnerable to loss than non-bereaved: 'the early bereaved may subtly prepare themselves for what they perceive to be another inevitable loss [i.e. of their spouses] by distancing themselves and relying less on their partners [avoidance]' but they are also 'more preoccupied with the relationship and its possible premature end'.

The fact that separation experiences are not necessarily associated with psychiatric problems indicates that there are some who can learn to cope despite and perhaps because of the separation. Indeed it is not long since it was thought beneficial to separate older children from their parents by sending them to boarding schools. They would there become both more independent but also learn to relate to their peers. As one who underwent just such a separation at the age of 9 I can look back on it as one of the most distressing experiences in my life. My parents, however, never doubted that it 'made a man of me'. It would be simplistic to dismiss this idea just because it is no longer 'politically correct'.

This research supports the contention that bereavement in adult life reflects and, to some extent, repeats the experience of earlier losses and gives rise to grief, both for the person lost and for the earlier losses. Early experience of loss can teach the child to cope with losses and thereby prepare them for such losses later in life. On the other hand, those who are insecure in their attachments may become sensitised to the effects of later losses and at greater risk of problematic bereavements. In this case the important task for therapists may be to imbue the client with sufficient security to undertake a much delayed positive learning experience. By taking stock, grieving and reviewing the implications of both the recent and the more remote losses it may be possible for the bereaved person to gain a new perspective that will lead to personal growth.

9   Trauma and bereavement

... and the war,
Goes on, and the moon in the breast of man is cold.
John Berryman (1914–1972) *The Moon and the Night and the Men*

My soul, like to a ship in a black storm,
Is driven, I know not whither.
John Webster *The White Devil* (1612) act 5, sc.6, 1.248

After the break-up of her second marriage Brenda Casebrook was left with her two sons, Len and Adam, now aged 22 and 18. Adam was the closest and she saw him as dependent upon her. Three years before I saw her, Adam had gone out with his friends for a drink at the pub. He was late returning and Brenda was alarmed when after midnight there came a knock at her door. A policeman and woman asked if they could come in. They told her that Adam had been stabbed to death in a fight.

For long after she had recovered from the shock of this news Brenda remained tense, anxious, depressed and haunted by visual images of her son's death. She missed him intensely and used alcohol as an anaesthetic. Her alcohol consumption increased and she began to go on binges for days on end. This behaviour undermined her relationship with her remaining son, Len, who threatened to leave her if she did not get help.

All bereavements are traumatic but some are more traumatic than others. In this chapter we shall look at the ways in which people die and how the more traumatic deaths influence the response to bereavement. We then go on to consider how these influences can be explained and how the attachment patterns, which were considered in earlier chapters, influence the response.

Death in the twentieth century

Despite the wars that have occurred and the advent of motor vehicles, the proportion of deaths from unnatural causes has fallen steadily in the western world and we can say that, for most of us, most of the time, the world is safer than it has ever been. In the USA men now have an expectation of life at birth of 76 years and women 82 years. The rest of the 'western' world is not far behind (World Guide 1999–2000). We no longer see the need to pray each night 'If I should die before I wake, I pray the Lord my soul to take.'

Each year we survive improves our chances and those who survive to the age of 75 can now expect another eight years of life. We shall then die, most of us from coronary heart disease, strokes, pneumonia or cancer. In the elderly even sudden deaths are seldom unexpected and improvements in palliative care have reduced the sufferings of the dying. This said, unexpected and untimely deaths still occur and substantial numbers of deaths are caused by accident and human agency. When they do take place we are less prepared for them than we would have been in the days when most children lost siblings, deaths took place at home and religion and culture placed ideas about death centre stage.

We saw in Chapter 2 how unexpected losses can shatter our assumptive world and undermine the most secure attachments, so too can multiple losses. People are seldom prepared for these, which means that they often but not always give rise to problematic bereavements. In disaster areas multiple deaths are likely to be sudden, unexpected, horrific and associated with social disorganisation and other mass disorder. They are particularly traumatic and complex (see Hodgkinson and Stewart 1991 for a review). Other multiple losses can be regarded as small-scale disasters. A car smash that kills a person's spouse and two children may not be a communal disaster but, from the survivor's point of view, the experience is much the same. Epidemics such as the current epidemic of AIDS (see Martin and Dean 1993) and armed conflicts may cause people to lose several friends or family members over a relatively short period. On the other hand, some multiple losses are spread out in time. A woman may suffer a succession of intrauterine and neonatal deaths or a family be afflicted by a congenital disease that kills off one person after another.

People who experience multiple losses not only suffer the cumulative effects of grief but their assumption that the world is a safe place where disasters do not happen is eroded and replaced by an expectation of further disasters. However some people learn to cope with repeated losses. Thus Znoj and Keller (2002) found that parents who had suffered a previous loss adjusted better to the loss of a child than parents with no such experience.

The commonest type of multiple loss is found in old age. As we get older, the number of funerals to which we are invited begins to outnumber weddings to the point where, among those who survive, most of their current generation are dead. In addition, old people suffer a number of other physical and psychological losses. Such multiple losses may have less impact because they have been anticipated and prepared for (see Moss *et al.* 2001).

Attachments, as we have seen, serve the function of keeping us safe in the world. It seems likely, therefore, that they will influence the ways in which we cope when our security is threatened by traumatic losses that undermine our safety and the safety of those we love. With this in mind we can turn our attention to traumatic losses in the current study and, in particular, the influence of childhood attachments on preparing people for or sensitising them to later traumatic bereavements. As we have seen, many of them had negative experiences during their childhood. Did this make them better prepared for trauma later in life or worse?

Trauma in the current study

If traumatic experiences contribute to cause psychiatric problems, we can expect more distress in bereaved people who experience traumatic bereavement than in those whose bereavement was less traumatic (see Appendix 9 for details). We also expect a higher incidence of traumatic losses in people who seek psychiatric help after bereavement than in those who do not. Both of these expectations are confirmed by the data from this study. People with high Trauma scores were significantly more distressed (on the Overall Distress score) than people with low scores and traumatic losses were much more frequent in bereaved psychiatric patients than in Ward's bereaved non-patients.

Figure 9.1 shows the mode of death as reported in the age-matched women in the psychiatric and non-psychiatric bereaved samples. Unexpected and multiple deaths are particularly common in the psychiatric sample (Figure 9.1a) and deaths by murder, manslaughter and suicide are prominent. Among the bereaved young women in Ward's non-psychiatric comparison group (Figure 9.1b) only one had suffered bereavement by suicide and two by manslaughter or murder. Being a young age group the proportion of unexpected deaths in the bereaved group was high but still much less than the proportion in the age-matched bereaved psychiatric patients. Only four (11 per cent) in Ward's group had suffered multiple (more than two) bereavements compared with a third of the matched psychiatric group. These four are too few to justify including multiple losses in the statistical comparison of psychiatric and non-psychiatric groups.

In the full sample of 181 bereaved people who sought psychiatric help, nearly three-quarters (73 per cent) had suffered one or more of these traumatic types of loss. These figures confirm other studies which indicate that traumatic types of bereavement are more likely to give rise to psychiatric referral than less traumatic bereavements.

(a) Psychiatric Bereaved

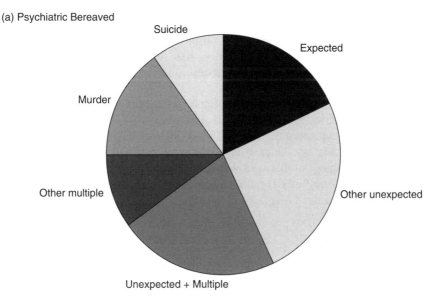

(b) Matched non-Psychiatric Bereaved

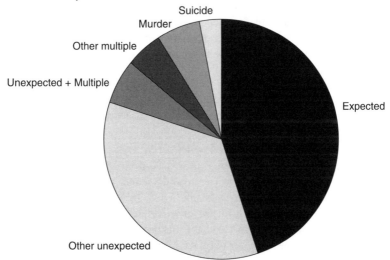

Figure 9.1 Mode of death (a) psychiatric bereaved. (b) matched non-psychiatric bereaved.

Diagnoses and symptoms associated with traumatic bereavement

As we have seen (pp. 32–4), previous research suggests that reactions to trauma include high levels of anxiety accompanied by avoidance of reminders of the traumatic event and occasionally post-traumatic stress disorder (PTSD).

When, in the current study, the clinical diagnoses following traumatic bereavements were compared with those that followed less traumatic losses, clinical anxiety state, was the most common. This diagnosis was made in 80 per cent of the traumatised group and 71 per cent of the less traumatised, but because of the small number of less traumatised this difference only reached a borderline level of statistical significance.

Contrary to expectation, the Trauma score was not correlated with any increase in the Anxiety/Panic score, perhaps because some people respond to trauma by becoming numb or exerting a rigid control over such feelings. On the other hand, the Grief/Loneliness score was significantly correlated with Trauma and the clinical diagnosis of chronic grief was confined to the traumatised group in whom it was diagnosed in 16 per cent of cases. It seems that although other studies have shown that, in the short term, grief may be inhibited after trauma (Parkes and Weiss 1983), in the current study the long-term effect of traumatic bereavement was to increase the intensity and duration of grieving.

Post-traumatic stress disorder was only found in those people who had experienced one or more traumatic circumstances attending the death. This is hardly surprising since the experience of trauma is an essential criterion for PTSD. However, the diagnosis was only made in 15 out of 97 cases (16 per cent). It was most frequent in the group of ten people bereaved by murder or manslaughter; of these three met criteria for a diagnosis of PTSD.

> Brenda Casebrook, as we saw above, illustrates all of these problems. After her son was killed she suffered severe clinical anxiety, chronic grief, post-traumatic stress disorder and alcohol problems.

Although Trauma was associated with a tendency to turn in when at the end of one's tether, the avoidance that accompanies PTSD was not of sufficient magnitude to influence the overall scores of Emotional Inhibition/Distrust or the incidence of Delayed Grief. Indeed, trauma was found to increase the intensity and duration of grief and to contribute to a clinical diagnosis of chronic grief. Since these are best seen as attachment problems it is reasonable to seek for an explanation in the interaction of trauma and attachment.

Insecure attachment and traumatic bereavement

In the psychiatric bereaved sample who, it is reasonable to assume, all had problematic bereavements, two possibilities need to be considered. If, on the one hand, traumatic experiences are sufficient to cause psychiatric problems regardless of prior vulnerability, we might find less evidence of attachment problems (i.e. a lower Insecure Attachment score) in those who sought psychiatric help after traumatic bereavements than in those whose bereavements were less traumatic (whose need for help may have resulted from insecurity of attachment). In other words, some people may have come for help because of trauma and others because of vulnerability.

Alternatively, if trauma interacts with insecure attachments to cause psychiatric problems, we would expect to find that the Trauma score and Insecure Attachment score are positively correlated. In fact there was no significant correlation, either positive of negative, between Insecurity of Attachment score (or any one of its constituent scores) and the Trauma score. It seems that both of the above factors may be operating to cancel out any overall effect.

Since both trauma and insecure attachments contribute to overall distress, it is no surprise to find that the highest scores of Overall Distress are found in those people who have high scores of both Trauma and Insecure Attachment. Trauma was found to add to the effect of the Avoidant Attachment pattern on the current Alcohol Problems scores and Disorganised Attachments interacted with Trauma to produce the highest levels of Overall Distress. In the light of this it is worth asking if it is mainly through their interaction with trauma that insecure attachments cause lasting problems after bereavement. Here we can again make use of hierarchical analysis in order to determine the chain of causation (see Appendix 9, pp. 354–5 for details).

The Insecurity of Attachment score was highly correlated with Overall Distress from the outset. Although both the Trauma and Problematic Coping scores were significantly associated with Overall Distress, the overall effect of Insecurity of Attachment on Overall Distress is mainly independent of trauma. It seems that insecure attachments do not act solely by increasing vulnerability to trauma, nor is the correlation of trauma with distress explained by its influence on coping.

Despite these overall findings some interaction effects were found when the individual patterns of insecure attachment were examined. Thus, scores of Avoidant Attachment interacted with Trauma to influence the Alcohol Problems score. Those with low scores of Avoidant Attachment did not report any more problems with alcohol after trauma than they did after other types of bereavement. But higher scores on Avoidant Attachment were associated with a disproportionate increase in the Alcohol Problem score after traumatic bereavements. It appears that the coping strategies adopted in adult life by people who have experienced avoidant attachments in childhood leave them particularly inclined to use alcohol as an escape following traumatic types of loss.

The most striking interaction between attachment and trauma was that between the Disorganised Attachment score, the Trauma score and current Overall Distress. People with low scores of Disorganised Attachment reported no more current distress after traumatic than after lesser bereavements; on the other hand, those with moderate to high scores of Disorganised Attachment had high scores of Overall Distress only if they also had moderate to high

Trauma scores. This suggests that the experience of a disorganised attachment in childhood leaves people less well able to cope with traumatic bereavement in adult life than more securely attached people.

> Brenda Casebrook had experienced just such a disorganised attachment. She had been an unwanted child. Her mother she describes as an insecure worrier who was unable to express affection and tended to drink too much. When Brenda was only 7 years of age her father was killed in the war and her mother and her maternal grandparents subsequently brought her up. Often her mother would become depressed and cling to Brenda who felt that she had to be a parent to her own mother. At such times her mother would threaten to commit suicide or give Brenda away. Brenda's greatest fear was that her mother would die, she became fearful of any separation.
>
> She grew up an anxious, unhappy and insecure child who performed poorly at school and was often tearful. Although she describes herself as lacking in self-confidence and unable to cope, she could not ask others for help. Indeed she was seen by them as tough, stubborn, aggressive and bad tempered.
>
> Her RAQ showed a high level of Insecure Attachments with high scores on Disorganised and Avoidant (9 and 6) and fairly high Anxious/Ambivalent Attachment scores (9).
>
> Brenda's insecure, close but ambivalent relationship with her mother persisted during her adult life and interfered with her other relationships. Two marriages ended in divorce and her relationship with her own two children (now aged 22 and 18) was stormy.
>
> She described her older son, Adam as close but dependent on her. In many ways she seems to have repeated with Adam her relationship with her mother and he was always jealous of his grandmother's clinging relationship with Brenda. He was also critical of Brenda's tendency to drink too much. She found this oppressive and from time to time needed to get away from him.
>
> In recent years she developed an equally insecure relationship with Len, with whom she was still living at the time when she was referred to me.

It seems that Brenda's insecurity of attachment left her with little trust in herself or others and her tendency to cope with stress by using alcohol added to her problems. It is small wonder that the violent death of her son Adam gave rise to a response that led her to seek psychiatric help and included all of the symptoms that are associated with traumatic losses.

Trauma and the assumptive world

Jannof-Bulman's theory of shattered assumptions (pp. 33–4) might be taken to imply that the negative assumptions associated with disorganised attachments will be confirmed rather than shattered by the experience of stress. Those who expect things to go wrong will be less upset when they do than those whose positive expectations are shattered. If this is so, we can expect that people with a history of insecure attachments will cope better than 'secure' others after traumatic losses.

Our data suggest a more complex situation. At the level of stress associated with 'non-traumatic' bereavements, the negative assumptions associated with disorganised attachments may indeed minimise the emotional impact of the loss. At higher levels of trauma, however, it seems that the strategies for coping break down and lead to catastrophic disturbance of emotional adjustment. The data reported in Appendix 9 (pp. 353–5) also indicates that it is the tendency for those who report disorganised attachment to turn in on themselves at times of stress that explains their special vulnerability to traumatic loss.

> Brenda's replies to the RAQ confirm the clinical impression of a deeply disturbed lady who had few resources that might have enabled her to cope with stress. In reply to the question about how she would behave when at the end of her tether she checked all the boxes except those concerned with seeking help from friends or family. She even said that she would take an overdose or otherwise harm herself although she did not think that she would succeed in killing herself. This was as well for she also agreed that she had recently got to the end of her tether.
>
> It seems to have been Len's threat to leave her that persuaded Brenda to attend an appointment with me and she was able to tell me her story and agreed to accept my offer of further therapy. But I was not altogether surprised when she failed to turn up for subsequent appointments. Therapeutic relationships based on coercion are unlikely to endure, particularly when patients lack trust in themselves or others.

In the current study, bereavement following murder or manslaughter was associated with more overall distress than any other type of traumatic bereavement. In a separate study of 17 such cases I concluded:

> The combination of sudden, unexpected, horrific and untimely death, with all the rage and guilt which followed and, often, the overwhelming of the family as a support system to the bereaved, is bound to interfere with normal grieving. It does this in several ways: (a) by inducing post-traumatic stress . . . (b) by evoking intense rage toward the offender

and all associated with him at a time when there may be little opportunity to vent that rage effectively; (c) by undermining trust in others, including the family, the police, the legal system and God; and (d) by evoking guilt for having survived and for failing to protect the deceased.

(Parkes 1993: 51)

Brenda illustrates well the ways in which a poor attachment history can influence relationships in adult life and add to the devastating influence of a cruel and violent murder. It can also influence how lack of trust in self and others can undermine a person's motivation to seek help and to form a therapeutic relationship. Following Adam's death it was her relationship with him that filled her mind so much that her younger son, Len, felt excluded. Indeed, she seems to have been tangled up in a web of intense, competing, ambivalent and insecure relationships, which had been evident throughout her life, and it is no surprise that her two marriages ended in divorce.

To sum up, it seems that the negative expectations that have been learned by those who have experienced the hardships of disorganised attachments during their childhood reduce the emotional impact of those later losses that have been anticipated and prepared for. These findings explain one of the most surprising findings in this study, the lack of any difference between average scores of Disorganised Attachment in the psychiatric patients and Ward's bereaved comparison group. The latter, as we have seen, had experienced few traumatic bereavements, seldom turned in on themselves and did not seek psychiatric help.

When, however, the loss is unexpected or otherwise traumatic, the tendency of those who have experienced disorganised attachments in childhood to turn in on themselves at times of stress proves an inadequate way of coping. In this situation they may assume that they are weak and powerless and that other people cannot be relied on to help them in times of trouble. The more traumatic their bereavement, the greater the risk that feelings of helplessness and hopelessness will overwhelm them and may lead to extreme reactions of anxiety, panic, depression and chronic grief.

People who report avoidant attachments in childhood may also find that their ways of coping with stress by distancing or avoiding problems are put to the test by traumatic bereavements. The use of alcohol as a tranquilliser, which helps them to minimise distress, may become a problem in its own right and contribute to the need for psychiatric help.

Multiple losses

Forty-six people in the current study had suffered multiple losses. Their average age was 40 years, virtually the same as that of the rest of the sample (42). Bearing in mind the fact that the frequency of bereavements increases with age this strongly suggests that this sample is atypical of the population as a whole and that multiple bereavements are more likely to cause younger people to seek psychiatric help than older. In other words, it is deaths that are multiple and/or untimely that are the most traumatic.

In most respects those who had suffered multiple losses did not differ from the singly bereaved; the clinical diagnoses assigned to them (including PTSD) were no different and nor were their scores of Emotions and Symptoms. The fact that multiple losses did not give rise to worse overall distress than that reported by people with single losses, at least in terms of the measures which were employed here, suggests that other factors contribute to the outcome in the singly bereaved cases. As already observed, some repeated bereavements may help to prepare people for the bereavements that are to come. Alongside those who are overwhelmed by multiple losses there may be others who learn from their experience of grief how to cope better with the next bereavement. Even so, bereavements that evoke severe fear, helplessness or horror, the defining requirement for PTSD, are not more likely to arise following multiple losses than single.

Conclusions

Since the function of attachments is to provide the security that enables us to cope with the stresses of life, it is not surprising that they influence the way people react to major psychological stress. In this chapter it has been possible to show how different patterns of attachment give rise to different basic assumptions about the world, which then colour how people cope when they are affected by traumatic bereavements.

We are now in a position to look at some examples of the kind of basic assumptions that are made by people whose secure attachments and positive life experiences have left them with a positive view of themselves, others and the world at large and to compare them with those of people whose experience has been predominantly negative.

Basic assumptions of those whose experience of life has been positive

Most attachment theorists assume that insecure attachments in childhood will leave people predisposed to more psychiatric problems and more difficulty in coping with traumatic life events than secure attachments, but Rando (2002), in an article which she titles 'The "Curse" of too Good a Childhood', claims: 'In over twenty-five years of practice, I have treated numerous individuals who have had specific difficulties in coping with negative life events due to issues stemming directly from a relatively idyllic prior life that was too pleasant and which was missing, for lack of a better term, a healthy dose of misfortune.' She attributes this to two problems:

- Those who have positive expectations of themselves and others are more likely to be overwhelmed when these expectations are shattered.
- They lack experience of defending and revising their assumptive worlds.

Rando is not so naive as to deny that problems can also result from negative experiences during childhood but her observations throw doubt on the assumption which I and others have made that secure attachments in childhood inevitably protect people from the damaging effects of subsequent traumatic life events such as bereavements. We know, intellectually, that disasters happen, but if our experience teaches us that they happen to other people, they do not happen to me, then we will adopt this basic assumption and feel secure. When a disaster strikes us, whatever the cause, our basic assumption of the world being a safe place is shattered, quite suddenly it feels very unsafe.

We know that murder, robbery and violence happen, but if our experience teaches us that our parents, God, the police and the law will protect us, we are unprepared for such violence in our own lives. If our child is murdered, we lose not only our child but also our trust in authority and the basic assumption that the world is a just place where bad things do not happen to good people.

We know that sickness and accidents happen, but this knowledge may not prevent us from eating too much or from other self-indulgence, for our experience has taught us that our body is strong enough to look after itself. If we are suddenly struck down by a disabling illness or suffer a mutilating accident, we lose not only the use of a body part but also our assumption of ourselves as intact, strong and invulnerable.

We know that people die, but unless we have suffered a major bereavement this will not prevent us from acting and thinking as if we and the people we love will live forever. When a loss occurs we lose not only the person to whom we are attached but also our assumption of immortality. We are waiting for the next death. It may even be our own.

People whose parents protected them from all dangers and gave them an exalted idea of their own powers may be easily overwhelmed when faced with betrayal or situations that bring home their limitations. From these examples we can assume that those of us who have been raised in a secure environment and fortunate enough never to have been exposed to separations, sickness and other trauma, will be less well prepared for traumatic losses than those who have grown up in 'the school of hard knocks'. Indeed, children and adults who are brought up in parts of the third world in which people have large families because they expect many of the children to die, grieve less and are less traumatised by the death of a child than those whose expectations are very different (Scheper-Hughes 1992).

Basic assumptions of those whose experience of life has been negative

But this does not mean that the traumatised child is less anxious than other children. Anxiety may indeed be in the interests of survival. In fact, Brown and Harris's (1978) studies of the influence of childhood losses on the response to stressful events in adult life indicate that, far from being inoculated against the effects of later trauma, many children who have been traumatised in childhood are sensitised to later stressful life events.

We saw above how the experience of insecure attachments in childhood can impair the developing child's ability to relate to others and to explore their world. This may leave them relatively less capable of coping with stress and less willing to seek help than others. Their assumptive world may leave them worse, not better, prepared for many of the problems that they must face. Thus, children whose parents have failed to protect them from painful experience may grow up with the assumption that they can never rely on authorities. While this may encourage them to become independent, it leaves them ill-prepared for any situation in which they need to seek out and trust such authorities.

Children who have been abused and told that the abuse is a punishment may grow up with the basic assumption that they are bad and must be punished for any misfortune that occurs. When things go wrong they may blame themselves and seek for punishment. They may even mutilate or otherwise harm themselves.

A person who, in early life, suffered losses of people to whom they had become attached may assume that it is safer not to fall in love. Even if subsequent life experience teaches them that there are exceptions to this rule, their faith will easily be undermined by later losses.

These examples go some way to explain the great variations that are found between the ways in which individuals respond to stressful life experiences. To understand these it is necessary to go beyond simplistic theories that stress is bad for you and that the passport to mental health is a secure attachment in childhood. The very fact of having survived childhood leads most people who reach adult life to assume that they now have the capacity to survive and to leave their parental home. The negative assumptions that accompanied insecure attachments in childhood are gradually replaced with more realistic assumptions of relative security. This said, the old assumptive world does not disappear; it may remain as a dreaded world to which one can return at any time.

The assumption that others cannot be trusted and will not respond to appeals for help, leaves the avoidant person isolated in the face of danger. In those who experienced disorganised attachments in childhood, their low expectations and previous experience of stress sometimes enable them to cope with losses for which they are prepared. But their basic assumptions of safety, self-regard and trust in others are already minimal and may be more easily shattered by unexpected or other traumatic losses that both threaten survival and invalidate large sections of their assumptive world.

On the other hand, the very fact of having survived a loss is eventually reassuring and, whether the bereavements are multiple or traumatic, they offer people the opportunity to discover that they are stronger than they had assumed and that other people do care. Despite our doubts, love, the ultimate cushion against disaster, goes on. Even the most traumatic losses do not abolish it from the world. It is these discoveries that account for the gradual increase in confidence and trust reported by most traumatised people and this that makes it rewarding to help them through the painful process of transition.

It is clear that an understanding of the assumptive world of the trauma-tised person helps us to understand what it is that can be retained and what must be relinquished. The task of therapy may be both to help restore those positive assumptions that are appropriate and to correct the irrational negative assumptions which are left over from childhood. Either way the end result should be a more realistic and mature set of assumptions about the world.

10 The influence of gender on attachments and bereavement

All women become like their mothers. That is their tragedy.
No man does. That is his.

Oscar Wilde *The Importance of Being Ernest* (1895) act 1

Roger Harper was 38 when he was referred to me following the death of his wife. Although greatly upset by this event, Roger found it very difficult to cry. He became very tense, anxious and depressed feeling 'dead inside'. His anguish was such that he found himself unable to return to work and it was this that finally convinced him that he needed help.

In this chapter we shall consider how men differ from women in their attachments and their reaction to bereavement and go on to attempt an explanation for these differences and for the psychological problems to which they sometimes give rise.

The influence of gender on the reaction to loss

Given the fact that gender differences have been studied in practically every research project involving human beings, there is a remarkable lack of consensus regarding their influence on the reaction to bereavement. The reasons for this variation include cultural differences, variation in the way men and women respond to questionnaires and differences in help-seeking behaviour.

Anthropological studies of 78 different cultures have been reviewed by Rosenblatt *et al.* (1976). They showed that although there are many societies in which both men and women are said to cry while mourning and at funerals, whenever sex differences are reported it is the women who cry more than the men.

Recent reviews of the large literature on gender differences in the western world have been carried out by Archer (1999) and by Stroebe *et al.* (2001). They conclude that, at all times, women tend to score more highly than men on almost every measure of emotional disturbance, psychological symptoms and help-seeking behaviour. After bereavement such scores increase in both sexes. However, when compared with non-bereaved people of the same age and sex, widowers show less improvement than widows and take longer to return to married levels following bereavement. Thus, in the Harvard Bereavement Study (Parkes and Brown 1972) young women reported more symptoms than men in both widowed and married control groups. Indeed, non-bereaved married women reported levels of depression equivalent to widowed men 14 months after bereavement. Nevertheless, it was the men rather than the women who still showed significantly greater depression two to four years after bereavement when compared to married people of the same sex. Furthermore, men are much more likely than women to die of cardiac conditions (the proverbial 'broken heart') during the year following the death of their wives (Parkes *et al.* 1969; Stroebe and Stroebe 1983).

One explanation for these findings is that men are inclined to avoid or inhibit the natural expression of separation distress and other emotions. This, it is assumed, impairs the process of grieving, delays recovery and may aggravate the effects of pre-existing heart disease. An alternative view is that it is their reluctance to seek help which makes it harder for men than for women to obtain emotional support from their family and peer group following bereavement and explains the delay in returning to normal functioning that was reported above. Of course, both of these explanations may play a part.

Several studies suggest that men are more inclined than women to cope with stress by adopting instrumental or problem-solving approaches. On the other hand, women more often make use of emotion-focused coping strategies (Billings and Moos 1981). In terms of Stroebe's Dual Process Model (see pp. 34–5) men tend to adopt a 'Restoration Orientation' and women a 'Loss Orientation'. Women tend to cope with stress by sharing their feelings with peers and, when bereaved, expressing their grief. Men may not show feelings but they cope well with the practical issues that they face after bereavement, replanning their lives and actively engaging with the problems of revising their assumptive world. Indeed, studies have shown that young widowers are much more likely than young widows to engage in dating and move sooner towards remarriage (Parkes and Weiss 1983).

Each of these coping strategies has its advantages and disadvantages. Problem solving is obviously less likely to help if a problem is insoluble. It will not enable a bereaved person to get back the person who has died. Emotion focusing may facilitate the expression and working through of grief but will not help bereaved people to replan their lives.

These considerations are consistent with the results of a comparative study of two methods of intervention in problematic grief. Schut *et al.* (1997b) assigned people who sought help from an experimental bereavement service at random to one of two methods of interventions and a waiting list control group. The interventions comprised a problem-focused group, aimed at helping people to rethink and replan their lives, and an emotion-focused group, in which people were encouraged to share feelings. On follow-up, people in both of the intervention groups had a better outcome than those in the control group. When the sample were analysed by the gender of the participants it was found that the bereaved men had responded better to emotion-focused therapy while the women had responded better to problem-focused therapy. Given a choice, the men would probably have selected the problem-focused intervention and the women the emotion-focused intervention. In the event the sexes benefited from learning to make use of the coping strategy that they were least good at.

A similar study by Sikkema *et al.* (2004) was confined to HIV positive men and women who were assigned at random either to a cognitive behaviour therapy (CBT), resembling Schut's problem-oriented therapy, or to traditional psychiatric treatment. At the end of therapy the women who received CBT had improved while those receiving traditional support had not. The men, however, benefited from both types of intervention. Again, it appears that it is women who benefit most from a problem-oriented approach.

In the copious literature about the differences between men and women, it is widely assumed that, despite important anatomical differences, most psychological differences are acquired rather than being innate. There is some recognition that sex hormones play a part in causing sexual behaviour but most other psychological characteristics are assumed to be culturally derived. This is most apparent in the area of stress and bereavement where differences are usually taken to be the consequence of learned coping strategies rather than inborn tendencies.

Gender differences in non-human species

Doubt is thrown on this assumption by studies of non-human animals in which innate behaviour patterns are easier to identify. These provide us with much information about gender differences and it is not possible here to give examples of all of the generalisations that follow. A good review is given by Archer (1999). In all social animals the differences between the sexes include a rich variety of social behaviours. With a fair amount of variation from one species to another, adult males tend to be more competitive, dominant and aggressive than females. They often range more widely over a larger territory and spend less time at their nest/home base than females. Adult females, particularly mammals, spend more time in caring for young. They tend to be more affiliative, submissive and gentle than males, stay closer to home and occupy a smaller territory. These gender differences are not present from birth and develop in the course of maturation. Like all innate behaviour patterns they are influenced by learning from the time of their inception. Hence they influence behaviour but do not dictate it.

Attachments are also influenced by gender. In general females are more strongly attached to their young than males and in many species fathers do not know their own children. On the other hand, the attachment of young males and females to their mother is similar regardless of the child's sex. Pair bonding for life is a relatively infrequent pattern and in most mammals dominant males mate with and become attached to a number of females and their children. Females, on the other hand, tend to remain attached to one male for relatively long periods of time.

Studies of separation and loss in non-human species have been largely confined to mothers and infants. In general it appears that mothers cry and search for their young when lost and children of both sexes cry and search for their mothers; sometimes they appear to become depressed. Two accounts have been published of male infant vervet monkeys (Kaufman and Rosenblum 1969) and two of adolescent male chimpanzees who pined away and died after the death of mothers to whom they had made unusually dependent attachments (Goodall 1971; Scarf 1973). In several species, adult males have been reported to cry and search for lost partners and, in species in which the father plays a significant part in child rearing, for lost children.

In those species that are constantly on the move such as vervet monkeys (that forage from tree to tree) a variety of calls is used to maintain contact and to reunite individuals of both sexes who have become separated from the group (Struhsaker 1967).

Gender in human beings

As in non-human species, most women play a very much larger part in child rearing than men and the intensity of their attachment to their children seems to reflect this and to be associated with greater grief at the death of a child than is found in fathers (Littlefield and Rushton 1986). This is particularly the case when death occurs in early childhood and Fish (1986) has shown that, whereas mothers grieve for the loss of a child regardless of its age, fathers grieve more for the loss of adult offspring than they do for those of younger age.

Sex differences have also been reported in children following the death of a parent. By the time they reach school age boys react to the death of a parent with more aggressiveness and restlessness than do girls (Brown 1958). In later years daughters have been shown to express more grief than sons after the death of an elderly parent (Moss *et al.* 1997).

Although no differences have been demonstrated between boys and girls in the patterns of attachment which are identified in the Strange Situation Test (Ainsworth 1991), differences do emerge in later years and the 'romantic' attachment patterns identified in adult life by means of the RSQ (see pp. 22–4) are gender related (Bartholomew and Horowitz 1991; Brennan *et al.* 1991). More men than women are found with the pattern which Bartholomew terms 'dismissing of relationships' and which resembles the avoidant pattern of childhood, while women are more likely than men to be assigned to his 'fearful of intimacy' pattern, which resembles the disorganised pattern.

Gender in the current study

We turn now to a consideration of the gender differences that were found in the current study. These enable us to see how men and women compare when they seek psychiatric help after bereavement. Table 10.1 shows the numbers who attended my clinic after each type of bereavement. Women outnumbered men in a ratio of 7 to 1 and this applied over most categories of bereavement. This confirms the findings of other studies, which indicate that women are more likely than men to come to a psychiatrist after bereavement. As we shall see in Chapter 16 (pp. 215 and 377), the preponderance of women was not found in a comparable sample of 96 psychiatric patients who had not suffered a bereavement.

We saw in Chapter 3 (p. 60) that although gender had no influence on the Attachment Pattern scores or the Childhood Vulnerability scores, it did have some influence on the type of parenting reported. Men saw their mothers as rather more overprotective than did women. Details of the analyses that follow are given in Appendix 10 (pp. 356–7).

When we look at the way in which the bereaved men and women cope in adult life an important difference emerged. Men scored significantly higher than women on Emotional Inhibition/Distrust. Their scores on Aggressiveness/Assertiveness, however, were only slightly higher than those of the women and the difference did not reach statistical significance.

Exploring the individual questions which make up the Emotional Inhibition/Distrust score, it appears that it is not feelings of distrust that distinguish men from women but the inhibition of feelings. Among the bereaved men nearly two-thirds answered 'Yes' to the questions 'Do you find it hard to show affection for people who are close to you?' and 'Do you find it hard to express feelings of sadness or grief?' Only a third of women gave this answer. It seems that men, in our sample, are much more likely than women to say that they find it hard to express affection, grief or sadness and that they never cry.

Table 10.1 Gender of bereaved person × relationship to deceased person

Deceased person	Male	Female	Total
Spouse	6 (18%)	28 (82%)	34
Intrauterine death	0 (0%)	4 (100%)	4
Child 0–17 years	3 (20%)	12 (80%)	15
Child 18+	1 (10%)	9 (90%)	10
Mother	5 (23%)	17 (78%)	22
Father	1 (11%)	8 (89%)	9
Sibling	2 (17%)	10 (83%)	12
Other	7 (58%)	5 (42%)	12
Multiple	4 (12%)	29 (88%)	33
Total	29 (19%)	122 (81%)	151

As to the scores of symptoms and distress that contributed to the respondent's decision to seek psychiatric treatment, only one distinguished the sexes. The Grief/Loneliness score was slightly higher in women than men but this difference only reached a borderline level of significance.

Over three-quarters (78 per cent) of the bereaved women and two-thirds (66 per cent) of the bereaved men were assigned a diagnosis of anxiety state. The difference, although statistically significant, is not dramatic and seems to indicate that women are rather more likely than men to admit to problems involving anxiety.

More highly significant was the finding that 26 per cent of men and only 4 per cent of women were assigned a diagnosis of personality disorder. Personality disorders are enduring patterns of inflexible thought and behaviour that impair a person's relationships and their ability to function socially, occupationally and in other ways. Rooted in genetic endowment and childhood experience they are evident from early life and cannot, therefore, be caused by bereavement in adult life. On the other hand, they are often aggravated by bereavement and other stresses and this may bring people with personality disorders into psychiatric care. A similar preponderance of personality disorders in men was also found in the non-bereaved psychiatric patients (see Chapter 16) and confirms that this is a general trait rather than one resulting from bereavement.

Using the diagnostic classification adopted in the *DSMIV* (American Psychiatric Association 1994), the following types of personality disorder were diagnosed in the bereaved men seen in this study. In order of frequency they were Avoidant (4 out of 43 cases), Borderline (3 cases), Antisocial (2 cases) and Histrionic Personality Disorder (1 case).

By avoidant personality disorder (see also pp. 235 and 242) is meant 'a pervasive pattern of social inhibition, feelings of inadequacy and hypersensitivity to negative evaluation . . . present in a variety of contexts' (APA 1994: 664). These were present in many of the people seen in this study and, from the amount of emotional inhibition found, it seems likely that the condition was under-diagnosed.

In borderline personality disorder (see also p. 243) the emphasis is on fear of abandonment or loss which gives rise to 'a pervasive pattern of instability of personal relationships, self-image, and affects [emotions], and marked impulsivity . . .'. These too are likely to result from the types of insecure attachment that were commonly reported in this study and it is easy to see why a bereavement can aggravate the condition.

There was a trend for women to be diagnosed as having chronic grief more often than men, but the numbers were small in both sexes and do not allow statistical comparison. Other disorders were not markedly associated with either sex. Because Ward's comparison group was confined to women we have no data on the ways in which men who have not sought psychiatric help respond to the RAQ.

Discussion

These findings confirm the expectation that women will seek psychiatric help after bereavement much more frequently than men and that this is a consequence of the bereavement. In most other psychiatric settings men are as numerous as women.

The findings confirmed those of other studies, which show that men tend to inhibit their feelings. They also showed that this is unlikely to be a consequence of a greater tendency to avoidance in childhood. As boys, the males in this study had no greater tendency to report more avoidant attachment in their childhood than girls. Other possible explanations for the male tendency to inhibit feelings in adult life are:

- innate predisposition becoming manifest in adolescence
- acculturation by peers and/or others.

Our figures do not enable us to decide between these influences, all or both of which may contribute to the inhibition of feelings. Contrary to expectation, the inhibition of feelings in men did not lead to any greater frequency of the diagnosis of delayed grief. This (as we saw on pp. 356–7) can result from a number of causes which have no particular relationship to gender. There was, however, a tendency for women to have higher scores on Grief/Loneliness than men and to be more often diagnosed as suffering anxiety state and occasionally chronic grief.

The greater incidence of personality disorder in men is in keeping with general psychiatric experience and may itself reflect the tendency of men to inhibit feelings and to act out their problems. This is particularly the case with avoidant personality disorders which, as we have seen, are characterised by social inhibition.

From the practical point of view the findings fit well with Schut's finding that men benefit more than women from help aimed at enabling them to express feelings whereas women have few difficulties of this kind. Women, on the other hand, may need help in stopping grieving and rethinking their lives.

An example of insecure attachment and masculine grief

Roger Harper, whose grief at the death of his wife was described above, was the second of three children of an academic whose work took him abroad a great deal and his wife, a secondary school teacher. Both parents were nervous, insecure worriers who depended on each other. Neither showed affection for Roger and they alternately teased and overprotected him. All of his RAQ Attachment scores were high (Anxious/Ambivalent 13, Avoidant 8 and Disorganised 9.5).

Perhaps because of his insecurity of attachment, Roger hated all his schoolteachers whom he saw as 'insensitive'. He took a long time to fulfil the promise of his high intelligence, dropped out of university and, after several years of globetrotting and many menial jobs, finally became a science teacher. He had many of the features of borderline personality disorder including a tendency to idealise some relationships and denigrate others.

At the age of 21 he fell in love with an older woman for whom he 'carried a torch' for many years. Perhaps because he found himself unable to share his feelings she never reciprocated his love and eventually broke off the relationship.

At the age of 31 he met and six years later married Jean, a highly intelligent woman. Unfortunately she suffered from epilepsy and, five months before Roger's referral to me, died of liver failure caused by the toxic effects of medication.

As we have seen, Roger found it very difficult to express the grief that he felt, but his depression, tension and feelings of unreality were such that he was unable to work.

In therapy he gradually began to relax and to express feelings of grief, not only for his wife but also for the other losses in his life. With great distress, he recalled a childhood memory of being locked in a lavatory by his mother. His condition improved and he was able to return to work, but his problems were deep-seated and he now felt motivated to tackle them. He accepted referral to a psychotherapist for further treatment.

Roger exemplifies several of the problems that are met with in men who seek psychiatric help after bereavement. His bad experiences as a child had aggravated the masculine tendency to inhibit the expression of feelings and impaired his relationships with teachers and others. Unable for many years to commit himself to any steady relationship or job, he at last found a measure of security with Jean and committed himself to a teaching career. His wife's death threw him off course, but also triggered a request for therapy of which he had long been in need. In that setting he discovered that it was possible to express feelings without being totally overwhelmed and this enabled him to begin to 'turn over the stone' of other unresolved griefs.

Conclusions

Despite the differences between the sexes, which become most obvious in adolescence, it seems that there is little significant difference between boys and girls in their patterns of childhood attachment. This justifies us in combining the sexes for most purposes in the current study.

The research confirms and to some extent explains the inhibition of feelings that is commoner in men than women in our society. Perhaps as a consequence of this inhibition, men are less likely to seek psychiatric help after bereavement and, when they do, they are rather less likely than women to complain of anxiety and intense grief. On the other hand, they are more likely to be seen as suffering from personality disorders, particularly those that reflect emotional inhibition.

When we consider these findings and note their resemblance to the gender differences in non-human species, we may draw the conclusion that the core differences are inherent in origin although much influenced by cultural experience. Patterns of parental attachment play little part in explaining gender differences, although they may contribute to the problems that then arise and the treatments that are required.

11 Loss of a parent in adult life

> The relationship between a mother and child is a most unnatural one; other species have the good sense to banish their young at an early age.
>
> John Rae *The Custard Boys* (1960) ch. 13

Fourteen months before Sharon Herbert, aged 48, was referred to me, her mother had died suddenly of a 'stroke'. Sharon was told that the stroke had been caused by stress and blamed herself for contributing to her death by leaning on her mother. At the time when I first saw her she was tearful, depressed, anxious, lonely and insecure. She felt that she was at the end of her tether and was inclined to panic. She recognised that she desperately wanted someone to look after her and was clinging to her unmarried daughter. At the same time she felt full of regret and fearful of becoming a burden to her daughter.

Is the loss of a parent in adult life a likely cause of psychological problems?

Most people who reach the age of 50 are orphans; they will have lost one or both parents. Are they at increased risk of psychiatric disorder as a result? Although there have been many studies of the psychological effects of the loss of a parent, the majority of these are confined to children of school or pre-school age, when the death of a parent is relatively uncommon (for a critical review see Oltjenbruns 1999). In general it appears that in this age group lasting problems are more likely to result from inadequate subsequent parental care than from the loss itself (Harris *et al.* 1986). Such losses lie beyond the scope of this volume.

The most likely explanation for the paucity of research in the older age group is the general assumption that loss of parents in adult life is timely and 'normal'. It is, therefore, unlikely to have serious psychological consequences. Indeed, this assumption is supported by research findings. Norris and Murrell's community study (1990) found no evidence of any increase in depression, from pre-bereavement levels, in a sample of 58 adults whose parent had died. Comparing another 85 adults who had lost a parent with 434 who had lost a spouse and 39 who had lost a child, Owen *et al.* (1982) conclude 'the death of elderly parents is less disruptive, less emotionally debilitating and generally less significant for surviving adult children . . . than for the other two groups'. In a recent review of the literature Moss *et al.* (2001) conclude that 'complicated or pathological grief tend to be rare for surviving adult children'.

On the other hand, some studies have shown increased rates of depression (Birtchnell 1975; Cleiren 1991) and suicide (Bunch *et al.* 1971) following the death of parents. Umberson and Chen (1994) followed up a large national sample that included 207 adults who lost a parent during the course of the study. They reported more distress, more alcohol consumption and greater decline in physical health in the parent-bereaved than in the non-bereaved persons. The marriages of parent-bereaved people were also more often conflicted. This they attributed to difficulty in sharing feelings or communicating with the partner about the loss.

Although the UK national organisation Cruse Bereavement Care was originally set up to serve widows, in recent years it has opened its doors to people with other types of bereavement. The death of a parent is now the most common single reason for people to seek its help (Cruse 2004). How can these conflicting findings be explained? Once again we have to consider the possibility that some adults will suffer lasting distress as a consequence of the loss of a parent, while others may even find their emotional state improved.

Why do some adults get into difficulties after the death of a parent?

The increase in suicides after bereavement reported by Bunch *et al.* (1971) was largely confined to adult men who had never married and continued to live with their mothers. This raises the possibility that some of the problems of adults who lose a parent may result from longstanding clinging or other insecure attachments.

Support for this theory comes from a comparison by Horowitz *et al.* (1981) of 35 adults who had sought psychological treatment after the death of a parent with 37 parent-bereaved adults who had not sought help. In the treatment group a larger proportion were young women (for whom the death of a parent was untimely), and unmarried men and women who had had intense 'partnership' relations with the dead parent.

On the other hand, Umberson and Chen (1994) found that those adults who reported negative childhood memories of parents had less distress after that parent died than those who reported happy memories. Douglas (1990), in a qualitative study of 40 adults who lost a parent, states: 'Those who were happy as children were emotionally closer to their parents as adults and had stronger reactions to their deaths than those who were distant from their parents as children' (p. 135). Of course, it may be that the distress which Douglas is describing is normal grief and it would be a mistake to assume that the expression of grief is a problem. Indeed, it may be that the individuals who showed less distress were at greater risk of later psychological problems than those whose distress was expressed more intensely at the time of their bereavement.

Old people often become physically and mentally dependent on their children and clinical experience suggests that this can re-arouse previous attachment problems and spoil the last years with the parent. One diagnosis which gives rise to particular problems is dementia. This can be a great burden on the family and a cause for grief long before the death of the parent (Theut *et al.* 1991). Death, when it comes, may be a relief but may also give rise to self-reproaches and conflicts within the surviving family.

Other factors that deserve systematic attention but have received very little are the interaction between the gender of the parent and that of the child. Scharlach and Frederiksen (1993) showed few differences between reactions to the death of 63 mothers and 51 fathers, but in another study Douglas (1990) reports that, although daughters were more likely than sons to be distressed by the death of a father, sons and daughters both expressed similar levels of distress following the death of a mother.

Because women marry men older, on average, than themselves and men die at a younger age than women, most people lose a father before they lose a mother. It is possible that the greater distress expressed after the death of a mother reflects the fact that they have now lost both parents; they were now themselves 'at the head of the queue'. There is nothing like the death of a parent to bring home the prospect of one's own mortality.

Alongside the evidence of problematic reactions to parental bereavement there is also evidence that the death of a parent is often followed by personal maturation. For some the death of a parent may let the child 'off the hook' and convince them that, for the first time, they can survive without the parent. Other bereaved children treasure their memories of their lost parent and continue to make use of them as an internal source of reassurance and strength. For a more detailed review of this literature see Moss and Moss (1997).

Parental loss in the current study

This study provides us with an opportunity to explore the ways in which childhood attachments, as recollected in adult life, influence later attachments to parents and to identify the psychological problems that sometimes arise when those parents die. It was not expected to tell us much about the people for whom the death of a parent is a positive or growth promoting experience, for they were unlikely to seek help from a psychiatrist. Even so, as we shall see, such outcomes were certainly found in some of the psychiatric patients.

The study also provides us with an opportunity to shed light on the conflicting views expressed above. If Umberson and Chen (1994) and Douglas (1990) are correct we may find that, unlike the rest of our sample, people with most evidence of unsatisfactory parenting (high Problematic Parenting scores) will report lower levels of Overall Distress and Grief/Loneliness following the death of a parent than people who have suffered other types of bereavement. Since all of these people had asked for psychiatric help for their problems we might expect that the problems of adult orphans with low Grief/Loneliness scores will more often result from trauma than from personal vulnerability. On the other hand, if Horowitz *et al.* (1981) and Bunch *et al.* (1971) are correct, the opposite will be the case and the people in the current study who suffered parental bereavement and unsatisfactory parenting will have more lasting distress and less evidence of trauma than those with good parental relationships.

All in all it seems likely that people who have experienced anxious/ambivalent or clinging types of relationship with their parents will continue to do so in adult life and this group may show the greatest distress when bereaved.

We saw (on p. 59) that after loss of a spouse, loss of a parent was the second most frequent type of bereavement reported by the psychiatric patients and constituted 21 per cent of the bereaved sample. Twenty-two people (17 daughters and 5 sons) had been referred for psychiatric help for problems related to the death of a mother and 9 a father (8 daughters and 1 son). Further statistical details are reported in Appendix 11.

Timely and untimely deaths

The average age of people losing a parent was 37 years, seven years younger than the average for the rest of the bereaved sample. This difference is to be expected given the fact that children are younger than their parents and of a similar age to most partners, siblings and friends who die. Even so, these figures imply that the parents themselves were relatively young at the time of death. Although we have no figures for the age of these parents at death, it is not unreasonable to guess that they were about 25 years older than the bereaved person. This would give them an average age of 62, well below the expectation of life for their generation. This strongly suggests that many of these parental deaths were untimely and that the timely death of parents in later old age is relatively less likely to cause their children to seek for psychiatric help.

Loss of parent compared with other types of loss

As we saw in Chapter 9, unexpected deaths are commonly reported in bereaved psychiatric patients. In this and most other respects those seeking help after the loss of a parent did not differ from people who asked for help after other types of bereavement. They had similar overall proportions in each of the attachment patterns and their marital relationships, their ways of coping and their reactions to bereavement did not differ from those reported by people who had suffered other losses. There was a slight tendency for people who had lost a parent to say that they cling more after bereavement but this did not reach statistical significance.

It seems, from this evidence, that among those seeking psychiatric help the influence of insecure attachments to parents is no greater or less when that parent dies than it is when other attached persons die.

Loss of mother compared with loss of father

Those who sought help after losing a mother were significantly more likely than others to say that, as a child, they had been 'unusually close' to her, but this tendency was not sufficient to increase the Anxious/Ambivalence scores of the parent-bereaved group to a significant degree. The parent-bereaved were not unusually close to their fathers.

Within the age-matched comparison groups of 35 bereaved psychiatric and 35 non-psychiatric women, only two (6 per cent) of the non-psychiatric compared with ten (29 per cent) of the psychiatric patients had lost a mother. Figures for loss of father were four (11 per cent) non-psychiatric and five (14 per cent) psychiatric. Although the numbers are too small for statistical analysis to be useful, these findings suggest that the death of a mother is more often a cause of psychiatric referral than the death of a father.

Sharon Herbert described her mother as an over-anxious, over-protective woman who babied her and saw her as precious, but delicate and fragile. Her father was a similarly over-anxious man who drank too much. Sharon was unusually close to both parents and worried a great deal about them, fearing that they would both die. She felt that she had to look after them and her younger siblings. She describes herself as an unhappy child who cried a lot and was stubborn, bad tempered, bossy and rebellious. She never did well at school. Her RAQ scores showed above average scores of Anxious/Ambivalence (9) and Disorganised Attachment (6) with average Avoidant Attachment (3).

It seems that the death of her parents confirmed Sharon's lifelong fear that she would be left without support or protection. Her reaction was much like that of a child who has been abandoned.

Attachments in adult life

Only three (14 per cent) of the 22 people who sought psychiatric help after the loss of a mother were married and three others were cohabiting with a partner. On the other hand two-thirds (6/9) of those who had lost a father were married. It is possible to compare these figures with UK population figures in which 83 per cent of people aged 35 to 44 are married (Office of Statistical Censuses and Surveys 1992). It seems that people who seek psychiatric help after the death of a mother are more likely than the rest of the population to be unmarried. Half of those mother-bereaved persons who were not married or cohabiting were separated or divorced and the other half had never married.

Although seven of the nine people (including only one man) who sought help after the death of a father had partners, marital stresses were often present and there was usually a history of an ambivalent relationship between the bereaved person and the father. Four of the fathers were described as having problems with alcohol; two were depressives and three anxiously overprotective of the respondent. It is attachments like these that are most often associated with self-reproaches and conflicted grief. In addition, the father's death was usually unexpected and took place along with other stresses that contributed to the problems causing the person to seek help.

Among those who were separated or divorced at the time of their mother's death, the break-up of their marriages sometimes seems to have resulted from a continuing clinging attachment to their mother. In other cases it was the break-up of the marriage that caused them to become unusually close to their mother. Again, both factors are likely to have played a part in the problems that followed the mother's death.

> Sharon had married at 22 to a former soldier, now a gardener, who was never happy in civilian life. She describes him as a strict, dominant man who was often violent towards her and their two daughters. Even so, for a while, she was very close to him and sees them as having been mutually dependent on each other. She also remained close to her mother in whom she often confided, but this closeness was a bone of contention with her husband throughout their marriage. Sharon coped well with the death of her father five years ago and was able to support her mother but at the cost of increasing distance from her husband.
>
> Three years ago her eldest daughter left home to get married and shortly thereafter Sharon's husband left her for another woman. She missed him a great deal but was supported by her mother and by her younger daughter who remained at home.

Sharon illustrates well the problems that can arise when an adult child maintains a close insecure attachment to her mother. Her continuing relationship with her mother was one of the factors impairing her relationship with her husband. He had problems of his own, which he dealt with in a typically masculine manner. After leaving the macho, secure world of the army he attempted to keep control of himself and others by adopting a strict discipline and dominating his wife and family. This created a family myth of his independence, strength and superiority in which, at first, his wife colluded. Nevertheless, her continuing attachment to her mother created a rift between them. This increased after Sharon's father died and may have contributed to her husband's decision to seek for another relationship.

> I saw Sharon only three times but she made good use of our meetings. It was obvious to me that she was a very capable person who had no need to feel guilty or inferior. Her eldest daughter needed her help with her two grandchildren and this encouraged her to leave the house and find new and satisfying roles as a grandmother. In this situation her self-esteem rapidly improved as she discovered, perhaps for the first time in her life, that she did not need to depend on anybody else.

It seems that Sharon needed to get clear of her husband, her father and her mother before she could discover her true potential. In the end, her husband's desertion and her mother's death provided her with a real but terrifying opportunity to escape from the trap into which she had been born.

Conclusions

Overall our findings support the view that insecure attachment patterns contribute to the problems that follow the death of a parent, as they do those that follow other types of bereavement. The finding that mother bereaved are likely to report being unusually close to their mothers may explain the findings of Umberson and Chen (1994) and Douglas (1990) that distress after parental bereavement is greatest when the relationship has been a close one. These researchers may not have given sufficient weight to the problems associated with unusual closeness. The data also support the expectation that psychological problems are more likely to follow the death of a mother than a father.

It seems that we all retain, at some level, elements of the attachment to our parents that was established during our childhood. For most of us the process of maturation, which enables us to achieve autonomy during our adolescence, can be expected to prepare us for the changes in our lives that will follow their death. We do not stop loving our parents, but we no longer rely on their nurture in order to survive.

The evidence reported here suggests that there is a minority for whom this autonomy may not be fully achieved while the parents are alive. Unusually close attachments may persist, reducing the chance of making new relationships and spoiling those that are made, hence the large proportion of adult orphans in this study who were unmarried or in conflict with their partner. When at last the parent dies, the event may constitute a threat to mental health. On the other hand, it may also provide the orphans with opportunities to discover their true worth, strength and potential.

12 Loss of a child

Grief fills the room up of my absent child,
Lies on his bed, walks up and down with me,
Puts on his pretty looks, repeats his words,
Remembers me of all his gracious parts,
Stuffs on this vacant garment with his form:
Then have I reason to be fond of grief.
                                        William Shakespeare
                    King John III (1591–8) act 3, sc. 4, l.93

It was a wet night and Moira O'Rourke (aged 55) tried to persuade her son not to go out on his motor cycle. Sadly, he insisted and late that night she learned that he had been killed in a road traffic accident.

Moira suffered a severe and lasting grief reaction. Four years later she was still keeping his ashes in her spare room. When seen in my clinic she was preoccupied with thoughts of her son's death and her facade of independence had crumbled. She was now anxious, depressed and close to panic, feeling that she could cope no longer and needing someone to look after her.

Considered only in practical or instrumental terms we might think that the death of a child, particularly one who is no longer dependent on parents, would be less stressful to the surviving parents than the death of a spouse. After all, it does not disrupt the lives of the parents so much as the loss of a spouse. Parents normally separate from their children at adolescence and the parents of younger children are often young enough to replace any who die. Yet intuition and the evidence from both clinical and comparative research tell a different story. To most people in the west, the death of a child is the most agonising and distressing source of grief.

Reviewing four comparative studies Stroebe and Schut (2001) conclude: 'The loss of an adult child results in more intense, or more persistent, grief and depression than the loss of a spouse, parent or sibling.' Why should this be? One explanation comes from Archer (1999), who adopts a psycho-biological perspective. He suggests that the strength of an attachment and the intensity and duration of the grief that results when that attachment is severed is proportionate to the genetic value of the lost person. Since a child is the chief means of perpetuating our genes we should expect that the death of a child would lead to severe and lasting grief. We are losing our genetic immortality.

This theory is supported by several studies reviewed by Archer, which show that the intensity and persistence of grief is inversely proportional to the age of the child who dies (younger parents are more likely to be able to have more children) and that the death of only children is more traumatic than the death of one child among several.

None of the studies reviewed by Stroebe and Schut were carried out in third world countries, where women continue to have large families because they expect many of their children to die. Reports from these countries, such as Nancy Scheper-Hughes' book *Death Without Weeping* (1992), suggest that in these environments the death of a child, particularly in infancy, is less devastating in its psychological effects than it is in other countries.

A factor that may contribute to parental grief in the medically privileged world is that here the death of children is untimely and outrages normal expectations. These deaths are often caused by trauma and may be sudden, unexpected and, in cases of sudden infant death syndrome (SIDS), inexplicable. On the other hand, to us all deaths of children are traumatic and Miles (1985) showed no difference in the grief of parents whose child died from chronic disease and those whose child died in an accident. But a similar study in Turkey, in which reactions to the death of young adult sons from leukaemia were compared with reactions to the death of sons who had been killed in armed conflicts, showed higher rates of chronic grief and persisting 'traumatic stress' in the parents of those who had been killed (Yüksel and Olgun-Özpolat 2004).

Given these influences Moira O'Rourke's reaction to the death of her son comes as no surprise. Yet the fact remains that most mothers who lose a son do not seek psychiatric help and it is reasonable to ask why some people are more vulnerable to such losses than others. The clinical literature suggests that the death of a child is the acid test of the family as a support system for its members. It can make or break a family. Some are drawn together in mutual support but for others it may be the last straw. Thus, Cornwell *et al.* (1977) found evidence of serious marital difficulties in one-third of couples following sudden infant deaths and Nixon and Pearn (1977) reported parental separation within five years in 25 per cent of families following the death by drowning of an older child.

To a greater extent than with other types of loss, gender differences can cause problems (Dyregrov 1990). A mother who is in desperate need of emotional support may find her husband dealing with his grief by avoidance.

Consequently, when she needs him most he is not there for her. Reactions of anger can disrupt a family, particularly when people blame each other, rightly or wrongly, for the death. Those who are unable to find support within the family may seek for help from outside it and this in turn may lead to or be seen as infidelity. In general, intrauterine and perinatal losses affect the mother more than the father while losses in later childhood have more equal influence (Fish 1986).

Much has been written about the permanent nature of the 'shadow grief' that can follow the loss of a child (Peppers and Knapp 1980). Despite this, having reviewed five studies, Kissane and Bloch (2002) conclude that 'giving birth to a subsequent child is strongly correlated with reduced grief, less depression and improved outcome for the family'. While this may confirm Archer's theory, it should not blind us to the fact that the subsequent pregnancy may be a consequence rather than a cause of emotional recovery.

Loss of a child in the current study

Although no formal predictions were made before our data were analysed (see Appendix 12 for further details), from these considerations it seemed likely that among those seeking psychiatric help after bereavement, the proportion of people who have lost a child would be greater than expected from their numbers in the wider population; and women would be more numerous than men, particularly following intrauterine, perinatal and infant deaths. (There were no respondents who had lost a child in Ward's control group. This may reflect the young age of that group.)

It is reasonable to expect that the patterns of insecure attachment, which predict the various types of bereavement outcome in the full sample studied here, will also influence the type of outcome found in the parents who come for psychiatric help after the death of a child. In particular it seems likely that the combination of anxious/ambivalence in the mother and avoidance in the father will be associated with high levels of marital conflict and high levels of grief and distress in the mother after the death of a child. By the same token support given to the family following the death of a child can be expected to reduce these risks. This last consideration will be examined, along with other aspects of support in Chapter 14.

In the current study 29 people came for help after the death of a child; that is 16 per cent of the total sample of bereaved people. There were 25 mothers and only 4 fathers, a ratio of 6:1. Their mean age was 44 years, no different from the rest of the sample.

Table 12.1 shows the sex and age at death of the child by the gender of the parent who sought psychiatric help. This shows that, although it is only women who sought help following miscarriages, terminations and stillbirths, the problems of child-bereaved fathers are not confined to losses of older children.

From the mortality tables for England and Wales it is possible to calculate the proportion of deaths of boys and girls of various ages among bereaved

Table 12.1 Age and sex of child who has died × gender of respondent

	Father	*Mother*	*Total*
Miscarriage	0	2	2
Termination of pregnancy	0	1	1
Stillbirth	0	1	1
Death of son in first year of life	1	1	2
Death of daughter in first year of life	0	1	1
Death of son aged 1–17 years	1	5	6
Death of daughter aged 1–17 years	1	5	6
Death of son over age 17	1	6	7
Death of daughter over age 17	0	3	3
Total deaths of sons	3	12	15
Total deaths of daughters	1	9	10
Total deaths of children	4	25	29

people in the general population and to compare these with the proportions in our sample of bereaved people (see Appendix 12). They indicate that deaths in later childhood were 13 times more frequent in the psychiatric sample than the rest of the bereaved population. On the other hand, deaths in the first year of life were only twice the expected number.

The numbers in our sample who sought help after stillbirths, miscarriages and termination of pregnancy are too few to justify statistical analysis, but this in itself suggests that they are not often a cause of psychiatric problems.

The sex of the child is also reported in the mortality tables. In our sample there were 7 losses of daughters and 8 losses of sons, the expected number of daughters is 0.84 and of sons 1.27. In other words the death of both daughters and sons gave rise to similar increases in requests for psychiatric help.

Comparisons between the child-bereaved group and those suffering other bereavements are also shown in Appendix 12. These confirm our supposition that the causes of death of children are usually 'traumatic'; in fact there was only one child whose death did not fall into one of the traumatic risk categories described in Chapter 9.

The patterns of childhood attachment were similar in respondents who lost a child to those associated with other losses, but the scores of Rejection/ Violence by and Separations from the mother after the age of 5 were much higher in those seeking help after the loss of a child than they were following other types of loss. Separations from father after age 5 were also significantly more common in the child-bereaved patients. About a half of the child bereaved had been separated from their mother and the same proportion from their father between 6 to 10 and 11 to 16 years of age. (This is about double the number of separations from parents among people who suffered other bereavements.)

These findings, which had not been anticipated, suggest that women who have suffered rejection, violence and/or separation from their mother in childhood are more vulnerable to the death of a child of their own than they are to other types of bereavement. This influence cannot be attributed to an increase in the Disorganised Attachment score despite the fact that the Rejection/Violence score is a constituent of that score.

In other respects those who came for help after the death of a child showed few differences from other bereaved psychiatric patients. Their methods of coping with stress in adult life were much the same. After bereavement their scores of current symptoms and distress were not significantly different from those of other patients. Certainly there is no reason to regard them as more grief stricken than those who sought help after other types of bereavement.

To sum up, these figures support the view that the death of a child, particularly after the first year of life, is more likely to cause women, and to a lesser extent men, to seek psychiatric help than other types of bereavement. Those most vulnerable to the loss of a child are women who have suffered rejection, violence and/or separation from their mothers, and/or separation from their fathers during their own childhood. Their levels of grief and other reactions are no greater than those of other bereaved psychiatric patients despite the fact that their bereavements are more likely to have been of a traumatic type.

The influence of rejection and violence on the development of nurturance

In seeking for an explanation for these findings we need to reconsider the nature of attachments. Attachment theory suggests that the attachment which a parent makes to a child, in Chapter 1 referred to as 'nurturance', is different from the attachment which the child makes to the parent. The biological functions of the two types of attachment are quite different, the aim of 'nurturance' being the survival of the child and the aim of child/mother 'attachment' the survival of the self. If that is so, then it is reasonable to expect that the reaction to the loss of a child will differ from the reaction to the loss of a parent.

The patterns of child–mother attachment, as measured in Ainsworth's Strange Situation and the RAQ, influence the assumptions that the developing child makes about the world and itself within it. These assumptions, as we have seen, colour the way in which in later years the adult copes with and reacts to bereavements.

'Nurturance' is not measured by either of these indices of attachment. It may, however, be indirectly assessed by Main and Goldwyn's (1984) Adult Attachment Interview which (as we saw on pp. 19–21) correlates with the attachment patterns that the children of these mothers show in the Strange Situation. Certainly their work seems to indicate that the way adults view their parents influences the way they, in their turn, parent their children. If this is so then a mother's nurturant ability is not purely instinctive but is, to a large extent, a reflection of the parenting that she received herself as a child.

Our data shows that the Maternal Rejection/Violence score predicts particular vulnerability to the loss of a child. Let us look again at the constituent questions of this score and ask ourselves what kind of a model of nurturance is likely to follow. The score is obtained by adding together answers to the following questions:

- I/10 Did your parent ever assault or injure his/her partner?
- I/13 Did your parent drink more alcohol than was good for him/her?
- I/25 Was your parent inclined to tease you or make you feel small?
- I/26 Did your parent beat or physically punish you more often than most parents?[1]

Clinical experience suggests that women and men who recall these kinds of traumatic parenting are likely to be sensitised by them and very unsure of themselves as parents. They may want to be better parents but have no model of good parenting to guide them. They may become extremely close to their child but, particularly at times of stress, may find themselves behaving just like their parents and abusing their own children. This last consequence is amply supported by evidence from the literature on child abuse.

When their children become sick or distressed these parents are reminded of their own suffering and suffer along with them. It is this that Klass (1988) and others refer to as 'identification' with the child. Klass sees in it a cause of many of the problems experienced by parents bereaved of a child.

When, on the other hand, their children are happy, these parents may feel unexpectedly jealous. At all events their view of themselves as parents is sure to be influenced by such experiences and it seems very likely that, when things go wrong, they will become confused and highly anxious.

> Moira had been the third of ten children, brought up in Ireland in a Roman Catholic family. Neither parent expressed affection for her or provided her with consistent parenting; nor did her numerous siblings. They were competing with her and each other for the limited attention and care of their parents. Their father was a heavy drinker who often became violent towards his wife when drunk. From an early age Moira was afraid that he would, one day, kill her mother and she did her best to defend her against him. Mother received psychiatric treatment for depression.
>
> In the circumstances it is not surprising that Moira grew up an insecure, anxious child. She never did well at school where, she

---

1 Question I/27, which concerns sexual abuse, can be disregarded since none of the respondents said that either parent had treated them in this way. Questionnaires are not the most reliable source of such information.

says, she tended to bully other children and to act in stubborn and rebellious ways. So bad was her behaviour that she was expelled from school at the age of 12 years.

In keeping with this history Moira's RAQ attachment pattern was highly Avoidant (score 10) while her scores of Anxious Ambivalence (4) and Disorganisation (5) were average.

At 20 she took a job in England where she met and at 22 married a heavy-drinking labourer. She sees him as a weak man who depended on her. They had seven children. Money was always short and her husband's tendency to spend it on alcohol led to frequent quarrels. They divorced when Moira was aged 36.

Having learned to stand on her own two feet at an early age, Moira remained a compulsively independent person who distrusted others and tended to turn in on herself and to become irritable at times of stress. Her closest relationship was with her unmarried youngest son who had always been her favourite child.

His death was a great loss and made her aware of her alienation from others. It brought home to her the extent of her own childhood losses and, at the time of our first meeting, she acknowledged that she felt desperately 'alone'.

When she came again three weeks later she had regained her sense of independence and control. She told me that she had a longstanding but ambivalent relationship with a male lodger in her house who had stuck by her over many years. She was, however, fearful of too close an involvement with him. She expressed a similar uncertainty about continuing in psychotherapy with me and I was not altogether surprised when she failed to attend for further interviews.

Moira's avoidant attachment pattern made it difficult for her to trust others enough to commit to any lasting relationship. Her son seems to have been the one person whom she did not see as a threat and, just as she had stood by her mother against the threat of her father, so her son had stood by her in the conflicts with his father and remained with her after the break-up of the marriage. Mother and son understood and identified with each other. His death brought back the feelings of isolation and loneliness that had bedevilled her childhood.

Her brief therapy may have helped Moira to understand better the nature of her predicament. By the time of the second interview she was clearly reviewing the possibility of committing herself to her faithful 'lodger' and it may be that she decided that it was safer to turn to him for support than to entrust herself to the dangers of a therapeutic relationship with an unknown psychiatrist. Or maybe she settled, as she had done before, for an 'independent' existence.

The influence of separations from parents

We saw above that, in addition to the experience of maternal rejection and violence, separations from parents after the age of 5 were also associated with increased vulnerability to the loss of a child of one's own. In the current study, separations were often associated with rejection and violence within the family. We can conjecture that both because parents were often absent when needed and because when she was present the quality of parenting given by the mother was poor, those respondents with high Separation scores lacked a consistent model of parenting from which to learn effective nurturance. A second case study may help us to understand this chain of causation.

Referred at the age of 32, after the death of her son, Elizabeth Buxter-Hughes was a dignified, attractive and well-spoken woman who came from an army family. Her father had owned estates in the Far East where she had been born. As in many expatriate families, Elizabeth was cared for by a nanny and saw her parents as distant figures who drank more than was good for them and were often away. She was ambivalent towards her mother whom she describes as a nervous woman, inconsistent, critical and inclined to tease and denigrate her. Both parents were mutually dependent on each other and inclined to alternate between neglect and overprotection of Elizabeth.

The political situation was unstable, her parents worried about her safety and she about theirs. During much of her childhood she was sent to boarding schools where she did less well than expected. Seen as stubborn and tougher than she felt, she attempted to dominate and control others. She missed her family a great deal and looked forward to the holidays, despite the fact that both she and her younger brother had experienced sexual assaults by a servant and been disbelieved when they told their parents.

From the RAQ she emerges as very insecurely attached, with high Separation score (8), high Disorganised Attachment score (8) and moderately high Anxious/Ambivalent score (8).

She came to school in the UK at age 13 and stayed on to enter an art college. She subsequently returned to the east where she met and married a business executive on whom she was inclined to depend. They went on to have four daughters and a son. Although she felt that she could cope with the daughters, she described her relationship with her infant son as having been 'unusually close' and mutually dependent.

When Elizabeth was 28 she moved to a new home in England,

close to her husband's parents. His forceful mother never took to her and this, along with stresses attributed to her husband's continuing work and absences overseas, led to marital tensions.

She was 30 when her two-and-a-half-year-old son was killed in an accident while playing outside the house. Elizabeth was greatly upset by this, blaming herself and others for the accident. When she consulted me, two years later, she was still missing her son a great deal, very anxious and depressed, sleeping badly and finding it hard to cope. She was inclined to panic and filled with regrets. She even thought of suicide but dismissed the idea for the sake of her family.

She found that she could not bear to talk to her husband about their son, nor could she share her own or tolerate his grief. He blamed her for her withdrawal (Marital Disagreement score 6).

Although she came only once Elizabeth made good use of a lengthy assessment meeting. This reduced her fears and helped her to regain a feeling of being in control of her life. When followed up two years later she was at ease and no longer unduly anxious or inclined to panic. Although she still missed her son a great deal and continued to regret his death, she said that she no longer needed to talk or cry about that event. Her relationship with her husband had improved, although he still spent too much time away from home and her difficulties with her mother-in-law continued.

For a woman of Elizabeth's undoubted competence, to say that she was 'dependent' on her little son is remarkable. Her closeness to him seems to reflect a wish to give him, and vicariously to experience with him the warmth and closeness which she never received from her own mother. By the same token, in her despair at his death she seemed to re-experience her own feeling of childhood loss.

In the light of previous chapters it is no surprise that her lifelong insecurity is reflected in her own marital relationship. She chose for a partner a man who, like her father, was often away from home. When after her son's death she most needed her husband, she found herself unable to come close to him, fearing the intensity of both her own and his grief.

I suspect that any benefit which she received from her consultation with me stemmed from the fact that I was able to provide her with the opportunity to talk through her problems and to receive the same non-judgemental support which most of us expect to receive from our family. It did not resolve her grief or produce any very deep change in her attachment pattern, but may have helped her to understand and to live with these sources of continuing pain.

Conclusions

It seems that nurturance is not something parents do to or for their children, but something they do with them. In losing our children we lose the opportunity to share their lives, their future, their joys and successes as well as their love for us. Archer's (1999) theory, which relates our psychological investment in others to their genetic value, can now be endowed with emotional content. The child I love represents me both genetically and symbolically.

Previous chapters have shown how the intensity of love relationships between adults is determined partly by our genetic closeness and partly by our experience of earlier secure or insecure attachments. This chapter has shown that the same can be said to extend to nurturance.

If our own experience of attachment has been deficient, and particularly if we lack the memory of warmth and nurture, either because of separation from or rejection by our parents, we grow up in dread of the possibility that love and security will not last. Our children are less often perceived as a threat than adults, and the love which we give to a child may be our strongest experience of a love that is unqualified and reciprocated. It may help to redress the imbalance of our own deprivation. If we then lose that child we are doubly bereaved and our dreaded world becomes our assumptive world.

The peculiar passion of the reaction to separation from or loss of a child results not only from the threat that this represents to the child's survival but also from the threat that it represents to our survival through them. In this sense they are our immortality or, as Klass (1988) cogently puts it: 'The child is part of the psychic structure of the parent.'

13 Loss of a spouse or partner

I love thee with the passion put to use
In my old griefs, and with my childhood's faith
Elizabeth Barrett Browning
Sonnets from the Portugese (1850) no. 43

The secret sympathy,
The silver link, the silken tie,
Which heart to heart, and mind to mind,
In body and in soul can bind.
Walter Scott *The Lay of the Last Minstrel*
(1805) canto 5, st.13

Hannah Appleyard described her relationship with her husband as mutually dependent. She was 68 years of age when he died, suddenly and unexpectedly. She grieved deeply for him and became extremely anxious and lonely. When she first attended my clinic 18 months later, she was still extremely anxious, inclined to panic and feeling isolated and lonely. She was using alcohol as a tranquilliser and, although she was sober when attending the clinic, she admitted that she often drank more than was good for her.

If the bond between a child and a parent constitutes an 'attachment' relationship, and the bond between parent and child a 'nurturant' relationship, how shall we categorise the bond to a partner or spouse? (The term 'partner' will be used hereafter to include spouses.) The term 'romantic attachment' is too emotionally loaded to be entirely satisfactory. It reflects the fact that much of the research into attachments in adult life has involved studies of university students whose relationships have not yet matured and may indeed fit the term 'romantic' rather better than do the more lasting and mature, but less passionate, bonds that have stood the test of time.

As we have seen, there is no doubt that the attachment patterns established in childhood do influence adult attachments but the influence is not a simple one. Measures of insecure attachments in childhood do, to some extent, predict insecure conjugal attachments in adulthood but do not enable the particular subtype of attachment to be reliably predicted. Bearing this in mind we may ask to what extent these insecure attachment patterns predict the reaction to the death of a partner?

There is no shortage of research into the psychological consequences of losing a partner. In fact most of the research into the prediction of risk after bereavement has been carried out on widows and widowers in the English-speaking world. In that setting the reaction to the loss of a spouse has come to be seen as the norm for grief. For a full review of the field the reader is referred to *Bereavement: Studies of Grief in Adult Life* (Parkes 1996).

The loss of a spouse is the most frequent type of bereavement to lead to psychiatric referral. In a study of the case notes of 3245 patients admitted to two psychiatric units in London between 1949 and 1951, I found that the proportion whose illness had come on within six months of the death of a spouse was six times greater than expectation given the death rate in the population (Parkes 1964b). Deaths of a parent were much less often recorded in these psychiatric patients. (The absence of any respondents who had lost a partner in Ward's control group may be a reflection of the young age of that group.)

Among the factors which have been shown to predict problematic reactions to the death of a partner in several studies are an ambivalent or dependent relationship with the partner. Thus, in the Harvard Bereavement Study, which was a longitudinal study of young widows and widowers (Parkes and Weiss 1983), high levels of reported marital conflict were associated with little distress during the first few weeks of bereavement, but after the first month the grief of the conflicted group tended to become severe and protracted and two to four years later these widows and widowers still expressed a surprising amount of continued pining for their lost partner. Dependent relationships were also associated with longlasting grief, but in that case the grief was intense from the outset.

More recently Waskowic and Chartier (2003) have shown that widows and widowers classed as 'insecurely attached' to their spouse (using Griffith and Bartholomew's 1994 RSQ), suffered more anger, social isolation, guilt, death anxiety, somatic symptoms, despair, depersonalisation and rumination than more securely attached persons. These assessments were made an average of 8.6 years after bereavement and reflect lasting problems in adjustment.

It is not only the attachment to the spouse that influences the reaction to the loss of a spouse. The support of family and friends can also be expected to mitigate loneliness and lack of such support is particularly common in old age when children have left home and decreased mobility makes it more difficult to maintain social relationships outside the home. Fulton and Owen (1977), comparing the reactions to the death of a spouse, parent and child, found that although people who had lost a child were more grief stricken and preoccupied by thoughts of the loss, it was those who had lost a spouse who were most lonely. This, he suggested, reflects the fact that widows and widowers were more likely to live on their own than people who had lost a child.

Loss of a partner in the current study

The details of the statistical analysis of this group are given in Appendix 13. The research leads us to expect that loss of a partner will be one of the most frequent bereavements to precede psychiatric referral and that this group will report high rates of marital disagreements and/or dependence on their partner with subsequent social isolation, grief and loneliness. Anxious/ambivalent attachments to parents in childhood may have primed the pump of dependency in adult life and sowed the seeds of chronic grief after the loss of a partner.

In the event 28 women sought help after the death of a male partner while 6 men had lost a female partner. This makes people who had lost a partner the largest single group in our sample, with those who had lost a parent a close second. The mean age of the partner-bereaved group was 49 years, ten years older than the rest. As expected, their scores of Grief/Loneliness were significantly higher than they were among those who suffered other losses. This confirms the findings of other studies showing that loss of a partner gives rise to more severe and protracted grief and loneliness than do other bereavements. Other current symptom scores did not differentiate the groups. Looking more closely at the questions that make up the Grief/Loneliness score, 77 per cent (26) of those who had lost a partner said that they are now 'very lonely' by comparison with 48 per cent of those who had lost a child (p. = 0.015*) and 52 per cent of those who had lost a parent (p. = 0.047*). It seems that the grief following loss of a partner is associated with more loneliness than other types of loss.

The conjugal attachments of the widow(er)s are of particular interest. All of the partner-bereaved group said that they had been 'unusually close' to their partner. Out of the 34, 27 (79 per cent) answered 'Yes' to the question 'Were you rather dependent on your partner?' and 24 (71 per cent) said that their partner had been dependent on them. In all of these respects they differed from people who had lost other relatives and friends. By contrast they had marginally fewer marital disagreements than the others and their Aggressive/ Assertiveness scores were significantly lower.

What can account for the intensity of these conjugal relationships? I was surprised to find that although many of these patients had experienced insecure attachments in childhood, the frequency of these did not differ from those whose problems followed other types of bereavement and, in particular, they were no more or less likely than the others to have experienced anxious/ ambivalent attachments. Despite this finding these unusually close relationships with (mostly male) partners often reflected similarly close relationships with their father during childhood. This finding only reached a borderline level of statistical significance. There is a one in ten probability that it occurred by chance.

This 'unusual closeness' would no doubt be attributed by psychoanalysts to infantile sexuality but the attachments which arise between parents and children have a very different function, that of providing security. If children find security in an intense attachment to their father, it is likely that they will attempt to find a similar security with a father-substitute in adult life. The small number of men who lost a spouse (6) rules out the possibility of assessing whether or not it is loss of a father or loss of a parent of the opposite sex that influences future closeness to partner.

A half of those who lost partners were now living alone and this was much larger than the proportion (one-fifth) who lived alone after other bereavements. On the basis of Fulton's research we would expect that this explains their loneliness. To my surprise, this was not borne out by the data. The proportion of partner-bereaved who said that they were 'very lonely' was no greater in those who lived alone than it was in those who lived with others. We can conclude that living with others did not substantially reduce the loneliness reported by those who had lost a partner.

Another problem thought likely to be associated with loneliness was lack of a confidante, but despite the number who lived alone, partner-bereaved people were no more likely to answer 'No' to the question 'Do you have anyone in whom you can confide your inmost thoughts and feelings?' than others. Among the 20 partner-bereaved who said they had a confidante, two-thirds were still 'very lonely' as was every one of the 12 who have no confidante. This compares with the loneliness reported by 40 per cent of the others who had a confidante and 67 per cent who had none. It seems that having someone to confide in does little to reduce 'loneliness' in those who have lost a partner.

Summing up these findings

People who were referred for psychiatric help after the death of a partner were, on average, older and more often left to live alone than were people referred after other types of loss. Although they were no more or less insecurely attached to their parents, they were rather more likely than others to report having had an unusually close relationship with their fathers. Both sexes also reported significantly higher rates of unusual closeness to and mutual dependence on their partners, less aggression and assertiveness and, in keeping with Fulton and Owen's (1977) study, greater 'loneliness' after bereavement. This 'loneliness' was not relieved by living with others or by having someone in whom they could confide.

The picture that emerges is of people who are intensely bound up with their partner in a passive and mutually dependent way. Even so they are no more or less likely than others in the sample to have experienced anxious/ambivalent or other insecure attachments in childhood or to cling to anyone except their partner. In fact their attachment is exclusive and, although as we shall see in subsequent chapters social support can mitigate some of the effects of bereavement, no substitute for a lost partner is acceptable.

Monotropism in adult life

John Bowlby (1958) coined the term 'monotropic' for such exclusive relationships. They are a feature of all attachments, but seem to be particularly pronounced in conjugal attachments. For these people the term 'loneliness' denoted not so much a wish for company but for the company of a particular person who was no longer present; they were pining for their spouse. This is the key feature of 'grief' (as proposed on p. 30) and particularly for this group 'loneliness' is rightly lumped together with grief in the Grief/ Loneliness score.

Once again we need to remind ourselves that it takes two to make a partnership. It may be that the mutual dependency that characterised this group reflected the needs of the partners as much as it did the respondents. If that is the case it is likely that although anxious/ambivalent attachments played no greater a part in the problems of people losing a partner than they did after the loss of other types of relationship, insecurely attached persons of all patterns may seek out partners with whom they can find the security of a very close relationship. When they do this they run the risk of severe grief if that relationship should be interrupted by death.

An example of an unusually close but 'secure' relationship with parents (according to the RAQ score) that left a child poorly prepared for the losses which were to come in her life was Sarah Green (whose case is described on pp. 74–5). As we have seen, she chose for her partner a man with whom she could form a similarly close relationship, so much so that when asked why they never had children she replied, 'We were far too bound up with each other to consider it.'

But there were other widows whose childhoods were less idyllic. One was Hannah Appleyard, whose reaction to the death of her husband was described at the start of this chapter.

> Hannah was the younger of two children of parents who both suffered from depression. She had an ambivalent relationship with her father whom she describes as a rigid, gloomy civil servant. He was overprotective of Hannah and tended to cling in a dependent way to his wife.
>
> Hannah describes herself as an anxious child with little confidence in herself. She tended to cling to both of her parents in a dependent way and in the RAQ she scored highly on Insecure Attachment (17), Anxious/Ambivalent Attachment (7) and Disorganised Attachment (4).
>
> During the war years, when Hannah was in her teens, her father

was abroad on National Service and Hannah was sent to a boarding school in Wales where she was very homesick. At 16 she became clinically depressed and this was attributed to separation from her parents. Despite these difficulties she was not lacking in intelligence and went on to obtain good clerical and editorial jobs.

She married at 27 to Mark, aged 41, and describes their relationship as mutually dependent. He was an actor whose work often took him away from home and he sometimes drank too much. Hannah describes herself as an anxious pessimist and found the separations from Mark hard to bear. She had problems with her blood pressure and also suffered from catarrh. They had three sons who were a constant source of anxiety to Hannah.

When she was 30 her mother died and her father subsequently transferred his dependence onto Hannah who found this very hard to bear. She became so anxious and distressed that her doctor prescribed an antidepressant and her father was persuaded to live with Hannah's sister.

Two years before I saw her one of her grandsons was found to have Down's syndrome and shortly thereafter Hannah was retired from a rewarding job because of her age. In the same month Mark suddenly collapsed and died of a myocardial infarction leaving her alone in her home.

Her intense and lasting grief has been described above. When she entered therapy she was only too aware of wanting to find someone to look after her but afraid of alienating her children and friends by clinging to them.

Hannah was a bright lady who made good use of five therapeutic interviews with me in the course of which she took stock of her life and regained her self-confidence. I was pleased at the progress she had made but disappointed with the results of the follow-up questionnaire three months later when there was little change in her reported symptoms.

It appears that Hannah's intense, mutually dependent relationship with an older man reflected her lifelong need for security. Throughout their marriage she had been intolerant of separation from him and his death provoked both severe grief and alarm.

The ending of her career had also removed a large and rewarding section of her assumptive world, a source of reassurance of her own competence and a place where she might have escaped from the reminders of her loss. In therapy with me she responded rapidly to reassurance of her personal worth and the emotional support that I was able to give, but it was perhaps optimistic of me to have expected this to outlast the ending of our relationship.

This group resembled the group who had lost a parent more closely than it did the child-bereaved group and it seems likely that both of these groups are people whose adult ties contain more of child–parent attachment than parent–child nurturance.

Final conclusions

All attachments have the biological function of fostering security and, as we have seen, the special problems that arise following bereavement and which cause people to seek help often reflect the failure of that function. We saw in Chapter 11 that many of the psychiatric problems of adults losing a parent reflect the continuation into adult life of dependent attachments to a mother in childhood. In Chapter 12 we found that the problems of parents losing a child are often complicated by the lasting effects which absence or neglect of parenting have on subsequent nurturant relationships with those children.

In the current chapter the problems of adults who lose a partner have sometimes been found to reflect the replication, with an adult partner, of an unusually close attachment to a parent of the opposite sex. At other times relationships in adult life seem to have taken on added intensity because they met a need for love that was craved for, but never found, in childhood. In either case the relationships that resulted were both very intense and very insecure. So exclusive is this kind of love that no one else can share it.

When such relationships are severed by bereavement they do not come to an end but become the focus of the bereaved person's continuing wish to nurture and be nurtured by the particular person who has died. This leads to severe and lasting loneliness, a loneliness that cannot easily be assuaged by family, friends and, as we shall see in Chapter 16, counsellors.

14 Social isolation and support

Man seeketh in society, comfort, use and protection.
Francis Bacon *The Advancement of Learning* (1606) bk. 2, ch. 23, sect. 2.

After the children grew up and left home May Bristow and her husband centred their lives on each other. They assumed that they had no need for friends and both had health problems that made it difficult for them to leave the house.

May was 71 years of age when her husband died, peacefully, from cancer. She had had every opportunity to prepare herself for this event but she reacted very strongly, becoming extremely anxious, depressed and lonely. Her diabetes, as so often at times of stress, became hard to control and this added to her fear.

Although the ties that cement families together differ from those which attach us to friends and workmates, all human relationships have something in common and it would be surprising if the support that we receive from our fellows did not mitigate some of the distress which follows the loss of people to whom we are more closely attached. By the same token, the basic assumptions that we make about those to whom we are attached are likely to colour less intimate social relationships.

Reviewing the influence of social support on bereavement, Stroebe and Schut (2001) conclude that some studies show that social support has a 'buffering effect' on bereavement while others show no such influence. The positive 'buffering effect' is most evident in studies of older bereaved people and Stroebe concludes that this results from the special needs of older people to be cared for by others.

We must beware of assuming that, in such studies, it is necessarily the lack of social contact and support that causes the later problems. Social support does not come about by chance, it happens for a reason. Securely attached individuals have been found to be more likely than the insecurely attached to seek support at times of need (Larose and Boivin 1997). Conversely, people who adopt a paranoid basic assumption that other people are not to be trusted are likely to avoid social interaction and, consequently, to lack social support; their paranoia causes their lack of social support rather than vice versa.

Particular patterns of attachment can influence social support in several ways. Simpson *et al.* (1992) showed that in an anxiety-provoking situation avoidant adults are less likely than others to seek help and less likely to offer their partner reassurance and support. These researchers also found that anxious/ambivalent individuals were more likely to be overprotective towards their partners. Another study showed them to be less warm, responsive and dependable than others (Collins and Read 1990).

Some relationships are more supportive than others. Thus, young children in the home may be seen as providing distraction from grief, but they may also be a burden if people are so preoccupied by grief that they have insufficient emotional reserves to meet the demands and needs for nurture of their children. One of Main's predictors of disorganised attachment in children is the experience of a loss by the mother shortly before or after the birth. Even mothers who are not bereaved can find small children a burden and Brown and Harris (1978) showed that working-class women with children at home were twice as likely to be depressed as those without. This said, children can give meaning to life at a time when other meanings are shattered.

What of our ties to non-human objects? Can they also be influenced by the basic assumptions arising out of our primary attachments and do they, in turn, influence our reaction to loss? Two kinds of attachment will be considered here, attachments to companion animals and attachment to God.

Although dogs can protect us from burglars and cats from mice, such protection is not the main reason for keeping a dog or a cat. In a survey of 53 people taking pets to a veterinary surgeon, 83 per cent described their relationship to their pet as 'love' and 94 per cent perceived their pet as a member of their family (Moffat 2000). The main function of pets is as objects of nurturant attachment. Pets are small people who satisfy our needs for an affectionate other who will reward us with affection for the nurture and attention we give them. Since pets themselves become attached to human beings they grieve when we leave them, just as we grieve when we lose them (Stewart 1999).

As with other types of loss, women are more likely than men to seek help after the death of a pet. Among 1000 people who phoned the UK Pet Bereavement Helpline, 87 per cent were women. Although no questions were asked about their attachments to humans, a third were living alone and many others spoke of having unsatisfactory marriages (Woods 2000). Clearly this is an important area for future research.

Another relationship that is usually characterised as one of love is attachment to a divine being or 'God'. Kirkpatrick (1999) points out: 'Perceived relationships with God meet all of the defining criteria of attachment relationships and function psychologically as true attachments.' This is evident in proximity seeking (going to church, prayer, meditation, household shrines or sense of presence), turning to God at times of danger or sickness, perception of God as providing a secure base or 'rock', and seeing separation from God as the ultimate punishment, for example, in excommunication. People who leave cults may mourn for their loss.

In general, children's views of God seem to reflect their views of their parents and even in adult life views of God are coloured by the individual's patterns of attachment. Using Hazan and Shaver's self-report measure (see p. 22), Kirkpatrick and Shaver (1990) found that people who classed themselves as 'secure' were more likely than those who classed themselves as 'avoidant' to see God as loving. The 'secure' were also more likely to see themselves as having a personal relationship with God and to be evangelicals, while the insecure saw God as distant.

The 'avoidant' were more often agnostic and the 'ambivalent' (corresponding to the anxious/ambivalent category) most likely to see God as punitive. Among Pentecostals, the 'ambivalent' were more likely than others to 'speak with tongues' (glossolalia). Summarising the research literature on speaking with tongues (glossolalia), Kirkpatrick (1999) concludes: 'Something like ambivalent attachment may be associated with this extreme form of attachment behaviour expressed towards God.'

It does seem that a relationship with God provides those who have little reason to trust themselves or others with a parent-figure whom they can trust. This being so we may expect that faith in God would mitigate some of the distress of bereavement. The results of research are inconsistent, but having reviewed this evidence Stroebe and Schut (2001b: 358) conclude: 'Taken together, these studies offer some support for the assumption that religious beliefs can be helpful in coping with the death of a loved one.' In addition to the reasons given above, research by Noelen-Hoeksma and Larson (1999) suggests that another important factor is the social support that often accompanies religious observance.

Social relationships in the current study

We start by examining the correlates of living alone and social support. Since our measures of these two variables did not correlate with each other (Social Support scores in those living alone were no lower than they were in those living with other people) it makes sense to consider them separately (details of this analysis are given in Appendix 14).

Living alone

Of respondents 60 (33 per cent) were living alone. Their average age was 46 years, seven years older than those living with others, but still an age group unlikely to need the physical care of others. The expectation that insecure attachments might lead to isolation from others was not borne out by the current study. Insecure Attachment scores were not significantly higher in those who lived alone than they were in those who lived with others (see Appendix 14).

It was also anticipated that living alone would be associated with higher scores of Grief/Loneliness and indeed, in contrast with the negative findings in the subgroup of bereaved spouses reported in Chapter 13, living alone was significantly correlated with Grief/Loneliness after bereavement, though not with other Emotions and Symptoms. This correlation was highest in people over the age of 50. This is surprising when we remember that, in general, grief tends to be lower in older bereaved people than in younger. In the current study, however, this finding is limited to people who live with others. Among those who live alone, the mean Grief/Loneliness score rises steadily in each age group over aged 40 (see Figure A.14.1, p. 368 for details). The increase is mainly attributable to replies to the question 'Are you very lonely?' and confirms the findings of geriatric practice which indicate that loneliness is a common problem among elderly bereaved people who live alone (Pitt 1974).

As we have seen (p. 179), this correlation was not found in those who had lost a spouse. The 'loneliness' of which they complain is unaffected by living with others, whereas the loneliness of other solitary bereaved people can, at least to some degree, be alleviated by the presence of others. Since the 'other' is most often a spouse it seems that it is the presence of a spouse that is most effective in reducing loneliness.

The young age of Ward's comparison group makes them unsatisfactory as a control group for these older psychiatric patients. Young women living alone reported rather more Grief/Loneliness than those living with others, but the numbers were too small for this difference to reach statistical significance.

Social support

As we saw in Chapter 13, social support in the form of confiding relationships and social contact in the form of living with others are two different things. Brown and Harris (1978) showed that confiding relationships protect against the psychiatric sequelae of traumatic life events only if the confidantes live together. In the current study, although both confiding relationships and living with others are associated with lower levels of Grief/Loneliness, the relationship is additive rather than exclusive.

Nearly two-thirds (60 per cent) of the bereaved psychiatric patients said that they would not turn to their family when at the end of their tether and nearly a half (48 per cent) would not turn to their friends. Indeed, a third (38 per cent) answered 'No' to question III/6 'Do you have anyone in whom you can confide your inmost thoughts and feelings?' As we expect, people who have no confidante are less likely to turn to friends or family when at the end of their tether. (These questions together make up the score of Social Support.)

The End of Tether Turn In score includes two questions that also contribute to our score of Social Support (At end of tether would seek help from friends and/or family). This highlights the impossibility of disentangling social support from coping. Seeking help is an important way of coping with stress.

All scores of Insecure Attachment in childhood, but particularly, Avoidant Attachments, were associated with poorer Social Support in adult life. This confirms our expectation that insecure people are less likely to make and maintain the relationships which might protect them from stressful influences. The interaction of these variables can be seen more clearly if we return to the case of the elderly May Bristow.

Throughout her childhood both of May's parents had consumed too much alcohol and their relationship was stormy. May described her mother as an insecure woman who suffered from depression and, on several occasions, threatened suicide. She also suffered from diabetes and May was always afraid that she would die. Both May and her sister inherited this disease.

May always tried to support her mother. She had been an anxious child and her RAQ showed her to have a high score of Disorganised Attachment (9) and average scores of the other two attachment patterns.

She was 17 years old when her mother became sick and died. May was supported in her bereavement by an older man whom she married three years later. This was a close and mutually dependent relationship. They went on to have two children, both girls. Her husband and children always saw May as a vulnerable person.

During her youth May's sister died of diabetes and her only surviving sibling, her brother, committed suicide. May found all of these bereavements hard to bear but was well supported by her husband and family.

When she was referred to me, ten months after the death of her husband, May was living with one of her daughters and had been unable to return home. She was accompanied to the clinic by both daughters each of whom was apprehensive that she would be 'lumbered' with full responsibility for caring for their frail, clinging mother. The situation had become very tense.

May herself found it hard not to cling. When the effect of clinging was discussed in therapy she acknowledged the situation. With considerable apprehension she gritted her teeth and returned to her empty home for the first time. This brave action had immediate consequences. Her daughters responded by becoming much more supportive and the vicious circle of May's clinging and her daughters' self-protective withdrawal was broken. Only three interviews

and one telephone call were needed to effect a dramatic improvement in her mental state.

As so often happens in old age, the older members of May's family had died
and her reduced mobility had restricted her circle of friends. May's attachment problem, her tendency to cling, had had the effect of undermining the
limited social support that her two daughters were able and willing to give.
Only when she succeeded in controlling this tendency did she discover that,
despite the fact that she now lived alone, she had an adequate support system.
Indeed, it was only because she had accepted the need to live alone that her
daughters felt able to give her their willing support.

Among the bereaved psychiatric patients who completed the RAQ, lack
of Social Support was associated with increased Grief/Loneliness, Overall
Distress and, at borderline significance, Anxiety/Panic and Depression/
Medication. This seems to confirm the buffering influence of social support
but may simply reflect the fact that both poor social support and increased
distress have a common origin in insecure attachment. Unlike living alone,
Social Support was not correlated with age and older people were no more or
less likely to seek help from their family and friends or to confide in others
than younger people.

Clinical data indicates that, even in the absence of prior insecure attachment patterns, negative social influences are associated with increased grief
and loneliness and are, in turn, aggravated by the losses in people's lives. An
example was given of just such a reaction in Sarah Green, an elderly lady
whose social isolation was brought about and aggravated by successive
bereavements (pp. 74–5).

It seems that people who say that as children they avoided or clung to their
parents and who were suspicious of others are less likely, later in life, to have
anyone in whom they can confide or to whom they will turn at times of
trouble. This is reflected in a significant correlation between high Social
Support and disagreement with the statement 'I find it hard to trust other
people'. People who do not trust others cannot expect social support at times
of bereavement.

Social relationships in the non-psychiatric sample

When the social supports of Ward's young women were compared with those
of the matched group of young women who sought psychiatric help (pp.
370–1) an interesting difference was found. The psychiatric sample were
significantly less likely to say that they have someone in whom they can
confide their inmost thoughts and feelings. This suggests that a distinctive
feature of the comparison group who did not seek psychiatric help after
bereavement is their ability to confide in the other sources of help that are
available to them.

Even women in Ward's comparison group who had high scores of Anxious/

Ambivalent and/or Disorganised Attachment had retained this ability and these obtained lower scores of Overall Distress than the psychiatric group. This suggests that the experience of these insecure attachments in childhood allows some children to develop social skills and it is possible that, in some cases, attachment strategies developed by those with these attachments feed into subsequent social relationships. For example, a person who has learned to avoid closeness may meet and befriend others who are similarly 'independent' and those who need to depend may become skilled at meeting the nurturant needs of others.

The avoidant attachment pattern, social variables and grief/loneliness

The early thinking about bereavement was much influenced by Lindeman's claim that problems in grieving were attributable to the repression of grief and that they could be relieved by therapies that encouraged its expression. In recent years this theory has been challenged (Wortman and Silver 1889). Our data provides a test of this hypothesis. We saw that scores of both Avoidant Attachment in childhood and Emotional Inhibition/Distrust in adult life were correlated with increased scores of Grief/Loneliness after bereavement (p. 336). Three possible explanations will be considered here:

1 Avoidant attachment leads to emotional inhibition and that this, in keeping with Lindeman's thinking, delays or represses the grief process (the repression hypothesis) leading to delay in the onset of grief which then lasts longer than expected.
2 Avoidant attachment, emotional inhibition and distrust of others all lead to lack of social support after bereavement and that this, in turn, causes grief to persist (the social support hypothesis).
3 Avoidant attachment sensitises the person to the later effects of testosterone or other influences that come about during adolescence and postpone the expression of grief in males (the testosterone hypothesis).

Only a multivariate analysis can resolve this kind of issue. Variables likely to influence the expression of grief are Avoidant Attachment in childhood, male sex, Emotional Inhibition/Distrust in adult life, the Aggressive/Assertiveness score and Social Support, each of which was included in this analysis (details are given in Appendix 14).

When they were entered in turn into a hierarchical regression, the Avoidant Attachment score was significantly correlated with Grief/Loneliness at the outset and was unaffected by the addition of male sex. This implies that the influence of these two variables on the Grief/Loneliness score are independent of each other. It suggests that Avoidant Attachment does not act by priming the body to the effects of testosterone or other influences that come about during adolescence. The correlation dropped below significance, however, when Emotional Inhibition/Distrust was added. This suggests that, regardless of the sex of the individual, avoidant attachments in childhood increase persisting grief/loneliness by bringing about emotional inhibition and/or distrust in adult life. The addition to the equation of Aggressive/Assertiveness and Social Support scores had little further impact, implying that these played a relatively small part in the sequence. This supports the 'repression' rather than the 'social support' or the 'testosterone' hypotheses. It should not, however, be taken to indicate that the inhibition of grief is the sole cause of psychological problems in bereavement.

Other relationships

In keeping with the Brown and Harris's (1978) findings, those with children under the age of 16 at home scored significantly higher on Anxiety/Panic than those without. It would appear that among the people who sought psychiatric help after bereavement the presence of young children at home was often more of a burden than a blessing. Problems included mothers becoming more anxious about and overprotective of their children and children becoming 'clingy' after a parent's death. These problems sometimes stopped the surviving parent from working and created both social and financial difficulties. This said, there were a few people bereaved of a spouse who said that they could not have survived without the children. Although the death of a pet is rarely a cause of psychiatric problems, those that do occur, in my experience, are usually delayed reactions to the loss of a human being.

> One young lady was referred to me after the death of her horse. She had 'loved' horses from her adolescence. When she left school she obtained work in a riding stable where she fell in love with the owner, a married man. Eventually he told her that the relationship had to end and, in compensation, gave her a horse.
>
> She had always managed to keep her relationship to the married man secret and when it ended she seems to have transferred her affection to the horse, which she saw as a continuing link with her lost man friend. As long as she had the horse she had no need to grieve.
>
> Several years later the horse died. This event precipitated intense grief and anger, so much so that her friends became alarmed and persuaded her to seek psychiatric treatment. In the course of psychotherapy it became very clear that her grief and anger belonged more appropriately to the loss of her man friend than to the death of the horse. Therapy gave her the opportunity to express these feelings and to recognise the need to replan her life. When she did this her symptoms soon improved.

It seems, from this case that transferring one's attachment to a pet is one way of dealing with what Doka calls 'disenfranchised grief' (1989).

No systematic attempt was made, in the current study, to examine the influence of religious faith on the reaction to bereavement, but we saw (on pp. 110–11) how Mollie McKay's conversion to a Pentecostal sect and her discovery that she could 'speak in tongues' were associated with a transient improvement in the grief and insecurity which had followed the death of her parents.

Conclusions

It seems that with the exception of those who have lost a spouse or partner both living with others and social support can mitigate some of the intensity of grief and loneliness. The observation that this effect is most pronounced in older people may be attributed to the fact that when children leave home their parents are likely to live alone and this leads to more loneliness after bereavement. This study included only four people aged over 69 and the increased loneliness reported above would seem to be a reflection of isolation rather than the needs of the elderly for physical care.

Regardless of age, bereaved people for whom living alone is a relatively new experience are likely to feel insecure, anxious and panicky. If, in addition, their childhood attachments were insecure, they are likely to find themselves both more in need of social support after bereavement and less likely to get it, an example of the 'inverse care law' (Hart 1971). The presence in the home of children under 16 years of age was more likely to add to the burden than to relieve it.

The relatively low levels of Overall Distress in the non-psychiatric group of bereaved young women can reasonably be attributed to their good social supports. Even those who had experienced insecure attachments in childhood usually retained such supports and when they did their distress levels were low.

15 Other influences on the reaction to bereavement

They bore within their breasts the grief
That fame can never heal –
The deep, unutterable woe
Which none save exiles feel
W. E. Aytoun
The Island of the Scots (1849) st. 12

The stait of man does change and vary,
Now sound, now seik, now blith, now sary,
Now dans and merry, now like to dee;
Timor mortis conturbat me.
William Dunbar
(c.1465–1513) *Lament for the Makaris*

In this chapter we examine some other influences on the reaction to bereavement, which have only been touched upon in earlier sections of the book, although research indicates that they can be important. These are losses of home, environment and culture and the effects of illnesses and disabilities.

Immigration

> Bess Kingston, now aged 30, was born in the West Indies and came to England to join her mother at the age of 15. After her only baby died of a 'cot death' four days after delivery, Bess reacted severely, becoming extremely tearful and unable to sleep. When seen in my clinic three months later she appeared depressed and miserable. Her appetite was poor and she had lost a great deal of weight.

In this section we consider the problems faced by immigrants such as Bess and the influence that these may have on their reaction to bereavement.

Konrad Lorenz once referred to partners as having 'home valency'. By this he meant 'having the same emotional value as the home' (1963: 186). This observation suggests a link between attachments to people and places. Although we tend to be less strongly attached to places than we are to people, the concept of 'home' as a safe place to which we can retreat when we feel in danger is deep-seated and may well share a similar biological origin to our attachments to people.

Human beings, like most social animals, occupy territories and within these territories build nests or other defensible places in which it is safe to rear their young. They will fight to defend these places and their loss is likely to undermine security and evoke distress. Homesickness has much in common with Separation Anxiety and, according to a review by Van-Tilburg *et al.* (1996), commonly co-exists with separation and loss of home, lifestyle and roles. Marc Fried (1962), who studied the reaction to relocation of slum dwellers in the East End of Boston, writes: 'While there [is] . . . considerable variability in the loss experience, it seems quite precise to refer to the reactions of the majority as grief.' He describes both preoccupied and avoidant patterns of reaction to the loss which resemble the anxious/ambivalent and avoidant patterns of attachment under consideration here.

Others have found similar reactions to forced migration and Munoz entitles his paper on Chilean immigrants to Britain 'Exile as Bereavement' (1980). He refers to the 'loss of roots, the geography, the emotional support, the cognitive world and the status which they [the emigrants] had enjoyed prior to exile'. There is a copious literature on the psychology of migration, which lies beyond the scope of this volume. Like most stressful life events, migration is not uniformly traumatic and there are some for whom the experience is life enhancing and enjoyable. Much depends on the reasons for the migration, the preparation for the psycho-social changes which follow, the magnitude of the changes and the circumstances in which they take place.

Those who have experienced secure attachments and who are accompanied by the people to whom they are attached may be expected to cope better with the challenges involved in migration than people who are separated from their families or whose experience of insecure attachment has undermined their confidence in themselves and others. Most studies indicate that the risks to mental health of immigration are greatest during the first year or so. Once they have adjusted to life in their new country most immigrants are no more troubled than their hosts.

Immigrants in the current study

Most of the 20 immigrants who sought help after bereavement in the current study had been in the UK for many years. Only one was over the age of 30 on arrival in the UK and the mean age at immigration was 20 years. Of these immigrants 16 were female and 4 male. The numbers are too small for fine-grained statistical analysis but those findings that are statistically significant imply quite large differences between the immigrant and native populations (details of these are given in Appendix 15).

Over a third of the immigrants (compared with 8 per cent of the natives) answered 'Yes' to the question 'Was your family subjected for a long time to serious danger or persecution?' They also reported significantly more separations from their parents and a slightly higher score on Anxious/ Ambivalent Attachment, which only reached borderline levels of significance, as did the resulting Insecure Attachment score. Despite this they showed no more or less childhood vulnerability than the non-immigrants and their scores on adult current emotions and symptoms were not significantly different from the rest of the sample. Why should this be?

To find answers I went back to the case notes of the immigrants and examined each in turn. The high Separation scores seem to result from the fact that many of the immigrants came from large families in which one or both parents were absent and they were largely brought up by older siblings and/or grandparents. The parenting that they received was not necessarily inadequate. Most had emigrated to the UK in their teens or young adult life in order to escape from poverty or danger whose origins lay outside the family. Moving to Britain often coincided with or was shortly followed by their marriage and the creation of a family of their own. Although they achieved a measure of security in the UK, their lives remained complicated by poverty and the difficulties of maintaining continuing ties, over great distances, to family members who remained in their country of origin. A wide range of bereavements and other stresses contributed to bring about the problems that caused them to seek psychiatric help. In Bess Kingston we can observe the influence of these interacting factors, which include migration to Britain and serious illness in childhood (to be considered in the next section).

Bess never knew her father and had been brought up, until the age of 15, by her maternal grandmother. She nearly died of a life-threatening illness during her early childhood and her grandmother subsequently treated her as fragile and delicate. She grew up an anxious, unhappy child who was often tearful, intolerant of separation and reluctant to visit new places, meet new people or do new things.

An under-achiever at school she distrusted other children and became a 'loner'. Out of necessity, she learned to stand on her own two feet from an early age and sees herself as having become stubborn, rebellious and bossy. She was suspicious of other people and reluctant to accept cuddles or other demonstrations of affection. In the RAQ she showed a high Separation score (5), high Avoidant (6), average Anxious/Ambivalent (6) and below average Disorganised Attachment score (2).

At the age of 15 she came to join her mother in London but her life situation did not improve. Her feelings about her mother had always been ambivalent and she describes her as an aggressive woman whose relationship with her second partner was stormy and at times violent.

In her youth Bess had a succession of boyfriends but no close relationships. She had the idea that a baby would give her someone to love and at the age of 30 she became pregnant by Dan, a man whom she had no intention of marrying. Her relationship with Dan, like all her relationships, was marred by ambivalence, and although she wanted closeness she could never tolerate it for long and would then find it necessary to get away, in order to reduce rising feelings of tension. During her pregnancy, she was extremely anxious that Dan would find some way to take the baby away from her.

When I first saw her Bess said that the death of her baby had brought home to her the loneliness of her life. Although she had cried a great deal in private she found it hard to cry in the presence of other people and wished that she could cry more.

One could not fail to admire the courage and determination of this lady who showed a plucky face to the world whatever fears lurked within her. She eagerly accepted the help that was offered and made good use of our time together.

In the course of 11 supportive interviews with a medical student interspersed with four interviews with me, Bess talked a great deal about her bereavement and her life situation. At the same time she made a striking improvement, her grief diminished, her appetite and weight were restored and she slept better.

When last seen it was clear that her relationship with her boyfriend had improved. On my advice, she had joined the Compassionate Friends, a mutual help group for parents who have lost a child, and was finding meetings with them very helpful.

The pattern of leaving children to be brought up by grandmothers while the mother works abroad is not uncommon in the West Indies. Men seldom take much part in child rearing and wives are often unsupported both emotionally and financially. One cannot assume that a tradition that is culturally 'normal' is therefore desirable and the burden on both grandmother and children can be considerable. A great deal depends on the capacity of the grandmother to provide the secure parenting that is needed.

In Bess's case it is clear that she suffered the consequences of an insecure, avoidant attachment, large family size and immigrant status. She had not received the parenting that would have enabled her to grow up with a reasonable degree of trust in others. Her distrust spoiled those relationships that she had and left her feeling isolated and lonely.

Her desire for a child was very strong and seemed to reflect this loneliness, but it also carried the risk that she would perpetuate the cycle of deprivation in another generation. The baby seemed to embody the hope that, by giving to her baby the nurturance that she had never received, she could somehow assuage her own isolation and loneliness. When her baby died her loneliness and depression returned in full measure.

While it would be unrealistic to suppose that Bess's problems had all been solved by therapy, she had at least taken stock of her life and gained insight into the roots of her insecurity. Much would depend on the tolerance and commitment of her boyfriend who attended several of our sessions and seemed to care about her.

Immigrants in Ward's non-psychiatric group

Although there were 23 young women in Ward's group (30 per cent) who had been born outside the UK, only one had suffered serious danger or persecution and their scores of Separation from their parents were no higher than those of the non-immigrants. Like the immigrants in the psychiatric sample their scores of Insecure Attachment were also no different from those of the native-born. Their Overall Distress scores were low (mean 3.57 compared with 4.52 in the native controls and 8.85 in the psychiatric immigrants) and there is no reason to regard this group as having suffered lasting psychological harm from their experience of migration.

Summary

The psychological effects of migration were closely affected by the life situation in which it arose. Separations from parents, poverty, persecution and danger all undermined security and contributed to make the people who sought psychiatric help vulnerable to subsequent losses. The immigrants in the control group had suffered fewer of these traumatic experiences and did correspondingly well.

Returning to the questions why, despite the history of separations, persecution and danger, these migrants did not report more evidence of childhood vulnerability and poorer outcomes than non-migrants. Their parents, of course, suffered from the same danger, persecution and poverty as the respondents themselves. Having more children than they could protect and care for, they solved that problem by finding others in their extended family who could provide the love and care that was needed and this may have mitigated the insecurity of the attachments made by these children. The children learned to expect and cope with trauma; they survived and this in itself may have given them confidence and made them aware of their own strength. Again it seems that the experience of hardship has its positive aspects. These people's tough lives left them better able than some to meet new challenges. I was impressed by their courage and determination to find a way through the many problems that they continued to face in their country of adoption.

Sickness and disability

The relationship between illness, attachment and grief is complicated by the fact that illness may be both a stressor and a consequence of stress; it may evoke attachment behaviour in parents and may itself be influenced by the attachment behaviour of the parents. Assumptions that a person is suffering from an illness and has grounds for complaining to a doctor are determined by psychological and social factors that involve the sufferer, parents, medical professionals and others. There is no space here to discuss the finer points of the warp and woof of mind/body relationships. For a challenging examination of the interaction of these factors Simon Wilkinson's book *Coping and Complaining: Attachment and the Language of Dis-ease* (2003) is recommended.

Illness in childhood

Bowlby (1969) included illness in the child as one of the life situations that evokes attachment behaviour in both children and parents. Children who are perceived as 'damaged' often need and evoke more nurturant love from their parents. In general the response is appropriate and supportive but some parents react to disease or deformity, such as the birth of a handicapped child, by becoming overprotective; others may reject or avoid getting close to a child who is perceived as imperfect (Tarnow 1987).

Wilkinson suggests that many of the problems associated with 'dis-ease' arise out of the attachments and coping strategies associated with particular childhood situations. Thus, those who have learned 'preoccupied' or 'anxious/ ambivalent' strategies may complain of bodily symptoms because they have found that their parents then give them the attention that they craved. Those whose parents are unresponsive to such strategies, the 'avoidants', instead of seeking help when they feel sick, may adopt obsessive rituals of hand washing or other excessive hygiene in an attempt to control the uncontrollable.

Childhood illness and disability in the current study

The influence of physical illness in childhood is assessed in II/5 'Did you suffer from severe illness which threatened your life before the age of five?' and II/6 'Or a similar illness from 6 to 16?' These were added together to give a single score of Childhood Illness (details of the statistical analysis of these variables are given in Appendix 15).

Of the respondents 20 (11 per cent) reported life-threatening illness before the ages of 6 and 17 (9 per cent) in later childhood. Taken together 33 (18 per cent) reported such illness at some time before the age of 17 but only four

(2.2 per cent) reported illness during both time spans. Only 8 per cent and 4 per cent of Ward's control group reported childhood illness and the small number involved (11) does not justify statistical analysis.

Although the questionnaire does not include a space for recording the nature of the life-threatening illness, it was usually possible in the psychiatric patients to obtain information about this from the case notes. Diagnoses covered a wide range from asthma, bronchitis, diphtheria, tuberculosis and other respiratory conditions to poliomyelitis, rubella, head injuries and thyrotoxicosis. One group at special risk were six immigrants who had suffered life-threatening illness in childhood, prior to their migration to Britain. These included typhoid, malaria and the effects of malnutrition.

As is to be expected, childhood illness often gave rise to separation from parents and this explains why increased Childhood Illness scores were associated with increased Parental Separation scores. Illness in early childhood was associated with significantly higher scores of both Anxious/Ambivalent Attachment and Avoidant Attachment with Disorganised Attachments just missing significance.

This research helps us to understand how these early illnesses influence the relationship between parents and children. Thus, the association between sickness in early childhood and Anxious/Ambivalent Attachment confirms Tarnow's assertion (1987) that some parents cling to and become overprotective of a sick child. By contrast the association between sickness and Avoidant Attachment confirms his finding that other parents recoil from sickness and may distance themselves from a child who is seen as 'damaged', thereby creating or aggravating an avoidant attachment.

The example of Bess Kingston, reported above, illustrates both of these elements. She was treated as fragile because of her life-threatening illness in early childhood but seems also to have become fearful of closeness, perhaps because her grandmother gave physical care without the warmth that is so important a source of secure attachment.

Illness in later childhood was not associated with the Anxious/Ambivalent Attachment score. This suggests that parents are less likely to cling anxiously to older sick children than they are to sick infants, hence the Anxious/Ambivalent pattern is established before the age of 6, an observation that is supported by Ainsworth's work. Illness in later childhood was, however, associated with higher scores of Avoidant Attachment. Since avoidant attachment is also likely to have become established by the age of 6, this suggests that the avoidant attachment may have contributed to make the child more vulnerable to illness. Possible explanations for this will be considered below.

Whatever the influence of illness on attachments and vice versa, these were not great enough to make a significant impact on the reaction to bereavement in adult life. Illnesses, early or late in childhood, were not associated with any increase in scores of current Distress, Symptoms or Emotions. Once again it is possible that, across the sample, the negative effects of the stress of illness, on some children were balanced by positive effects on others, in whom the experience of illness increased their confidence in the protection of their parents and their ability to survive. We must also remember that only 33 of our respondents experienced these illnesses. In a group of this size the magnitude of the influence would have had to be large to reach statistical significance.

In those who reported illnesses between 6 and 16 years of age the adult Disability score was more than twice as high as it was in those who said their childhood was healthy. We should not assume, however, that in these cases the childhood sickness was persisting into adult life, a rare occurrence. It seems rather that it is the vulnerability to illness that continues into adult life.

Illness in adult life

Tessa Johnson, aged 33, was referred to me six years after her husband Hal died, suddenly and unexpectedly, from a cerebral haemorrhage. With hindsight it seems likely that this was not his first. She showed little grief at the time and devoted herself to her work. She felt very lonely and soon began to cohabit, in an unsatisfactory relationship, with Bill, a divorcee,

Three years after Hal's death she began to suffer from pains behind the ears which closely resembled the headaches from which Hal had suffered. This type of symptom has been termed an 'identification symptom' (Parkes 1996), but Tessa's, like many 'psychosomatic symptoms', may also have had an organic component. The pains were associated with panic attacks and intense fear that she too would die.

The following year she developed back pain. She was diagnosed as having a slipped disc and forced to give up work. She became increasingly dependent on analgesic medication.

Illness in adult life can both influence and be influenced by the reaction to bereavement. The effects of bereavement on health have been much studied and there is no space here to discuss them in detail. Suffice it to say that both physical and psychosomatic disorders are likely to arise or get worse after bereavement and there is even an increase in mortality rates. For a more adequate review see *Bereavement: Studies of Grief in Adult Life* (Parkes 1996).

Much research has also been carried out into the grief that can be caused by physical ill health and injury in adult life. This is discussed in detail in *Coping with Loss* (Parkes and Markus 1998), which showed that following a wide range of serious illnesses and injuries reactions of grief are to be expected. It also showed that rehabilitation is often complicated, among other things, by two types of reaction which are similar to the chronic and the inhibited or delayed forms of grief. These are obsessive preoccupation with the losses caused by the illness, or denial of the illness or its implications. These reactions may impair the patient's ability to cope with subsequent losses, particularly if the illness is disabling.

To a large extent, our security depends upon the possession of an intact body and anything that damages this will evoke feelings of insecurity; indeed our very survival may be threatened. It follows that sickness and lasting disabilities can be expected to add to the other causes of insecurity that have been considered in this volume and to contribute to the problems which accompany bereavement. Some support for this supposition comes from studies by Perlin and Schmidt (1975) and Vachon *et al.* (1982), both of which found physical illness and disability to predict greater distress than usual after bereavement.

To make matters worse, the chronic symptoms caused by longstanding illness can easily be aggravated by bereavement. Thus, in one study (Parkes 1964b), older people were found to consult their GPs more often than usual after the loss of a spouse. They were more likely than younger widows and widowers to complain of aches and pains, such as those caused by osteo-arthritis, than they were to complain of psychological symptoms. (Note that this research was carried out in the early 1960s when old people may have been less inclined to seek help for psychological symptoms than they are today.)

Adult disabilities in the current study

Disabling physical illness in adult life is covered by question III/3 'Are you suffering from any physical illness or disability?' This is followed by a checklist of five ways in which it might have threatened life, caused lasting pain or impaired ability to function unaided. Together these five answers make up the Disability score.

One or more current physical disabilities were reported by a surprisingly large proportion (30 per cent) of the bereaved psychiatric patients, 54 people. Fifteen (8 per cent) said that their life was threatened, 31 (17 per cent) that they had suffered lasting pain, 29 (16 per cent) that they were unable to work, 36 (20 per cent) that they were unable to move about as much as they wished, and 34 (19 per cent) that their illness or disability interfered with their life in other important ways. These disabilities were caused by a wide variety of conditions, many of them long term, and diagnoses included:

- Nine patients with cancer, AIDS and other life-threatening illnesses.
- Eleven patients with a variety of chronic organic diseases such as spondylitis and diabetes.
- Seven patients with chronic conditions to which psychological factors may have contributed. These included slipped discs, osteo-arthritis, asthma, ulcerative colitis and premenstrual tension.
- Six had physical symptoms to which psychological factors commonly

contribute, e.g. migraine, diarrhoea, gastritis and hypertension, all of which can be aggravated by psychological circumstances.

- Seven complained of pains whose origin was not clear. Most of these involved a mixture of arthritic and rheumatic conditions aggravated by the psychological effects of bereavement.

In Ward's group of young women only 9 per cent (7 cases) reported having a physical disability. These are too few for further analysis.

The relatively large number with current physical disabilities in the psychiatric sample may result from the fact that the study was carried out in a large London teaching hospital and some of my referrals were made by consultants working in other departments.

The Disability score, as we might expect, was higher in older people. Despite their frailty, people with disabilities were more likely than the able bodied (and younger) respondents to live alone and were not more likely to seek social support (i.e. they were not more inclined to seek help from friends or family or have someone in whom they could confide).

There was an unexpected association between insecure attachments in childhood and disabilities in adult life. As with the illnesses of later childhood, a significant though not large correlation was found between the score of Avoidant Attachment and the Disability score. Disability in adult life was also associated with Disorganised Attachments. While this may help to explain the social isolation (we saw above how people with these insecure attachment patterns have difficulties with close relationships in adult life), it was not at first clear why avoidant and disorganised attachments should be followed by greater disability than more secure attachments. Before answering this question, let us take a closer look at the case history and clinical data.

Tessa was the second of five children. Her father, a policeman, is described as a strict, over-anxious man who was inclined to depression. He could never express affection but Tessa felt close to him and worried about him, fearing that he would die. Her mother was jealous of Tessa's relationship with her father. She was even more distant and unaffectionate than father and Tessa had very mixed feelings towards her.

Tessa was not popular at school where she was seen as tough and was teased for being tall and plump. Wary of closeness she could not ask for help and now sees herself as having been aggressive, rebellious and stubborn. She was often tearful and sometimes wished she was dead. In the RAQ her Attachment scores place her high on Avoidance (7) and average on both Anxious/Ambivalence (8) and Disorganised Attachment (5).

Tessa's avoidant attachment to both parents reflects their own avoidant strategies and her fear that her father would die indicates that she was apprehensive about mortality from an early age. It is likely that Tessa's plumpness as a child was itself a consequence of 'comfort eating'. This both reflected and aggravated her insecurity and social isolation.

Further examination of case summaries of the more isolated individuals shows that most became isolated because they were insecure people who in later life were separated or divorced. The effects of their disability were aggravated by both the insecurity and the social isolation. Thus, people living with others were less likely than those alone to want to move about or leave the house and they may have been better able to tolerate any pain caused by their illness. This may have influenced their replies to the questions that made up the Disability score.

Given the special dangers and difficulties associated with illness it comes as a surprise to discover that Disability scores did not predict any of the scores of problematic coping or of current Distress, Symptoms or Emotions. It appears that the influence of these disabilities was not so great as to outweigh the other factors which contributed to the distress of these patients. As we have seen, most of the disabilities were longstanding and it may be that, like the immigrants described above, the respondents had adjusted to their disabilities long ago. Indeed they may have learned the hard way to tolerate suffering and even to trust others to care for them.

Because of the wide range of physical and psychosomatic disorders found in these patients, it is not possible to identify individual cases which exemplify them all. Tessa's case shows how an avoidant attachment can influence later psychosomatic disorder after bereavement.

On leaving school Tessa took work in a store and in a few years was promoted to become manager. At 21, against the opposition of her parents who subsequently 'disowned' her, she married Hal, a gentle giant. They had two children both of whom suffered from asthma and eczema.

She seems to have found in Hal someone who would not challenge her need for independence and with whom a degree of closeness was possible which she had never before experienced. Even so she may have passed on her avoidant tendency to her children and it is not unreasonable to suppose that their asthma and eczema were psychosomatic in origin.

In later years Hal's personality changed. He began to suffer from headaches becoming bad-tempered and prone to outbursts of violence in the course of which his speech was slurred. Tessa suggested that he seek medical advice but he refused. Nevertheless she was unprepared for his death.

As we saw above, she at first expressed little grief but before long became increasingly lonely and suffered from pains in her head and back.

When I first saw Tessa she came across as an intelligent and attractive young lady who was anxious, depressed and smoking 15 cigarettes a day. In the course of short-term therapy she recognised the link between her husband's symptoms and 'focusing on my head'. She was also much helped by reading Claire Weekes's 'brilliant' book *Self-help with your Nerves* (1984), which explains anxiety symptoms and gives clear advice how to manage them. At the end of therapy she was much more relaxed, her head pains had diminished in frequency and intensity and she had stopped smoking.

On follow-up three years later she was still severely disabled by her back problem and, although no longer depressed, she reported continuing tension and anxiety. She still missed Hal and her relationship with Bill was impaired by her continued difficulty in expressing affection.

As is typical of the avoidant attachment pattern, Tessa dealt with her traumatic bereavement by keeping busy and denying its implications. When at last this defence began to crumble her symptoms took the form of an identification syndrome rather than delayed grief. This was associated with intense fear that she too would die, perhaps a reflection of her fear of losing control.

Bibliotherapy and other 'self-help' techniques are often favoured by people with avoidant tendencies. Claire responded rapidly to emotional support and her use of 'self-help' enabled her to get back in control. At this point she discontinued therapy, still without expressing grief for Hal's death. In this circumstance it is hardly surprising that the results of follow-up were disappointing. She remained insecure and anxious, was still taking medication for her nerves and finding difficulty in expressing both affection and grief. Even though her back pain was attributed to a displaced intervertebral disc it is very likely to have been aggravated by anxiety, a well-recognised factor which 'opens the gate' to pain and lowers the pain threshold (Melzack and Wall 1965).

The findings reported above indicate that life-threatening illnesses in early childhood are associated with anxious/ambivalent, avoidant and possibly disorganised attachments to parents. It seems that, in these cases, the illness contributed to bring about the insecure attachment. In older children, however, it is avoidant attachment alone that is associated with illness and in this case it seems more likely that the insecure attachment caused or contributed to the illness. Avoidant and disorganised attachments in childhood may also sow the seeds of disabilities in adult life. Because of the small number of physical disorders in the control group it is not possible to say whether or not these findings are peculiar to my psychiatric sample.

At all ages a history of childhood avoidant attachment was associated with increased scores on measures of life-threatening and disabling illness. Three factors need to be considered to explain this finding:

- the possible influence of avoidant attachments on bodily health
- the sufferer's perception of themselves as ill
- their perception of the healthcare system as an acceptable source of help.

The research was not set up to test these hypotheses and any conclusions drawn are speculative and inconclusive.

The influence of avoidant attachments on bodily health

Avoidance of emotional expression has often been blamed for psychosomatic and somatic symptoms and some of these may be very serious. For instance, repression of grief has been postulated as contributing to the increased mortality from heart disease following bereavement, which is commoner in men than in women (Parkes *et al.* 1969; Stroebe and Stroebe 1983).

While the chain of causation is not fully understood, it has been shown that bereavement commonly gives rise to impairment of the immune response system and the neuro-endocrine control of bodily functions, both of which influence health. The impairment of lymphocyte functioning that follows bereavement has been shown to correlate with measures of depression rather than grief (Hall and Irwin 2001). This may be associated with a history of insecure attachment. Insecure attachments may also influence habits such as diet, smoking and alcohol consumption which all increase the risk of ill health.

Clearly more research is needed to establish the intermediate links between avoidant attachments and disease. We also need to consider the other factors that influence perceptions of illness as life threatening, disabling and requiring medical help.

The influence of avoidant attachment on perceptions of illness

Although some avoidants may see sickness as a weakness to be denied, it provides others with a relatively blame-free explanation for limitations which cannot be avoided. For example, one man was referred to me after a minor coronary infarction from which, in the opinion of the cardiologist, his heart had recovered although he remained seriously disabled. It soon became apparent that this very controlling businessman needed to remain 'sick' in order to escape responsibility for the failure of his family business. Only when his wife and family rallied round to reassure him of their continuing respect and support did his 'cardiac' symptoms improve to the point where he could return to work.

Similar factors can influence the persistence and severity of back pain, such as that suffered by Tessa Johnson. In such cases there is seldom any doubt that the patient's symptoms are rooted in physical illness, they are rarely 'purely psychological'. On the other hand, psychological factors that are often unrecognised or unacknowledged by the patient contribute to aggravate or prolong the physical disability.

The influence of avoidant attachment on seeking medical care

Given the tendency of avoidants to turn in on themselves and avoid help seeking we might expect them to avoid acknowledging illness or seeking for medical help. In this study the opposite seems to be the case. Once again we need to remind ourselves that the aim of avoidant attachment in childhood is not to separate from parents but to keep at a safe proximity. Any independence achieved is more apparent than real. The parents may be unable to touch their children, and may even punish clinging or tearfulness, but they will care for the child when sick. Children in such a relationship may indeed find that becoming sick or injured is one way of obtaining the care that they crave. This may explain some risk-taking behaviour by avoidant children who stand to benefit whether the risk taking succeeds or not. If it succeeds they get credit for bravery and skill; if it fails and they are injured they get care and attention.

Those who are perceived as sick commonly get 'tender loving care' and this is particularly likely if the illness is seen as life threatening. Indeed, one patient in St Christopher's Hospice described cancer as 'a drawing together illness' (C.M. Saunders, personal communication). Medical care often involves bodily contact without emotional closeness and this may be better than nothing to those for whom emotional closeness feels dangerous. This applies whether the care is given by parents or healthcare professionals and it may well persist from childhood into adult life. Both of these factors are likely to influence the inclination of people who have experienced insecure and avoidant attachments in childhood to perceive their illnesses as life threatening, to worry excessively about them, and to seek and accept medical care.

Conclusions

Nurturant love is evoked by expressions of weakness, helplessness or distress in others and those who suffer may be rewarded for their suffering. For some the reward is worth the pain and sickness may become a strategy. Hence, physical illness and disability are sometimes linked in complex ways with insecure attachments. In turn, they both influence and are influenced by social isolation. Physicians need to take the time and trouble that is needed to tease out these various interacting factors. As Wilkinson elegantly puts it, we need to learn 'the music that the patient is dancing to, the form of their complaining' (Wilkinson 2003).

The stresses associated both with migration and with illness interact with the effects of separations and attachment insecurity in childhood, but their consequences are not all bad. They also provide people with opportunities to learn to cope with stress and their overall effect on the person's reaction to later bereavements is not necessarily impaired.

In the next chapter we widen the focus still further to ask whether the influences that have been discussed in the preceding chapters contribute to the wider range of non-death losses which cause people to seek medical and psychiatric care.

Conclusions from Part III

The function of attachments is to provide security and the opportunities for exploration and learning that allow the child to develop strategies to cope, with varying success, with the stresses, losses and other challenges that emerge. We saw in Part II that the strategies adopted by those who have experienced insecure attachments may themselves prove either harmful or helpful according to circumstances.

The evidence presented in Part III has focused on the life situations and events that contribute to problems following bereavement. We found that these present us with a tapestry of fascinating interactions, which we are still only beginning to understand.

In Chapter 8 separation from or loss of a parent in childhood was found to be associated with persisting fears of later loss and of the grief that then results. This sometimes deters people from making fresh attachments. It may also aggravate any reported insecurity of attachment. Separations from parents were also found to add to the problems of many immigrants and to those of people who suffer major illness during their childhood. All of these factors contribute to the problems that arise after bereavement in adult life although they may also provide opportunities for maturation.

Chapter 9 showed how unexpected, multiple and other traumatic losses shatter basic assumptions of security and may be sufficient to cause psychiatric problems in their own right. We saw how they also interact with insecure, particularly disorganised, attachments to aggravate any vulnerability attributable to these causes.

Contrary to expectation, the self-assessments reported in Chapter 10 did not show boys to be any more likely than girls to report avoidant attachments to their parents during their childhood. In later life, however, men reported more inhibition of expressions of love and grief than did women.

It seems likely that innate predisposition plays a part in the psychological differences between male and female human beings as they do in other species. These become more active in adolescence and persist thereafter.

Among the problems that brought men into psychiatric care after bereavement, a quarter were thought to reflect lasting personality disorders, most of which are likely to have resulted from inhibition of feelings and communication. These disorders were then aggravated by the bereavement.

In Chapters 11, 12 and 13 we examined the particular responses to loss of a parent, a child and a spouse. The reaction to the death of a parent in adult life shows most clearly how the attachment patterns forged in childhood may persist into adult life. This was most obvious in girls who said that they had been unusually close to an overprotective mother. Many of them had been seen as very precious and fragile. Having grown up with the basic assumption that their survival depended on their parent they had never achieved autonomy.

The attachment of a parent to a child is a different kind of attachment from that of a child to a parent; its primary aim is the nurture of another person, the child. Our data suggest that these nurturant ties are powerfully influenced by the nurture that the parents received in their own childhoods and create special problems if the child should die.

Separation, rejection and violence in childhood played a larger part in the attachment histories of people who subsequently sought psychiatric help after the death of a child than they did prior to other types of loss. It seems that these types of parenting predispose people to create exceptionally strong nurturant ties to their own children. The children's deaths evoked a mixture of renewed grief for the parent's earlier losses and sympathetic identification with the children now dead.

People who report separation from or rejection by their own parents may attempt to redress the balance by giving to their own child the love and security which they lacked. But their own lack of personal security is such that their love is tinged with dread. The death of such a child is a particularly cruel blow, which confirms the parent's fear that the world is cruel and that nothing lasts; what started as a dread now becomes an assumption.

People seeking help after the death of a spouse or partner were less likely than others to have been in conflict and more likely to see themselves as having been very close to and dependent on that partner. After the partner died they experienced more grief and loneliness than others. Their problems were increased by the fact that most of them were also older and more likely to live alone. This said, those who did not live alone were no less lonely.

The influence of childhood insecurity of attachment was no greater or less after conjugal bereavement than it was following other types of loss, nor was there any evidence that anxious/ambivalent attachments played a greater part in creating dependent attachments in adult life. Rather it seems that all types of insecure attachment predispose some people to seek out partners who will provide them with the security and closeness that they did not find with their own parents. When these partners die the grief of the survivor is not greatly assuaged by the presence or support of others. Love is not transferable.

Chapter 14 examined the effects of two social variables, social support and living alone. Except in those who lost a partner, these were found to be associated with increased grief and loneliness after bereavement. Lack of social support is associated with low trust in others and has special importance in old age when people are also more likely to live alone and to suffer physical disabilities. Although social relationships are influenced by childhood attachment patterns and themselves influence grieving, multivariate analysis showed that they are not the main explanation for the influence of these attachment patterns on grief and loneliness.

In Chapter 15 two other types of circumstance, migration and illness, were examined. Many immigrants in this study had come from large families to whom they remained tied. Although some had been separated from or neglected by their parents, the parenting that they had received from grandparents or others had, to some extent, mitigated the effects of this. Even so, continuing poverty and the difficulties of retaining attachments and obligations to distant families, many of whom remained in danger, contributed to the immigrant's current problems after bereavement.

The data reported here suggest that illness can both cause and be caused by insecure attachments. Thus, life-threatening illnesses in early childhood correlated with a history of insecure, particularly anxious/ambivalent and avoidant attachments. Disabilities in adult life may also cause and be caused by attachment and other social problems. Those who reported avoidant and disorganised attachments in childhood also reported higher rates of disabling illness in adult life. Disabilities increased with age and may have played a part in bringing about psychiatric referral, although the overall measures of symptoms and emotional reactions after bereavement were no worse or better in disabled people than in people without disabilities. Social isolation and disabling disorders both contributed to the loneliness of older patients.

Avoidant Attachment scores were associated with increased levels of disability at all ages and this observation supports the theory that inhibition of emotions increases the risk of psychosomatic and possibly, somatic illness.

While each of the factors considered in Part III contribute to influence the reaction to bereavement, none of them has emerged as the main cause of the distress suffered by bereaved people. Rather it is the interaction between them that creates or undermines security. This is perhaps best explained by the confirmation or disruption of what Peter Marris (1974) calls the 'structure of meaning' which results from a worldview in which the proximity of loved others is a main source of security. Although each attachment is unique and irreplaceable, a person's capacity to 'recover' from bereavement stems not from their ability to forget the lost person, but to build upon and remodel their assumptive world in a way which includes and draws upon the treasure of the past.

It seems from the evidence of this and other studies that patterns of loving make an important contribution to the formation of personality and influence how people react to bereavement in adult life. While these influences have become clear after bereavement it is reasonable to ask whether or not bereavement is the only type of loss event to be affected by patterns of loving.

In Part IV we go on to extend our frame of reference to include people seeking psychiatric help who had not been bereaved. We then ask if these patterns justify us in recognising a new category of psychiatric disorder, Attachment Disorders. Finally we examine the implications of the foregoing chapters for the prevention and treatment of psychological problems.

Part IV

Disorders of attachment, other psychiatric problems and their prevention and treatment

16 Attachments in non-bereaved psychiatric patients

> What man that sees the ever-whirling wheel
> Of Change, the which all mortal things doth sway,
> But that thereby doth find, and plainly feel,
> How Mutability in them doth play
> Her cruel sports, to many men's decay?
> > Edmund Spenser
> > *The Faerie Queen* (1596) bk. 7, canto 6, st. 1

In Ellen Glazer's case it was not bereavement but pregnancy that triggered mental illness. Her first depressive illness occurred during her first pregnancy, At that time, she had been admitted to hospital overnight after she got drunk, overdosed on sleeping tablets and put her fist through a window. When a baby son was born she at first 'felt nothing for him'. Subsequently they became 'very close'.

This depression undermined her relationship with her partner John, yet they stayed together. During the next six years Ellen remained somewhat depressed. Then, aged 36, she became pregnant again and her depression returned in full force causing her to accept referral to my clinic. I found her an anxious, tense, unhappy lady who adopted a challenging attitude to the world.

Although the study of attachments has contributed to our understanding of the way people react when attachments are severed by bereavement, it is not unreasonable to consider that they may also influence the reaction to some of the other life events and circumstances which cause people to seek help from a psychiatrist. Losses of one sort or another are not uncommon and the reaction to them is often characterised as 'grief'. Indeed, we have already seen how the reactions to loss of physical health (pp. 199-200) can give rise to many of the psychological responses that are found after bereavement by death and sometimes give rise to lasting problems.

Research into the causes of psychiatric disorder has been going on for a long time and the field is a large one, too large to be fully reviewed here. Brown and Harris's well-conducted studies of the incidence of significant 'life events' in the pre-illness histories of women with clinical depression (1978) and Paykel's examination of the precursors of a wider range of mental illnesses (1974) revealed the magnitude and frequency with which negative events of lasting impact (i.e. major losses) contribute to cause mental disorders. This being the case, we should not be surprised to find that the insecure attachments and other factors that have been shown to contribute to problems after bereavement contribute, in a similar way, to the reaction to these other losses.

Most of the systematic studies of the influence of attachments on mental health have been confined to children and adolescents. In addition, several studies have focused on attachment patterns in mentally disordered offenders. One such by Frodi *et al.* (2001) used the Adult Attachment Interview (AAI) to study 24 psychopathic offenders in a forensic psychiatric hospital and medium-security prison. None was found to be securely attached and the largest single group were in the 'Dismissing of Attachment' category (which resembles the avoidant attachment of childhood). Other studies using the AAI have looked at the prevalence of insecure attachments in adult life in psychiatric outpatients and inpatients. Van Ijsendoorn and Bakermans-Kranenberg (1991) in a meta-analysis of this literature, found that only 8 per cent of these patients could be classed as 'Autonomous-Secure'. While these studies are of interest, the AAI cannot (as pointed out on p. 21) be taken as a measure of former childhood attachment patterns (see Schuengel and van Ijsendoorn 2001 for a critique of this literature).

Losses, as we have seen, may contribute to psychiatric problems but they are rarely assumed to be their sole cause. In general it is the interaction of life events and prior vulnerability that, taken together, are thought to explain much psychiatric disorder. This conclusion, as we have seen, also applies to the problems that follow bereavement.

Vulnerability to mental illness is itself generally attributed to two interacting factors: innate predisposition and damaging influences in childhood. These act together to increase the risk of later disorders. Just how they do this has been the topic of much debate and a great number of theories. Some of these have been touched upon in the foregoing chapters. They include psychoanalytic theory, coping theory, cognitive theories and various interpersonal and social theories.

There is no way in which all of these theories can be considered here and I make no assumption that they compete with the theory to be advanced. Rather I shall take a deliberately myopic approach and ask to what extent the attachment theory model, which enabled us to predict some of the psychiatric problems that follow bereavement, may also be found to predict psychiatric problems not associated with bereavement. We shall then have to decide whether or not an explanation based on attachment theory is useful and how, if at all, this theory fits with others.

If the correlations between Attachment Pattern scores and the various current Symptoms and Distress scores, which confirmed my predictions regarding the bereaved group, are also found in non-bereaved psychiatric patients, then it seems likely that the theoretical model that has been derived to explain problematic reactions to bereavement can also be applied to other psychiatric problems.

The non-bereaved psychiatric patients

Who were these psychiatric patients and why were they referred to me? During the course of this study, I was an honorary consultant psychiatrist at the Royal London Hospital with responsibility for providing psychiatric services, under the National Health Service, to the community of Tower Hamlets, in the East End of London. People were referred to my outpatient clinic by their general practitioners or by specialist consultants, who were requesting help for a wide range of psychiatric issues. As a community psychiatrist I had no inpatient beds, consequently I saw few psychotic patients; nor did I see many elderly people, most of whom were referred to the psycho-geriatric service. A few people were referred because of my special interest in helping people with life-threatening illness. In other respects the sample was that of a general psychiatric clinic in a downtown area.

Ninety-seven non-bereaved people completed the RAQ before their first attendance at my clinic. Unlike the bereaved sample, but like other psychiatric outpatients in Tower Hamlets, there were almost as many men (40) as women (57) among them. This difference from the bereaved group is statistically highly significant and suggests that the large proportion of women in the bereaved group is indeed attributable to bereavement (see pp. 153–4). The mean age of the sample, 37 years, was slightly younger than that of the bereaved group (41 years).

Comparison of non-bereaved and bereaved psychiatric samples

The statistical analysis of this comparison is reported in Appendix 16. The comparison between the 97 non-bereaved and 181 bereaved psychiatric patients is complicated by the fact that the questions about a dead person cannot be answered in the non-bereaved group. These questions and the scores derived from them have been omitted from the analysis that follows.

The clinical diagnoses showed the non-bereaved sample to have a smaller proportion of anxiety disorders, depression and post-traumatic stress disorder (PTSD) than the bereaved sample. These findings confirm those of earlier studies (such as Parkes 1964a; Jacobs 1993) that people who seek psychiatric help after bereavement are more likely than others to receive a diagnosis of affective (emotional) disorders and PTSD than other psychiatric patients. The non-bereaved psychiatric patients received a wide range of diagnoses and were less likely than the bereaved to have suffered both anxiety and depressive disorders at the same time.

Further confirmation of this comes from the scores of Current Emotions and Symptoms. Non-bereaved patients reported significantly lower Grief/Loneliness and Depression/Medication scores than the bereaved. There was a trend suggesting that non-bereaved patients may be more inclined to abuse alcohol, but this did not reach statistical significance.

Despite this, the Overall Distress scores were very similar in both groups, so were the Coping scores, apart from a slight tendency for the non-bereaved to say that they were more likely to seek help when at the end to their tether. This finding did not reach statistical significance.

It would seem from this that the overall magnitude of the distress, which brought people to seek psychiatric help after bereavement, was no more or less than that found in other psychiatric patients. Their ways of coping with stress were also much the same, although the non-bereaved may have been rather more ready to ask for help, perhaps because they had more hope of finding a solution to their problems than bereaved people.

Turning now to consider the attachment patterns of the two groups, do insecure attachments contribute more to the problems of people who seek psychiatric help after bereavement than they do to those of other psychiatric patients? If so we would expect to find higher scores of Insecure Attachment in the bereaved patients. In fact, the average scores of non-bereaved respondents on each measure of Insecure Attachment were very similar to those of the bereaved respondents. Non-bereaved had slightly lower scores on Anxious/Ambivalent Attachment, but this difference did not reach statistical significance. This suggests that insecure attachments played as great a part in the lives of my non-bereaved psychiatric patients as they do in the bereaved patients.

The question remains: Are the childhood attachment patterns associated with the same patterns of coping and emotional state in the adult lives of non-bereaved psychiatric patients as they are in bereaved patients? Are the predictions that were confirmed in the bereaved group also confirmed in the non-bereaved? By and large, the answer is yes. When the attachment scores in the non-bereaved group were correlated with the same variables with which they had been found to be associated in the bereaved group, similar results were obtained. Thus the Insecure Attachment score continued to predict the Current Overall Distress score suggesting that insecurity of attachment in childhood influences overall distress when people come for psychiatric help in adult life, to a similar degree in both groups.

In both groups Anxious/Ambivalent Attachments correlate with current grief and loneliness, but as we would expect grief is less of a problem in non-bereaved than it is in bereaved people. Scores of Avoidant Attachment in childhood correlate with Emotional Inhibition/Distrust in adult life in non-bereaved psychiatric patients to the same degree as they do in the bereaved.

Likewise there is a similar association between Avoidant Attachment and Aggressiveness/Assertiveness in both groups.

Similarly Disorganised Attachment predicted the End of Tether Cope by Turning Inward score in both groups and, although the correlation with the Anxiety/Panic, Depression/Medication and Alcohol Problem scores did not reach statistical significance, the trends were in the expected direction. We find many similarities between the two groups in the attachment patterns reported by Ellen Glazer, whose problems after the birth of her two babies were described above.

Ellen had been the eldest of four children of a heavy-drinking engineer who was sometimes violent when drunk. Although he worried about her, saw her as 'fragile' and was overprotective towards her, he was unable to show affection and Ellen's feelings towards him were ambivalent. Her mother was an insecure, anxious woman who also suffered from recurrent depression for which she received psychiatric treatment. Ellen worried about her and felt that she had to protect her from her father's physical assaults. As a child, Ellen suffered from asthma and was an insecure, anxious and unhappy girl who lacked confidence in herself and trust in others. A passive, inconspicuous loner she never did as well at school as expected.

Her RAQ showed her to have high scores of Anxious/Ambivalent (16) and Avoidant Attachment (8), and average Disorganised Attachment (4).

It seems that Ellen reported similar insecurity of attachments to those that we have found among bereaved psychiatric patients.

She was sent to a boarding school at the age of 8 years. At first she suffered severe anxiety at being separated from her parents but she then turned in on herself and would not be comforted or allow others to come close to her. In her teens she became stubborn, rebellious and aggressive.

At the age of 28 Ellen became insecurely attached to John, an Irish painter and decorator. She describes him as a 'chauvinist pig', as insecure as herself and inclined to panic. He 'pushed his problems onto me' and could not be relied upon to support her when she needed him. It seems that each felt the need for nurture but was unable to give it in return.

Although John proposed to Ellen she refused to marry him. Her intolerance of closeness spoiled their sexual relationship but did not prevent her from getting pregnant. As we have seen the pregnancy triggered her first serious depression. After she gave birth to a daughter there was some improvement in her depression but she remained tense and inclined to panic when left alone. She would not let her partner touch her, even after she underwent tubal ligation to prevent further pregnancies. Her 6-year-old son became very difficult and jealous of his little sister.

Ellen attended once before the baby was born and three more times during the succeeding year. Her partner John refused several requests to attend my clinic with her and I was not surprised when he separated from her. Despite this Ellen coped well without him and found it possible and rewarding to centre her life on her children. It was difficult for her to make the journey to the hospital and she failed her last appointment with me but accepted referral for counselling in her general practitioner's surgery, which was near her home.

The consequences, in adult life, of Ellen's childhood attachment problems resemble many of those with which the reader will now be familiar. Her mixture of anxious/ambivalence and avoidance continued into her adult life and probably influenced both her choice of an equally insecure partner and her difficulties in relating to him. She oscillated between clinging and avoiding John and we may suspect that she also oscillated between avoidance of and clinging to her own children. This started during pregnancy and after the birth of her first child when she 'felt nothing', then became 'very close'. Her son's jealous and difficult behaviour after his sister was born confirms the expectation that he would develop an insecure attachment to his mother.

Ellen's depression seems to have been the manifestation of feelings of helplessness and hopelessness, which emerged at a time when she felt overwhelmed by demands that she could neither fulfil nor fight. Thus pregnancy to her was a traumatic life event, a threat to her survival, which shattered her feeling of being in control of her world and undermined her security. It was only after she discovered that she could survive it and meet the needs of her children without John's help that her depression began to improve. Therapy, by providing her with a relatively 'secure base', where she could 'hold the line' and talk through her problems, may have helped to bring this about

Although my measures of parenting and childhood vulnerability imply that these factors play as large a part in the current distress of non-bereaved psychiatric patients as they do in bereaved, the way in which they do this sometimes differed in the two groups. Whereas, in bereaved people, anxious/ ambivalent attachments were more often associated with interpersonal problems of clinging and marital disagreements, this was less often the case in the non-bereaved sample. This is hardly surprising given the fact that, in the bereaved group, the person who died had often been the person with whom the survivor had had an ambivalent relationship.

Unlike the bereaved patients, the Disorganised Attachment score in the non-bereaved did not predict a reply to the End of Tether question indicating that the person might 'Take an overdose or otherwise harm yourself'. It seems that bereaved may be more tempted to suicide than non-bereaved psychiatric patients. In both groups, Disorganised Attachment correlated with Overall Distress and this was mainly attributable to a high correlation of Disorganised Attachment with Grief/Loneliness. On closer inspection it transpired that in the non-bereaved patients but less so the bereaved patients reports of Disorganised Attachment in childhood were associated, in adult life, with social inhibition (high EoT Turn In), social isolation (living alone), and, presumably as a result of these, current loneliness. It was these social factors that explained the Grief/Loneliness score in the non-bereaved group.

It seems that the experience of Disorganised Attachment in childhood leaves some non-bereaved psychiatric patients less able to form social relationships and more likely to end up on their own and lonely. This finding expands and confirms the results of the research (reported on p. 183), which indicates that social support can sometimes act as a buffer against psychiatric illness.

Overall it appears from these findings that issues directly related to attachments made in adult life are less often problematic in the non-bereaved sample than in the bereaved. Rather, the influence of attachment patterns in non-bereaved people seems to result from the indirect influence of two important basic assumptions about the world, trust in self and others. We saw in Chapter 9 that traumatic life events (which occur in non-bereaved as well as bereaved people) undermine assumptions of personal safety, worth and control. These assumptions are likely to be more easily undermined in people whose current negative view of the world results from previous insecurity of attachment.

Non-bereaved respondents in the non-psychiatric sample

We can compare the findings in these non-bereaved psychiatric patients with the non-bereaved women in Ward's comparison group, who had not sought psychiatric help. In Ward's control sample of young women who had not sought psychiatric help, 40 answered 'No' to the question 'Has any person close to you died in the last five years?' Twenty-six of them could be matched by age with the same number of non-bereaved young women who had sought psychiatric help. The small number (26) in these matched groups meant that only large differences between the groups can be expected to reach statistical significance. The comparison will, however, give us some idea of how large a part is played by insecure attachments in the emotional lives of these young women (details of the relevant statistics are given in Appendix 16).

The figures show that, as we would expect, most of the Symptoms/Distress scores are about twice as high in the non-bereaved psychiatric patients as they are in the non-bereaved control group. These findings confirm the validity of the Symptoms/Distress scores as indicating greater distress and symptoms in people who seek help for psychiatric problems.

As in the bereaved groups, the non-bereaved control group were more likely than the non-bereaved psychiatric group to have good social support, that is to say, they reported that they would turn to friends, family and others if at the end of their tether and be less likely to turn in on themselves or be aggressive. This indicates that the psychiatric patients are less likely than the non-psychiatric to seek help when under stress and less willing to trust others. It adds weight to the conclusion that lack of trust in self and others is a special problem in psychiatric patients. As we have already seen (p. 120), this is often attributable to insecure, particularly disorganised, attachments. Although scores of Avoidant Attachment, Disorganised Attachment and Separations from Parents during childhood were rather higher in the psychiatric patients than the controls, the differences were not large enough to reach statistical significance.

Within the full sample of 40 non-bereaved women in Ward's non-psychiatric group the same patterns of attachment are associated with the same patterns of adult relationships and feelings as those found in both the bereaved members of this control group and the bereaved psychiatric patients. This provides further confirmation that these influences are consistent, valid and cannot have arisen by chance. Thus, reported Anxious/Ambivalent Attachments in childhood were associated with Clinging and Anxiety/Panic in adult life, Avoidant Attachments were associated with Emotional Inhibition and difficulty in expressing feelings of sadness/grief and Disorganised Attachments with Overall Distress, and an increase in the End of Tether Turn In score.

There were a few anomalous findings. Those non-bereaved controls who received high scores of Disorganised Attachment differed from non-bereaved patients (but resembled both bereaved patients and the bereaved controls) in reporting increased levels of anxiety and alcohol consumption. On the other hand, they showed little of the loneliness and grief reported by the other three groups. This suggests that it is possible for people who have experienced disorganised attachments in childhood to develop coping strategies that enable them to obtain the social support that usually protects them from loneliness and psychiatric disorder. Even so, this support does not protect them from anxiety. They remain liable to use alcohol as a tranquilliser and, if they should suffer bereavement, they remain vulnerable to intense grief and loneliness.

Attachment and trauma

Returning to the psychiatric sample, although attachment problems played as large a part in the histories of non-bereaved as bereaved patients there was great variation in the problems to which they gave rise and it would be misleading to take the case of Ellen Glazer as our sole example. Another substantial group were people whose illness was triggered by a manifestly traumatic life event. One such was Philip Edwards.

Philip (aged 39) was referred to me three years after the discovery that he had a malignant pelvic tumour. Subsequently, he had become anxious, tense, irritable and depressed.

The only child of a furniture restorer and his wife, who worked shifts in a factory, both parents were inconsistent and neither could show affection. Philip was he says, 'pampered but not loved'. His mother worried about money and worked unsociable shifts. He describes her as a 'career person', by which he seems to mean that she cared more about her work than she did him. She was seldom there when needed. Philip was left in the care of his ageing paternal grandmother.

When he was 6 years of age Philip's mother was injured in a road traffic accident. Thereafter he became preoccupied with the fear that she would die. He could not concentrate on his work at school and did less well than his intelligence led people to expect.

An insecure, timid child, Philip suffered from nightmares, bit his nails and grew up solitary and distrustful of others. On the RAQ he received moderately high scores of Anxious/Ambivalent (12) and Avoidant Attachment (6). His Disorganised Attachment score was low (1).

Leaving school he obtained a clerical post in the civil service and did quite well. He achieved regular promotion, but he worried a lot about his work and found the added responsibilities, as he grew more senior, an increasing source of stress.

Against his mother's advice, he married, at 25, to a fellow clerk and they had two children. His wife was a kind, tolerant person and he describes their relationship as 'unusually close'.

The discovery of cancer was a shock, which undermined his fragile confidence and triggered severe anxiety and panic, but this was an operable tumour and he subsequently made a good recovery. During the course of his illness he took time off work. This removed a major source of stress and his emotional symptoms improved greatly, only to return when he went back to work.

When I saw him three years after his diagnosis he was physically recovered but remained depressed, anxious and inclined to use alcohol on his way home from work in order to relieve tension. He admitted that he was drinking more than was good for him and this had created a rift with his wife. He felt guilty about his behaviour and made matters worse by attempting to assuage his guilt by buying 'silly gifts' which he could not afford. He often felt at the end of his tether and in his RAQ indicated that at such times he was inclined to shut himself away from other people, drown his sorrows with alcohol, become irritable and bad tempered and turn his frustration inwards, feeling guilty and self-reproachful. He found it difficult to show both affection and grief and wished he could cry more than he did.

During our first three meetings we made little progress. He refused to tell his wife that he was seeing a psychiatrist or to talk to her about his problems. Tensions were building up at work and things came to a head when his wife found him shut in his garage with the engine of the car turned on. This event had a singular effect on his family who suddenly began to take seriously his need for help. It was also at this time that he was able to acknowledge his need for his wife's support. He invited her to attend our meetings and she accepted.

In the course of the next year he accepted an offer from his employers of retirement on medical grounds, following which he found a new and rewarding role for himself as 'house husband' and nurturer of the children. He stopped drinking and agreed to take an antidepressant drug, Lofepramine, but before the drug could take effect he was already beginning to feel very much better.

When followed up a year after the ending of therapy he had stopped all medication. The RAQ confirmed that he had improved in many ways. Although he was still sometimes anxious, lacked confidence and found it hard to show affection and grief, he was no longer depressed, tense or using alcohol. He had lost his former shyness and isolation and felt that he was able to cope with his responsibilities. He was no longer inclined to turn in on himself if at the end of his tether.

His relationship with his wife had improved and he was now able to confide in her. The two of them had become very close and he described them as mutually dependent.

Work seems to have been a central issue in Philip's life. He blamed his mother's lack of care on her devotion to her career. He then disappointed her by his failure at school and in later life found no satisfaction in his own career, believing that he had been promoted above his ability. His failure to confide in his wife may reflect an assumption that, as the man of the family, he should succeed as well as her. This was matched by a deep-seated expectation that he would fail. Although he never admitted it, he may also have begun to worry about the effect on his two young children of having two parents who, like his own, had demanding careers.

His illness was terrifying at first and a real threat to his survival. It disrupted an assumptive world that was already insecure and provoked severe and disabling anxiety. But it also provided him with an opportunity to escape for a while from the stresses of work. This resulted in a temporary improvement in his symptoms, but when he returned to work his fragile sense of security again collapsed and he was driven to a dramatic 'cry for help'. Fortunately his cry was heard and subsequent events enabled him to discover a new identity. For a while there was a real danger that his temporary solution to his problem, the adoption of a sick role, would lead to chronic disablement; but in devoting himself to the care of his wife and children he was able to give them the unstinted nurture that, as a child, he had lacked. He also seems to have discovered that it was safe to confide in his wife and, although his attachment problems did not disappear, he found it much easier to tolerate them.

Philip's mother seems to have instilled in him the assumption that he was doomed to fail in the most important thing in life, work. His illness taught him that he could survive, not only cancer but also unemployment. In taking on a nurturant role, which is more commonly assigned to women in our society, he discovered a new world in which he could succeed as father and husband.

Both of these cases exemplify the Mixed Attachment patterns (discussed on pp. 119–20). They confirm our expectation that it is not only after bereavements that insecure attachments can give rise to psychiatric problems. Although in both cases they were triggered by life events, in Ellen's case pregnancies and in Philip's a malignant tumour, the significance of these events can only be understood in the special context in which they took place. In both cases the successful adoption of nurturant roles went some way to counteract the influence of insecure attachments in childhood.

Conclusions

In this study bereavement has turned out to be a spotlight that has enabled us to identify important antecedents of mental illness and other psychological problems. These influences are most clearly seen in psychiatric patients when an attachment is interrupted by bereavement, but the evidence presented in this chapter suggests that attachments contribute to a variety of other problems and disorders whether or not the sufferer experiences a bereavement and/or seeks psychiatric help.

Across all four samples, bereaved and non-bereaved, psychiatric patients and non-psychiatric, the patterns of parenting, childhood vulnerability, coping strategies and emotions in adult life with which they are associated show marked similarities. This suggests that these patterns of attachment are consistently and reliably associated with these consequences. They are not a peculiarity of the minority of bereaved people who seek psychiatric help.

People who report secure attachments in childhood make secure attachments in adult life and remain more secure. Those with anxious/ambivalent attachments in childhood continue to lack confidence and express more anxiety in adult life. Those with avoidant attachments remain emotionally independent and distrusting. Those with disorganised attachments remain inclined to turn in on themselves and are more easily distressed.

Although these patterns were found in the non-psychiatric comparison group as well as the psychiatric, the social support that, as we have seen, distinguished the bereaved controls from the bereaved psychiatric group also distinguished the two non-bereaved groups. It seems that only those people who, either through misfortune or lack of social skills, are unable to find the support that they need from friends and family eventually seek it from psychiatric sources. These social supports are themselves part of the web of love in which we are all entangled.

Given the fact that those patients in the psychiatric group who had attachment problems requested psychiatric help, it is important to ask whether their psychiatric problems justify recognition as disorders of attachment. Can love become a disorder?

In the next chapter we shall consider whether or not insecure attachments in childhood can give rise to disorders of attachment in adult life that justify the designation of new categories of psychiatric diagnosis.

17 Disorders of attachment

Griefe all in sables sorrowfully clad,
Downe hanging his dull head with heavie cheare,
Yet inly beine more, ten seeming sad,
A paire of pincers in his hand he had,
With which, he pinched people to the heart,
That from thenceforth, a wretched life they lad,
In wilful languor and consuming smart,
Dying each day with impair'd wounds of dolors dart.
                    Edmund Spenser *The Faerie Queen* (1596)

We have seen how attachment patterns can contribute to problems in both bereaved and non-bereaved people. In this chapter we consider the question: Are the problematic patterns of insecure attachment that have emerged from this study sometimes so distinctive, severe and disabling as to justify the designation of a diagnosis of attachment disorder? If so, how do they equate with established psychiatric diagnoses? (Details of the statistical analysis relevant to these questions are given in Appendix 17.)

Before attempting to answer these questions I must confess to some reluctance to undertake this enterprise. My reluctance stems from a fear that by identifying certain types of problematic attachment as indicating an 'attachment disorder' I shall do more harm than good. The popular prejudice against psychiatric illness is such that there is a danger that people identified as suffering from such a disorder may find themselves stigmatised, denigrated and treated as 'abnormal'. Indeed it is widely believed that psychiatric disorders represent deviation from the 'norm' and that the aim of therapy is to restore normality. Psychiatric disorders are treated as a 'weakness' to which only those of inferior stock are liable.

An alternative view, which I hold, is that the more we understand about the situations faced by people who seek psychiatric help, the more we find that all of us are vulnerable. Indeed, most psychiatric patients are normal people faced with abnormal situations. They deserve our sympathy for their suffering and our respect for their attempts to face up to their problems. The aim of therapy is to relieve their distress and restore functioning. Of course, there are a few psychiatric patients who are suffering from diseases of the brain but this is not their fault. They are a small minority and they too deserve our sympathy and support rather than our condemnation.

If we allow our fear of the stigma of mental illness to deter us from making an appropriate diagnosis we collude with and perpetuate the stigma. On the other hand, if we grasp the nettle and make it plain to our patients that none of us is immune to problems of love and grief and that, at such times, some will need and benefit from specialist help, we shall open the door to a more humane society.

While the risk of stigma is real it may not outweigh the advantages of a psychiatric diagnosis. People who are recognised as suffering from such disorders are entitled to receive help. Health and social services become available to them and they may be excused, for a time, from responsibilities that they are currently unable to fulfil. In a recent study, Prigerson found that '95 per cent of persons who meet our criteria for CG [complicated grief] claim they would be helped in a variety of ways and not hurt [victimised, stigmatised] by the label'. Asked 'If you were diagnosed with a mental illness, would you be interested in receiving treatment for this condition?' 100 per cent replied 'Yes' (personal communication). It seems from these figures that people are quite capable of making up their own minds about whether or not they are prepared to accept any possible stigma that may arise and they have a positive attitude to treatment. Even so, in my view, such diagnoses should be reserved for people whose problems cause intolerable distress or are impairing their ability to function effectively in the fields of human activity that make life worthwhile.

In order to justify most psychiatric diagnoses, the authors of the fourth volume of the *Diagnostic Statistical Manual* (*DSMIV*) demand evidence of 'clinically significant distress or impairment in social, occupational or other important areas of functioning' (American Psychiatric Association 1994). These criteria are likely to be met by people who are no longer able to cope with their responsibilities in life, who are at the end of their tether and/or who rely on medication, alcohol or other drugs to enable them to cope with stress. In the RAQ these are covered by the questions that make up the Dysfunction score (see p. 310). This score was found to distinguish the psychiatric patients from Ward's non-psychiatric controls more clearly than any other score. Indeed, it would seem that it was their awareness of their own inability to continue to function effectively that caused most of these people to accept the help of a psychiatrist. Of the psychiatric sample 84 per cent had a Dysfunction score of two or more compared with only 19 per cent of controls. On this basis it seems justifiable to use a Dysfunction score of two or more as one of our criteria for diagnosing attachment disorders. Other criteria will be discussed below.

Established psychiatric diagnostic categories

We start by considering the existing diagnostic categories as formulated in *DSMIV* and will then ask to what extent they resemble categories derived from the current study. We shall find that, with modification, several of them could indeed be regarded as disorders of attachment.

DSMIV adopts a multi-axial system for assessing psychiatric disorders. In Axis I are placed most of the clinical disorders that we commonly think of as mental illnesses. These are distinguished from the Axis II disorders, which include personality disorders and mental retardation. This distinction recognises that many personality disorders co-exist with and may underlie the more obvious Axis I disorders that come to clinical attention. For example, a paranoid personality disorder may predispose people to paranoid schizophrenia.

Other disorders that may co-exist with and contribute to an Axis I disorder are general medical conditions and these are referred to in the multi-axial classification as Axis III. Thus hypothyroidism, which produces a deficiency of thyroid hormone, is an Axis III disorder, which may cause major depression (an Axis I disorder).

Finally it is recognised that many psycho-social problems and traumatic events, including bereavement, may also contribute to Axis I disorders. These are categorised as Axis IV problems but are not themselves diagnostic categories.

The preceding chapters reveal the sometimes complex interaction of the variables that contribute to the reaction to the Axis IV problem bereavement. Although some questions remain unresolved, the overall pattern is reasonably clear and consistent.

The *DSMIV* lists two types of Axis I disorder that can reasonably be regarded as attachment disorders: 'Separation Anxiety Disorder' and 'Reactive Anxiety Disorder of Infancy or Early Childhood'. Both of these originate in childhood and, it is claimed, rarely persist into adult life. They are described below.

Brennan and Shaver (1998) claim that two thirds of the underlying dimensions of adult personality disorders reflect adult patterns of attachment and the *DSMIV* lists four types of Axis II personality disorders which resemble the adult form taken by childhood attachment disorders (although they make no acknowledgement of this link): these are Dependent, Schizoid, Borderline and Avoidant Personality Disorder. They too will be considered below.

Is there an anxious/ambivalent attachment disorder?

Gladys Arnold was 25 years of age when she was referred to me for the assessment of longstanding feelings of separation anxiety. Her desperate need to cling had undermined a series of relationships and had repeatedly led to her being abandoned. Every time this occurred she had suffered an episode of severe depression and had come close to suicide. Far from her learning from experience, repeated rejection only caused her to cling harder and by the time she was referred to me this tendency had become so great that she would follow her latest boyfriend to the lavatory and wait outside the door until he came out.

Separation Anxiety Disorder is listed in *DSMIV* under 'Other Disorders of Infancy, Childhood, or Adolescence (309.21)' and is characterised by excessive anxiety on separation from home or from those to whom the child is attached. This interferes with social, academic and/or other important areas of functioning. It is often associated with severe homesickness, fears for the survival of parents or fears of being lost or otherwise separated from them. Children with this disorder often refuse to go to school or to other places necessitating separation. When separated their anxiety impairs their ability to concentrate or learn. Often they are afraid to be sent to bed and may have nightmares of disasters affecting their parents. Separation often causes physical symptoms reflecting anxiety and tension.

Although *DSMIV* does not make parental influence an essential criterion for the diagnosis, children with Separation Anxiety Disorder are recognised by *DSMIV* as coming from families that are unusually close; sometimes their mother is said to suffer from a panic disorder. The condition is reported in about 4 per cent of children and young adolescents. It may come on at any time but is particularly common after bereavements, illness in the child or parent, or change of home or school.

Separation Anxiety Disorder is said to be rare in adult life but I have my doubts. Liotti (1991) sees intolerance of separation from attachment figures as the essence of the common condition of agoraphobia (phobia of going out of the home). In each of 31 cases he claimed that 'early patterns of insecure-anxious attachment were the starting point of the development of agoraphobia'. According to Greenberg (1999) 'Separation Anxiety Disorder' is a risk factor for a number of adult psychiatric disorders, including depression, agoraphobia and panic disorder. In addition, the description in *DSMIV* of the Axis II category Dependent Personality Disorder (301.6) sounds much like an adult version of childhood Separation Anxiety Disorder: 'a pervasive and excessive need to be taken care of that leads to submissive and clinging behavior and fears of separation'. This is said to come on in early adulthood and no mention is made of a possible link to Separation Anxiety Disorder of childhood. We may suspect that the authors of this part of the DSM had not read the section on childhood disorders.

In the current study, the evidence presented in Chapter 5 indicates that, if their recollections are reliable, many of the people who scored highly on Anxious/Ambivalent Attachment would have met DSM criteria for Early Onset Separation Anxiety Disorder. Indeed, scrutiny of the wording of the questions suggests that a high score on Anxious/Ambivalent Attachment could be taken as an approximate measure of Childhood Separation Anxiety Disorder. Thus, it includes agreement with the following questions, I/17 (Did either parent give you the impression that the world is a very dangerous place in which children will not survive unless they stay very close?), II/14 (Were you afraid to be left alone or easily upset by separation from your parents?), II/17 (Did you feel helpless and unable to cope?), II/18 (Did people baby you and regard you as sweet and appealing?) and II/19 (Did people regard you as a delicate or fragile child?). In addition, the Unusual Closeness score was high in this group indicating that these children had been unusually close to their parents.

Returning to Gladys, she was the younger by seven years of two children of a carpenter and his wife. Her father she describes as an aloof, distant man who had never wanted a daughter. He suffered from an industrial disease, which caused increasing disability, dependence on his wife and, in later years, on Gladys. This brought them closer together in an anxious, mutually dependent relationship.

Mother was a dominant woman who both 'smothered' and denigrated Gladys. She was inconsistent and overprotective, discouraging Gladys from playing with other children. Gladys's mother preferred and idolised her older brother, Gerald. But he was also an insecure child who disliked and abused Gladys.

A positive influence in Gladys's early life was that of her maternal grandfather, whom she loved and trusted, but he died when she was 6 years of age. Gladys remembers vividly the occasion of his death. Hearing a noise she crept downstairs to find strange people doing extraordinary things to him. She mistook the attempt to resuscitate him for an assault and tried to interfere; the doctor shouted at her to go away. 'My world came to an end,' she says. Thereafter, she kept mistaking the identity of people in the street as her grandfather and getting a shock when she realised her mistake. At night she experienced recurrent dreams of him being resuscitated.

From this time she became extremely anxious that other members of her family would die. So fearful was she of separation from her parents that she malingered in order to avoid going to school.

In her replies to the RAQ she revealed herself as having been an insecure, anxious and unhappy child who was fearful of separation from her parents but distrustful of them and of all adults throughout her childhood. She was reluctant to visit new places, an under-achiever at school and a passive child, waiting for others to tell her what to do. She had a very high score of Anxious/ Ambivalent Attachment (24, the highest in the sample), and above average scores of Avoidant Attachment (6) and Disorganised Attachment (8).

Gladys shows much evidence of having suffered a childhood Separation Anxiety Disorder to which both her Anxious/Ambivalent Attachment to her parents and the death of her grandfather contributed.

Do the Separation Anxiety Disorders of childhood continue into adult life?

As we have seen, our data suggest that they sometimes do. Anxious/ Ambivalent Attachment in childhood was associated with higher scores of current Grief/Loneliness and Anxiety/Panic in adult life than were found among other patients, both bereaved and non-bereaved (see pp. 82–4). In bereaved people it also predicted the score of Clinging, which includes positive replies to the questions: 'Do you sometimes rely on others more than you should?' (IV/15), 'Do you often wish that someone would look after you?' (IV/16) and 'Have you recently got to the end of your tether?' (IV/18). These tendencies may also explain the association of Anxious/Ambivalent Attachment with increased levels of Marital Disagreements.

At the age of 16 Gladys engaged to marry an equally insecure young man who became addicted to drugs and violent towards her. They soon separated and in desperation she took an overdose but suffered no serious damage to her health. Her security was further undermined when her parents told her that they would both kill themselves if she tried again!

She then started training as a nurse and before long formed a relationship with a male nurse by whom she became pregnant. By the time her son was born this relationship was very rocky and following the birth she suffered a severe post-natal depression and was unable to care for the baby. Her boyfriend chose this time to leave her for another woman. While she was grieving for this loss, another man, who was sympathetic towards her supported her. She clung to him and before long they were cohabiting. But Gladys was distrustful, suspicious of his fidelity and experienced severe panic attacks, with hyperventilation, if separated. He was the partner whom she would follow when he went to the lavatory.

Gladys received courses of psychotherapy and hypnotherapy without benefit and was referred to me in the hope that I would help her come to terms with the death of her grandfather. By this time her clinging had destroyed the relationship with this partner, who left her after our first interview.

Gladys suffered quite the most severe Separation Anxiety Disorder that I have met. This was manifested, in childhood, by clinging to her mother after her grandfather's death and by her refusal to go to school. In adult life it was apparent in her intense clinging to the men in her life, most of whom found this intolerable. Her choice of partners was not good and may have reflected her desperation and low valuation of herself. The pattern of clinging and rejection was repeated several times and each rejection left her more anxious and more inclined to cling to the next man who came her way.

Gladys knew very well that her treatment of her boyfriend was unreasonable and her decision to seek psychiatric help implies that she was prepared to accept any stigma that resulted. Her boyfriend had been pushing her into therapy and his choice of this time to leave her implies that he felt that he could now get 'off the hook', leaving her in the hands of someone more expert than himself. However unreasonable this rationalisation, there is no reason to believe that he would have stuck by her if she had refused referral.

Although separation from her boyfriend gave rise to great distress and to threats of suicide, Gladys soon began to improve. Her parents lived nearby and she was able to spend her evenings with them. She felt that she was not the only party to benefit from this. 'I am their life,' she remarked. It was at this time that she chose to tell her mother about the abuse which she had experienced from her brother. Mother confessed that she too had been abused by *her* brother as a child and had also had a 'suffocating' relationship with her own mother. Clearly the anxious/ambivalent attachment had been passed through two generations. I saw the two of them together for a while and was impressed by their ability to make sense of the problems that they shared.

Gladys made repeated attempts to relate to and nurture her baby but her lack of confidence was very apparent and, on one occasion, she lost her temper and slapped the child. She then rushed from the house. As time passed, however, she tried again and began to find satisfaction in the relationship although she remained an anxious mother.

Things improved rapidly when she met another young man. He

accompanied her to an interview with me and held her hand throughout the session. She had been warned of my coming retirement and coped surprisingly well with that event.

It is hard, at this time, to know whether this improvement resulted from the psychotherapy (which focused on helping her to understand her attachment problems), the antidepressant medication (Fluoxetine) that was prescribed, the intensive support that she received from her parents, or to a combination of all these things.

Two years later I received a letter from Gladys reporting that things had been going well for her until her father had suddenly died. 'I am totally devastated,' she wrote and 'finding it so hard to cope with not only my grief but that of my mother and Gerald' [her brother]. I referred her to an experienced bereavement counsellor and heard nothing more.

It is clear, from these details that, Gladys's dependent personality disorder was the continuation into adult life of a childhood separation anxiety disorder. It seriously impaired her ability to function effectively in her relationships with members of the opposite sex and with her own children, as well as leading to disabling anxiety and depression whenever her relationships foundered or she suffered bereavement. It is particularly poignant that the very behaviour that spoiled her relationships, and eventually drove away her partners, had arisen as a means of staying close to her mother and achieving a measure of security.

It seems reasonable to conclude, from the evidence presented here, that anxious/ambivalent attachments may continue into adult life, provoking conflicts and predisposing people to cling and to grieve intensely when separated or bereaved. These findings suggest that problems of separation anxiety do not come to an end with adult life and that they often become more evident after bereavement.

My own interest in separation anxiety disorders arose from recognising the part that they play in chronic grief. This is the commonest form of complicated grief and is characterised by painfully intense and protracted pining for the lost person, which continues for a great length of time and may be associated with suicidal motivation. A problem that exists in making this diagnosis is the difficulty in distinguishing it from anxiety, depression and other psychiatric disorders. Although not yet accepted by DSM, clear diagnostic criteria which overcome this problem, have been formulated by Prigerson *et al.* (1996) and Jacobs (1999) whose definition of complicated grief includes both chronic and delayed reactions. Unfortunately their work was not published until after this study was carried out and I was unable to make use of their diagnostic criteria in the analysis of my own data. I collaborated with members of this group in carrying out a study that confirms an association between childhood separation anxiety and complicated grief. This showed that bereaved people who obtained high scores of Childhood Separation Anxiety also had high scores on Prigerson's measure of Complicated Grief after bereavement (Vanderwerker *et al.* 2006).

In the current study the best indicators of chronic grief are, in my opinion, high scores of Grief/Loneliness, Anxiety/Panic and Clinging. All of these were significantly correlated with high scores of childhood Anxious/ Ambivalent Attachments and it seems that it is these attachments that most often contribute to chronic grief. This does not mean that they are the sole cause of chronic grief. Indeed the clinical diagnosis of chronic grief did not correlate with the Anxious/Ambivalent Attachment score. Among 25 individuals who had been diagnosed as having chronic grief, 10 had low scores on all three measures of insecure attachment. However, scrutiny of the case notes in these ten cases showed that in only three was there no evidence of attachment problems. In all of the others, attachment problems were very evident but these were associated with bereavements in later childhood and/or idealised relationships with parents, both of which are compatible with low scores of Insecure Attachment.

Criteria for a separation anxiety disorder of adult life

The RAQ was not designed as a diagnostic instrument and the criteria that follow should not be treated as definitive. Further research is needed to improve them. However, they do enable us to begin the process of 'guessing and testing' from which diagnostic criteria can be developed.

The Clinging score and the Anxiety/Panic score correlated highly with the Dysfunction score. There was also a significant association between increased Dysfunction score and positive answers to question IV/11 'Are you very lonely?' (see Appendix 17, p. 384). This suggests that a combination of these scores could reasonably be taken as an indicator of Separation Anxiety Disorder. As a first step in using the RAQ to identify Separation Anxiety Disorders in adult life, irrespective of bereavement, an arbitrary decision was made to use the following criteria all of which had to be met:

- IV/47 Clinging score of 2 or more.
- Answers 'Yes' to IV/11 'Are you very lonely?'
- IV/44 Anxiety/Panic score of 3 or more.
- IV/50 Dysfunction score of 2 or more.

Although the question about loneliness comes from the Grief/Loneliness score the full score has not been included. This has been done to make the instrument more useful in non-bereaved populations.

Another factor, which has been shown to correlate with Grief/Loneliness (p. 328), is a dependent relationship with a partner. But this has not been included as a diagnostic criterion here because many respondents did not have partners and it would be inappropriate to limit the diagnosis to those who have. It may be that the inclusion of the full Grief/Loneliness score and a measure of dependence on partners would improve the diagnosis of Separation Anxiety Disorder in bereaved and partnered subgroups. Indeed, it is likely that in clinical situations the disorder would be easier to diagnose after bereavement.

Bearing this in mind, it came as a surprise to find that, using these criteria, Separation Anxiety Disorder of adult life was found just as commonly in non-bereaved as in bereaved psychiatric patients. Nineteen (20 per cent) of the non-bereaved and 25 (14 per cent) of the bereaved psychiatric patients met these criteria for Separation Anxiety Disorder. The difference is not statistically significant.

When the analysis was confined to the matched bereaved psychiatric and control samples, 31 per cent of the psychiatric and only 5.7 per cent of the controls met criteria for Separation Anxiety Disorder in adult life; this difference is statistically significant. It confirms the expectation that the disorder is much more common among people seeking psychiatric help than among the controls.

As was to be expected there was a significant correlation between the childhood Anxious/Ambivalent score and Separation Anxiety Disorder in adult life. This said, not all people with Separation Anxiety Disorder had received high scores of Anxious/Ambivalent Attachment in childhood and many who had high scores of Anxious/Ambivalent Attachment did not subsequently develop a Separation Anxiety Disorder in adult life.

It is not possible, from these data, to know how well people with Separation Anxiety Disorders of adult life would have met *DSMIV* criteria for Dependent Personality Disorder, nor does the clinical data allow us to distinguish between the various personality disorders. This said, I can see no reason to separate the two diagnoses without further evidence.

Women with Separation Anxiety Disorders outnumbered men in both bereaved and non-bereaved psychiatric groups, but the differences were greatest in the bereaved group. This gender distribution resembles that of bereaved and non-bereaved patients without Separation Anxiety disorders. Those with Separation Anxiety Disorders also resembled the other psychiatric patients in their average age (39 years) and year of birth.

Conclusion

In general it seems that there is no need to formulate a separate category of Separation Anxiety Disorder of adult life, but to classify both Separation Anxiety Disorder of childhood and Dependent Personality Disorder of adult life within the rubric of Attachment Disorders. Further research is needed to discover how often and why Dependent Personality Disorders in adult life sometimes occur without a previous Separation Anxiety Disorder in childhood. This research begins to explain the origin of such disorders and should help us to develop effective preventive programmes and treatments.

Is there an Avoidant Attachment Disorder?

Although there is no diagnosis in *DSMIV* comprising a severe form of the Avoidant Attachment of Childhood in the way that Separation Anxiety Disorders of Childhood reflect the Anxious/Ambivalent Attachment, there is reason to believe that such a disorder exists. Thus Juliet Hopkins (1991) gives a vivid description of what she calls 'failure of the holding relationship'. The following case study comes from that paper.

> Clare, aged 6 when referred for therapy, was the only child of a mother who had found her physically repellent from birth. To avoid touching her child she had propped Clare's feeding bottle on a pillow and kept her in her playpen all day. Clare became extremely independent, refusing cuddles and never asking for help or crying, even when hurt. She was referred because of recurrent nightmares about lepers. Clare explained that lepers were contagious which meant that 'if they touch someone they die'. She thought that they could be cured by the laying on of hands.
>
> In therapy she came to see that she felt herself to be a leper that no one wanted to touch because she would kill them and was tortured by her longing to touch and be touched by the therapist and by her terror of it.

The paper goes on to describe how Hopkins was able to work sensitively with both the child and mother to gradually overcome the child's fears. More recently the value of 'therapeutic holding' has been recognised and made use of by other therapists (Welch 1988; Fahlberg 1990; Howe and Fearnley 1999).

An adult approximation to this disorder is included in *DSMIV* as Schizoid Personality Disorder (301.20). This is characterised by 'a pervasive pattern of detachment from social relationships and a restricted range of expression of emotions in interpersonal settings'. This condition is assumed to begin in early adulthood but it contains many of the features that, in the current study, were associated with avoidant attachments in childhood. The criteria make no clear distinction between people who lack feelings (the emotionally cold), and people who have feelings but are unable to express them, perhaps because such a distinction is not easy to make. Nevertheless I would argue that this distinction is crucial. In the current study there was evidence to support the diagnosis of Avoidant Attachment Disorder in both childhood and adult life.

Frederick Emerson was 42 when referred to me eight months after the accidental death of his son. He told me that he had always been a solitary person and added, 'Life is an act . . . I don't know what the real me is.' When asked what he would do when at the end of his tether, he said he would not seek for help from his family or friends but would drown his sorrows in alcohol and become irritable and bad tempered.

The death of his 17-year-old son resulted from youthful risk taking and was totally unexpected. Fred started drinking heavily because he found that he could only express grief when he was under the influence of alcohol. He needed this disinhibition and then felt better. But his wife felt unsupported and objected to his drinking. At one point she left him, but he waited for her at their son's graveside and persuaded her to return.

In childhood, parents who were reported to have high Parental Insensitivity scores, which included agreement with the statement that a parent had been 'Unable to show warmth or to hug or cuddle you' had children who assigned to themselves high Childhood Aggressiveness/ Distrust scores. This included agreement that, as a child the person would 'find it hard to accept cuddles or other demonstrations of affection' (II/26), would distrust adults through much of their childhood (II/20), would be controlling, 'bossy' (II/28), bad tempered (II/29), stubborn (II/31) and in trouble for aggressive or antisocial behaviour (II/30). Taken together these replies comprised the Avoidant Attachment score

Frederick had been the eldest of seven children of an Irish street trader who had teased him and, at times, beat him more than most parents. Neither parent had been able to show warmth or to hug or cuddle him and Fred had grown up unable to accept cuddles or other demonstrations of affection. He was seen as tough and stubborn but under the surface he felt fearful. At the age of 13 he was sexually abused by an older youth but kept this to himself. His RAQ showed him to have an above average score on Avoidant Attachment (5), and below average Disorganised Attachment (2) and Anxious/Ambivalent Attachment (3) scores.

At 16 Frederick met and three years later married Betty, a girl whose background was as deprived as his own. From time to time he would binge on alcohol and this, along with his tendency to overspend money, led to marital disagreements. He admitted that he found it hard to show affection for Betty and for other people close to him.

In Chapter 6 we saw that people who reported high childhood Avoidant Attachment scores, also reported difficulties in later life in expressing both affection and grief (as reflected in high scores of Emotional Inhibition/ Distrust). They also saw themselves as more aggressive and assertive than others in their relationships (with high scores of Aggressive/Assertiveness).

Both the Emotional Inhibition/Distrust and the Aggressive/Assertiveness scores were significantly correlated with the Dysfunction score. This seems to imply that people with high scores on all three of these measures may well be suffering from an adult Avoidant Attachment Disorder. To examine this further an arbitrary decision was made to include in the putative diagnostic category, Avoidant Attachment Disorder, those who met the following criteria:

1   Emotional Inhibition score 3 or more.
2   Aggressive/Assertive score 2 or more.
3   Dysfunction score of 2 or more.

The proportion in both the bereaved and non-bereaved psychiatric samples was 14 per cent. There was only one person among the 35 young women in Ward's matched non-psychiatric control group who met these criteria compared with six (18 per cent) in the psychiatric group.

The average scores of Avoidant Attachment in childhood were six in the group with Avoidant Attachment Disorder and three in those without it. The difference is significant, but is still only a moderate level of correlation. This seems to imply that although avoidant attachments in childhood are associated with Avoidant Attachment Disorder in adult life, they do not fully explain them.

Another factor expected to contribute to Avoidant Attachment Disorders was male sex but this did not prove to be the case. The proportion of men with Adult Avoidant Disorder (18 per cent) was virtually the same as that of women (16 per cent). Those with Avoidant Attachment Disorder had slightly fewer marital disagreements than those without. They may have been better able to avoid quarrels. Even so, no less than 70 per cent say that they are 'filled with regret for things which they did or said but cannot now put right' (IV/24). This statement was agreed by under a half (45 per cent) of the other psychiatric patients.

An unexpected finding was that the average age of those with Avoidant Attachment Disorders in adult life was six years younger than that of the rest (mean 35 and 41 years) and this difference was statistically significant. But even more significant than age was the correlation between Avoidant Attachment Disorder and year of birth. Figure 17.1 shows that among the psychiatric patients born before the end of the Second World War Avoidant Attachment Disorder comprised less than 8 per cent of the sample, whereas in each decade born after the war 15–20 per cent fulfilled the criteria for this diagnosis. These figures are taken from the full psychiatric sample but

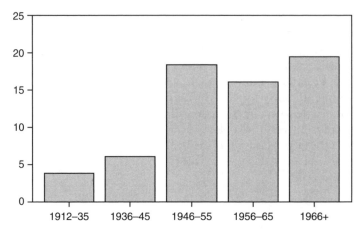

Figure 17.1 Percentage of Attachment Disorders in each decade of birth (full sample
of psychiatric patients n = 277)

were also statistically significant when bereaved respondents were analysed
separately.

A similar picture emerges when we look at the relationship between year of
birth and the average childhood Avoidant Attachment score. Here again
there is a significant correlation with people born before the First World War
having the lowest Avoidant Attachment scores and those born after 1965 the
highest. This suggests that it may have been the changes in child rearing that
began during and became more influential after the Second World War that
explains both the increasing numbers of avoidant attachments and the
increased risk of Avoidant Attachment Disorder. It is tempting to attribute
this to changes in child rearing, but the sheer number of other social, eco-
nomic and cultural changes that have come about over this period of time
makes it dangerous to speculate.

Summary of statistical findings

The evidence presented here supports the hypothesis that there is an Avoidant
Attachment Disorder in adult life that is often associated with avoidant
attachments in childhood. The affected people find it hard to express emotions, particularly those of affection and grief. Their fear of relying on
others makes it hard for them to ask for help and their relationships
with others are often based on control and aggression rather than affection.
Other people tend to assume that they do not care, but the evidence
suggests that avoidant people are attached and that they care as much
as others. Most blame themselves because they are unable to show it.
They are hurt by attributions of coldness. It seems that both avoidant
attachments in childhood and Avoidant Attachment Disorders of adult life

have become more frequent in people who have been born since the Second World War.

The case notes indicate that the 'romantic relationships' of people with Avoidant Attachment Disorders are singularly unromantic. Their partners complain that they do not express affection and will not talk things through. They may be adroit at avoiding quarrels but this does not mean that their partners are happy. Some have chosen partners equally intolerant of closeness. In that event they may organise their lives in such a way that they seldom touch each other. When they do meet, issues of dominance and control are likely to spoil their interactions. The children of such unions are exposed to the same avoidant attachments and this may perpetuate the problem from generation to generation.

People with Avoidant Attachment Disorders are not unaware of the 'childish' roots of their problems. In fact they often blame themselves for their inability to show feelings or to confront emotional issues. Some recognise that their apparent independence is a sham. At the same time they blame themselves for being unable to control themselves and circumstances as they should. Far from the compulsive independence which they show to the world, they live in fear of breaking down, panicking or allowing powerful emotions to break through.

At first, some people in the current study with strong Avoidant Attachment Disorders appeared to cope well with bereavements. Their lack of overt grief and their reluctance to ask for help led others to assume that they did not need support. Only later did it become apparent that their compulsive independence was a cover-up. At this point some experienced a breakthrough of delayed grief or turned in on themselves and became depressed. Some developed psychosomatic symptoms reflecting chronic anxiety and tension, others became irritable and subject to outbursts of anger or rage. Yet others reacted immediately to the bereavement but found the break-through of emotion extremely distressing and did their best to inhibit or conceal it. Indeed, some experienced severe anxiety and panic but were quite unable to cry. Expressions of grief and anger, which others would see as appropriate, gave rise to fear and were seen as a sign of incipient mental collapse. People often feared that if they 'broke down' and showed feelings they would indeed have a 'nervous breakdown'.

When I first met him Frederick was very lonely and afraid, inclined to panic and fearful that he might give vent to feelings of grief and rage that welled up inside him. To express anger would make him like his father, an identity that he rejected.

Fred's wife attended with him for three sessions in which, for the first time, he was able to cry and to share other feelings as well as to take stock of his life. He substantially reduced his consumption of alcohol and was able to deal sensibly with a crisis, which arose when he discovered that his surviving son was having an affair with his best friend's wife.

On follow-up, two months after our final meeting, he was less anxious and grieving less. He felt that he was now able to share grief and affection for his wife.

It would be easy to attribute Fred's problems to alcoholism but he needed alcohol because it enabled him to overcome the emotional disability from which he suffered. His Avoidant Attachment Disorder stultified his emotional life and prevented him from grieving for his son. His childhood experience had left him wary of spontaneity, life was 'an act'. The aim of therapy was not to stop him from drinking, but to help him and his wife to understand that it was safe for them to share their thoughts and feelings. When they did this the need for alcohol as a means of dissolving emotional inhibition diminished.

A possible explanation for the failure of the authors of the DSM to include Avoidant Attachment Disorder as a separate category lies in its social acceptability. In a society in which many parents take little part in educating their children (who are separated from them in schools and taught to be independent, to control emotions and to achieve distinction by intellectual effort), and in which adults are expected to work at a distance from their parental homes and to keep their emotions to themselves, the characteristics of control, unflappability and detachment are seen as virtues, while spontaneity, emotionality and involvement are evidence of weakness. This value system, as we saw in Chapter 10, is most pronounced in men.

Conclusion

In common with other diagnostic categories, avoidant behaviours only justify the designation of a 'disorder' if they lead to 'clinically significant distress or impairment in social, occupational or other important areas of functioning'. Among the people who, like Fred, sought psychiatric help in the current study, it was clear that this was indeed the case. It seems that there are grounds for recognising an Avoidant Attachment Disorder both in childhood and adult life.

Is there a Disorganised Attachment Disorder?

Disorganised disorders in childhood

Much has been written about the damaging effects on children of parental neglect and separation. In *DSMIV* this has given rise to a diagnostic category Reactive Anxiety Disorder of Infancy or Early Childhood (313.89). This requires both grossly pathological parenting and disturbance of social relatedness in the child. The problems in parenting include persistent disregard of the child's physical or emotional needs (for comfort, stimulation and affection) and/or repeated changes of primary caregiver such that the child is unable to form a stable attachment. The disturbance of relatedness in the child may take one of two forms:

1   The *Inhibited type* in which the child fails to initiate or respond to most social interactions in an appropriate way. He or she shows a pattern of inhibited, hypervigilant or highly ambivalent responses to others.
2   The *Disinhibited type* in which the child exhibits indiscriminate sociability or a lack of selectivity in the choice of attachment figures. This may place the child at risk of abuse that may, in turn, aggravate the disorder.

In addition to the problems of parenting, extreme poverty and lengthy hospitalisation are mentioned as predisposing to this disorder, which may be accompanied by other evidence of abuse or neglect. The condition is said to begin before the age of 5 years and tends to persist unless there is improvement in the quality of child care. In many ways this disorder is less distinctive and clear-cut than the foregoing disorders, which makes it less satisfactory as a diagnosis. By lumping together several causes and two patterns of response the authors have created a catch-all diagnosis.

Many of the parenting characteristics seem to resemble those reported here in the Disorganised group. The designation of Reactive Anxiety Disorder of Infancy as an anxiety disorder, despite the absence of anxiety as a diagnostic criterion, may reflect recognition of the part played by insecurity in this condition. Few of the features of the disorder, as described above, were included in the RAQ but they were often reported in the case notes. The Inhibited form may have included some people who, in the current study, met criteria for the avoidant pattern.

It seems that children brought up in families in which there were high levels of violence, rejection, danger and/or depression tend to be unhappy and to lack trust in themselves and others. They show the negative aspects of both anxious/ambivalence and avoidance. Thus their lack of confidence in themselves causes them to cry and at times to cling to others, but distrust of others spoils their relationships and they end up isolated and anxious. Having nowhere to turn they remain at high levels of anxiety which impairs their ability to learn so that they perform less well at school than expected. Some of them invert the parenting relationship and becomes compulsive carers of their own parents and others.

From her account of her childhood Barbara Fulton, now aged 50, may have suffered from the Inhibited form of Reactive Anxiety Disorder during her childhood.

She was the youngest in a large family. She described her mother as an alcoholic whose drinking made her an unreliable parent. A persistent worrier, mother had clung to her husband in a dependent way. She worried about Barbara's health and safety but was inconsistent and often ignored her needs for attention and affection. Barbara's father was similarly anxious and inconsistent and there were frequent quarrels at home both between her parents and her siblings. One gets the impression that, in this large family, there was little mutual support.

Barbara grew up insecure, anxious and unhappy. She cried a lot and lacked self-confidence but was inclined to be suspicious and distrustful of others. She felt helpless and unable to cope but was afraid to ask for help. Her anxieties grew so great that she refused to go to school and at the age of 9 was sent to a children's home. This only increased her fears and on several occasions she ran away from the home but was brought back.

Her RAQ showed her to have high scores of Disorganised (10) and Anxious/Ambivalent Attachment(16) and an average score on Avoidant Attachment (3).

Barbara illustrates the finding in the current study that people who describe their parents as so preoccupied with their own emotional needs that they are alternately unresponsive to and over-anxious about their child often describe themselves as unhappy children who may even have wished themselves dead (see p. 53). This justifies us in inferring that their attachment was disorganised and they could, as we have seen, be assigned to the imprecise category of Reactive Anxiety Disorder of Early Childhood. Even so many of their responses did not fit this category and are too unspecific to justify us in terming high scorers as suffering from a specific Disorganised Attachment Disorder. Further research is needed to clarify this issue.

Disorganised disorders in adult life

Among the disorders of adult life *DSMIV* includes an Axis II Avoidant Personality Disorder (301.82) that does seem to correspond to an adult version of the Inhibited form of Reactive Anxiety Disorder of Childhood. The condition is distinguished by '. . . a pervasive pattern of social inhibition, feelings of inadequacy, and hypersensitivity to negative evaluation'. The authors acknowledge that this disorder 'often starts in infancy or childhood with shyness, isolation and fear of strangers and new situations'. These people become increasingly shy and avoidant of social relationships during adolescence. This diagnosis would fit some of the people in the current study with high scores of Disorganised Attachment, especially if accompanied by a high Separation score; others would probably better fit the Avoidant Attachment category.

Another disorder described in *DSMIV* that may represent an adult form of disorganised attachment is Borderline Personality Disorder (310.83). This is distinguished by 'a pervasive pattern of instability of interpersonal relationships, self-image and affects' with impulsivity and most commonly 'frantic efforts to avoid real or imagined abandonment'. It is distinguished from Dependent Personality by 'feelings of emotional emptiness, rage and demands' in response to threats of loss rather than submission and appeasement. Other common features of Borderline Personality Disorder are unstable patterns of attachment alternating between idealisation and denigration, shifting self-image, goals and aspirations, recurrent suicidal or self-mutilating behaviour and episodes of irritability and anxiety often associated with inappropriate outbursts of anger. The condition begins by early adult life and commonly follows a childhood history of 'physical and sexual abuse, neglect, hostile conflict and early parental loss or separation'. It is hardly surprising that several studies have found that people with AAI patterns of Disorganised (Unresolved) Attachment are particularly likely to be diagnosed as having a Borderline Personality Disorder (Patrick *et al.* 1994; Barone 2003).

If, as seems clear from Chapter 7, disorganised attachments undermine a person's trust in themselves and others and leave them with few strategies for coping with stress, they are likely in adult life to be vulnerable to a range of psychiatric problems. In the current study, the recollection of a disorganised attachment pattern in childhood was associated, in adult life, with lack of trust in self and others. These adults remain insecure and feel unable to cope but, when faced with stress, they cannot ask for help; instead they turn in on themselves and feel frustrated and self-reproachful. After bereavement they react with severe anxiety or depression. A significant proportion used alcohol as an escape.

In adult life Barbara remained shy, insecure and fearful. She found it hard to trust people and her relationships were marred by ambivalence. At the age of 18 she became pregnant and had a son by a man who had no intention of marrying her.

Later she met and at 22 married Jim by whom she had a second son. There was much violence between the partners and the marriage ended in divorce 15 years ago since when she had remained on her own.

Barbara's first son was also inclined to aggression and violent outbursts and, in later years, was charged with murder. Although the charge was dropped he became depressed and took a non-fatal overdose of medication.

Barbara remained close to her mother from whom, despite her ambivalence, she found even short periods of separation distressing. But she was alone in her affection for, even when mother became ill, the rest of the family 'didn't want to know'.

After her mother's death Barbara blamed herself for not caring enough and grieved very intensely. Her longstanding anxiety increased and she had several panic attacks. She also felt very depressed and unable to cope. She had difficulty sleeping and admitted that she often took too many sleeping tablets. Although she wished that someone would look after her, in response to the question 'What would you do if you got to the end of your tether?' she said she would not turn to any living person but would shut herself away from other people, become irritable and bad tempered and turn her frustration inwards, feeling guilty or self-reproachful.

Barbara illustrates the consequences of a disorganised attachment, which continued into adult life and made her vulnerable to bereavement. Her parents had undermined their child's trust in herself and others. She expected rejection and often received it. Study of the case notes indicates that, like Barbara, those who score highly on Disorganised Attachment in childhood find it hard to make relationships with others. Those that they do make are to similarly insecure people and are complicated by ambivalence.

In adult life they tend to be afraid of their own children and are likely to be insensitive to the child's needs for autonomy. They often over-identify with their children, treating the child as they would wish to have been treated as a child. This makes them particularly vulnerable to separation and loss of these children (as shown in Chapter 12). Following bereavement they immediately suffer severe anxiety with a tendency to panic. Some turn to alcohol or other drugs as a means of escape, others may become depressed.

Seen in the clinic, Barbara at first appeared wary and defensive. It had taken a lot to persuade her to come and she was very apprehensive. Only when it was clear that I respected her priorities and had no hidden agenda did she begin to relax and tell me about her many problems.

Contrary to my initial expectation she responded well to a combination of antidepressant medication (Lofepramine) and four sessions of supportive psychotherapy aimed at helping her to understand the roots of her difficulties and to get them in proportion.

In psychotherapy she was able to understand the nature of the problem and to obtain a modicum of control for which she was grateful. However, she ended therapy without dealing with issues of ambivalence and I had the feeling that she wanted to get out of therapy while she was still winning; to continue was just too dangerous.

While Barbara's account includes features typical of disorganised attachments it also includes features of the other two groups. It may be more logical to think of disorganised attachments in adult life as a combination of the other two insecure attachment categories and regard them as a non-specific disorder of attachment rather than a specific disorganised attachment disorder.

Conclusion

These patterns help to explain the diagnoses described above but do not yet, in my opinion, have sufficient specificity to justify us in using the RAQ as a means of diagnosing a Disorganised Attachment Disorder. The problem is not that disorganised attachments do not cause problems but that many of the problems they cause are of a more variable and non-specific character than those which follow the other two patterns of attachment.

De Clérambeault's Syndrome

This rare attachment pyschosis is, misleadingly termed 'erotomania'. It shares with the disinhibited form of childhood Reactive Anxiety Disorder, a lack of sensitivity to the need for reciprocity in attachments, but in this case, of psychotic intensity. It is characterised by episodes of passionate attachment to senior or famous authorities, often doctors, who are unavailable, unresponsive and unwilling to reciprocate the patient's declarations of love. Patients hold to the delusion that their love is secretly welcome and they often harass the object of their attentions.

Final conclusions

It seems that love may not make the world go round but it can make it go 'pear shaped'. The conclusions reached in this chapter should be seen as a tentative first attempt at formulating diagnostic characteristics of Attachment Disorders. Based as they are on retrospective data applied to an atypical population, much further work will be needed if they are to become part of our accepted diagnostic system. I have little doubt that the patterns of attachment that underlie these attachment disorders are not the only relevant patterns, but will leave it to others to elucidate these.

Up to this time, the diagnosis of psychiatric disorders has relied mainly on accurate delineation of symptoms rather than on the identification of causes. It resembles the descriptive diagnoses of eighteenth-century medicine rather than the cause-related categories of the twentieth century. The diagnosis of post-traumatic stress disorder broke the mould and it is hoped that the attempt to delineate categories of attachment disorder which has begun in recent years and which continues here will take the process a step further.

Attachment disorders should be regarded as Axis II disorders that can contribute to a number of Axis I psychiatric disorders. In a similar way arterio-sclerosis can contribute to cause coronary thrombosis, strokes and many other physical illnesses. Perhaps the physical disorders most similar to attachment disorders are the vitamin deficiencies. Just as the functions of vitamins were discovered by studying what happens when they are absent from the diet, so the functions of attachment are clarified by studying bereavement. Just as malnutrition causes illnesses that are attributable to several deficiencies, so the mixed pictures which follow insecure attachments are attributable to several deficiencies. Table 17.1 sums up the categories of attachment disorder that have emerged from the analysis reported above and the *DSMIV* categories that overlap with them.

It would be misleading to suggest that all of the bereaved people included in this study were suffering from attachment disorders and no attempt has been made to define these so precisely that their frequency in this or other populations can be firmly established. Even so it does appear that, even in unselected, non-bereaved, psychiatric outpatients, attachment disorders are surprisingly common. The most common was Separation Anxiety Disorder, which was found in a quarter of non-bereaved and the same proportion of bereaved patients. Avoidant Attachment Disorders were less common but even they were found in 14 per cent of each group. Disorganised Attachment Disorders cannot at this time be clearly specified but may emerge from future studies as a distinct category.

Attachment disorders are closely related to complicated grief and the evidence presented here supports the work of Jacobs and his colleagues

Table 17.1 Classification of Insecure Attachments and related disorders

Insecure Attachment Pattern	Attachment Disorder	DSMIV and other in childhood	Categories in adulthood
Anxious/Ambivalent Attachment Pattern	Separation Anxiety Disorder	Separation Anxiety Disorder (309.21)*	Dependent Personality Disorder (301.6)*
Avoidant Attachment Pattern	Avoidant Attachment Disorder	Failure of the Holding Relationship (Hopkins)	Schizoid Personality Disorder (301.20)*
Disorganised Attachment and Mixed Patterns	Non-Specific Attachment Disorder	Reactive Anxiety Disorder (313.89)*	Avoidant and Borderline Personality Disorders (301.82, 301.83)*

* Figures refer to the numerical codes used in the 4th edition of the *Diagnostic Statistical Manual (DSMIV)*.

(Jacobs 1999; Vanderwerker *et al.* 2004), which suggests that complicated grief reactions should be regarded as distinct Axis I disorders that are commonly but not always a consequence of an Axis II attachment disorder. This evidence also indicates that the attachment disorders can be subdivided into two disorders (Separation Anxiety Disorder and Avoidant Attachment Disorder) corresponding to and often following on from the Anxious/ Ambivalent and the Avoidant Attachment Disorders of childhood, with a possible third category which contains elements of the other two.

It will also be apparent from the bereaved case examples given above that attachment disorders are apparent long before bereavement and that there are some cases in which the bereavement which triggered a request for help was only one incident in a long series of problems.

The poetry and prose of love is replete with praise of the ideal romantic love between men and women, yet any kind of relationship that is unconventional is denigrated. Homosexual love is a 'perversion', grown-ups who persist in loving their parents in the way they learned as children are condemned as 'dependent', and the mother or father who chooses to stay home in order to nurture children or an elderly relative is 'lazy'. Similar condemnation may also be directed at members of the caring professions who enjoy caring for others and are therefore 'over-involved', or if the client is a child suspected of paedophilia.

Society has many ways of expressing its disapproval and one of these is to label such unconventional attachments as 'sick'. It is important therefore to recognise that the aim of formulating criteria for diagnosing attachment disorders is not to confirm such labels, but refute their misuse. The term should be reserved for those whose attachments, far from fulfilling their needs, are frustrating and preventing them and those they love from achieving the peace of mind and satisfaction that they need.

The case of Philip Edwards (described in Chapter 16), illustrates this. In a work-oriented society, his decision to retire from work and become a 'house husband' might have been seen as a symptom of his attachment disorder. In fact it was the means by which he cured it. His children benefited from the nurture that they received, his wife was free to pursue her career and he achieved peace of mind, not by denying or altering his attachment pattern, but by finding a way of living with it.

18 Prevention, therapies and outcome

Love is a sickness full of woes,
All remedies refusing . . .

Samuel Daniel (1562–1619) *Hymen's Triumph*

Prevention

It is seldom possible to prevent bereavements and other disasters although the more we understand about the chains of events which lead to psychiatric problems the more we should be able to prepare people for the losses and other stresses that are to come, to reduce the risk and mitigate the worst consequences.

As a psychiatrist it has been my role to attempt to help people whose psychological problems have not been prevented and there will always be a need for some specialists to take this role. On the other hand it may well be the case that fewer people would need psychiatric treatment if the causal chains that lead to psychiatric disorders could be broken at an earlier point in the sequence. Since this book is concerned with such causal chains it makes sense to look at the implications of our findings for the prevention as well as the treatment of psychiatric problems, particularly those that follow bereavement.

It is not unreasonable to suppose that, if something has been learned, it can be unlearned. If, as the research reported here indicates, many people who seek psychiatric help after bereavement and other stresses have learned a distorted view of themselves and others, then it should be possible to correct those misperceptions. In this chapter we shall consider why this task is not quite as simple as it sounds and how it may, even so, be carried out.

Up to now, attempts to prevent psychiatric problems after bereavement have focused on the development of services for bereaved people that enable them to obtain early help with their problems without the need to 'go sick'. These range from various types of mutual help (or 'self-help'), to the provision of bereavement counsellors and other supporters who may or may not be professionals.

Changing patterns of attachment

Studies of attachment open the door to types of programme that might effectively reduce the risk of problematic bereavement by modifying attachments. The findings reported here indicate that, if successful, these benefits would have wide-ranging consequences and these would not be limited to bereavement. Such programmes range from developing ways of preparing parents for the birth of a child, improving the quality of parenting, identifying children at risk of attachment problems at an early age and intervening to reduce that risk. In adult life it includes helping people to understand and modify their assumptive worlds. In the field of bereavement and other loss, it includes preparing people for the losses that are to come, particularly in those individuals who are at special risk. None of these programmes fall within the province of the psychiatrist although other medical practitioners may have useful parts to play. They should not be seen as an attempt to medicalise normal life crises. Rather they hold out promise of reducing the need for such interventions.

There is good evidence that stillbirths are associated with an increased risk of clinical depression, anxiety and post-traumatic stress disorder (PTSD) in the mother. This has caused some authorities to recommend that mothers should be encouraged to see and hold their stillborn babies on the grounds that they are then less likely to suffer unresolved grief. But recent research has shown that holding and cuddling a dead baby is associated with an increase in anxiety, depression and PTSD, particularly at the time of the next pregnancy. On the other hand, mothers who opt not to see or touch their dead baby are less prone to these problems (Hughes *et al.* 2002). In addition these researchers have also shown that mothers who see and hold a dead baby are more likely than those who do not to develop a disorganised attachment with their next baby (as shown by the SST). If Main is right (see p. 14), this suggests that their grief for their dead child remains unresolved.

Given that seeing, holding and touching contribute to cement attachment between mothers and babies (see pp. 11–12), it may be that mothers who have not held or seen their baby become less attached to it and cope better with the loss. Furthermore, we have seen (p. 33) that witnessing horrific events, such as the face of a dead baby, can increase the risk of PTSD. It may well be the conjunction of these two factors that explain Hughes's findings. For further discussion of these issues see Reynolds (2004).

Another example of early intervention aimed at modifying mother–child attachments has been evaluated by Cicchetti *et al.* (1999). They measured attachment patterns and depression in 61 mothers who had suffered major depression since the birth of their child, now a toddler aged c.21 months. Of the depressed mothers 27 were given toddler–parent psychotherapy (TPP) aimed at increasing 'maternal understanding of the effects of prior relations on current feelings and interactions'. This resulted in a reduction in the proportion of insecure attachments among these toddlers from 44 per cent insecure to 26 per cent. Meanwhile the proportion of insecure toddlers in the comparison group of depressed mothers (n = 34) who did not receive TPP increased.

Similar results were found in a study by Lieberman *et al.* (1991) of infant–mother dyads at risk for abuse, neglect and relationship disorders (a substantial proportion of whom met criteria for reactive attachment disorders). They were assigned at random to either an infant–parent programme 'to free [mothers] and their baby from old "ghosts" that have invaded the nursery', or a control non-treated group. When followed up the intervention group showed improved empathy in the mothers and in the children less avoidance, resistance and anger towards their mothers.

Treatment

As we have seen, many of the problems that bring people into psychiatric care arise when a large section of our assumptive world is found to be obsolete or too many of our patterns are challenged. The fit between the world that is and the world that should be is lost. At such times, it is the role of psychotherapists, counsellors and others to help the sufferer to relinquish one pattern and discover another.

To do this we can make use of two very different types of technique, analytic and palliative. The analytic aims to help clients to identify and understand the pattern of their assumptive world and, if necessary, to discover a new, more satisfactory pattern. It includes both broadly oriented techniques such as psychoanalysis and more focused cognitive and similar therapies. Palliative therapies aim to mitigate the symptoms and distress associated with psychiatric disorder, including psychotropic drugs and supportive psychotherapies.

Analytic therapies suffer from several difficulties. Not only are the relevant patterns complex and the process of analysis difficult, but it is often hampered by the intense anxiety and fear to which the process of analysis gives rise. As we have seen elsewhere in this book, it is hard and feels dangerous to change our basic assumptions.

Palliative therapies are often deplored as a cop-out on the part of over-stretched services, and they may be misused as a cheap alternative to more radical therapies, but they do have certain advantages and may indeed make analytic therapy unnecessary. The aim of palliation is to mitigate psychological pain, provide reassurance, promote self-esteem and give people the emotional support that they will need if they are to begin the daunting process of relearning their assumptive world. Viewed in this way, palliation is a precondition for therapy and may bring people to the point where they can find their own way without further help from us.

Both psychotropic drugs and supportive therapies can reduce mental pain and most psychotherapists accept that analytic work is seldom possible until a degree of palliation has been achieved.

What are the implications of our understanding of attachments for intervention after loss? If, as the research reported here indicates, many people who seek help after bereavement have learned a distorted view of themselves and others, then it may be possible to correct these misperceptions. On the other hand, those problems that are rooted in childhood attachment patterns go back a long way and may not be open to change. There is evidence that assumptions associated with the child's earliest memories (implicit memories) are more difficult to access and change than those associated with later memories (LeDoux 1996). Indeed there is evidence that, in rats at any rate, the experience of repeated separations of juveniles from their mothers can result in anatomical changes in the brain (Kehoe *et al.* 1995). Furthermore, the disorders of attachment that were discussed in Chapter 17 can be regarded as personality disorders, and personality disorders are among the most intractable psychiatric disorders. Indeed many psychiatrists regard them as untreatable and decline to offer help to this group of patients.

These considerations might lead us to expect that bereaved people whose problems are most closely related to unsatisfactory attachment experiences will respond less well to treatment than those whose problems are not attachment related. This expectation, however, was not supported by Fonagy *et al.* (1996) who found that 93 per cent of psychiatric inpatients classed in the Adult Attachment Interview as 'Dismissing of Attachment' (the adult form of the avoidant attachment category) improved while receiving psychotherapy. On the other hand, only 41 per cent who fell into the 'Preoccupied' category (which resembles the anxious/ambivalent category of childhood) showed similar improvement. There were only nine patients rated as 'Secure' in this sample and only three (33 per cent) of these improved.

In this chapter we shall consider the current samples in the light of this and other research, and ask whether an understanding of attachment issues can be of help to people faced with losses of one sort or another. We recall that the members of Ward's control group reported levels of insecure attachment, which were just as high as those of the psychiatric patients, without themselves seeking psychiatric help or suffering the same high levels of distress as the psychiatric patients. This suggests that there are many people in whom a history of insecure attachment is not a forerunner of serious problems. Clearly they have found ways of coping with life despite or perhaps because of their childhood experiences. Can therapeutic interventions help others to do the same?

We look first at the evidence for the effectiveness of the various interventions that are currently recommended for helping bereaved people. We then examine the sample of bereaved people who took part in the research reported here and ask who did well and who badly. Finally we attempt an integration of these findings in the light of the attachments made in childhood as recalled by these people.

The prevention and treatment of problematic bereavement

In recent years the reasonable demand for cost effectiveness in therapies of all kinds has put pressure on therapists to justify both the effectiveness and the cost of their interventions. Expensive therapies of unproved value, such as traditional psychoanalysis, have come under a cloud and a wide range of shorter term psychological therapies and methods of counselling have come to the fore along with an increasing number of psychotropic drugs. Several programmes aimed at helping bereaved people have been developed and many of them have failed the test of scientific evaluation. On the other hand, some of them have passed such tests and encourage us to continue. Indeed, the lessons that have been learned from studying bereavement have wide implications for other stressful life situations.

Having reviewed this literature Schut *et al.* (2001) reach a surprising conclusion: 'The more complicated the grief process . . . the better the chances of intervention leading to positive results.' They confined their review to well-conducted studies in most of which bereaved people were assigned at random to intervention or none. No less than 12 studies of various types of counselling, provided to unselected bereaved widows and/or widowers, and four studies of counselling to unselected parents who had lost a child or suffered a stillbirth, showed no benefits from intervention. On the other hand, a number of services offered to 'high risk' groups or to bereaved people with psychiatric problems have obtained good results.

Two random-assignment studies of family therapy to bereaved children (themselves a high risk group), one of group support to bereaved pre-adolescents (aged 7–11) and three in which bereavement counselling was offered to adults at special risk, showed favourable results in the counselled groups. In all of these therapies particular attention was paid to attachments and other relationships within the social unit.

A variety of more specific therapies has also been successfully evaluated, although some showed only marginal benefits. These included Mawson *et al.* (1981) and Sireling *et al.*'s (1988) studies of 'guided mourning', an active form of therapy aimed at helping people with 'pathological grief' to confront the reality of their loss, and Brom *et al.*'s (1989) comparison of hypnotherapy, dynamic therapy and systematic desensitisation. In all of these studies a control group of untreated people was compared with each of the therapy groups and benefits were found in the therapy groups.

Perhaps the most impressive study of this type is reported in several papers by McCallum and Piper (1990) and McCallum *et al.* (1993). They compared the results of psychotherapy for the treatment of prolonged or delayed grief triggered by bereavement or in a few cases divorce, with waiting list controls. The treated group did better on measures of self-esteem, neuroticism, depression and life satisfaction.

The overall conclusion to be drawn from these studies is that there is little evidence that counselling given to unselected bereaved people is either needed or effective. On the other hand, services that are selective have often proved to be of value. These services are offered:

- to people at special risk by reason of traumatic loss, personal vulnerability or lack of social support
- to the minority of bereaved people whose grief falls outside the range of what is regarded as culturally normal
- to people who have evidence of psychiatric disorder.

Other scientific studies have used random assignment to compare one method of treatment with another. These include Schut *et al.*'s (1997a) comparison of cognitive psychotherapy (problem solving) combined with art therapy (focusing on emotional issues), and cognitive psychotherapy alone. Those who received the combined therapy benefited most. In another study, individual therapy was found more successful than a self-help group (Marmar *et al.* 1988), and in another Islamic culturally sensitive therapy proved more successful than therapy that ignored cultural/religious issues (Azhar and Varama 1995). Together these findings suggest that the most effective therapies embody a personal relationship with the client that is sensitive to emotional, cognitive and cultural issues.

On the whole, individual and family therapies have proved their worth more often than group interventions but few adequate evaluations of groups have been carried out at this time. Because the successful therapies used a combination of techniques and/or medications for a variety of problems, it is hard to know which particular elements were responsible for the improvement. This said, two approaches seem to be of particular value: therapies which facilitate emotional expression in those who cannot grieve; and therapies which facilitate the restructuring of the assumptive world in people who cannot stop grieving.

These were well illustrated in two, very different random allocation studies by Schut *et al* (1997b) and by Sikkema *et al.* (2004). Schut found that Dutch men who seek help after bereavement benefited most from a therapy aimed at helping with emotional expression, women, on the other hand benefited from a more cognitive therapy. Women also benefited from cognitive therapy in Sikkema's study of bereaved HIV positive men and women. Here men improved following both cognitive therapy in a group and traditional psychiatric help whereas women only improved after the cognitive therapy. As we have seen, these findings can be explained in the light of the studies of attachment reported here.

Turning to the use of psychotropic drugs following bereavement, these have given rise to much controversy but little serious research. The benzodiazepine group, of which diazepam (Valium) is the best-known example, were very popular at one time but have come under a cloud in recent years, largely thanks to the danger of habituation. There is also some anecdotal evidence that they may interfere with the course of grief. This said, the only systematic study of the use of diazepam in bereavement that is known to me showed no such consequences although the duration of treatment was short and the dosage low (Warner *et al.* 2001).

There is evidence from several studies, that antidepressants can be helpful to the minority of bereaved people who are clinically depressed (Pasternak *et al.* 1991; Reynolds *et al.* 1999; Zisook *et al.* 2001). In none of these studies was there any evidence that the antidepressant impaired grieving and in Reynolds's study, which was confined to depressed elderly bereaved people, those treated with nortriptyline (with or without psychotherapy) improved more than those treated with psychotherapy alone. The general consensus among psychiatrists today is that antidepressants should only be used after bereavement if there is clear evidence of major depression.

On reflection it seems unlikely that any one 'blockbuster' treatment will be found that solves all of the problems of bereaved people. The better we become at identifying and understanding the problems for which help is needed and the interventions that are most likely to succeed, the better our chances of obtaining good results.

Changes on follow-up in the current study

In my own practice I adopt an eclectic approach, using whatever methods seem appropriate to the particular problems I meet. My interest in attachments has caused me to favour psychotherapeutic approaches that include exploring, with my patients, the ways in which their view of the world has developed over the course of their lives. In this process of exploration the RAQ has proved to be therapeutically useful and several patients have indicated that it has opened their eyes to possible causes for their problems. (For further information about this section see Appendix 18.1.)

The current study was not set up to test the efficacy of any treatment that was provided to the people who sought my help. These were, as we have seen, an atypical group most of whom had already received counselling and/or therapies of various kinds before being referred for a specialist opinion. Forty-five bereaved patients were followed up for an average of 20 months after their initial consultation, at which time we can obtain some idea of how well or badly they were fairing from their scores of Symptoms and Distress. We have no means of knowing how well they would have done without my help.

My role as a consultant was to assess and advise and only 41 per cent of my bereaved patients were offered therapy by me and seen more than three times. Twenty-three of these were included in the follow-up study. At this time 12 (52 per cent) showed definite (two or more points) improvement in their Overall Distress scores and 5 (22 per cent) were definitely worse (−2 points or less). Depression/Medication scores had definitely improved in nine (39 per cent) but three (13 per cent) were now worse. These numbers are too small to justify statistical analysis.

Similar results were obtained in the full sample of 45 bereaved people who were included in the follow-up study. Eighteen (40 per cent) of them recorded Overall Distress scores that were definitely better and 11 (24 per cent) worse on follow-up. This improvement in the Overall Distress score only reached borderline levels of significance, perhaps because of the small numbers involved.

There was a statistically significant improvement in the Depression/Medication score on follow-up and, at borderline levels of significance, in the Alcohol Problems score. Improvement in Depression/Medication was confined to bereaved people under the age of 50. Older people had slightly lower levels of Depression/Medication at the outset but had not improved on follow-up. Could the improvement in the Depression/Medication score result from antidepressant drugs, which had been prescribed for 16 people? The evidence suggests not (see Appendix 18.1, p. 388). Initially those 19 who did not receive antidepressants had just as high scores of Depression/Medication as those who did, despite the extra weight given in this score to prescriptions of medication.[1] The Depression/Medication scores of those who received antidepressants improved less on follow-up than those who did not receive these drugs. But the difference did not reach statistical significance and the small numbers involved make it unwise to draw firm conclusions from this finding.

The association between increasing age and persisting depression is attributable to the fact that older people are more likely to live alone. In fact, the 18 people who lived alone showed no improvement on Depression/Medication or any of the Symptoms and Distress scores and their Clinging score tended to get higher, but again the numbers were too small for statistical comparisons to be valid.

To my great disappointment, there was little evidence to suggest that Anxiety/Panic or Grief/Loneliness scores were lastingly improved. This lack of significant improvement is surprising. Even without treatment, we might have expected grief and anxiety to improve over time. However, our initial assessments of Grief/Loneliness were seldom made before the end of the first year of bereavement and other studies, including the Harvard Bereavement Study (Parkes and Weiss 1983), have indicated that although grief levels diminish sharply during the course of the first year after bereavement, any subsequent improvement is slow.

Although the numbers are too small to justify statistical analysis it appears that it is the people who were not referred until over five years had elapsed who did least well. It would seem that grief and loneliness which persist for more than five years can become chronic and these figures suggest that they may not then respond to therapy.

Although I had not expected to find much change in the Coping scores,

---

1 There were another ten in whom we cannot be sure, from the case notes, that they did not receive antidepressant medication from GPs or other sources.

there was a highly significant increase in the mean End of Tether – Seek Help score. People said that they were more ready to seek help from others at follow-up than they had been when first referred.[2] There was also a trend, which did not reach statistical significance, for them to score more highly on Aggression/Assertion on follow-up. It would be unwise to draw firm conclusions from this but it may be that these bereaved people became more assertive over time as well as more willing to seek help. If anything, their experience of therapy seems to have convinced them that other people can be of help.

The follow-up study also enables us to look at changes in outcome associated with particular attachment patterns. On the whole higher scores of insecure attachment patterns were associated with high scores of initial symptoms but many of these improved on follow-up. Perhaps because of the small numbers involved, none of these changes reached statistical significance. All-in-all it would appear that those who experienced insecure attachments in their childhood did not respond less well to therapy than those who were more secure.

If, as the studies reported at the beginning of this chapter suggest, therapies which help emotionally inhibited people to become less inhibited are beneficial, we may expect that improvement on follow-up in scores of Emotional Inhibition/Distrust will be associated with improvement in the scores of Symptoms and Distress. On the other hand the opposite could also follow. People who become less inhibited might suffer more emotional distress as a consequence. In the event decreases in the Emotional Inhibition/Distrust score were significantly associated with improvement in the Overall Distress score (see Appendix 18.3, p. 388). This was attributable to highly significant decreases in scores of Grief/Loneliness, Anxiety/Panic and, to a lesser extent, Depression/Medication.

There was also a significant association between expressed willingness to seek help when at the end of one's tether (increase in the EoT Seek Help score) and improvement in the level of Grief/Loneliness although it is not possible to know whether the improvement in grief resulted from seeking help or whether people who were now grieving less were more willing to seek help as a result.

The implications of attachments for counselling and therapy

Regardless of the attachment pattern, in the current study, therapy was often associated with improvement in trust in others as reflected in change in the EoT Seek Help. This, in turn, may have helped to reduce levels of depression

---

2 Note that the reliability of the Seek Help score is uncertain and this score, more than others, is likely to be influenced by social influences including the respondent's wish to express appreciation for the help given.

and alcohol consumption. It follows that therapists should pay particular attention to establishing a trusting relationship with their clients.

It has long been recognised by psychotherapists that the relationship between the therapist and the client is an important influence on the outcome of therapy. This is nowhere more likely than when the problems that bring people into therapy are attachment problems. Bowlby has written in some detail (1988) about the importance of therapists providing their clients with a 'secure base' (i.e. a relationship in which they feel secure enough to consider and share the thoughts and feelings which make them insecure). In theory, it should not be difficult for us to provide such a secure base for we have no hidden agenda. Our aim is much the same as that of a good parent, to be sensitively responsive to our client's needs, being available to give protection if it is needed and to encourage autonomy when it is not. Since our clients are seldom in actual danger it is the latter function to which we give priority.

But the paucity of improvements in Anxiety/Panic in the current study suggest that, in practice, our clients may see things very differently and their priorities may be very different from ours. A secure base is not a simple thing to provide to people whose main problem is their insecurity. They probably have little reason to trust themselves or us and their experience has taught them not to. Somehow we have to use a subtle mixture of sensitivity to and understanding of their assumptions about the world with a willingness to 'hang in' as they begin, slowly and painfully to think and talk about the things that are most difficult to think and talk about. As John Bowlby put it in the last paper he wrote:

> A well-known observation . . . is the constant interaction of, on the one hand, the patterns of communication, verbal and non-verbal, that are operating within an individual's mind and, on the other, the patterns of communication that obtain between him and those whom he feels he can trust. The more complete the information that a person is able to communicate to someone he trusts the more he himself becomes able to dwell on it, to understand it and to see its implications – a process well illustrated by the adage 'How can I know what I think until I hear what I say?' Conversely, the more adequately a person can process information on his own the more capable will he be of communicating it to some other person. A key word here is trust. Without trust that the confidant will understand and respond helpfully, communication between self and other is blocked, with a corresponding blockage placed on intra-psychic communication.

(Bowlby 1991: 293)

Here he sums up the essence of much counselling and psychotherapy. Therapy is concerned with helping people to feel safe enough to change their minds, to review their current assumptive world and to discover new perspectives. Following bereavement this is termed 'grief work' but it is not essentially different from other situations in which, for whatever reason, people need to take stock, to give up some basic assumptions and to develop others. While they are explaining themselves to us they are explaining themselves to themselves and this, it seems, is a therapeutic experience.

One of the consequences of therapy may well be to help people to relate more successfully to their family and friends, but this may be of little use to those who are socially isolated. The poor results found here in older people who live alone suggest that they are the group least likely to respond to therapeutic endeavours.

The particular problems that our clients meet are likely to be influenced by the basic assumptions that have resulted from particular insecure attachment patterns. It would seem reasonable to make the following links between particular attachment patterns, the basic assumptions to which they give rise and the effects that these will have on therapy.

People who have experienced anxious/ambivalent attachments are likely, in later life, to view the world as a place in which exploration is dangerous and those more powerful than themselves must be persuaded to provide protection. Lacking basic trust in themselves, they are driven to rely on others, however ambivalent they may feel about this. They are likely to have developed skills at soliciting help from others, trusting them and being loyal, while keeping a watchful eye open for external danger and expressing early warnings. Thus they may be the 'worrier' in the family, thereby saving others the need to worry and setting them free to do the exploring. In certain circumstances these are real assets and should be recognised as such. For these people anxiety is the norm and they may see injunctions to relax as a threat to their security. Like the herbivores, whom they resemble, they feel relatively safe as long as they remain on guard.

These strengths and weaknesses have important implications for counsellors/therapists. Our empathy for our clients may cause us to see the anxious/ambivalent as the endangered child that they see themselves to be. The moment we do this we feed into their fears and perpetuate the problem for which they need our help. On the other hand, if we can retain our objectivity, we will soon come to recognise their true potential. It will be our respect for their value and strength that is of most use to them, not our pity for their weakness.

People who have experienced avoidant attachments may see it as dangerous to get close to others and to trust them to provide the care and protection that they think they need. With varying degrees of success, they may seek safety by attempting to control their world and others. Feelings of shame and guilt may alternate with aggressive assertion and complicate their relationship with others including ourselves. On the positive side, they have learned to stand on their own feet and their apparent strength may enable them to achieve status and power over others. Such powers are much appreciated in settings in which assertion and control are valued.

Counsellors/therapists should not allow our admiration for our clients' struggles for independence, or our fear of their attempts to control us, to blind us to the insecurity that makes it necessary for them to exert control when none is needed. Their apparent independence is a bluff and, at one level, they know it; why else would they seek our help? If we understand the true nature of their compulsive self-reliance, and respect their underlying fear, we shall find it easier to provide the reassurance and the secure base that they need. We must beware of violating their space, but may well find that they will themselves get closer to us once they understand that this is safe.

Those who have experienced disorganised or mixed attachments are often the most difficult to help. Lacking trust in themselves and others, they may oscillate between approaching and avoiding both us and the problems that they need to tackle. They miss sessions, turn up late and over-react if we draw attention to their behaviour. They are likely to be sensitive people who take nothing for granted and, as such, may become skilled at treading a narrow path between assertion and submission. They may be apologetic and even ingratiating, but this does not mean that others will find it easy to take advantage of them for they are wary of all relationships. Their skills at controlling themselves and others may suit them for roles as intermediaries, where a mixture of suspicion and compliance is needed.

We shall, perhaps, help these people best by holding fast to our faith that the world is not the dangerous place which they feel it to be; that they are not the useless creatures which they feel themselves to be, and that they can place a reasonable degree of trust in us and others. We must be prepared to tolerate their ambivalence and help them to understand it rather than punishing their negativity. Neither closeness nor distancing is punishable, and they can safely oscillate between the two strategies. When it is necessary for us to set limits, for instance, by insisting that they arrive on time for appointments, this should be done with gentleness and restraint for it will often be misperceived as rejection.

We have seen how disorganised attachments can give rise to assumptions of helplessness and hopelessness, which are themselves precursors of anxiety and depression. There is now copious evidence that mild to moderate levels of depression can be resolved by the use of cognitive therapies (Beck 1995). These techniques are systematic ways of modifying negative assumptions about the world and they have the effect of reducing helplessness and hopelessness (see Dobson 1989 for a meta-analysis of a large literature on this subject). Although these require specialist training, the principles that underlie them, that negative assumptions can be replaced by positive ones, can be of value in all therapies.

Is psychotherapy a love relationship?

Despite the similarity between the relationship between child and parent and that between client and therapist, there is also an important difference. Therapists, no matter how caring, can only offer a temporary attachment that is limited to the time which they spend with the client, and this is no substitute for the real thing. Most clients know this, although both they and their therapists sometimes forget it and 'transference' can be very strong.

Perhaps the best way to view such therapy is as a special situation in which, for a time, the client can become attached to another kind of parent in order to test out new models of the world and new assumptions. The therapist may need to remind the client, from time to time, the limits of the attachment. To speak personally, while I am with my clients they are the most important people in my life and I am fully committed to their welfare; but the moment they step outside my door the situation changes; they must go back to the world from which they came and I to mine.

The counsellor's attachment pattern

Of course, it is not only clients who have attachment patterns. Counsellors and therapists have their own patterns of attachment and it is reasonable to ask how these influence the therapy. In an ingenious study, Dozier *et al.* (1994) asked clients and therapists to complete the AAI. Clinicians who scored as 'insecure' perceived 'dependent' clients as needing them more than 'avoidant' clients. On the other hand, 'secure' clinicians saw 'avoidant' clients as more needy. Given the tendency for avoidant clients to deny or minimise their needs, this seems to imply that the more secure clinicians have a greater capacity to hear what is not being spoken and a greater tendency to be objective about what is. It seems likely that therapists who have insight into their own attachment patterns are less likely to misperceive the attachment needs of their clients than those who lack this insight.

In working with those who have an anxious/ambivalent history and a tendency to cling, we need to recognise and control our own nurturant needs. We like to care for people, why else would we become a carer? Like our patients, we may be in a state of conflict between our needs for closeness and distance, and our feelings are a pale reflection of their suffering. Yet there is a real danger that, like the parent and child in an anxious/ambivalent relationship, we shall get trapped if we allow our own need to nurture to blind us to our client's need for autonomy. Conversely, once we understand the client's true need and distinguish it from our own, we shall be better able to help them and may even help ourselves. Viewed in this way the experience of intervention may become transforming for us as well as for our clients. This, in essence, is the privilege of therapy and it is one of the things that makes it a worthwhile experience for both therapist and client.

Psychotherapy for disorganised attachment – a case study

Eve Barrola, aged 32, was born in Australia, the younger of two children of a psychologist father who was a heavy drinker and seldom present throughout her childhood. Her mother was unable to show warmth or to get close to her. She describes mother as a nervous, insecure alcoholic who was often depressed and, on several occasions, threatened suicide. At such times she would cling to Eve 'My angel', who was favoured over her brother, the 'black sheep' of the family.

Eve was an anxious, unhappy child and fearful of separation from her parents. She wet her bed through much of her childhood and lacked confidence in herself. Her RAQ showed her to have high scores of Disorganised (9), Avoidant (9) and Anxious/Ambivalent Attachment (8).

She was also rebellious and stubborn, trying to dominate others and thought of as tough. Despite these difficulties she did well at school both academically and at sports. But her later life was chaotic and typical of a disorganised attachment disorder. When she was 16 years of age she 'blew up like a balloon' due to thyroid deficiency. Under treatment she soon blossomed into an attractive young woman. Even so, her lack of self-esteem inclined her to choose men who were as insecure as herself and her relationships regularly ended in disaster with herself as the victim. Her distrust in herself and others was such that she had difficulty in settling into employment and tended to flit from job to job.

At 18 she was sexually abused by a doctor and shortly thereafter began taking drugs, under the influence of a boyfriend. Her father found out and subjected her to the ordeal of nightly 'psychotherapy'. In the same year she was raped by another boyfriend. When she complained to her permissive father he dismissed the incident.

She came to the UK from Australia in order to escape from another abusive relationship and over the next few years moved back and forth between the two countries. She was fond of the theatre and, while training as an actress, met and later married one of her tutors, an older man whom she regarded as a 'father figure'. Both of them were inclined to drink too much and they disagreed about many things, including her continued tendency to cling to and quarrel with her parents. After a year or so Eve left her husband. By now she had established a pattern of running away from her problems by changing continents whenever a relationship foundered, which it regularly did, assisted by the influence of ambivalence, drink and/or drugs. As she put it, 'When the chips are down I want to go away.'

Four years before referral she was again raped while under the influence of alcohol. This event brought her up short and caused her to take stock of her life. She subsequently managed to stop drinking. She then met a sensitive artist, Graham, who persuaded her to undertake a form of group therapy, which included 'rebirthing'. Shortly thereafter her father had a massive stroke and she flew to Australia and was with him when he died. She returned to England but ten months later her mother also became ill. Once more she flew to Australia in time to be at the bedside when her mother died. She found that event very distressing, but returned yet again to the UK in order to be with Graham who had 'stuck by me through thick and thin'.

It was at this time that she was referred to me. She was missing her mother a great deal but found it difficult to express her grief and wished she could cry. Anxious and inclined to panic, she had no confidence in herself and little trust in others, yet she wanted desperately to find someone who would look after her. She had got to the end of her tether and oscillated between clinging to her friends and shutting herself away from them. At such times she would become irritable and self-reproachful, feeling she was unworthy of affection.

Despite her feelings of inferiority there was no doubt of her above average intelligence and ability. She had managed to stay off alcohol and drugs and her relationship with Graham was continuing. Her biggest fear at this time was that she would spoil this relationship, as she had spoiled others in her life.

Rather to my surprise she maintained a commitment to come for therapy and, over the next three years attended for 20 meetings. In the course of these she re-examined her relationship with her parents and came to see how their problems had influenced her view of herself and her world. She was confused by the ambivalence that she felt for her mother but, as time passed, she felt that she was becoming 'disentangled'.

Initially she found it very difficult to settle to a job, but she gradually came to recognise that this too was a consequence of her uncertainties about herself and others, and of her tendency to drop out of situations and relationships that she feared she could not handle. Her relationship to Graham matured and she took a major step forward when she engaged to marry him and undertook in vitro fertilisation for infertility. Although this was not successful, it represented a change in her attitude to the future, which was now very positive. At the same time she accepted employment as a market researcher and stayed with this job.

Although she was not included in the follow-up study I was able to taper off the frequency of our meetings over the course of three years until I was satisfied that her improvement was solid.

Eve's story shows that disorganised attachments do not always give rise to intractable problems. The deaths of her parents, which triggered her request for help, may have stirred up distressing feelings but also presented her with the opportunity to escape from the ambivalent ties, which had kept her locked into entangled relationships with her parents. Fortunately for her, Graham was sufficiently secure to tolerate her confusion and disorganisation and to provide her with the secure base that she had always lacked. This enabled her to stay with the relationship with him, and with the therapist, until she had built up a new and more positive view of herself and others.

It will not have escaped the reader's attention that many of the people described in the case studies in this volume, who got better while in therapy, developed a new love relationship in their lives. This finding is borne out by other research. Parker (1994), like Brown and Harris (1978) found that those with uncaring parents who married a caring partner found that 'the earlier parental risk was "undone" to the extent of reducing the chance of adult depression by four fifths'. By contrast those with caring parents but uncaring partners had levels of depression almost as high as those with lack of care from all support figures. Parker concludes that 'the effects of distortions in parenting are not immutable'.

It seems that therapy may help to make new attachments possible, and to reduce the chance that they will founder. In the long run, however, it was probably the relationship with the partner that was more important to these people than the relationship with the therapist.

Working with families

Another important implication of attachment theory is the recognition of the continuing influence of the client's partner and other family who can aggravate or mitigate longstanding attachment problems. Family therapists such as Byng-Hall (1991) have shown how the distorted perceptions of the world that have been described here are shared within families. He uses the term 'family scripts' for these assumptive worlds and sees it as the overall aim of family therapy 'to help the family to establish their own sufficiently secure attachment pattern so that they can resolve problems when they arise'.

Even outside the field of family therapy it is, in my view, valuable to include spouses and other relevant family members in therapy whenever it is possible and appropriate to do so. This view is shared by Kissane and Bloch (2002) whose 'family focused grief therapy' is currently undergoing systematic evaluation. Family therapy can also benefit families in which unusually traumatic losses have undermined the security of more than one member of the family.

> Connie Perslake is an example of this. She describes her childhood as happy and her relationship with her parents as 'very secure'. Although somewhat lacking in confidence, she made friends, did well at school and grew up with a positive view of the world. In the RAQ, she received low scores on all attachment patterns.
>
> She was 16 years of age when her sister failed to arrive home from school. Her dead body was found a few days later; she had been abducted and then murdered. This event shattered Connie's safe, secure world. For months afterwards she was in fear for her own life. She was repeatedly glancing over her shoulder in case a killer should sneak up on her and this habit developed into a nervous tic. She was afraid to go to sleep at night and cried when left alone.
>
> I saw Connie at this time and referred her to a child psychotherapist for treatment while I worked independently to support her parents. From time to time we held joint meetings at which Connie, her parents and both therapists took part. Following the murder, Connie's parents were also at the end of their tethers. Her mother was tearful, agitated and depressed. Father, on the other hand, distanced himself from his wife and child for fear of being overwhelmed by their distress. His own distress was expressed in the form of anger, a reaction that was aggravated by the fact that the killer had not been apprehended.
>
> Their problems are well illustrated by the situation that arose each night at bedtime. Connie was frightened of being left alone and would at first cry aloud in her room and then come downstairs for comfort. Her mother was so close to being overwhelmed by her own grief that she found it hard to support Connie. Father, on the other hand, would attempt to regain control by telling Connie and her mother to pull themselves together and insisting that Connie return to her bedroom. He expressed the view that if he gave way to her unreasonable demands for attention her clinging behaviour would be perpetuated.
>
> In therapy it was Connie who proved most resilient. Her therapist provided her with a safe enough place in which she could share her thoughts and feelings about the terrifying event of her sister's murder and the shattering of her view of the world as secure. I was able to reassure her parents of the important role that they could play in

meeting her needs for comfort and protection. I suggested that her clinging was more likely to persist if they rejected her bids for attachment than if they gave way to them.

Once her parents recognised and responded to her needs for protection, reassurance and emotional support, for instance, by sitting with her for a while after she went to bed and responding rapidly by going to her room if she cried out at night, her tic soon disappeared and her sleeping pattern improved. She returned to school, made an apparent recovery and was discharged from therapy.

Sixteen years later, Connie returned to see me again and it was at this time that she completed the RAQ. She recalled that her parents had remained very overprotective and she had never lost the feeling that it should have been she who died rather than her 'good' sister. She continued to visit her sister's grave regularly and to miss her a great deal. Her sister had died when there was a full moon and it was at this time each month that Connie would become tired and depressed.

She grew up a 'loner' who found it hard to ask for help or to accept cuddles or other demonstrations of affection. In later years she remained fearful of making new relationships for fear that her partner would find out how unworthy she was and terminate the relationship. Her marriage at the age of 20 did not last, probably because of her difficulty in tolerating closeness.

In the end her decision to seek further help was precipitated by a burgeoning attachment to another young man, Albert. She was fearful that this would end in the same way as her marriage. Like Connie, Albert was inclined to denigrate himself, but he was able to show affection and stuck by her despite her difficulties. Connie was by now an attractive, intelligent young lady. She had a positive recollection of our meetings 16 years earlier and was ready to trust me and to re-examine the painful feelings that arose whenever thoughts of her sister's death came to mind. She spoke frankly about her feelings of unworthiness for having survived, and her fears of further loss, which made her hang back from a full commitment to Albert.

She made good use of our time together, recalling the memories of her sister's death and examining their influence on her view of the world and of herself in it. I needed to see her only three times. At the time of our last interview she was coping well and no longer felt guilty about her sister's death, although she still had some fear of losing her independence as a result of this new relationship.

Followed up nearly two years later she was doing very well. Her Overall Distress score had fallen from 5.5 to 0 and, when returning the form, she wrote in a letter that she had had a baby and moved into a new house with Albert. She added: 'I doubt that I would be in this situation now if it was not for my visits to you. You made me realise that I do deserve a happy life of my own, and I am grateful to you for that. I am still very independent, but I don't think that will ever change.' She added that she had now '. . . come to terms with the loss [of my sister] and my feelings about it. I still miss her and always will but the guilt has gone and it feels wonderful to love'.

We have no means of knowing if, prior to the murder, Connie's sister was equally secure but the chances are that, growing up in the same family, she was. It is even possible that the trust in others, which grew out of a secure attachment to her parents, put her at risk in the hands of the untrustworthy and may have contributed to her death.

Neither do we know if a less secure childhood would have left Connie better prepared for her sister's murder. That event, by shattering her trust and that of her parents in the world as a secure place, and of each other as reliable sources of security, gave rise to late-onset attachment problems. Connie became fearful of making relationships, compulsively independent and blaming herself for having survived. From now on she learned to stand on her own two feet. This meant that she did not have to trust others or to run the risk of losing them if she became attached. Seeing her sister's death as a punishment for her own badness reinstated in Connie a vestige of meaning and control in a world which had become meaningless and uncontrollable. But it also helped to undermine her trust in herself.

Fortunately the therapeutic relationship that resulted from our initial contacts was sufficiently good for her to choose to return 16 years later. With the support of her new boyfriend, who attended one of our meetings, she undertook the daunting task of revisiting, in a psychological sense, the scene of the crime. When she did that, she realised the extent to which her perception of the world and of herself had been influenced and distorted by that event. Her new perspective enabled her to give up the protective wall that she had built round herself.

The therapy may also have helped Connie to feel secure enough to risk another loss, by committing herself to her partner, and may have helped her partner to understand and tolerate her attachment problems. Once the new attachment had 'taken', the rewards that resulted from the relationship itself tended to make both partners feel more secure and to feed into a cycle of increasing security and satisfaction which soon made the therapist redundant.

Is the day of the volunteer counsellor past?

If, as Schut's review suggests, most bereaved people do not need and will not benefit from counselling, is there still a place for the volunteer-based bereavement service? Is it reasonable to expect volunteers to cope with the complex problems of the minority of bereaved people who are at special risk by reason of attachment problems, traumatic bereavements, social isolation, etc.

In my own study people who met criteria for 'high risk' after bereavement were assigned at random to proactive support by carefully selected and trained volunteers or simply informed of the availability of bereavement support (none made use of this). On follow-up there was a significant benefit in the supported group which was largely confined to the men (Parkes 1981). It is my impression, arising out of many years of working with volunteers, that the kinds of people who offer to work in this field and who pass the test of a proper process of selection, are particularly good at helping people with problems of attachment. When we consider the skills that are needed, the ability to provide reassurance, emotional support and the kind of security which we associate with good parenting; it may well be that carefully selected, trained and supported volunteers are sometimes better than clever professionals whose paper qualifications may outweigh their ability to handle human relationships with sensitivity and tact.

In the light of the difficulty which many clients have in trusting others, we might expect that people who see their family as unsupportive will be equally distrusting of volunteers and professionals, and unable to benefit from their help. This expectation was tested by Raphael (1977) who found no such influence. She showed that in a group of Australian widows who sought help for problems after bereavement perceiving their family as 'unsupportive' was a predictor of poorer outcome after bereavement. She also showed that people who perceived their families as 'unsupportive' made a good response to her supportive therapy. The most obvious explanation is that people who lack support from their families need it from outside the family. This suggests that an important component of counselling is the provision of the kind of help that most of us can expect to get from a supportive family. Volunteers may be well suited to provide this.

So, is it necessary for volunteers to be selected and trained by professionals or is there a danger that professionals will undermine the spontaneity and genuineness that is a characteristic of good families? Those professionals who work with volunteers argue that special skills are needed if people are to avoid getting sucked into collusive or harmful relationships, and special knowledge is needed to enable people to diagnose and refer on those at suicidal risk and those with clinical depression, post-traumatic stress disorder and other psychiatric problems. Experience indicates that it is quite possible to train volunteers in all of these skills. This said it is important that professionals recognise, value and encourage the quasi-parenting roles of the volunteers. Their aim should not be to produce a pseudo-professional.

One example of the misuse of ideas stemming from professional practice is the widespread use of the fixed term contract. This has been justified for two very different reasons, to prevent 'dependency' and to satisfy the needs of funding bodies who like to know exactly what they are paying for. Yet this kind of regimentation is the antithesis of a relationship that relies on security for its success. Since every relationship is different the needs of clients are bound to vary and any attempt to force them into the procrustean bed of a fixed term contract unlikely to succeed. The sensitive handling of dependency requires a gradual tailing off of the frequency of meetings as the clients' confidence increases rather than the imposition of impersonal rules. If we allow for a range of different responses to different needs we shall find that many clients do not need more than two or three sessions while others will need more. Funding bodies should be persuaded to recognise this variation.

Likewise the strict and abrupt ending of therapy at the end of a fixed contract may be counter-productive. Elkin *et al.* (1989) found that although 70 per cent of depressed patients had improved at the end of therapy, only 30 per cent had no further relapses in depression two years later. The provision of 'top-up' sessions doubled this figure to 60 per cent.

Although there is a place for volunteer support for bereaved people, this does not mean that professional skills are to be dismissed. The research evidence reviewed above suggests that some people will benefit from specialist therapies. It follows that the ideal bereavement service should be able to provide a range of skills. Many clients will benefit from the help of a volunteer, others will need more highly trained professionals.

What do professionals have to offer?

Professionals have important roles to play in assessing the need for specialist treatment and will work most effectively if they establish links with voluntary organisations who may also benefit from their help in the training of volunteers. It is not possible, in the space available, to describe the full range of therapies that may be needed by people who have suffered losses of one sort or another. Mention has been made of the need for specialist treatment of PTSD and of the use of cognitive therapies and antidepressant medication for the treatment of clinical depression and anxiety disorders, any or all of which may be caused by loss.

Cognitive therapies are the success story of clinical psychology and may turn out to have special value in bereavement. Up to now progress has been inhibited by the assumption that since 'the negative thoughts verbalised by these [bereaved] patients may reflect an accurate appraisal of their surroundings' they are not amenable to change by cognitive behaviour therapy (Moorey 1996). Fleming and Robinson (2001), however, have challenged this view. They point to the need for bereaved people to change their assumptions about the world and they suggest that cognitive methods may well be appropriate to this purpose. Certainly the results of my research support this view and it is to be hoped that others will develop the techniques that are needed.

Cognitive behaviour therapies attempt to change harmful assumptions without necessarily helping people to understand how those assumptions have arisen. Attachment-informed psychotherapy is more concerned with analysing the roots of harmful assumptions. This is a relatively new field that has been well described by Jeremy Holmes, whose own contribution has been considerable. He asserts:

> Psychotherapy is not just about a grim coming to terms with loss. Like poetry, it also, and necessarily, puts us in touch – physiologically, emotionally, cognitively – with our 'first world', so that, with luck, we can live more fully in our 'second'.
>
> (Holmes 2001: 118)

Attachment-informed psychotherapy employs methods of analysis derived from psychoanalysis that have been reinterpreted and modified in the light of research into attachments. Like psychoanalysis, it is time consuming, expensive and uncertain in its results. But it offers hope that at long last a scientific basis for analytical psychotherapy can be found. Although well-conducted research evaluations are lacking, it is reasonable to consider referring people with problems in attachment to these practitioners if their problems have not responded to less demanding types of therapy.

Since attachment problems are very common, all members of the caring professions need to take a special interest in this field, to understand the complex interweaving of parental and later influences, and the ways in which our clients avoid the very issues that they need to tackle. Bereavements and other major life events confront them with the need to change and make them more open to change. Some will need our help if they are to grasp that opportunity.

Self-help

The implications of an understanding of attachment problems for bereaved people

People reading this book who have suffered losses in their lives may reasonably ask what they can do to help themselves. Up to now the convention of writing in the third person plural may have given the impression that 'the bereaved' are a separate group from the volunteers and professionals who serve them. But we are all attached and we all suffer losses. To bring this home the paragraphs that follow will be written in the third person singular.

This book may have given us greater insight into our own assumptive worlds and enabled us to recognise the obsolete habits of thought and behaviour that continue to bedevil our lives. If we are aware of a tendency to cling we may find it wise to resist that temptation in any circumstance in which it is likely to create problems. Only by doing this will we find out that we never needed to cling in the first place. If on the other hand we find it hard to get close to people for fear of rejection or punishment, this book may persuade us to test out the validity of this assumption by taking the risk of closeness. In either case our experience is likely to reassure us that these attitudes of mind belong in the past not the present.

We shall not find that the fears that were instilled in childhood are easily dispelled, but the sense of liberation that can arise when we understand how these habits of thought were initiated will encourage us to persist. In the end 'nothing succeeds like success'. Once we begin to do the very things that we fear the fear will subside.

Other books that can be recommended to bereaved people are to be found in the references section under Tatelbaum (1997) and Collick (1986). This said, it should also be clear that our preference for self-help, over the help of others, may itself reflect an attachment problem. Does it arise out of an untested assumption that others cannot be trusted to care or give us the help we need? It is important to assess our need for help from others. If we have attachment problems, have experienced traumatic losses or lack social support we are likely to find it difficult to cope unaided with the loss of someone to whom we are attached. Rather than battling on alone, we have the right and the need to ask for help. A general practitioner or social worker should be able to advise us what kinds of support are available in our vicinity and to guide us in the selection of the right counsellor or therapist. Hopefully this book will also have shown how we can make the best use of the help we are given by shelving any doubts that we may have about the extent to which others can be trusted and recognising that we deserve any help we can get. We should at least give the helper a chance to earn our trust.

There are many aspects of bereavement that have not been adequately covered in this book. For a more detailed account of the field *Bereavement: Studies of Grief in Adult Life* (Parkes 1996) may be of value. For organisations and websites concerned with attachment and bereavement see Appendix 18.2.

Conclusions

It seems that love can both cause problems and facilitate their cure. For most people, the love and support that they get from their friends and family are all that is needed to get them through the problems of uncomplicated bereavement and in such cases help from outside the social network is not needed. Only if people are at special risk, is other care likely to be needed and beneficial. In this circumstance a number of different interventions have proved helpful. All of them provide the bereaved person with someone from outside the family with whom they can develop a therapeutic relationship. The relationship with the therapist is an integral part of the therapy and such relationships need to be sensitive to the cultural, emotional and cognitive needs of the client.

It follows that those who offer help to people at risk should be properly selected, trained and supervised to ensure that they understand these needs and respond appropriately. Academic expertise is not enough and experiential methods should enable trainees to become aware of their own attachment needs as well as those of their clients. Like all attachments the client–therapist relationship is a species of love relationship and like all such relationships it carries risks to both the client and the therapist. Pain there will be for, as Father Julio Lancelotti has put it: 'There is no love without pain.' But in most instances the pain is worth bearing and the potential benefit great for 'only love can heal that which it causes' (unpublished lecture, Centro de Defesa da Criança e do Adolescente, Sao Paulo, 2005).

The love relationship between therapist and client may lack the long-term commitment of other attachments but its very transience and the strict taboo on sexuality encourages clients to experiment, to play games, to try out alternative ways of behaving and construing the situation. In the relatively safe world of the therapeutic relationship they can take risks, laugh, cry, express anger, evoke the spirit of a lost love in the person of the therapist and learn to tolerate the pain of separation at the end of each session. For the same reasons we the therapists can bear with them, tolerate their pain and hang in when the going is tough. In the end we too may gain something from the privilege of the relationship.

While the research reported here has focused mainly on the needs of people bereaved by death, the finding that attachment problems influence the response to a wide range of other traumatic and life-change situations is a challenge to therapists. The success that can sometimes be achieved in the field of bereavement should give us grounds for hope. We can conclude that an understanding of love relationships and their consequences, throughout the life cycle can enrich and enhance all kinds of care.

The whole field of attachment research is currently developing at a rapid rate and organisations such as *The International Attachment Network* with its journal *Attachment and Human Development* are providing the academic base that should ensure that this takes place on a sound scientific basis (further details of these are given in Appendix 18.2).

Final conclusions

We of the twentieth century have witnessed some amazing advances in science and the creation, in cities and towns across the world, of environments that are largely man-made. As a result more people are alive today than ever before and for many of them the advances in medicine, public health, agriculture, transport, information systems and the large-scale organisation of society have brought about a world where we are healthier, safer and better nourished than ever before.

Unfortunately the psychological and social sciences have not kept up with the physical sciences. The large-scale systems of organisation that in the 'developed world' have taken over from the family as our principle source of security rely on workers of both sexes who are separated from their children throughout the working day and whose extended family, the traditional surrogate parents, now often live too far away to be of use. While teachers and others may be quite adequate to meet the attachment needs of many children, often they are not, particularly since the increase in sexual abuse by such carers has led to prohibition of the most effective sources of reassurance for distressed children of all ages, touching and cuddling. Thus the very social changes that have increased our objective security have undermined those functions of the family which maintain subjective security, the experience of a secure base for the developing child. We are only now beginning to discover the cost of this neglect and it is to be hoped that this volume will contribute to redress the balance.

Research into attachments has contributed to our understanding of child development and has become a field of study in its own right. At long last a scientific basis for studying the influence of the experiences of early childhood has been established and bids fair to bring about a rational basis for the prevention and treatment of the problems that arise from attachments.

Another consequence of the success of medical science has been the prolongation of life. While this is a worthy aim, it has often been pursued without regard for the quality of the life that is thereby prolonged. Pneumonia, once called 'the old man's friend' for its capacity to bring merciful relief from the sufferings of the wide range of diseases and disabilities that afflict the elderly, is now routinely treated with antibiotics. Cancers, which remain the third commonest cause of death, are treated by poisons which half kill the patient in order to fully kill or at least slow down the tumour. Our fear of death is such that many patients collude with this and may even press their doctors to prolong their lives at all costs. Yet despite all of the advances of modern science, 100 per cent of people still die.

In recent years a growing awareness of these issues has focused attention on the dying and on the families who care for and survive them. Hospices have led the way. They combine the best of physical care with psychological, social and spiritual care for people who are dying. So successful has this been that they have spread, within a few years, across the globe. These successes reflect both awareness of the problems and faith in possible solutions. As a result an entire new field of palliative medicine has come into being with its own journals and scientific literature.

Interest in the related topic of bereavement has also burgeoned but has grown more slowly. Within palliative medicine lip service has been paid to the importance of the patient's family both as a source of support to the dying patient and in its own right. After all, the patient's problems will soon be over; those of the family may just be beginning. On the other hand the blinkered outlook of professionals has not helped the development of an agreed theoretical understanding of bereavement from the various disciplines with an interest in the field. As a result we have theories derived from psycho-analysis, cognitive psychology, sociology and traumatology competing for the high ground and denigrating their competitors.

In the current volume I have attempted to draw together evidence from all of these fields, as well as from my own research, to propose an integrated model that embraces studies of attachment and loss extending across the life cycle. Where conflicting views or discordant evidence have become apparent I have attempted to suggest explanations and, although I do not doubt that further modifications to the overall model will be needed, the existing pieces of the jigsaw puzzle do seem to fit.

It is this, more than anything else that reassures us that the technical limitations of the study which were addressed in Chapters 3 and 4, the possible effects of retrospective distortion, the problems of missing informa-tion, the inadequacies of the measures of adult relationships and doubts about the reliability of the clinical assessments, do not seriously undermine the overall conclusions.

The focus on a group of people who came for help after bereavement has turned out to illuminate the whole structure and focus of our thinking about love and loss. Whatever genetic factors may have contributed to their prob-lems, these people are not freaks or curiosities. We find in them aspects of problems that we all face, for no family is perfect and no one immune to loss. But our conclusions are not limited to loss by death and the data reported in Chapter 16 makes it clear that attachment patterns, separations and the assumptive world to which they give rise influence how we cope with many of the losses of life and shed light on a wide range of psychiatric problems.

We started by examining the assessments made by our respondents of their parents and of themselves as children. The replies to the questions about parenting correlated with the measures of childhood and confirmed expectations based on Ainsworth and Main's systematic studies. This justified us in using measures reflecting their classification of the patterns of attachment as our principle predictors of later development.

We saw how problematic attachments in childhood and separation from parents, can undermine the developing child's views of the world as a safe place, of their own ability to cope by independent action (or by rewarding or coercing others), and of the extent to which they can trust others to protect, support and encourage them. Out of this mixture of expectations and assumptions emerges a set of strategies and a view of the world and of oneself within it that colours all of our relationships and our approach to novel or challenging situations. The loss of a close relative or partner emerges as one of the most challenging and one which brings home, more clearly than other life situations, the fallibility of our basic assumptions.

Even so, Ward's comparison group made us aware of the resilience of human beings. As in other studies of the effects of 'stress' on mental health, we found that many people who have been forced by circumstances to learn to cope with parenting that is less than ideal develop strategies for survival that prepare them for disappointments and other stresses, and often stand them in good stead in later life.

We found in the patterns of attachment derived from Ainsworth's Strange Situation a set of basic assumptions about the world and its meanings that made sense of many of the strange situations that we meet throughout our childhood and later life. Assumptions about ourselves, about our families and about the world at large enable us to interpret the meaning of each situation and to develop strategies that we hope will enable us to survive. If we do survive this is assumed to confirm the validity of the strategies.

Some bereavements are more traumatic than others, but even the most traumatic can only be adequately understood if we pay attention to the basic assumptions that are being overturned by the trauma. These basic assumptions arise from an experience of life that is very limited. The basic assumption that arises from secure attachment is that I am protected, worthwhile and secure. Much of the time it stands me in good stead for it gives me the confidence and trust to face strange and novel situations without undue anxiety. But it may let me down when disaster strikes and I am suddenly unprotected, weak and deskilled.

The basic assumption arising from anxious ambivalent attachments is that I am a weak vessel in a turbulent environment in which my only hope of survival in strange situations is to stay close to a greater power. As long as I can find my greater power I am safe enough, although the uncertainty inherent in this situation means that I must be sure to stay close. Without the greater power I am lost.

The basic assumption arising out of avoidant attachments is that I will survive if I maintain an appearance of strength and do not get too close to others. Much of the time this assumption holds true and I may even get status and credit for my performance. But this assumption is confounded by anything that brings home my weakness, reduces my status (i.e. my power to control others) or leaves me 'without a leg to stand on'. When this happens I may attempt to regain control by threats or, as the data on disability suggests, by 'going sick'.

The basic assumption underlying disorganised attachments is that I am weak and others cannot be trusted to protect me. Consequently I must be constantly on the alert for danger while remaining inconspicuous, staying in places of relative safety and avoiding any situation that might undermine my security. If this fails I panic, I may take to the bottle or I may even take an overdose.

Although many of these basic assumptions arise in early childhood, our data indicates that they are not immutable. Thus, in childhood, boys were no more likely than girls to make avoidant attachments but with the arrival of adolescence bodily and psychological changes lead to an increase in strength and aggressiveness with a corresponding change in basic assumptions about self and others which resemble those of the avoidant pattern. Thereafter, boys are much more likely than girls to respond to threat or loss by assertiveness, by inhibiting the expression of grief (and other feelings), and by refusing any help that might undermine their status. Although these strategies are sometimes successful, when they fail they are reflected in the personality disorders to which the bereaved men in our study were prone. The smaller number of men than women who sought help after bereavement may say more about men's reluctance to admit their need for help than it does about their actual need.

Each type of relationship has its functions, strengths and weaknesses that are themselves influenced by prior attachments. The weaknesses are sometimes reflected in disorders of attachment and they sometimes become apparent when the relationship is challenged by bereavement. This study has enabled us to compare the loss of parents, children and spouses. It has also thrown light on social relationships that turn out to play an important role at times of bereavement.

Relationships to parents may be vital to our survival during childhood, but with the advent of adolescence their importance normally diminishes, separation becomes possible and the nature of the bond gradually changes, often from attachment to nurturance. We saw how problematic reactions to the loss of a parent, more than other losses, commonly reflect the continuation into adult life of unusually close and clinging attachments to that parent in childhood.

The main function of nurturance is the survival of our genes through our children. This function is diminished once the children can survive without us. Separation then becomes desirable and the nature of the parent's nurturant bond may gradually change to one of attachment. The loss of a child is always painful but our study suggests that it is most likely to lead to requests for psychiatric help if it revives a dangerous assumptive world over which the child had little or no control and from which they could not learn a satisfactory model of parenting. This was most obvious in the people who had experienced disorganised attachments. They reveal the extent to which the assumptions that arise from attachment relationships in childhood are reflected in the nurturant relationships of adults.

Relationships with partners fulfil sexual, nurturant and attachment functions including the provision of a secure base in which to raise children. Although we have found that insecure attachments in childhood are associated with insecure attachments to spouses, these are not a slavish copy of the attachments to parents. Insecurity upsets the balance between giving and taking, nurture and attachment, which ensures the success of pair bonds between adults. In this study, problems following the loss of a partner often resulted from an exclusive, insecure and mutually interdependent relationship with the partner that gave rise to high levels of anxiety, grief and loneliness when the partner died.

In most societies the network of attachments to the extended family plays an important part in child rearing as well as providing physical and emotional support to the parents. In western society social and professional networks have largely subsumed these functions. The research reported here shows that both social support and living with others can mitigate some of the intensity of grief and loneliness, and social support emerged as one of the most salient factors distinguishing the psychiatric patients from Ward's controls. Even people who had experienced insecure attachments reacted to bereavement without lasting distress if their support networks were still intact.

Problems associated with social isolation and lack of social support were most apparent in old age. Sadly, those who had experienced insecure attachments, who are the people most in need of this support, were also the ones least likely to get it. Their lack of trust in others meant that they remained isolated and unsupported.

One group whom one might have expected to be insecure were the immigrants. Their history of persecution, poverty and separations from parents was such that it came as a surprise to find that their ability to cope and their reaction to bereavement in later life was no worse than that of the non-immigrants. It seems that many of them had the benefit of surrogate parents and extended family networks whose support had helped to mitigate these difficulties. It may also be the case that their experience of stress in childhood prepared them for some of the stresses to come.

Another source of insecurity is life-threatening illness. When, in the current study, this occurred in early childhood it affected the parents' treatment of the child and was associated with overprotection and anxious/ambivalent attachments or distancing and avoidant attachments. In later childhood and adult life it seems that an increased prevalence of avoidant attachments increased the risk of illness and disability. Illness in childhood often caused separations from parents, which also undermined security.

Given the high prevalence of disabilities and the numerous bereavements and other losses that occur in the lives of older people it is remarkable how many of them are able to lead reasonably contented lives. Among those older folk who sought psychiatric help in the current study, however, it seems that it was the combined effect of insecure attachments, physical disabilities and social isolation (many lived alone) which made the added burden of bereavement intolerable.

It will be obvious by now that parental love is difficult to get right. None of us can prepare our children for every eventuality, all we can hope to be is 'good enough'. The most perfect parents may not succeed in preparing their children for an imperfect world. Well-meaning parents who overprotect or over-control their children, parents who are intolerant of closeness and griev- ing or traumatised parents (whose overwhelming needs for nurture make it hard for them consistently to nurture their own children), all of these prob- lems in loving undermine the child's security and trust in itself and others. Few of these parents lack love for their child; it is the way they express or fail to express that love which causes problems.

Sometimes, as we have seen, the problems are so serious that they justify the diagnosis of an attachment disorder. We have seen how such disorders start in childhood and persist into adult life when they may increase the risk of complicated grief and a variety of other psychiatric problems that some- times arise after bereavement. But the influence of insecure attachments is not limited to bereavement and this study shows that they also play a part in psychiatric disorders arising in people who have not been bereaved. This important observation opens the door to a major advance in our understanding of mental illness and its causes.

Finally we come to the most important question of all: What can be done to put things right? This study was not set up to answer that question but the implications are clear. They include recognition of the importance of parent- ing and the implementation of a range of measures to free up, educate and support parents or their surrogates so that they can devote as much time and attention as is needed to provide each child with a reasonably secure base from which it can learn an appropriate degree of trust in itself and others. Early warning systems are needed to ensure that children with attachment prob- lems are recognised and that their parents receive the help which they will need to put things right. This does not imply that parents are to blame for their child's problems. As we have seen, their problems are often rooted in their own upbringing and they need understanding and support rather than condemnation.

In later childhood teachers and others have greater influence and must take every opportunity to provide effective antidotes to problematic attach- ments. For those whose attachment problems continue into adult life, bereavements and other critical life events constitute both a risk and an opportunity. Professionals and others who are around at times of loss and change can recognise those at special risk and act to reduce that risk. The loss of 'significant others' is both a cause for grief and a challenge to our basic assumptions about the world. Counsellors and others can provide the 'secure enough base' from which our clients can begin to explore what they have lost and what remains. Out of the wreckage of habitual assumptions can come a new view of the world that may be more appropriate and realistic than the one that preceded it. Those whose assumptive world was distorted by mis-trust of self and/or others have the opportunity to discover their own strength and the strength and goodwill of others.

Our role as carers is akin to that of the good parent who provides protec-tion when it is needed but also recognises that most of the time it is not needed and helps the child to believe the same. It then becomes safe for the child or client to think and talk about things that are unsafe, to do the things that will establish their strength and autonomy, and to take the risk of trusting others and forming new relationships.

Perhaps one of the most important and cheering aspects of the study is the recognition from both the control group and the follow-up study that even the most insecurely attached are not doomed. People can learn to cope with distressing circumstances and events, both those that result from insecure attachments and bereavement. Some will never need psychiatric help or coun-selling, but for those who do it is important that they receive help that recognises and facilitates the painful process of change.

The carer must be prepared to share in this process. We will suffer along with our clients and must hold fast to the faith that people have the capacity to pass through grief and achieve a new maturity. With time and experience we shall discover that, like parenting, therapy is worth the effort. Therapists have developed their own language for the attachments that our clients make to us and we to our clients. Terms such as 'transference' and 'countertransfer-ence', 'therapeutic alliance' and 'therapeutic relationship' recognise that this relationship is not a romantic attachment or a nurturant attachment; yet, if we are honest, we must admit that it contains elements of both these relationships; in the end, it is a species of love.

It seems that love and loss provide the point and counterpoint of a sym-phony whose first movement sets the colour and feeling tone of all that is to come. Succeeding movements introduce new themes, which may challenge, replace or develop the earlier themes but cannot wipe them out. Order alter-nates with chaos as the music of life progresses and the whole moves towards some kind of resolution that, in great music, is always unexpected, subtle and deeply moving. The greatest music, like the greatest drama, is the saddest, and its greatness stems from the emergence of meaning out of discord, loss and pain. The sublime in music, as in life, reflects the human search for meaning, the grasping at eternity, the transcendence of the littleness of I.

Appendices

Appendix 3.1: Retrospective Attachment Questionnaire (RAQ)

Section I About your parents*

		Mother	Father
1	Were you brought up by your true parents?	Yes/No	Yes/No
2	Are your parents still alive?	Yes/No	Yes/No
	If not, write in how old you were when they died.	———	———
3	Were you separated from either parent for more than a month before the age of 6 years?	Yes/No	Yes/No
4	Were you separated from either parent for more than a month between the ages of 6 and 10 years?	Yes/No	Yes/No
5	Were you separated from either parent for more than a month between the ages of 11 and 16 years?	Yes/No	Yes/No
6	During your childhood were you ever afraid that a parent would die or be killed?	Yes/No	Yes/No
7	Was either parent nervous, insecure or a worrier?	Yes/No	Yes/No
8	Was your parent subject to episodes of gloom or depression?	Yes/No	Yes/No
9	Did your parent ever receive psychiatric treatment?	Yes/No	Yes/No
	If so, was she/he ever admitted to a hospital for psychiatric treatment?	Yes/No	Yes/No
10	Did your parent ever assault or injure his or her partner?	Yes/No	Yes/No
11	Did either parent obtain your obedience by threatening to leave you or give you away?	Yes/No	Yes/No
12	Did either parent threaten to kill themselves?	Yes/No	Yes/No
13	Did either parent drink more alcohol than was good for them?	Yes/No	Yes/No
14	Was your parent often away or not available?	Yes/No	Yes/No
15	Was your parent inconsistent, sometimes responding, and at other times ignoring your needs for attention and affection?	Yes/No	Yes/No
16	Did either parent discourage you from playing with other children?	Yes/No	Yes/No

* If you were adopted these questions apply to your adoptive parents.

17	Did either parent give you the impression that the world is a very dangerous place in which children will not survive unless they stay very close?	Yes/No	Yes/No
18	Did either parent worry a great deal about your health?	Yes/No	Yes/No
19	Did either parent worry a great deal about your safety?	Yes/No	Yes/No
20	Was either parent overprotective?	Yes/No	Yes/No
22	Was your parent dependent on or inclined to cling to his or her spouse?	Yes/No	Yes/No
24	Were you unusually close to your parent?	Yes/No	Yes/No
25	Was either parent inclined to tease you or make you feel small?	Yes/No	Yes/No
26	Did either parent beat you or physically punish you more than most parents?	Yes/No	Yes/No
27	Did either parent sexually interfere with you or expect you to touch their genitals?	Yes/No	Yes/No
28	Was either parent unable to show warmth or to hug or cuddle you?	Yes/No	Yes/No
29	Was your birth planned and wanted by your parents?	Yes/No	Yes/No
30	Did you have mixed feelings of love and hate, affection and resentment, towards either parent?	Yes/No	Yes/No

Section II About your childhood

1	Were you, at any time before the age of 10, sent to a boarding school, orphanage or children's home for more than a few weeks?	Yes/No
2	Were you an only child for more than five years of your childhood?	Yes/No
4	Was your family subjected for a long time to serious danger or persecution?	Yes/No
5	Did you suffer from severe illness which threatened your life before the age of 6?	Yes/No
6	Or a similar illness from 6 to 16?	Yes/No
7	Would you describe yourself as an insecure child?	Yes/No
8	Would you describe yourself as an anxious child?	Yes/No
9	Would you describe yourself as an unhappy child?	Yes/No
10	Were you an under-achiever, never doing as well at school as your intelligence led people to expect?	Yes/No
11	Were you, as a child, always looking after others?	Yes/No
12	Did you lack self-confidence as a child?	Yes/No
14	Were you afraid to be left alone or easily upset by separation from your parents?	Yes/No
15	Were you timid and reluctant to visit new places, meet new people or do new things?	Yes/No
16	Were you a passive child, leaving it to others to tell you what to do?	Yes/No
17	Did you feel helpless and unable to cope?	Yes/No
18	Did people baby you and regard you as sweet and appealing?	Yes/No
19	Did people regard you as a delicate or fragile child?	Yes/No

20	Did you distrust most adults through much of your childhood?	Yes/No
23	Did people often think of you as tougher or more capable than you really were?	Yes/No
24	Were you a loner, avoiding others as a child?	Yes/No
25	Did you find it hard to ask other people to help you?	Yes/No
26	Did you find it hard to accept cuddles, or other demonstrations of affection?	Yes/No
27	Were you, as a child, inclined to be suspicious or distrustful of other people?	Yes/No
28	Did you find it important to be the one in control, were you 'bossy' or inclined to dominate your friends?	Yes/No
29	Did you have a bad temper?	Yes/No
30	Did you get into trouble for rebellious, aggressive or antisocial behaviour?	Yes/No
31	Were you stubborn?	Yes/No
32	How often did you cry?	Never/ Sometimes/ Often
33	Did you, as a child, often wish you were dead?	Yes/No
34	Were you born outside Britain?	Yes/No
35	If so, at what age did you immigrate or move permanently to Britain?	——

Section III About your life as an adult

1	Do you have children under the age of 16?	Yes/No
2	Do you live alone?	Yes/No
	If yes, for how long?	—— Years
3	Are you suffering from any physical illness or disability? If so:	Yes/No
	(a) Does it threaten your life?	Yes/No
	(b) Does it cause lasting pain?	Yes/No
	(c) Does it prevent you from working?	Yes/No
	(d) Does it prevent you from moving about as much as you would wish?	Yes/No
	(e) Does it interfere with your life in other important ways?	Yes/No
6	Do you have anyone in whom you can confide your inmost thoughts and feelings?	Yes/No
7	If you have, at any time, been married or had a lasting relationship with someone (not your parents) to whom you are or were attached, please answer the following questions. If you have had more than one important relationship these questions apply to the most recent.	
	(a) Were you or are you very close to this person?	Yes/No
	(b) Were you or are you rather dependent on this person?	Yes/No
	(c) Were/is this person rather dependent on you?	Yes/No
	(d) Most couples disagree about something. Which of the following were/are major areas of disagreement between you and your partner:	
	(i) Disciplining children?	Yes/No

	(ii)	Managing money?	Yes/No
	(iii)	Your parents?	Yes/No
	(iv)	Your partner's parents?	Yes/No
	(v)	Alcohol or drugs?	Yes/No
	(vi)	Infidelities?	Yes/No
	(vii)	Time spent away from home?	Yes/No
	(viii)	Sexual matters?	Yes/No
	(ix)	Other problems?	Yes/No

(e) Is/was this person more than five years older than you? Yes/No

(f) Do/did you regard him/her as more like a parent than an equal partner? Yes/No

(g) Do/did you find even short periods of separation from this person distressing? Yes/No

(h) Do/did you have mixed feelings of anger and affection towards this person? Yes/No

(i) Do/did you find it necessary to get away from this person from time to time in order to reduce tension? Yes/No

(j) Do/did you find it hard to get this person to talk about matters that were emotional or upsetting? Yes/No

8 Has a relative of yours died shortly after the death of another person in circumstances that made you suspect that grief might have contributed to their death? Yes/No

9 Has any person close to you died in the last five years? Yes/No

(a) If so, how many have died? ——
(If more than one has died, the questions which follow refer to the loss which you found most upsetting.)

(b) Was the death expected for more than a week before it took place? Yes/No
(c) Did you blame yourself in any way for what happened? Yes/No
(d) Did you blame other people for what happened? Yes/No
(e) Was the death caused by murder or manslaughter? Yes/No
(f) Was the death caused by suicide? Yes/No
(g) Was the person who died the person referred to in question 7? Yes/No
If Yes, ignore the rest of the questions on this page and continue overleaf.
If No:

(h) Would you say that your relationship with the person who died was particularly close? Yes/No
(i) Were you unusually dependent on this person? Yes/No
(j) Was the person unusually dependent on you (inclined to cling)? Yes/No
(k) Did you have mixed feelings of affection and anger towards the person who died? Yes/No
(l) Were there many things on which you disagreed? Yes/No
(m) Did you find even short periods of separation from this person distressing? Yes/No
(n) Was this person your father/mother
brother/sister
uncle/aunt
husband/wife
daughter/son
friend/other (specify)?
(Underline the relationship that applies)

Section IV About you now

1	Would you say that you are very anxious?	Yes/No
2	Would you say that you are very depressed or miserable?	Yes/No
3	Are you very tense or strung up?	Yes/No
4	Do you lack confidence in yourself?	Yes/No
5	Do you find it hard to trust other people?	Yes/No
6	Of the two, which is the bigger problem: trust in yourself or trust in others?	Self/Others/ Neither
7	Do you take medicines for your nerves? If so, do you take rather more than you should?	Yes/No Yes/No
8	Do you use alcohol to control anxiety or depression? If so, do you take rather more than you should?	Yes/No Yes/No
9	Do you find it hard to cope with your responsibilities?	Yes/No
10	Do you sometimes experience feelings of panic or acute fear?	Yes/No
11	Are you very lonely?	Yes/No
12	Do you sometimes behave in a childish or immature way?	Yes/No
13	Are you very shy?	Yes/No
14	Do you spend a lot of time pining or longing for someone or something you have lost?	Yes/No
15	Do you sometimes rely on others more than you should?	Yes/No
16	Do you often wish that someone would look after you?	Yes/No
17	If you got to the end of your tether would you:	
	(a) seek help from a friend?	Yes/No
	(b) seek help from your family?	Yes/No
	(c) seek help from a doctor?	Yes/No
	(d) seek help from some other person?	Yes/No
	(e) shut yourself away from people?	Yes/No
	(f) drown your sorrows with alcohol?	Yes/No
	(g) take an overdose or otherwise harm yourself?	Yes/No
	(h) become irritable or bad tempered with others?	Yes/No
	(i) turn your frustration inwards, feeling guilty or self-reproachful?	Yes/No
18	Have you recently got to the end of your tether?	Yes/No
19	How often do you cry?	Never/ Sometimes/ Often
20	Do you wish you could cry more than you do?	Yes/No
21	Do you find it hard to show affection for people who are close to you?	Yes/No
22	Would you describe yourself as aggressive or challenging?	Yes/No
23	Do you find it hard to express feelings of sadness or grief?	Yes/No
24	Are you filled with regret about something which you did or said, but cannot now put right?	Yes/No

Thank you

Appendix 3.2: Instructions and permission form

Please complete this form and return it to me. Answer all the questions even if you think that they are not important to you. (I need to know what is *not* important as well as what is.)

All answers will be treated as strictly confidential and no names or other identifying information will be revealed if the replies are used for research or teaching purposes.

The best way to fill in the form is to answer each question quickly. Just underline the correct answer to each question. You can put a cross in the margin if you are unable to answer.

Although most people find it interesting, and possibly helpful, to fill in the form, this is quite voluntary and you will not be penalised in any way if you prefer not to answer any or all of the questions.

Your replies to the questions will be entered for analysis onto a computer under a code number. This means that if an unauthorised person should gain access to them they would not be able to discover who had completed the form. The key to the code giving names and addresses will be kept under lock and key and will only be accessible to me.

In accordance with the Data Protection Act you are entitled to read any data held about you on a computer in this way. If you wish to read this please contact Dr Parkes. The printout will only contain, in coded form, the replies that you have given to these questions.

CONSENT FORM

I give permission for the information given on this form to be used by Dr Parkes for research and teaching purposes on the understanding that my name will not be disclosed and that no other information which would enable me to be identified will be revealed in any publication of the results of this research.

Please sign here   Date

Appendix 3.3: Missing and unreliable data

Analysis of missing data

In all questionnaire studies some questions will remain unanswered and it is necessary to adopt consistent rules to minimise the risk of error. In the RAQ most questions required a dichotomous 'Yes' or 'No' answer. In sections I, II and III most responses were negative. Inspection of the data showed that although the questionnaire requested respondents to record negative as well as positive responses many failed to do so, underlining only the (relatively infrequent) positive responses. In these sections, therefore, missing data were treated as negative responses.

In section III, question 9, which covered any bereavement that had occurred in the last five years, was missed out or inadequate in many cases. The reasons for this were:

- In 36 cases, due to a clerical error, this question was omitted from the questionnaire.
- In a further 21 cases the bereavement which had given rise to the referral had occurred more than five years earlier.

These problems reduced the total number of bereaved people about whom details of the bereavement are known from 181 to 124. The subsection of question III/9 about dependence on and disagreement with the dead person may also have been influenced by the tendency of bereaved people to idealise the dead. These deficiencies will be taken into account in the analysis of the data.

The subsections of questions III/9k–n were added at a late stage of the study and answers to these questions have not been included in the analysis reported here. They are included in Appendix 3.1 for the benefit of any reader who wishes to make future use of the questionnaire.

In section IV both positive and negative types of response were obtained with similar frequency and any response set established in the preceding sections was soon corrected. Consequently most questions were answered and little data was missing. In this section, whenever data was missing the mean was substituted.

Reliability of individual questions

The test/retest reliability of those questions which concerned past rather than present issues; that is, the questions from sections I, II and some in section III of the questionnaire were tested by comparing the answers given to the RAQ when first completed with those given at follow-up. Only the 60 respondents who completed both questionnaires were included.

Seven dichotomous questions had exceptionally low reliability (kappa < 5.0) and have therefore been excluded from the questionnaire (hence the numbering of questions in Appendix 3.1 is not consecutive). These were:

I/21   When you were a child did either parent make you feel that you had to look after them?

I/23   Did your parents want you to grow up?
       (0 = Yes, 1 = No, 9 = NK)

II/3   Did you have five or more brothers and sisters older than yourself (including stepbrothers and stepsisters)?

II/13 Did you depend too much on others?

II/21 Did you distrust other children through much of your childhood?

II/22 Did you learn to be independent, to stand on your own two feet, at an early age?

III/5 By comparison with most families in this country, would you say that your own family:
       (a) are sentimental, showing their feelings easily and freely?
       (b) are controlled, concealing their feelings, cool, laid back?
             are neither of these?

Other questions, whose reliability lay between kappa 0.7 and 0.5, have been included in composite scores.

Finally, question III/4 (Are you an immigrant from another country) was deleted as it is covered by question II/34.

Appendix 3.4: Data reduction

After eliminating unreliable scores, as described above, those that remained were examined with a view to reducing the total number of variables for analysis. The simplest were the four checklists. These are mainly found in section III (Adult Life). Replies to questions on these lists were summed together as shown below.

II/36c. A *Childhood Illness Score* was obtained by summing replies to questions II/5 (life-threatening illness before aged 6) and II/6 (life-threatening illness from 6 to 16 years).

III/3f. A *Disability Score* was obtained by summing replies to III/3a to III3e (replies to checklist of types of disability).

III/7d.i–ix. A *Marital Disagreement Score* was obtained by summing replies to question III/7d.i–ix (major areas of disagreement with partner). Since disagreement with the deceased person was assessed by only one question (III/9l) the marital disagreement score can be regarded as the more sensitive measure.

III/7. The Marital Disagreement Score was summed with replies to question III/7b (Were you or are you rather dependent on this person?) and III/7c (Were/is this person rather dependent on you?) to make a *Marital Disharmony Score*.

Three questions that were replied to in related ways were IV/17a and IV/17b (If you got to the end of your tether would you (a) Seek help from a friend? (b) Seek help from your family?) and question III/6 (Do you have anyone in whom you can confide your inmost thoughts and feelings?). As we would expect, people who have no confidante are less likely to turn to friends or family when at the end of their tether. After rescoring III/6 so that a Yes response scores 1 and a No response 0, the result can be added to the replies to IV/17a and b to make a *Social Support Score*.

IV/50 Current Dysfunction Score. Sum of: IV/7a (Do you take medicine for your nerves?), IV/7b (If so, do you take rather more than you should?), IV/8a (Do you use alcohol to control your anxiety or depression?), IV/8b (If so, do you take rather more than you should?), IV/9 (Do you find it hard to cope with your responsibilities?) and IV/18 (Have you recently got to the end of your tether?).

Some factual questions and questions of low communality could only be treated as unique and remain in the questionnaire in their own right.[1]

Factor analysis

The remaining items from section I (Parenting), II (Childhood) and IV (Current State) were subjected to factor analysis as a means of determining the extent to which they covary. Most of the factors that resulted corresponded to clusters that had been anticipated on clinical and theoretical grounds. This justifies us in adding them together to form groups each of which gives rise to a different score. When items emerged in more than one factor the decision about which group to place them in was reached on clinical and theoretical grounds. Each group was assigned a different number for purposes of identification. These numbers are given below.

Section I – Parents

This section was complicated by the fact that each question was asked twice, once for each parent. For this reason two factor analyses were carried out, one for questions relating to mother and one for questions relating to father. Each included 28 variables. Bartlett's test of sphericity (p = 0.00000 for each parent) and the Kaiser-Meyer-Olkin (KMO) measure of sampling adequacy (Father 0.75 Mother 0.70) were satisfactory in both analyses indicating that the data was suitable for principle axis factoring.

Seven factors having eigenvalues > 1.0 were emerged out of the questions appertaining to father and eight factors from those applying to mother. Between them these factors accounted for 54 per cent (Father) and 57 per cent (Mother) of the variance.

Because there were many questions in both analyses which gave loadings >.3 on more than one factor, Varimax rotation was undertaken. Convergence occurred in 14 and 25 iterations. There were now four factors about father and four about mother with eigenvalues > 1.0. They accounted for 31 per cent and 29 per cent of the variance.

On inspection it is clear that the first factor contained virtually the same variables about father as did the first factor for mother. Other factors too showed considerable overlap although they did not follow the same sequence of factors. Very few questions were found with loadings > 0.3 in more than one factor.

Table A.3.4.1 lists the variables and factor loadings (in italics) that were

---

1   III/9u. A *Bereavement Trauma Score* can be obtained by summing the replies to questions III/96.e and f. This is mentioned since it may be useful as an index of bereavement risk, but it is not relevant to the current volume and will not be referred to again here.

Table A.3.4.1 Factor loadings of variables concerned with Father and Mother

Father #	Load	Mother #	Load	Title
Factor 1		**Factor 1**		
11	0.57	11	0.37	Threat to Leave
(15)	0.62	15	0.56	Inconsistent
16	0.52	16	0.42	Discourage Play
28	0.54	28	0.48	Unable Touch
(25)	0.33	(25)	0.47	Teased
(14)	0.43			Often Away
(26)	0.40			Beat
		30	0.53	Ambivalent
		29	0.34	Unwanted Child
Factor 2		**Factor 4**		
3	0.68	4	0.45	Separated 0–6 years
4	0.78	4	0.45	Separated 7–11 years
5	0.60	5	0.49	Separated 12–16 years
14	0.40	14	0.55	Often Away
		(25)	0.32	Teased
Factor 3		**Factor 6**		
10	0.68			Violent
13	0.46			Alcohol
(25)	0.41	(25)	0.41	Tease
(26)	0.48			Beat
27	0.37			Sex Abuse
(15)	0.34			Inconsistent

Father #	Load	Mother #	Load	Title
Factor 4		**Factor 2**		
17	0.47	17	0.58	Family in Danger
18	0.53	18	0.59	Worry Health of Child
19	0.67	19	0.61	Worry Safety of Child
20	0.61	20	0.66	Overprotective
Factor 5		**Factor 6**		
7	0.67	7	0.49	Worrier
8	0.61	8	0.68	Depressive
9	0.56	9	0.52	Psychiatric Therapy
12	0.32	12	0.44	Threat Suicide
		22	0.39	Dependent

Variables in brackets occur in more than one factor.

found in each factor relating to father and mother. The numbers refer to the questions listed in Appendix 3.1, pp. 281–5.

Factor 1 about father and factor 1 about mother seems to reflect controlling, inconsistent parents who are intolerant of closeness. Factor 2 about fathers corresponded to factor 4 about mother and draws together various indicators of separation from parents. Father's factor 4 corresponds to mother's factor 2 and seems to imply parents who see the world as a dangerous place in which their child is at special risk, consequently they are overprotective of that child. Father's factor 5 and mother's factor 3 includes depressed parents some of whom threatened suicide and/or received psychiatric treatment. A difference between the clustering of attributions about parents arose in factor 3. about fathers. This identifies a cluster of variables reflecting alcoholism, outright rejection and/or violence both towards mother and towards the child. The only component of this which is reported in mothers is question I/25 (Teased). I/25 is also found in both sexes in factor 1. It appears that this cluster of variables is largely confined to fathers.

On the basis of this analysis the following scores have been derived for further analysis. Each is scored for both parents separately and together. Because of the similarity between the characteristics attributed to mother and father, for most purposes, the combined scores for both parents will be used. The full wording of each question is given in the Appendix.

Scores of parenting

I/40 Parental Distant Control Score (based on factor 1 in both parents). Sum of : I/11 (Parent obtained obedience by threat to leave or expel child), I/15 (Inconsistent, sometimes responding, other times ignoring child), I/16 (Discouraged play with other children), and I/28 (Unable to show warmth, hug or cuddle).

I/41 Parental Overprotection Score (based on Mother factor 2 and Father factor 4). Sum of: I/17 (Parent saw world as dangerous, stay close), I/18 (Worry a great deal re health), I/19 (Worry a great deal re safety), I/20 (Overprotective).

I/42 Parental Depression/Psychiatric Problem Score (based on Mother's factor 3 and Father's factor 5). Sum of: I/7 (Parent nervous, insecure or worrier), I/8 (Episodes of gloom or depression), I/9a (Psychiatric treatment), I/9b (Admission for psychiatric care), I/12 (Threatened to kill self).

I/43 Parental Separation Score (based on Mother's factor 4 and Father's factor 2). Sum of: I/1 (Not brought up by true parents), I/3 (Separated for > 1 month before aged 6 yrs), I/4 (Separated aged 6–10 yrs), I/5 (Separated 11–16 yrs), I/14 (Parent often away).

I/44 Parental Unusual Closeness Score (based on Mother's factor 5 and Father's factor 6). Sum of: I/6 (Afraid parent would die or be killed), I/24 (Unusually close to parent).

I/45 Parental Rejection/Violence Score (based on Father's factor 3). Sum of : I/10 (Parent assaulted or injured partner), I/13 (Drank more alcohol than was good for them), I/25 (Inclined to tease child or make them feel small), I/26 (Beat or physically punished child more often than most parents), I/27 (Sexually interfered with or expected child to touch parent's genitals).

I/46 Overall Problematic Parenting Score. Sum of above parenting scores (I/40–I/45).

Question I/2 (Are your parents still alive?) does not necessarily apply to childhood and had low communality in regard to both parents. Consequently it has not been included in any of the scores. Neither has question I/23 (Did your parents want you to grow up?) which also had low communality.

Question I/30 (Ambivalence) differed from the rest in reflecting the child's feelings about the parent(s). Thus it should be regarded as a dependent variable when studying the effects of parenting. For this reason it has not been included in any of the scores listed above.

Section II – Childhood

Twenty-four questions about childhood personality, reactions and behaviour were included in this analysis. Bartlett's test (p = 0.00000) and the KMO test of sphericity (0.85) were both satisfactory. Principle axis factoring showed that six variables had eigenvalues > 1.0. Together these accounted for 56 per cent of the variance with 25 per cent explained by factor 1. Because of the number of variables appearing in more than one factor Varimax rotation was carried out. In the final analysis two factors had eigenvalues in excess of 1.0 and between them they accounted for 30 per cent of the variance with 22.5 per cent explained by factor 1. Convergence took place after 7 iterations.

Table A.3.4.2 shows the factor loadings of variables in the six factors which emerged. Factor 1 seems to reflect overall insecurity and timidity. Factor 2 indicates an aggressive, controlling attitude to others. This seems to resemble factor 3, which implies distrust of others. Difficulty in accepting cuddles and other demonstrations of affection is found in both these factors. Thus, it seems justified to amalgamate factors 2 and 3 to make a single score. Factor 4 describes the classical 'Dresden Vase', a prized but fragile child who fears separation from parents. Factor 5 is depressed and tearful child while factor 6 describes what Bowlby (1980: 156) calls a 'compulsive caregiver'. From these factors the following scores have been derived for further analysis:

New scores of childhood variables

II/40 Childhood Timidity Score. Sum of: II/7 (Describes self as an insecure child), II/10 (Under-achiever), II/12 (Lacked self-confidence), II/15 (Timid child), II/16 (Passive child), II/24 (Loner, avoiding others), II/25 (Found it hard to ask for help).

II/41 Childhood Aggressiveness/Distrust Score. Sum of : II/20 (Distrusted adults through much of childhood), II/26 (Hard to accept cuddles or other affection), II/27 (Suspicious and distrustful), II/28 (Controlling, 'bossy',

Table A.3.4.2 Factor Loadings of variables concerned with Childhood

#	Load	Title	#	Load	Title
Factor 1			*Factor 4*		
7	0.57	Insecure Child	14	0.51	Fearful of Separation
10	0.48	Under-Achiever	18	0.41	Sweet Child
12	0.75	Lacked Self-Confidence	19	0.45	Delicate/Fragile Child
15	0.61	Timid Child	(8)	0.37	Anxious Child
16	0.57	Passive	(17)	0.43	Helpless
24	0.60	Loner			
(8)	0.31	Anxious Child			
(17)	0.43	Helpless			
(26)	0.30	Hard accept cuddles			
(25)	0.61	Hard ask for help			
Factor 2			*Factor 5*		
28	0.48	'Bossy'	9	0.50	Very Unhappy Child
29	0.53	Bad Tempered	32	0.50	Often Cried
30	0.68	Aggressive Child	33	0.48	Wished self dead
31	0.62	Stubborn			
(23)	0.30	Others mistook as tough			
(26)	0.39	Hard accept cuddles			
Factor 3			*Factor 6*		
20	0.71	Distrusted adults	11	0.45	Always looked after others
27	0.64	Suspicious	(23)	0.49	Others mistook as tough
(26)	0.36	Hard accept cuddles	(25)	0.39	Hard ask for help

Variables in brackets occur in more than one factor.

dominating friends), II/29 (Bad tempered), II/30 (In trouble for aggressive or antisocial behaviour), II/31 (Stubborn).

II/42 Childhood 'Dresden Vase' (Precious Child) Score. Sum of: II/8 (An anxious child), II/14 (Afraid to be left alone or separated from parents), II/17 (Felt helpless, unable to cope), II/18 (Babied, seen as sweet and appealing), II/19 (Seen as delicate or fragile).

II/43 Childhood Unhappiness Score. Sum of: II/9 (Sees self as an unhappy child), II/32 (Often cried), II/33 (Often wished self dead).

II/44 Childhood Compulsive Caregiving Score. Sum of: II/11 (As child, always looking after others), II/23 (Seen by others as tougher or more capable than really was).

II/45 Childhood Overall Vulnerability Score. Sum of above childhood variables II/40–44.

Questions not included were numbered II/1–6 and II/34–35. These covered events and circumstances of childhood and are not integral to patterns of attachment although they may influence later developments and relationships.

Section IV – Current coping and symptoms

Following preliminary analysis, the questions in this section have been divided into two categories: those concerned with the respondent's ways of coping and viewing the world at the time of completing the form (termed 'Coping Style and Personality Variables') and those concerned with current feelings and reactions (termed 'Symptoms and Distress Variables').

Although this division sounds clear the link between coping and symptoms was sometimes so close that it made more sense to score them together. Thus, coping question 17f in which the respondent agrees that, at the end of their tether, they would 'drown your sorrows with alcohol' correlated highly with symptom question 8 (Do you use alcohol to control anxiety and depression; if so do you take rather more than you should?). Similarly IV/15 (Do you sometimes rely on others more than you should?) sounds like a way of coping but was found to correlate highly with a positive response to the question 'Have you recently got to the end of your tether?' which is closer to being a symptom variable. For purposes of analysis all of these were included among the 'Symptoms and Distress' variables.

Question IV/19 (How often do you cry – Never/Sometimes/Often?) sounds like a simple measure of current feelings and reactions, but preliminary factor analysis of pooled variables from this section showed that people who replied 'Never' to this question were found to adopt a coping style characterised by inhibition. For this reason replies to this question were subdivided into two dichotomous questions: IV/19a (Never Cries – Score: Never = 1, Sometimes and Often = 0) and IV/19b (Often Cries – Score: Often = 1, Sometimes and Never = 0).

Replies to question IV/23 (Do you find it hard to express feelings of sadness or grief?) could be regarded as a personality variable in non-bereaved populations but has a rather different meaning to bereaved people in whom it comes closer to being a distressing feeling.

In the final analysis it is important to recognise that major life events such as the loss of a loved person are likely to influence the way people view and cope with the world. This attempt to separate coping styles and reactions, as if the former was an immutable aspect of personality, should be treated with caution. This said, there is some value in attempting to separate the two since coping is likely to influence reaction and may have important implications for intervention programmes.

IV/A Current coping and personality

Twenty questions about ways of coping with stress and about personality were included in this analysis. The KMO of 0.71 and Bartlett's test (P = 0.00000) indicates suitability for factor analysis. Five factors emerged with eigenvalues above 1.0. Together, these explained 53 per cent of the variance. The first factor accounted for 19 per cent. Because many items appeared in more than one factor a Varimax rotation was undertaken. Convergence occurred after 13 iterations.

Table A.3.4.3 shows the rotated factor loadings. These suggest that four clusters of variables occur. The first, factor 1, is concerned with the inhibition and control of feelings and the second, factor 2, with aggression and challenging others. Factors 3, 4 and 5 all cover replies to the multiple choice list in question IV/17 (If you got to the end of your tether would you . . .?). Factor 3 includes four questions indicating that the respondent would seek help from others, Factor 4 comprises the two questions concerned with turning in on oneself and factor 5 a single question on drowning one's sorrows with alcohol.

Question IV/17g (At end of tether – would take overdose) contributes in a negative way to factor 3 implying that people who would turn to others are less likely to harm themselves than those who do not, but the factor loading was not high and this question has not been included in any of the coping or reaction scores to be described below.

Questions IV/17j–l were only added to the questionnaire at a late stage. The numbers completing the questionnaire were not sufficient to meet criteria for factor analysis. The scores derived from this analysis are as follows.

IV/40 Cope – Emotional Inhibition/Distrust Score. Sum of: IV/5 (Finds it hard to trust other people), IV/19 (Never cries), IV/20 (Wishes could cry more), IV/21 (Finds it hard to show affection), IV/23 (Finds it hard to express sadness or grief). This last will also be treated as a symptom/feelings variable

Table A.3.4.3 Factor loadings of Coping/Personality variables

#	Load	Title	#	Load	Title
Factor 1			*Factor 4*		
5	0.40	Hard trust others	17e	0.45	At EoT – Shut self away
21	0.86	Hard show affection	17i	0.47	At EoT – Turn inwards
23	0.55	Hard express grief	(17d)	−0.36	At EoT – Seek Others
Factor 2			*Factor 5*		
12	0.40	Childish/Immature	17f	0.66	At EoT – Drown sorrows with alcohol
17h	0.65	At EoT – Irritable/ Bad-tempered			
22	0.50	Aggressive/Challenging			
Factor 3					
17a	0.43	At EoT – Seek Friend			
17b	0.35	At EoT – Seek Family			
17c	0.45	At EoT – Seek Doctor			
17g	−0.31	At EoT – Take Overdose			
(17d)	0.51	At EoT – Seek Others			

Variables in brackets occur in more than one factor.

in Chapter 6 where it is used as a measure of inhibition of grief after bereavement.

IV/41 Cope – Aggressive/Assertive Score. Sum of: IV/12 (Sometimes behaves in a childish or immature way), IV/17h (At end of tether – irritable or bad tempered), IV/22 (Describes self as aggressive or challenging).

IV/42 Cope – End of Tether (EoT) – Seek Help Score. Sum of: IV/17a (At EoT – seek help from friend), IV/17b (At EoT – seek help from family), IV/17c (At EoT – seek help from doctor), IV/17d (At EoT – seek help from other).

IV/43 Cope – EoT – Turn Inward Score. Sum of: IV/17e (At EoT – shut self away from people), IV/17i (At EoT – turn frustration inward, feeling guilty).

As indicated above the question on drowning one's sorrows with alcohol was treated as a reaction variable and included in IV/48 below.

IV/B Current symptoms and distress

Seventeen questions about current feelings, reactions and emotions at the time when the questionnaire was completed, after referral for psychiatric treatment, were included in this analysis. A KMO score of 0.78 and Bartlett test (p = 0.00000) indicated their suitability for factoring.

A principle components analysis showed that six factors reached eigenvalues > 1.0. Together they accounted for 58 per cent of the variance, factor 1 explained 21 per cent. Because many variables with factor loadings > 0.3 were found in more than one factor a Varimax rotation was undertaken. This converged after 18 iterations.

Table A.3.4.4 shows the factor loadings for variables in the six main factors. Factor 1 includes questions about anxiety, fear and loss of confidence, factor 2 pining and loneliness (the essential features of grief), factor 3 gives high loadings on depression, tension and psychotropic medication but also overlaps with anxiety and pining. Factor 4 seems to imply helplessness and dependency. Factor 5 describes people who cannot cry and wish they could. Thus it resembles factor 1 in the coping and personality section above. For this reason the questions in factor 5 have been included in the 'Coping: Inhibition/Distrust' Score (IV/40) described above.

Question IV/8 was a combined score derived from the question 'Do you use alcohol to control your anxiety or depression? If so, do you take rather more than you should?' This emerged as the main component of factor 6 with a low association with IV/24 (Filled with regrets). The latter is more powerfully included in factor 2 while IV/8 seems to belong with the 'coping' question IV/17f (At end of tether – drown sorrows in alcohol). These two (IV/8 and IX/17f) were therefore assigned to the same 'Symptom/Distress' score (IV/48 below). The scores derived from this analysis are as follows.

IV/44 Anxiety/Panic Score. Sum of: IV/1 (Very anxious), IV/4 (Lacks confidence), IV/9 (Hard to cope), IV/10 (Sometimes feels panic or acute fear).

IV/45 Grief/Loneliness Score. Sum of : IV/11 (Very lonely), IV/14 (Much time pining), IV/24 (Filled with regret).

Table A.3.4.4 Factor loadings of Emotions/Symptoms variables

#	Load	Title	#	Load	Title
Factor 1			*Factor 4*		
1	0.76	Very Anxious	15	0.69	Dependent
4	0.66	Lacks Confidence	16	0.70	Wish cared for
(9)	0.54	Hard to cope	(9)	0.35	Hard to cope
(3)	0.38	Very Tense	(18)	0.49	Recently at end of tether
(10)	0.65	Panic/Acute Fear			
Factor 2			*Factor 5*		
11	0.68	Very Lonely	19a	0.80	Never cry
14	0.64	Pining	19b	−0.66	Often cry
(24)	0.66	Filled with regrets	(20)	0.59	Wish could cry more
(2)	0.43	Very Depressed			
Factor 3			*Factor 6*		
7	0.42	Medication	8	0.85	Excess Alcohol
(2)	0.59	Very Depressed	(24)	0.38	Filled with regrets
(3)	0.66	Very Tense			
(10)	0.32	Panic/Acute Fear			
(14)	0.35	Pining			
(18)	0.45	Recently at end of tether			
(20)	0.34	Wish could cry more			

Variables in brackets occur in more than one factor.

IV/46 Depression/Medication Score. Sum of: IV/2 (Very depressed), IV/3 (Very tense), IV/7a (Takes medicines for nerves), IV/7b (Takes more than should).

IV/47 Clinging Score. Sum of: IV/15 (Relies too much on others), IV/16 (Wish someone would look after me), IV/18 (Recently got to end of tether).

IV/48 Alcohol Consumption Score. Sum of: IV/8a (Uses alcohol to control feelings), IV/8b (Takes more than should), IV/17f (At end of tether would drown sorrows with alcohol).

IV/49 Overall Distress Score. Sum of IV/44–48.

The Kolmogorov-Smirnov Test was used on all scores to determine their normality. Only the Childhood Overall Vulnerability Score was greater than 0.05 in both the initial and follow-up scores. For this reason non-parametric statistics have been used, whenever appropriate, to analyse this data.

Appendix 3.5: Reliability of scores

The *internal reliability* or consistency of all scores was tested by calculating the alpha coefficient. The results of this analysis are shown in Table A.3.5.1. As might be expected the highest reliability is found in scores which were created from the start to measure aspects of the same variable: the Disability (α 0.88) and Marital Disagreement (α 0.99). Other scores that reach or come close to the 0.8 level are Parental Overprotection, Parental Separation and Childhood Timidity.

The rest have lower levels of internal consistency. This is hardly surprising given the fact that the questions were chosen to cover the widest possible range of variables rather than to fit particular scores. For example, the Marital Disharmony score was set up to include two very different kinds of risk factor, marital disagreements and dependency. Marital Disagreements were measured using a checklist and, as we have seen, was found to have high internal reliability. Dependency was measured in two questions, one assessing the respondent's dependence on the partner and the other the partner's dependence on the respondent. These two also had high reliability (α 0.99) but the reliability dropped to 0.46 when all three items were scored as one score. Even so it is reasonable to retain the Marital Disharmony score because previous research has found that all of these disparate variables contribute to problems both before and after the ending of the relationship in question.

The fact that most variables were found by factor analysis to cluster together also reassures us that the scores derived in this way are likely to be meaningful. The proof of that particular question, of course, must await examination of the extent to which they confirm or contradict the hypotheses that the study set up to test.

Test/retest reliability is a more satisfactory way of assessing the extent to which respondents reply consistently to the same questions. It was tested on a sample of 60 respondents who completed the questionnaire a second time over 2 months and a mean of 19 months later. Only those scores that would not be expected to change over time (mainly the Parenting and Childhood scores) could be included. The score of each respondent at the time of first completing the questionnaire was compared with their score at follow-up and Spearman's Coefficient (*rho*) calculated. The coefficients resulting from this

Table A.3.5.1 Reliability of scores

Parenting scores	Mother		Father		Both	
	Alpha	Rho	Alpha	Rho	Alpha	Rho
(I/40) Distant Control	0.80	0.56	0.85	0.74	0.86	0.75
(I/41) Over protection	0.85	0.75	0.85	0.74	0.85	0.74
(I/42) Depression/Psy	0.83	0.71	0.78	0.64	0.78	0.64
(I/43) Separations	0.88	0.78	0.90	0.81	0.91	0.83
(I/44) Unusual Closeness	0.76	0.62	0.80	0.57	0.76	0.61
(I/45) Rejection/Violence	0.78	0.53	0.73	0.58	0.77	0.63
(I/46) *Problematic Parenting*	0.87	0.77	0.85	0.74	0.85	0.76
Childhood Vulnerability			Alpha	Rho		
(II/40) Timidity			0.88	0.78		
(II/41) Aggressiveness/Distrust			0.82	0.69		
(II/42) Dresden Vase (Precious Child)			0.87	0.77		
(II/43) Unhappiness			0.69	0.52		
(II/44) Compulsive Caregiving			0.86	0.76		
(II/45) *Overall Vulnerability*			0.90	0.82		
Attachment scores						
Anxious/Ambivalent Attachment			0.91	0.83		
Avoidant Attachment			0.80	0.67		
Disorganised Attachment			0.87	0.77		
Insecure Attachment Score			0.94	0.89		
Adult circumstances			Alpha	Rho		
(III/3f) Disability			0.90	0.81		
Coping and Personality						
(IV/40) Emotional Inhibition/Distrust			0.64	0.59		
(IV/41) Aggressive/Assertive			0.49	0.42		
(IV/42) End of Tether – Seek Help			0.48	0.52		
(IV/43) End of Tether – Turn Inward			0.38	0.47		
(IV/50) *Problematic Coping*			0.65	0.55		
Current Symptoms and Feelings						
(IV/44) Anxiety/Panic			0.68	N/A		
(IV/45) Grief/Loneliness			0.54	N/A		
(IV/46) Depression/Medication			0.47	N/A		
(IV/47) Clinging			0.52	N/A		
(IV/48) Alcohol Consumption			0.66	N/A		
(IV/49) *Overall Distress*			0.62	N/A		

Notes: N/A Not applicable to retest. Alpha-Coefficient of Internal Reliability n. 278. Rho-Spearman coefficient obtained on Test/Retest on follow-up n. 60.

analysis are shown in Table A.3.5.1 with the significant findings in italics (all were significant).

Most *Scores of Parenting* are in the satisfactory range with Spearman coefficients > 0.65. Scores relating to the relationship with mother had coefficients very similar to those relating to father. Lowest coefficients (both alpha coefficients and rho) are those reflecting Parental Unusual Closeness. Although the reliability of the scores for Mother and Father separately are improved when both are summed to make a combined Unusual Closeness score. These scores rely on only two questions neither of which has a high factor loading. Since the alpha coefficients for this score is also low, the reliability of the measures of Unusual Closeness is in doubt and this will have to be taken into account in those analyses which make use of this variable.

Most coefficients of scores derived from section II of the questionnaire, Childhood State and Relationships, fall into the same satisfactory range with the exception of the Childhood Unhappiness score, which only reached 0.52. This score is based on three questions from the fifth factor, which emerged with relatively low factor loadings. The highest correlation (0.82) in this section derived from the Overall Childhood Vulnerability score. In this instance it was appropriate to use the Pearson Correlation.

The *Attachment scores* were reasonably reliable with the overall scores rho 0.89, the Anxious/Ambivalent score correlations rho 0.83 and the Disorganised Attachment scores rho 0.77. The lowest correlation was that of the Avoidant Attachment score (rho 0.63).

Only one score in section III, Adult State, was suitable for testing. This was the Disability score, which was found reliable with a coefficient of 0.79. The Marital Disagreement score and the Marital Disharmony score had lower correlations (0.62 and 0.42) but these may well have changed over the time between the completion of the first and second questionnaires.

None of the scores in section IV, Symptoms and Distress, were suitable for test/retest reliability testing because all are likely to have been affected by therapy or by the passage of time. Even the Coping Style and Personality scores are likely to change and unlikely to prove reliably constant. The Spearman correlation on retest of the overall Problematic Coping score was 0.55 with the constituent scores ranging from 0.49 (Cope – Aggressive Assertive) to 0.67 (Cope – Emotional Inhibition/Distrust).

Appendix 3.6: Intercorrelation and reliability of attachment pattern scores

Ainsworth's concept of secure attachment would seem likely to be reflected in low scores of 'Problematic Parenting' and 'Childhood Vulnerability'. This is confirmed by a reasonably high and highly significant correlation between 'Problematic Parenting' score and the 'Childhood Vulnerability' score (r 0.64). The two scores can be combined to give a score of 'Insecurity of Attachment'. A low score on the combined variable is taken as an indicator of 'Secure Attachment'.

Ainsworth and Main's three types of insecure attachment are also reflected in this data. 'Anxious/Ambivalent Attachment' is reflected in scores of 'Unusual Closeness' to parents, 'Overprotection' by parents, 'Childhood Timidity' and 'Dresden Vase' (Precious Child).

Table A.3.6.1 shows the intercorrelation between these four variables. 'Overprotection' is highly correlated with 'Childhood Timidity' and 'Dresden Vase' scores, 'Unusual Closeness' less so. On balance it seems reasonable to sum the four scores together in order to produce a score of 'Anxious/Ambivalent Attachment'.

'Avoidant Attachment' is reflected in the 'Parental Distant Control' score (which included agreement with the statement that a parent had been 'Unable to show warmth or to hug or cuddle you') and the 'Childhood Aggressiveness/Distrust' score (which included agreement that, as a child the person would 'find it hard to accept cuddles or other demonstrations of affection'). The two scores are correlated (r 0.42) and can be summed to make a

Table A.3.6.1 Intercorrelation of components of Anxious/Ambivalent Attachment score

	Unusual Closeness to Parents	Overprotection	Childhood Timidity	Dresden Vase
Unusual Closeness	X	0.18**	0.09	0.27**
Overprotection		X	0.25**	0.50**
Childhood Timidity			X	0.48**

** p < 0.01

single measure of 'Avoidant Attachment'. Because only two variables are involved a multivariate analysis is not needed.

Although not included in the score a positive answer to the question 'Did you learn to be independent, to stand on your own two feet, at an early age?' (II/22) also correlated (Spearman's rho 0.13) with this Avoidant Attachment score to a small but significant degree (sig one-tailed 0.037).

'Disorganised/Disoriented Attachment' was less easily measured. The mothers described by Main had suffered severe loss, stress and depression. The nearest approximation to this in the RAQ seemed to derive from the question 'Was your family subjected for a long time to serious danger or persecution?' (II/4), plus the parental 'Depression/Psychiatric' score and the parental 'Rejection/Violence' score. The children in Main's study had reacted by becoming unhappy and helpless. In the RAQ the 'Childhood Unhappiness' score seems to capture this reaction.

Despite the research (reported on p. 16) that suggests that people who have experienced disorganised attachments in early childhood subsequently develop coercive ways of controlling others, it has been decided to place replies to question II/28 'Did you find it important to be the one in control, were you "bossy" or inclined to dominate your friends?' in the Avoidant Attachment category. The justification for this comes from finding that positive replies to this question correlated Spearman's rho = 0.32 with the other questions which make up the Avoidant Attachment score (p = 0.000) whereas its correlation with the Disorganised Attachment score was only 0.15 (p = 0.021). It seems that attempts to dominate require more self-confidence than was commonly found in our sample.

On the other hand, the strategy of selfless caring for others, which is reflected in the Compulsive Caregiving score, was significantly correlated with the scores of Parental Depression/Psychiatric, Parental Rejection/Violence and Childhood Unhappiness though it did not correlate with positive replies to the question on Family Danger.

The intercorrelation of these scores is shown in Table A.3.6.2. Most correlations are significant and moderately high. For the purposes of our research it seems reasonable to combine the scores to make a single measure of 'Disorganised Attachment'.

The reliability of the three insecure attachment scores was tested in the 45 bereaved people who were followed up by comparing their initial scores on these variables with the scores on follow-up. The test/retest reliability of the attachment scores was high as confirmed by the scores of Cronbach's alpha in Table A.3.6.3.

Table A.3.6.2 Intercorrelation of components of Disorganised/Disoriented Attachment score

	Parental Depression/ Psych Disorder	*Parental Rejection/Violence*	*Childhood Unhappiness*	*Childhood Compulsive Caregiving*
Family Danger/ Persecution	0.16*	0.25**	0.18**	0.02
Pt. Depression/ Psychiatric Dis.	X	0.42**	0.31**	0.30**
Pt. Rejection/ Violence Score		X	0.34**	0.28**
Childhood Unhappiness			X	0.13*

** p < 0.01, * p < 0.05

Table A.3.6.3 Test/retest reliability of the Attachment scores

Secure/Insecure Attachment	0.91
Anxious/Ambivalent Attachment	0.91
Avoidant Attachment	0.86
Disorganised Attachment	0.81

Appendix 3.7: RAQ scoring instructions

Missing questions (see also Appendix 3.3, p. 287)

Because data regarding age and sex of the respondent were available from case notes these question were omitted from early versions of the questionnaire and should be added. (These are included as questions III/10 and III/11 in later versions.)

Some questions were found to be unreliable on test/retest. They have been deleted but the question numbers remain unaltered to avoid confusion in analysing earlier versions of the RAQ.

In some early versions of the RAQ question III/9 (about bereavement) were numbered as III/8.

Missing data

Four rules of thumb have been adopted:

1 When it is clear that, in answering a particular series of Yes/No questions, a respondent has only made Yes responses and left other responses blank, blanks to be scored as No.
2 *Dichotomous data*:
   - When over three-quarters of the replies given are in one category (0 or 1), blanks to be scored as the majority.
   - When over a quarter and under three-quarters of the responses are in one category (0 or 1), blanks to be scored as intermediate (i.e. 0.5).
3 *Continuous data*: Missing data to be scored as the mean for this question.
4 When large amounts of data are missing from a part of the questionnaire, as when the questionnaire was changed, those respondents who did not complete these parts to be excluded from the analysis of these parts.

Section I: Parents

- I/2a Mother/Father alive Missing = 0 (Alive).
- If Parent Dead (I/2a = No) in all remaining questions (I/3–I/30) Missing = 0.

Section II: Childhood

- II/12, II/23, II/25, II/31 Missing = 0.5 (approximate mean substitution).
- II/34 (R. born outside Britain) score missing data as 0 (No).
- If II/34 = Yes then, if II/35 (Age at immigration) is missing, substitute mean for your sample.

All other questions in section II score Missing data as 0 (No).

Section III: Adult Life

- III/2a (Do you live alone?) Missing to be scored 0 (No).
  If III/2a = Yes (Living alone) then if III/2b (Years alone) is missing substitute mean for your sample.
- III/3a–e (Physical illness or disability?) Missing to be scored 0 (No).
- III/6 (Confidante) Missing data scored 0.5.
- If III/7a–d (Questions re partner) are all scored 0 or missing, rescore both Missing and 0 as 8 (= No partner). If one or more of these are scored 1 (Yes), score Missing = 0 (No).
- III/7e–j are recently added to the questionnaire and require further analysis using above rules of thumb.
- If III/9 (Bereaved) is scored 0 or 1 (Yes or No) and 3.9a (How many have died?) is missing, score 0.
- If III/9a is 0, then, if III/9b–h (Bereavement risk VARs) is missing = N/A (Not applicable).
- If III/9a is 1 or more, then if III/9b,c,d Missing = 0.5 and if III/9e,f Missing = 0 (No) and if III/9g (Was this partner?) is missing, check if any of 7 questions indicate there was a partner. If No score III/9g = 0.
- If III/11 (Age in years) is missing, substitute mean for your sample.

Section IV: Now

- Questions IV/1–IV/5, IV/9–IV/16, IV/18 and IV/20–IV/24 Missing data to be scored 0.5.
- IV/7a (Medication) and IV/8a (Alcohol) Missing data to be scored 0 (No).
- If IV/7a (Medication) = 0 (No) then IV/7b (excess medication) = 9 (N/A).
- If IV/7a = 1 (Yes) score and IV/7b is missing = 0 (No).
- If IV/8a (Alcohol) = 0 (No) then, if IV/8b (excess alcohol) is missing = 9 (N/A).
- If IV/8a = 1 (Yes) missing data in IV/8b = 0 (No).
- If one or more questions IV/17a–i are scored 1 (Yes) *and* none are scored 0 (No), then score missing data as 0 (No).
- If both Yes (1) and No (0) answers to IV/17a–i score missing data as 0.5.
- If any of IV/17j–l were answered Yes (1) or No (0) *and* if one or more

questions IV/17a–l are scored 1 (Yes) *and* none are scored 0 (No) then score missing data as 0 (No).

- If both Yes (1) and No (0) answers to IV/17a–l score missing data as 0.5.
- IV/19 (Tearfulness) if missing or not known rescore as Sometimes (see below for scoring).

Scoring individual questions

Numeric questions (e.g. I/2b Age at Mother's/Father's death__Years) should be scored as such. Most *Yes/No questions* are scored Yes = 1, No = 0, except questions:

- I/1 Were you brought up by your true Mother/Father?
- I/2a Are your Mother/Father still alive?
- I/29 Was your birth planned and wanted by your Mother/Father?
- III/6 Do you have anyone in whom you can confide?
- III/9b Was the death expected?

These are all scored Yes = 0, No = 1.

- I/32 (How often did you cry Never/Sometimes/Often?) is subdivided into I/32a Never Cry = 1, Sometimes or often = 0, and I/32b Often Cry = 1, Never or sometimes = 0.
- If the reply to question III/9g (Was the person who died the person referred to in III/7 above?) is Yes then score III/9h (Were you unusually dependent?) as III/7b (Were/are you rather dependent?).
- Score III/9i (Was the person unusually dependent on you?) as III/7c (Was/is this person rather dependent on you?).
- III/9l (Were there many things on which you disagreed?) If III/7d × Marital Disagreement score (*v.i.*) >1 score III/9l as 1, if not score III/9l as 0.
- IV/19 (How often do you cry? Never/Sometimes/Often) is subdivided into IV/19a Never Cry = 1, Sometimes or Often = 0 and IV/19b Often Cry = 1, Never or Sometimes = 0.

Combining scores

The following scores are obtained by adding together other scores.

Section I

Parenting scores are obtained by adding individual scores for Mother to scores for Father.

- *I/40 Parental Distant Control Score.* Sum of : I/11 (Parent obtained obedience by threat to leave or expel child), I/15 (Inconsistent, sometimes responding, other times ignoring child), I/16 (Discouraged play with other children) and I/28 (Unable to show warmth, hug or cuddle).

- *I/41 Parental Overprotection Score.* Sum of : I/17 (Parent saw world as dangerous, stay close), I/18 (Worry a great deal re health), I/19 (Worry a great deal re safety) and I/20 (Overprotective).

- *I/42 Parental Depression/Psychiatric Problem Score.* Sum of: I/7 (Parent nervous, insecure or worrier), I/8 (Episodes of gloom or depression), I/9a (Psychiatric treatment), I/9b (Admission for psychiatric care), I/12 (Threatened to kill self).

- *I/43 Parental Separation Score.* Sum of: I/1 (Not brought up by true parents), I/3 (Separated for > 1 month before aged 6), I/4 (Separated aged 6–10), I/5 (Separated 11–16 yrs) and I/14 (Parent often away).

- *I/44 Parental Unusual Closeness Score.* Sum of: I/6 (Afraid parent would die or be killed) and I/24 (Unusually close to parent).

- *I/45 Parental Rejection/Violence Score.* Sum of : I/10 (Parent assaulted or injured partner), I/13 (Drank more alcohol than was good for them), I/25 (Inclined to tease child or make them feel small), I/26 (Beat or physically punished child more often than most parents) and I/27 (Sexually interfered with or expected child to touch parent's genitals).

- *I/46 Overall Problematic Parenting Score.* Sum of above parenting scores (I/40–I/45).

Section II

- *II/36c* A *Childhood Illness Score* is obtained by summing replies to questions II/5 (Life-threatening illness before aged 6) and II/6 (Life-threatening illness from 6 to 16 years).

- *II/40 Childhood Timidity Score.* Sum of : II/7 (Describes self as an insecure child), II/10 (Under-achiever), II/12 (Lacked self-confidence), II/15 (Timid child), II/16 (Passive child), II/24 (Loner, avoiding others) and II/25 (Found it hard to ask for help).

- *II/41 Childhood Aggressiveness/Distrust Score.* Sum of : II/20 (Distrusted adults through much of childhood), II/26 (Hard to accept cuddles or other affection), II/27 (Suspicious and distrustful), II/28 (Controlling, 'bossy', dominating friends), II/29 (Bad tempered), II/30 (In trouble for aggressive or antisocial behaviour) and II/31 (Stubborn).

- *II/42 Childhood Dresden Vase Score.* Sum of : II/8 (An anxious child), II/14 (Afraid to be left or separated from parents), II/17 (Felt helpless, unable to cope), II/18 (Babied, seen as sweet and appealing) and II/19 (Seen as delicate or fragile).

- *II/43 Childhood Unhappiness Score.* Sum of : II/9 (Sees self as an unhappy child), II/32 (Often cried) and II/33 (Often wished self dead).

- *II/44 Childhood Compulsive Caregiving Score.* Sum of : II/11 (As child, always looking after others) and II/23 (Seen by others as tougher or more capable than really was).

- *II/45 Childhood Overall Vulnerability Score.* Sum of above childhood variables (II/40–II/44).

Section III

- *III/3f* A *Disability Score* is obtained by summing replies to III/3a–e). (Replies to checklist of types of disability.)
- *III/7dx* A *Marital Disagreement Score* is obtained by summing replies to III/7d.i–ix (Major areas of disagreement with partner).
- *III/9u* A *Bereavement Trauma Score* is obtained by summing the replies to III/9b, e, f.
- *III/7xi Marital Disharmony Score.* The Marital Disagreement Score is summed with replies to III/7b (Were you or are you rather dependent on this person?) and III/7c (Were/is this person rather dependent on you?).
- *III/9i Disharmony with deceased.* Sum of: III/9h (Unusual closeness to deceased), III/9i (Dependent on deceased), III/9j (Deceased dependent on bereaved), and III/9l (Disagreements with deceased).

Section IV

Social Support Score. Rescore III/6 (Has confidante), so that a Yes response scores 1 and a No response scores 0. Then add replies to IV/17 (At end of tether would (a) Seek help from friend and (b) Seek help from family).

- *IV/40 Cope – Emotional Inhibition/Distrust Score.* Sum of: IV/5 (Finds it hard to trust other people), IV/19a (Never cries), IV/20 (Wishes could cry more), IV/21 (Finds it hard to show affection) and IV/23 (Finds it hard to express sadness or grief).
- *IV/41 Cope – Aggressive/Assertive Score.* Sum of: IV/12 (Sometimes behaves in a childish or immature way), IV/17h (At end of tether – irritable or bad tempered) and IV/22 (Describes self as aggressive or challenging).
- *IV/42 Cope – EoT – Seek Help Score.* Sum of : IV/17a (At EoT – seek help from friend), IV/17b (At EoT – seek help from family), IV/17c (At EoT – seek help from doctor) and IV/17d (At EoT – seek help from other).
- *IV/43 Cope – EoT – Turn Inward Score.* Sum of : IV/17e (At end of tether – shut self away from people) and IV/17i (At EoT – turn frustration inward, feeling guilty).
- *IV/51 Overall Problematic Coping Score.* Sum of: IV/40 (Cope: Emotional Inhibition/Distrust), IV/41 (Cope: Aggression/Assertion), IV/43 (Cope: EoT: Turn In) and IV/17 (Cope: EoT Overdose) *and subtracting* IV/42 (Cope: Seek Help).
- *IV/44 Current – Anxiety/Panic Score.* Sum of : IV/1 (Very anxious), IV/4 (Lacks confidence), IV/9 (Hard to cope) and IV/10 (Sometimes feels panic or acute fear).

- *IV/45 Current – Grief/Loneliness Score.* Sum of : IV/11 (Very lonely), IV/14 (Much time pining) and IV/24 (Filled with regret).
- *IV/46 Current – Depression/Medication Score.* Sum of: IV/2 (Very depressed), IV/3 (Very tense), IV/7a (Medicine for nerves) and IV/7b (Takes more medication than should).
- *IV/47 Current – Clinging Score.* Sum of: IV/15 (Relies too much on others), IV/16 (Wish someone would look after me) and IV/18 (Recently got to end of tether).
- *IV/48 Current – Alcohol Consumption Score.* Sum of IV/8a (Uses alcohol to control feelings), IV/8b (Takes rather more alcohol than should) and IV/17f (At end of tether would drown sorrows with alcohol).
- *IV/49 Current – Overall Distress Score.* Sum of IV/44–IV/48.
- *IV/50 Current Dysfunction Score.* Sum of: IV/7a (Takes medicine for nerves), IV/7b (Takes rather more than should), IV/8a (Uses alcohol to control anxiety or depression), IV/8b (Takes rather more than should), IV/9 (Finds it hard to cope with responsibilities) and IV/18 (Recently got to end of tether).

Attachment scores

- *V/1 Insecure Attachment Score.* Sum of I/46 (Overall Problematic Parenting) and II/45 (Overall Childhood Vulnerability).
- *V/2 Anxious Ambivalent Attachment Score.* Sum of I/40 (Parental Distant Control), I/44 (Parental Closeness), I/41 (Parent Overprotection), II/40 (Childhood Timidity) and II/42 (Childhood Dresden Vase).
- *V/3 Avoidant Attachment Score.* Sum of : I/28 (Parents intolerant of closeness), II/26 (Child intolerant of closeness) and II/41 (Childhood Aggressiveness/Distrust).
- V/4 *Disorganised/Disoriented Attachment Score.* Sum of II/4 (Family suffered severe danger or persecution), I/42 (Parental Depression/Psychiatric Disorder), I/45 (Parental Rejection/Violence), II/43 (Childhood Unhappiness) and II/44 (Compulsive Caregiving).

Appendix 3.8: Measurement of retrospective distortion

If depression, anxiety and other emotions are crucial influences on scores derived from retrospective data we would expect that changes in our measures of these emotions would be associated with changes of similar magnitude in the retrospective scores. To test this the scores on follow-up of Depression/Medication, Anxiety/Panic and Overall Distress were subtracted in each case from their initial scores. This gives us measures of *Change in Depression, Anxiety and Overall Distress*.

Similarly the scores on follow-up of each retrospective measure were subtracted from their initial scores in each case giving indices of *Change in the Parenting Scores, Childhood Scores* and the *Disability Score*.

The Kolmogorov-Smirnov Test of normality was carried out on each of these new scores and all fell below the 0.5 level indicating that the scores were not normally distributed. For this reason Spearman's measure of correlation was used in the analysis of this data. Each of the Emotional Change Scores was then correlated with each of the changes in retrospective scores. It was predicted that if changes in emotion influence any of these retrospective scores, this will be reflected in a significant correlation between the two types of variable.

Table A.3.8.1 shows the Spearman correlations together with significance of all associations between changes in a retrospective variable and our three indicators of emotional change.

Contrary to expectation, change in the *Depression/Medication score* at follow-up was only associated with one significant change in a retrospective score. There was a small but significant (p >0.05) association between improvement in depression/medication and a reduction in the tendency to see parents as overprotective (as reflected in the Parental Overprotection score).

Improvement in the *Anxiety/Panic score* at follow-up was associated with small but significant changes in several scores. Significant at the 0.01 level were reductions in the respondent's view of their parents as overprotective (rho 0.37) and a more positive overall view of their parents (rho 0.36) and of themselves as children (rho 0.33). None of the component scores that made up the Childhood Vulnerability score reached significance. At the 0.05 level improved Anxiety/Panic was associated with more positive views of parents as

Table A.3.8.1 Spearman correlations – Emotional Change × Change in Retrospective scores

Change in Retrospective score	Depression Initial-FU	Anxiety Initial-FU	Overall Distress Initial-FU
I/40 Parental Distant Control	0.00	0.33*	0.20
I/41 Parental Overprotection	0.30*	0.37**	0.44**
I/42 Parental Depression/Psychiatric Prob.	−0.05	0.16	0.08
I/43 Parental Separation	0.02	0.05	0.07
I/44 Parental Unusual Closeness	0.15	0.14	0.20
I/45 Parental Rejection/Violence	0.05	0.32*	0.23
I/46 *Total Parenting Score*	0.09	0.36**	0.32*
II/40 Childhood Timidity	0.12	0.20	0.28*
II/41 Childhood Aggressiveness/Distrust	0.02	0.25	0.07
II/42 Childhood Dresden Vase Score	0.02	0.03	0.09
II/43 Childhood Unhappiness	0.03	0.18	0.30*
II/44 Childhood Compulsive Caregiver	−0.04	0.14	0.07
II/45 *Childhood Vulnerability Score*	0.15	0.33**	0.30*
III/3f Adult Disability Score	0.02	−0.01	−0.01

* p > 0.05, ** p > 0.01

less insensitive (rho 0.33) and rejecting (rho 0.32). This said, none of the correlations was high.

Since the *Overall Distress score* included both of the foregoing Emotional Change scores we would expect to find similar correlations. Improvement in Overall Distress score was correlated 0.32 (p >0.05) with a lower Total Parenting Score implying that parents were viewed in a slightly more positive light. The only individual score of parenting to be significantly associated with improved Overall Distress was the view of parents as overprotective (rho 0.44, p >0.01). Among the Childhood scores overall Childhood Vulnerability was seen as lower in those who improved in Overall Distress (rho 0.29, p >0.01) as were scores of Childhood Timidity (rho 0.28, p >0.01) and Unhappiness (rho 0.3, p >0.05).

In other words, this study suggests that among *parenting scores* the respondent's view of parental overprotection was influenced by depressive mood, anxiety and the level of overall distress in the respondents and it indicates that anxiety levels may also influence assessments of parental insensitivity and rejection. Although statistically significant, *none of these correlations was high*. The other parenting scores (Parental Depression/Psychiatric Problems, Separations from Parents and Unusual Closeness) were not influenced. Examination of a scattergram showing change in Anxiety plotted against change in view of parents as Overprotective shows outlying scores from two respondents who reported more anxiety on follow-up and who then saw their parents as much more overprotective than they had initially.

The respondents' specific *assessments of themselves as children* were not significantly influenced by changes in depression or anxiety but change in anxiety did influence the Overall Childhood Vulnerability score although the correlation was not high (rho 0.33, p >0.01). Self-perceptions of oneself in childhood as aggressive, a fragile 'Dresden Vase' or a compulsive caregiver were not significantly influenced and reports of childhood unhappiness were influenced to a small degree by overall distress (rho 0.3, p >0.05) but not by depression or anxiety alone. The Adult Disability Score was not significantly affected by any of the Emotional Change Scores.

Appendix 3.9: Comparison of questionnaire and clinical data

Since several of the variables that were assessed by questionnaire are similar to the clinical assessments obtained from the case notes, it is possible to test the validity of each by comparing it with the other. High correlations will suggest that both are measuring the same thing; low correlations will suggest that they are not, although they will not tell us which is the more valid measure.

A clinical diagnosis of depression was made in 63 per cent of cases. Figure A.3.9.1 shows the mean Depression/Medication score derived from the questionnaire at the time of referral for psychiatric care in respondents with and without this diagnosis. While the association between the two scores is highly significant ($p < 0.000$) the Spearman correlation is only 0.31. This suggests that although there is an overlap between them the Depression/ Medication score is not so closely associated with clinical depression that one can be taken as a measure of the other.

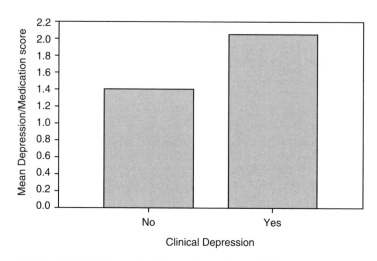

Figure A.3.9.1 Clinical diagnosis of Depression × Mean RAQ Depression/Medication score.

Anxiety state often accompanied depression. It was the commonest diagnosis and was made in no less than 76 per cent of cases. Although the mean Anxiety/Panic score was higher in the group diagnosed as clinically anxious this difference did not reach statistical significance and the Spearman correlation was low (0.02). Certainly these figures provide no confirmation of the validity of either measure though it is not possible to say which is at fault. My own impression, based on clinical experience and study of the case summaries, is that anxiety is so common a problem in these patients that it is likely to have been used as a catch-all diagnostic category.

More clear-cut is the diagnosis of alcohol or drug-related illness, which was made in 18 per cent of cases. Figure A.3.9.2 shows the mean Alcohol Problem score in respondents with and without this diagnosis. It shows a very much higher score in the diagnosed group and this is confirmed by the high Spearman correlation of 0.49 which is highly significant ($p < 0.000$). In this instance it does appear that the two methods of assessment are measuring similar but still not identical things.

The RAQ did not allow direct measures of pathological grief to be made but high scores on the Grief/Loneliness score were expected to be found in those assigned by clinical assessment to chronic grief. In the event those diagnosed as having chronic grief had slightly higher scores than the group not so diagnosed. The correlation between the two variables, however, is low and just misses statistical significance (Spearman's rho 0.07, $p = 0.072$). In seeking for an explanation for this finding we must look again at the diagnosis of chronic grief. This term implies that grief is both more intense and of longer duration than is to be expected.

Figure A.3.9.3 shows the Grief/Loneliness scores in 25 people (3 men and 22 women) diagnosed as suffering chronic grief who completed the RAQ at

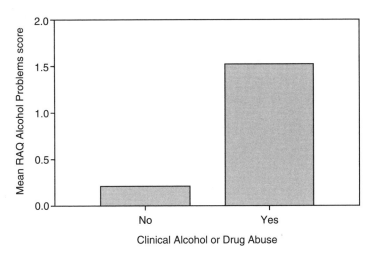

Figure A.3.9.2 Clinical Alcohol or Drug Abuse × Mean RAQ Alcohol Problems score.

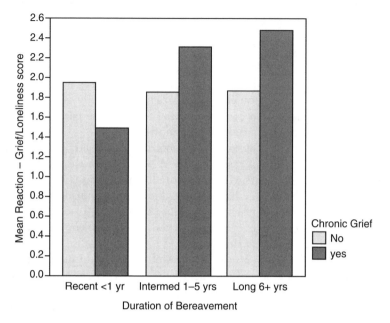

Figure A.3.9.3 Clinical Chronic Grief × Duration of Bereavement × Mean RAQ Grief/Loneliness score.

various periods after their bereavement. This is compared with those who were not so diagnosed. The Grief/Loneliness score is only elevated in those chronic grievers who have been bereaved for more than a year. When the four cases diagnosed during the first year (which included all three men) are omitted the correlation with Grief/Loneliness becomes statistically significant (Spearman's rho 0.18, p = 0.034). Even so, the correlation between the two variables is not high.

Appendix 3.10: Comparison between matched psychiatric and non-psychiatric samples

The 35 bereaved women who had sought psychiatric help from me were matched by age (plus or minus five years) with each of the control women from Ward's study who had answered Yes to the question 'Has any person close to you died in the past five years?' Since the data is not parametric the Wilcoxon Signed Ranks test was used to determine the significance of any differences.

Table A.3.10.1 shows the mean scores of Symptoms and Distress in the psychiatric and non-psychiatric groups. All except the Alcohol score were significantly higher in the psychiatric group.

Table A.3.10.2 shows the mean scores of Coping/Personality in the psychiatric and non-psychiatric groups. The members of the psychiatric sample were significantly *less* likely than the non-psychiatric to say that, when at the end of their tether, they would seek help from family, friends, doctors or others; this despite the fact that all of them had in fact sought help from doctors.

Table A.3.10.1 Mean scores of Symptoms and Distress in psychiatric and non-psychiatric samples

		Means		Z	Sig
		Psychiatric	Non-Psych.		
	n.	35	35		
Age (years)		25.6	27.1		N/S
Symptoms/Distress scores					
Anxiety/Panic		2.7	1.5	3.28	0.001**
Grief/Loneliness		2.0	0.9	3.33	0.001**
Depression/Medication		1.8	0.5	4.57	0.001**
Clinging		1.8	1.3	2.34	0.025*
Alcohol Problems		0.4	0.4	0.14	N/S
Overall Distress		9.2	4.6	4.27	0.000**

* p. < 0.05, ** p. < 0.01, N/S = Not significant.

Table A.3.10.2 Mean scores of Coping/Personality in psychiatric and non-psychiatric samples

		Means	*Z*	*Sig*
	Psychiatric n. 35	*Non-Psych.* 35		
Coping Scores				
Cope Emotional Inhibition	2.22	2.05	0.68	N/S
Cope Aggressive/Assertive	1.74	1.41	1.05	N/S
Cope End of Tether Seek Help	1.66	2.16	2.03	0.04*
Cope End of Tether Turn In	0.97	0.71	1.33	0.19

* p. < 0.05, N/S = Not significant.

Appendix 3.11: Influence of gender of parent and child on parenting, childhood vulnerability and attachment scores

There were no significant differences between the overall Problematic Parenting score in either male or female patients, nor were the Problematic Mothering scores significantly different from the Problematic Fathering scores. Significant differences did emerge, however, when each of the constituent scores of parenting were examined separately.

Table A.3.11.1 shows the mean parenting scores of each parent in male and female patients together with the significance of all differences between scores for mother and father in each sex. Because the distribution of scores is not parametric the Wilcoxon Signed Ranks test has been used as the test of significance.

In both sexes mothers were seen as having significantly higher scores of Depression/Psychiatric Problems and Overprotection while fathers were more likely to receive higher scores on Rejection/Violence. Female respondents also reported significantly greater Unusual Closeness to their mothers and more separation from their fathers. Males showed similar trends but these did not reach significance, perhaps because of the smaller sample size in males.

Allowing for this there were no major differences between men and women in their views of the parenting which they received, although men were rather more likely than women to see their mothers as overprotective. The mean Overall Childhood Vulnerability score was 7.3 in women and 8.1 in men, a

Table A.3.11.1 Mean Parenting scores by gender of child and parent

Mean scores	Male Child (n = 43)		Female Child (n = 138)	
	Mother	Father	Mother	Father
Distant Control	0.74	0.88	0.75	0.64
Depression/Psychiatric	1.21	0.84*	1.12	0.68***
Overprotective	1.51	0.79***	0.96	0.70**
Unusual Closeness	0.67	0.44	0.80	0.55***
Separations	0.84	1.09	0.72	1.34***
Rejection/Violence	0.33	0.63*	0.39	0.67***

Wilcoxon Signed Ranks test * p > 0.05, ** p > 0.01, *** p > 0.001.

difference which did not approach statistical significance. Neither did any of the differences between the constituent Childhood Vulnerability scores in male and female patients.

As shown in Table A.3.11.2 the mean Security of Attachment score was 16.6 in women and 18.0 in men. This difference did not approach statistical significance using the Mann Whitney Test, neither did any of the individual scores of Insecure Attachment.

Table A.3.11.2 Gender differences in mean Attachment scores

Scores	Males (n = 43)	Females (n = 138)
Security of Attachment	18.0	16.6
Insecure		
Anxious/Ambivalent	8.0	6.8
Avoidant	4.3	3.6
Disorganised	4.4	4.5

Appendix 4: Secure and insecure attachments

Parenting, childhood vulnerability and distress after bereavement

Given the highly significant correlation between Secure Parenting and low Current Distress, which is reported in Chapter 4 (p. 69), our first need is to consider the crucial question: *'Are patient's scores of Parenting related directly to Distress (for example, via the continuing influence of the parents in adult life) or indirectly through the influence of Parenting on Childhood Vulnerability?'*

This was answered by means of two path analyses (using Lisrel 8.52). The exogenous variable was the score of Overall Parenting (I/46) and the endogenous variables Childhood Vulnerability (II/45) and current Overall Distress (IV/49). Structural equation modelling was used because, unlike the hierarchical regression method which will be reported below, it includes error measurement. Cronbach's alpha for each variable was included in the calculation and the path coefficient between scores of Overall Parenting and Childhood Vulnerability was standardised at 1.00. The two path analyses comprise: an Indirect Model in which the link is assumed to run in sequence from Parenting to Childhood Vulnerability to Overall Distress, and a mixed Indirect and Direct Model in which an additional link is also included from Parenting direct to Overall Distress.

The results of these analyses are summarised in Figure A.4.1(a) and (b). The manifest variables are shown by the rectangles and the latent variables by ellipses. The figure shows that the proportion of error variance in the indicators are Parenting 0.15, Childhood Vulnerability 0.10 and Overall Distress 0.39. Taking these into account, the indirect effect of the latent variable of Parenting on Childhood Vulnerability is shown by a highly significant path coefficient of 0.76 ($t = 11.66$, $p < 0.001$, 2-tailed) and that of Childhood Vulnerability on Overall Distress is also highly significant at 0.59 ($t = 6.59$, $p < 0.001$ 2-tailed).

In the second model, which includes a possible direct influence of Parenting on Overall Distress, the path coefficient between these variables is only 0.13 and does not approach statistical significance ($t = 0.8$). Neither do the differences between Chi-squared measures of the two models. This means that the

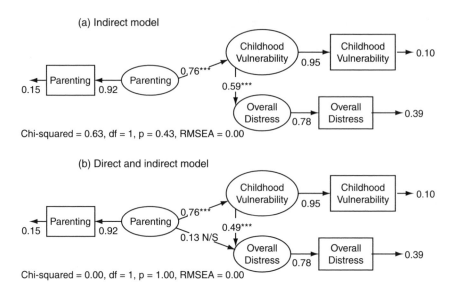

Figure A.4.1 Path diagrams with error correction linking Parenting × Childhood
Vulnerability × Overall Distress.

indirect model (a) is not a significantly poorer fit to the data than model (b).
Indeed the magnitude of the path correlations indicate that it is the indirect
model which best represents the data and confirms the supposition that
Parenting influences the outcome of bereavement by way of its influence on
Childhood Vulnerability. This provides further justification for the decision
to combine these two variables as a single measure of Insecure Attachment.

Predictions and correlations in bereaved psychiatric patients

Predictions

1 *People who indicate that they grew up secure will make secure relationships in
   adult life.* This will be reflected in significant correlations between low
   scores on Insecurity of Attachment and low scores on our various measures
   of problematic relationships in adult life.
2 *People who indicate that they grew up secure will, in adult life, cope better with
   stress, being less aggressive and more trusting in themselves and others.* This will
   be reflected in significant correlations between low scores on Insecure
   Attachment in childhood and low scores of adult Problematic Coping.
3 *Adults who have good relationships in adult life will suffer less distress
   following bereavement than those with problematic relationships.* Low scores on
   problematic relationships in adult life will correlate with low scores of
   Overall Distress after bereavement.

4 *Adults who cope well with stress will suffer less distress after bereavement than others.* Low scores on Problematic Coping in adult life will correlate with low Overall Distress scores after bereavement.

5 *Adults who indicate that, as children, they experienced secure attachments to parents will suffer less distress after bereavement in adult life than those whose parental relationships were insecure.* This will be reflected in significant correlations between low scores on our measures of Insecurity of Attachment and low scores on Overall Distress.

Results of testing these predictions

These are shown in Table A.4.1. All of the predictions were confirmed at highly significant levels. Low scores of Insecure Attachment predicted low scores of Marital Disharmony and Disharmony with Deceased (who was sometimes, but not always, one and the same person). These in turn predicted low scores of Overall Distress after bereavement. Similarly, high correlations

Table A.4.1 Results of tests of hypotheses re Secure Attachments

Hypothesis 1. *Children who grow up with secure attachments will make secure relationships in adult life.*	*Spearman correlation*	*Significance*
Low score Insecure Attachment → low score Marital Disharmony	rho 0.32	p. = 0.000
Low score Insecure Attachment → low score Disharmony with deceased person	rho 0.31	p. < 0.001
Hypothesis 2. *Children who grow up with secure attachments will cope better than others with stress in adult life.*	*Spearman correlation*	*Significance*
Low score Insecure Attachment → low score Problematic Coping	rho 0.44	p. = 0.000
Hypothesis 3. *Adults who have good relationships in adult life will suffer less distress following bereavement than those with problematic relationships.*	*Spearman correlation*	*Significance*
Low score Marital Disharmony → low score Overall Distress	rho 0.27	p. = 0.000
Low score Disharmony with deceased → low score Overall Distress	rho 0.24	p. = 0.007
Hypothesis 4. *Those who cope better with stress in adult life will suffer less distress after bereavement.*	*Spearman correlation*	*Significance*
Low score Problematic Coping → low score Overall Distress	rho 0.35	p. = 0.000
Hypothesis 5. *Children who grow up with secure attachments will suffer less distress after bereavement in adult life.*	*Spearman correlation*	*Significance*
Low score Insecure Attachment → low score Overall Distress	rho 0.40	p. = 0.000

were found between low Insecure Attachment scores and low Problematic Coping scores (r 0.45) and these also correlated with low Overall Distress.

From these data the Problematic Coping score emerges as the strongest intervening factor between Insecure Attachment in childhood and Overall Distress after bereavement. To examine these intermediate variables more closely a hierarchical regression was carried out in which Overall Distress was the dependent variable and the following independent variables were entered in turn Problematic Parenting by Mother, Problematic Parenting by Father, Childhood Vulnerability, Marital Disharmony, Disharmony with the Deceased Person, and Problematic Coping. Since the Overall Distress score was normally distributed and other criteria for this test were met it seems that the results should be taken as valid. Table A.4.2 shows the results of this analysis.

R squared for the combined effect of all independent variables is 0.33 indicating that, taken together, these variables account for one-third of the variance in the Overall Distress score. The beta correlation of 0.43 between Maternal Parenting and Overall Distress is highly significant when entered alone but drops sharply to borderline levels when Paternal Parenting (beta 0.23) is added. This suggests that the combined effect of both parents is greater than that of the mother alone. Both fade into insignificance in the face of the high beta correlation of 0.41 when Childhood Vulnerability is introduced, confirming that this is the intermediate variable. On the other hand, the beta correlation is very little affected by either Marital Disharmony or Disharmony with the person now deceased. Problematic Coping (beta 0.16), however, is associated with a drop in the beta values of all other variables although it fails to reach statistical significance in its own right.

It would seem from these data that problematic parenting by both mother and father contribute to the level of distress after bereavement and that childhood vulnerability and poor coping in adult life are the main intervening variables. Dysfunctional relationships play a relatively small part.

Further confirmation that Coping is the main intervening variable, and best explains the influence of Insecure Attachment on Overall Distress, was obtained by structural equation modelling. Detailed results can be obtained from the author.

Comparison with Ward's non-psychiatric group

Since the occurrence of bereavement in adult life was unlikely to influence the assessments of childhood attachments it was possible to increase the size of the psychiatric and non-psychiatric matched samples to 47 by including 12 controls and 12 matched psychiatric patients who did not report a bereavement. The mean scores and significance levels are shown in Table A.4.3. There were no significant differences between psychiatric and non-psychiatric samples in any of the mean attachment scores. Similar results were obtained when the bereaved psychiatric patients and bereaved controls were analysed separately.

Table A.4.2 Hierarchical regression – Parenting, Child Vulnerability, Adult Disharmony, Coping and Distress

Dependent Variable: Reaction – Overall Distress

Model		*Unstandardised Coefficients*		*Standardised Coefficients*	*t*	*Sig.*
		B	Std. Error	Beta		
1	(Constant)	6.687	0.536		12.472	0.000**
	Mo Total Parenting Score	0.389	0.087	0.428	4.463	0.000**
2	(Constant)	6.386	0.563		11.348	0.000**
	Mo Total Parenting Score	0.233	0.129	0.256	1.802	0.075
	Fa Total Parenting Score	0.221	0.136	0.231	1.624	0.108
3	(Constant)	5.671	0.561		10.107	0.000**
	Mo Total Parenting Score	0.147	0.123	0.162	1.195	0.235
	Fa Total Parenting Score	6.173E-02	0.134	0.064	0.459	0.647
	Childhood Vulnerability	0.239	0.065	0.408	3.681	0.000**
4	(Constant)	5.753	0.617		9.326	0.000**
	Mo Total Parenting Score	0.151	0.124	0.166	1.215	0.228
	Fa Total Parenting Score	6.559E-02	0.136	0.068	0.483	0.630
	Childhood Vulnerability	0.242	0.066	0.414	3.672	0.000**
	Marital Disharmony	−4.608E-02	0.140	−0.032	−0.330	0.743
5	(Constant)	5.834	0.669		8.726	0.000**
	Mo Total Parenting Score	0.151	0.125	0.166	1.211	0.229
	Fa Total Parenting Score	7.063E-02	0.137	0.074	0.514	0.608
	Childhood Vulnerability	0.241	0.066	0.412	3.637	0.000**
	Marital Disharmony	−5.916E-02	0.146	−0.041	−0.404	0.687
	Disharmony Dec'd Score	−9.821E-03	0.030	−0.030	−0.323	0.748
6	(Constant)	5.683	0.671		8.464	0.000**
	Mo Total Parenting Score	0.124	0.125	0.136	0.988	0.326
	Fa Total Parenting Score	8.078E-02	0.136	0.084	0.592	0.556
	Childhood Vulnerability	0.200	0.071	0.342	2.800	0.006**
	Marital Disharmony	−5.313E-02	0.145	−0.036	−0.366	0.716
	Disharmony Dec'd Score	−9.020E-03	0.030	−0.028	−0.298	0.766
	Problematic Coping	0.180	0.120	0.156	1.492	0.139

** p. < 0.01

Table A.4.3 Childhood Attachments of psychiatric and non-psychiatric samples

Childhood Attachment		Means		Z	Sig
		Psychiatric	Non-Psych		
	n.	47	47		
Anxious/Ambivalent Attachment		8.23	7.96	0.15	N/S
Avoidant Attachment		3.32	3.23	0.03	N/S
Disorganised Attachment		4.32	4.32	0.05	N/S
Insecure Attachment		18.9	18.8	0.22	N/S

N/S = Not significant.

Appendix 5: Anxious/ambivalent attachments: predictions and associations

Predictions

1 *Those who report insecure attachments of the anxious/ambivalent type during childhood will make dependent relationships in adult life.* These will be reflected in significant correlations between the Anxious/Ambivalent Attachment score and Yes replies to the question 'Were you unusually dependent on this person?' – of spouse or partner (III/7b) and of deceased person (III/9).

2 *Dependent relationships in adult life will be associated with intense and lasting grief after bereavement and a tendency to cling to others.* The measures of dependency listed above will correlate with high scores of current Grief/ Loneliness and Clinging and with an increased incidence of a clinical diagnosis of chronic grief.

3 *Those who made insecure attachments of the anxious/ambivalent type during childhood will report intense and lasting grief after bereavement and a tendency to cling to others.* The measure of Anxious/Ambivalent Attachment will correlate with each of the indicators of lasting grief and clinging listed above.

Results of testing these predictions

Table A.5.1 shows no appreciable association between Anxious/Ambivalent Attachment and replies to the single questions on Dependence on either the spouse or the deceased person. Prediction 1 is not confirmed.

Table A.5.1 Tests of Prediction 1

	Mann-Whitney U Z	Significance p.
Anxious/Ambivalence × Dependent on Spouse	1.56	N/S
Anxious/Ambivalence × Dependent on Deceased	1.33	N/S

N/S = Not significant.

Table A.5.2 shows that Prediction 2 is mainly supported with Dependence on the Deceased significantly associated with both Grief/Loneliness and Clinging. Dependence on Spouse was associated at a highly significant level with Grief/Loneliness but not Clinging.

Missing data reduced the number of people diagnosed with chronic grief whose dependence on the deceased could be assessed to 13 making statistical analysis inappropriate.

In Table A.5.3 the Anxious/Ambivalent score shows moderate and highly significant correlations with both Clinging and Grief/Loneliness. There was no significant correlation between high scores on Anxious/Ambivalence and a clinical diagnosis of chronic grief. To test the observation, based on case studies, that anxious/ambivalence predisposes to conflict in later relationships, I made the following *supplementary predictions*.

1(a)   *Those who experienced insecure attachments of the anxious/ambivalent type during childhood will make ambivalent relationships in adult life.* This can be tested by examining the correlations between Anxious/Ambivalent Attachment score and two variables, the Marital Disagreements score and positive replies to question III/9l (of the deceased person) 'Were there many things on which you disagreed?

1(b)   *Those who make ambivalent relationships in adult life will experience more intense and lasting grief after bereavement.* Marital Disagreements and

Table A.5.2 Tests of Prediction 2

	Mann-Whitney U Z	*Significance p.*
Dependent on Spouse × High score Clinging	1.20	N/S
Dependent on Spouse × High Grief/Loneliness	2.77	0.008**
Dependent on Deceased × High Clinging	1.96	0.05*
Dependent on Deceased × High Grief/Loneliness	2.37	0.01**

** $p. < 0.01$, * $p. < 0.05$, N/S = Not significant.

Table A.5.3 Tests of Prediction 3

	Spearman rho	*Significance p.*
Anxious/Ambivalence × Clinging	0.31	0.000**
Anxious/Ambivalence × High Grief/Loneliness	0.24	0.000**
Anxious/Ambivalence × Chronic Grief	Mann Whitney z −0.91	N/S

** $p. < 0.01$, N/S = Not significant.

Disagreements with Deceased will correlate with Grief/Loneliness, Clinging and a diagnosis of chronic grief.

In Table A.5.4 the predictions of significant correlations between Anxious/ Ambivalence and disagreements with spouse and deceased are confirmed and the predictions regarding ambivalence and clinging are confirmed at highly significant levels and those for Grief/Loneliness scores at lower but significant levels of correlation. The clinical diagnosis of chronic grief was not significantly associated with disagreements with spouse.

Although we now have a partial explanation for the high scores of Grief/ Loneliness and Clinging that were reported by those with high scores of Anxious/Ambivalence, I was surprised to find (see Table A.5.5) that neither the Anxious/Ambivalence nor the Marital Disagreements score significantly predicted the diagnosis of chronic grief. Unfortunately missing data had reduced the number of people with chronic grief whose disagreements with the deceased could be assessed to 12 making statistical analysis of dubious value. Other likely explanations for this will be considered in Chapter 17 (pp. 230–4), where the case for considering pathological grief as a disorder of attachment is examined.

Table A.5.4 Supplementary Prediction 1(a)

	Spearman rho	*Significance p.*
Anxious/Ambivalence × Marital Disagreements	1.56	0.000**
Anxious/Ambivalence × Disagreements with Deceased	Kruskal/Wallis Chi 13.40 1 d.f.	0.001**

** p. < 0.01

Table A.5.5 Supplementary Prediction 1(b)

	Spearman rho	*Significance p.*
Marital Disagreements × High Grief/Loneliness	0.18	0.01*
Marital Disagreements × High Clinging	0.24	0.001**
Marital Disagreements × Chronic Grief	Mann Whitney z 0.27	N/S
Disagreements with Deceased × High Grief Loneliness	rho 0.21	0.045*
Disagreements with Deceased × High Clinging	0.35	0.002**

** p. < 0.01, * p. < 0.05, N/S = Not significant.

Appendix 6: Avoidant attachments: predictions and correlations

As indicated on p. 310, the score of Avoidant Attachment was obtained by summing replies to questions about lack of expression of affection and intolerance of closeness in each parent, intolerance of closeness in the child and the Childhood Aggressiveness/Distrust score. Here we examine how this combined score correlated with each of the variables that had been predicted to be associated with avoidant attachment.

In this bereaved population the response to the question 'Do you find it hard to express feelings of sadness or grief?' (IV/23) seems to be our best measure of inhibition of grief, and in this section has been taken as a Symptoms/Feelings score. It is not, therefore, included in the coping score of Emotional Inhibition/Distrust.

Predictions

With this in mind the following predictions were made:

1 *Those who report avoidant attachments in childhood will, as adults, find it hard to show affection or to cry and will tend to be aggressive and assertive towards others.* Thus, scores of Avoidant Attachment were predicted to correlate with scores of coping by Emotional Inhibition/Distrust, Aggressive/ Assertiveness, Marital Disagreements and with positive answers to the question 'Do you find it hard to show affection for people close to you?' (IV/21), 'Were there many things on which you [and the deceased person] disagreed?' (III/91) and to reply Never to the question 'How often do you cry?' (IV/19).

2 *Adults who find it hard to show feelings and/or who distrust others, will inhibit or delay the expression of grief and/or be more liable to psychosomatic disorders after bereavement.* The scores and questions listed in (1) will be associated with clinical diagnoses of delayed grief and psychosomatic disorders and will answer Yes to the question 'Do you find it hard to express feelings of sadness or grief?' (IV/23).

3 *Adults who report avoidant attachments in childhood will inhibit or delay the expression of grief and/or be more liable to psychosomatic disorders after*

bereavement. High scores of Avoidant Attachment were predicted to correlate with clinical diagnoses of delayed grief and psychosomatic disorders and with a tendency to answer Yes to the question 'Do you find it hard to express feelings of sadness or grief?' (IV/23).

Results

Table A.6.1 shows that all of the first group of predictions are supported with high correlations, which are also highly significant. The childhood Avoidant Attachment score predicts coping in adult life by Emotional Inhibition/ Distrust and Aggression/Assertion. It seems that those with high scores of Avoidant Attachment in childhood find it hard, in adult life, to show affection and have more disagreements than others with partners and with the deceased person. They are significantly more likely to say that they never cry. This last finding is illustrated in Figure A.6.1 in which the mean Avoidant Attachment scores are shown in people who answered Never to the question 'How often do you cry?'

Those with high scores of Avoidant Attachments have high scores of Marital Disagreements and although disagreements with the deceased do not reach the same high level of significance this may be attributed to the smaller numbers involved (Figure A.6.2).

Table A.6.2 shows the results of testing the second group of predictions. Positive replies to the question 'Do you find it hard to express feelings of sadness or grief?' (IV/23) were found to be associated, at a highly significant level, with Yes replies to 'Do you find it hard to express affection for people close to you?' (IV/21) and the reply Never to 'How often do you cry?' (IV/19).

Only 22 people were diagnosed as having delayed grief and this number is too small for statistical analysis to show any except large differences. In the event none of the predictions of delayed grief were confirmed and the only

Table A.6.1 Tests of Prediction 1

	Test	*Significance*
Avoidant Attachment score × Emotional Inhibition/ Distrust	Spearman rho 0.47	0.000**
Avoidant Attachment score × Aggressive/Assertive	rho 0.38	0.000**
Avoidant Attachment score × Marital Disagreements	rho 0.29	0.000**
Avoidant Attachment score × Disagreement with Deceased	Kruskal Wallis Chi Sq. 7.4	0.025*
Avoidant Attachment score × Hard show affection (IV/21)	Mann Whitney z. 6.3	0.000**
Avoidant Attachment score × Never cries (IV/19)	Exact 1 tailed	0.027*

** p. < 0.01, * p. < 0.05

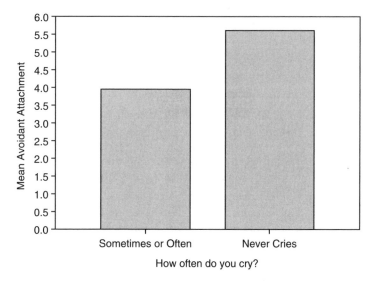

Figure A.6.1 Mean Avoidant Attachment × 'How often do you cry? Never' (IV/19a).

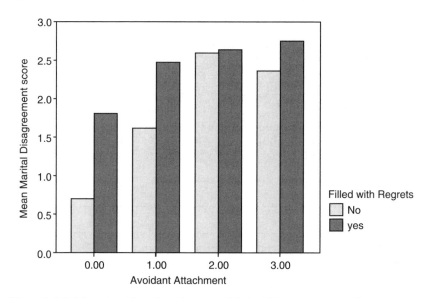

Figure A.6.2 Mean Avoidant Attachment × Marital Disagreements × Regrets.

prediction of psychosomatic disorder that came close to confirmation was the tendency for people diagnosed as having psychosomatic disorders to say they never cry. Thus, a half of the ten patients who answered Never to the question 'How often do you cry?' were diagnosed as suffering a psychosomatic disorder. This compares with a quarter of the rest.

Since disagreements with the deceased could be assessed in only eight

Table A.6.2 Tests of Prediction 2

	Test	Significance
Emot. Inhibition/Distrust† × Unable Express Grief	Spearman rho 0.53	0.000**
Aggressive/Assertive × Unable Express Grief	Spearman rho 0.53	N/S
Marital Disagreements × Unable Express Grief	Mann Whitney z. 0.33	N/S
Hard show affection (IV/21) × Unable Express Grief	Chi Squared 64.4, 1 df	0.000**
Never cries (IV/19) × Unable Express Grief	Chi Squared 25.2, 1 df	0.000**
Emotional Inhibition/Distrust† × Delayed Grief	Mann Whitney z. 72	N/S
Aggressive/Assertive × Delayed Grief	Mann Whitney z. 49	N/S
Marital Disagreements × Delayed Grief	Kruskal Wallis chi 1.3	N/S
Hard show affection (IV/21) × Delayed Grief	Chi Squared 4.7, 1 df	N/S
Unable express grief (IV/23) × Delayed Grief	Exact Test	N/S
Never cries (IV/19) × Delayed Grief	Chi Squared 5.1, 1 df	N/S
Emot. Inhibition/Distrust* × Psychosomatic Dis	Mann Whitney z 0.61	N/S
Aggressive/Assertive × Psychosomatic Dis	Mann Whitney z 0.89	N/S
Marital Disagreements × Psychosomatic Dis	Mann Whitney z 0.72	N/S
Disagreement with Deceased × Psychosomatic Dis	Chi Squared 7.38, 1 df	N/S
Never cries (IV/19) × Psychosomatic Dis	Fisher's Exact Test	0.05*

Notes †Unable express grief (IV/23) subtracted from Emotional Inhibition/Distrust score.
** p. < 0.01, * p. < 0.05, N/S Not significant.

people with delayed grief, statistical analysis of the influence of these two variables on each other is inappropriate.

Table A.6.3 shows the results of testing the third group of predictions. The Avoidant Attachment score strongly predicts self-assessments of difficulty in expressing sadness and grief and there is a trend towards a clinical diagnosis of delayed grief, which does not reach significance. Because of the small number who were diagnosed as suffering delayed grief the association would have had to be high in order to reach statistical significance. There is no approximation to a link with a clinical diagnosis of psychosomatic disorder.

Table A.6.3 Tests of Prediction 3

	Mann-Whitney U Test	Significance
Avoidant Attachment × Hard to Express Grief (IV/23)	z 4.38	0.00**
Avoidant Attachment × Clinical Delayed Grief	z 1.59	N/S
Avoidant Attachment × Clinical Psychosomatic Disorder	z 0.07	N/S

** p. < 0.01, N/S Not significant.

Other variables associated with avoidant attachments

Wish could Cry

Over a third (69/181) of the bereaved patients agreed with the statement 'Do you wish you could cry more?' Table A.6.4 shows that this reply was associated with high scores on Avoidant Attachment and a tendency to reply 'Never' to the question 'How often do you cry?'

Regrets

Over a half (95/181) of the sample answered 'Yes' to the question 'Are you filled with regret about something, which you said or did, but cannot now put right?' (IV/24). Table A.6.5 shows that this reply was significantly associated with Avoidant Attachment, Emotional Inhibition/Distrust, Aggressive/Assertive Coping and with many Marital Disagreements. It was not associated with Disagreements with the Deceased.

Table A.6.6 shows that those who spend much time pining also express deep regrets.

Table A.6.7 shows that Aggressive/Assertive Coping and, at lower significance, Emotional Inhibition/Distrust were significantly associated with the number of Marital Disagreements but failed to reach significant correlations with Disagreements with the Deceased Person (a less sensitive measure, see p. 46).

Among 31 with few disagreements and no regrets only two (6%) had high

Table A.6.4 'Do you wish you could cry more than you do?' (IV/20)

	Test	Significance
Avoidant Attachment × Wish I could cry more	Mann Whitney 3.2	0.001**
Never cries × Wish I could cry more	Fisher's Exact	0. 015*

** p. < 0.01, * p. < 0.05

Table A.6.5 'Are you filled with regret about something, which you did or said, but cannot now put right?' (IV/24)

	Test	Significance
Avoidant Attachment × Filled with regrets	Mann Whitney 2.4	0.017*
Emotional Inhibition/Distrust × Filled with regrets	Mann Whitney 3.5	0.000**
Aggressive/Assertive × Filled with regrets	Mann Whitney 2.6	0.008**
Marital Disagreements × Filled with regrets	Exact one tailed	0.028*
Disagreements with Deceased × Filled with regrets	Exact one tailed	N/S

** p. < 0.01, * p. < 0.05, N/S = Not significant.

Table A.6.6 Filled with regrets × Much time pining

		IV/14 *Much time pining*		
		Yes	*NK*	*No*
IV/24 Filled with regrets	Yes	79	8	10
	NK	9	5	7
	No	39	2	24

Pearson Chi Squared 28.3 4 d.f. Exact 2 sided p. = 0.000

Table A.6.7 Coping × Disagreements

	Spearman's rho	*Significance*
Emotional Inhibition/Distrust × Marital Disagreements	0.16	0.024*
Aggressive/Assertive Coping × Marital Disagreements	0.30	0.000**
Emotional Inhibition/Distrust × Disagreements Dec'd	0.02	N/S
Aggressive/Assertive Coping × Disagreements Dec'd	0.07	N/S

** p. < 0.01, * p. < 0.05, N/S Not significant.

scores on Avoidant Attachment, whereas among the 60 with many disagreements and regrets 19 (31%) had high scores of Avoidant Attachment. This difference is statistically significant (Chi squared 6.69, 1 d.f., p < 0.01). It would seem that Avoidant Attachments cause regrets because of their influence on relationships.

Dependency

It was anticipated that people with high Avoidant Attachment scores would choose partners whom they saw as dependent on them rather than themselves being dependent on their partners. To test this, the sample was divided into those with high scores (3+) on Avoidant Attachment and those with lower scores. In each group the replies to question III/7b 'Were you or are you rather dependent on [your partner]?' and III/7c 'Was/is [your partner] rather dependent on you?' were cross-tabulated.

Table A.6.8 shows dependence of respondent and partner in those with low and high scores of Avoidant Attachment. Overall, people with high Avoidant Attachment scores saw themselves as no more or less dependent on their partners than those with low scores, neither did they see their partners as more or less dependent on them.

An interesting difference emerges, however, when we examine the extent to which people score their own dependence on their partner in the same direction as they score their partner's dependence on them. Among those with high Avoidant Attachment scores 34/92 (37%) were concordant whereas

Table A.6.8 Dependence × Avoidant Attachment

In those with Low Avoidant Attachment score (0–2.9)		Partner Dependent		
		No	*Yes*	*Total*
Respondent	No	18 (29%)	5 (8%)	23 (37%)
Dependent	Yes	14 (23%)	25 (40%)	39 (63%)
	Total	32 (52%)	30 (48%)	62 (100%)

Chi Squared 10.4 1 d.f. p < .001

In those with High Avoidant Attachment score (3 +)		Partner Dependent		
		No	*Yes*	*Total*
Respondent	No	19 (21%)	17 (19%)	36 (40%)
Dependent	Yes	31 (34%)	25 (27%)	56 (60%)
	Total	50 (55%)	42 (46%)	92 (100%)

Chi Squared Not Significant

among those with low Avoidant Attachment scores 33/62 (53%) were concordant (Chi squared = 4.00, 1 d.f., p < 0.05). It seems that mutual dependence and mutual independence were significantly less common in those with high Avoidant Attachment scores than in those with lower scores.

Avoidant attachment and persisting grief/loneliness

Avoidant Attachment correlated rho 0.21 with the Grief/Loneliness score (p 0.005 2-tailed) and Cope: Emotional Inhibition/Distrust correlated rho = 0.24 with Grief/Loneliness (p 0.001 2-tailed). This suggests that grief that is inhibited or repressed is more likely to be reported as persisting than grief that is not inhibited.

Table A.6.9 Coping strategies associated with Marital Disagreements and Current Symptoms/Emotions

	Emotional Inhibition/Distrust	*Aggressive/Assertive*
Marital Disagreements	0.16*	0.30**
Anxiety/Panic	0.25**	0.16*
Grief/Loneliness	0.23**	0.08 N/S
Depression/Medication	0.19**	0.08 N/S
Clinging	0.20**	0.25**
Alcohol Problems	0.09 N/S	0.11 N/S
Overall Distress	0.32**	0.22**

** p. < 0.01, * p. < 0.05, N/S Not significant.

Coping strategies and their correlates

Although none of the correlations is high, Table A.6.9 shows that Coping by Emotional Inhibition/Distrust is correlated significantly with most Symptoms/Distress scores. Aggressive/Assertive Coping is correlated more highly with Marital Disagreements and Clinging but less highly with Anxiety/Panic and not to a significant extent with Grief/Loneliness and Depression/Medication. Neither score is correlated with alcohol problems.

Appendix 7: Disorganised attachments: predictions and correlations

In the RAQ the question 'If you got to the end of your tether would you . . .' followed by multiple choices (IV/17) was intended to identify those people who turn in on themselves rather than asking for help when faced with situations which they cannot tackle. The 'Turn In' score seems to constitute an indicator of passivity or helplessness in adult life. The line between passivity and helplessness is not easy to draw and it may be that this score can be an indicator of either or both.

Predictions

1   *Adults who as children made disorganised attachments will in adult life adopt passive ways of coping.* This will be shown by significant correlations between Disorganised Attachment scores and a tendency to turn in on themselves (high Turn In score) rather than seeking for help (low Seek Help score) when at the end of their tether.

2   *Adults who adopt passive coping will react to bereavement by becoming depressed, helpless and potentially suicidal.* This will be shown by significant correlations between the above measures of lack of trust in self and others and scores of Depression/Medication, Anxiety/Panic, Alcohol Problems and a tendency to overdose or otherwise harm themselves when at the end of their tether (IV/17g).

3   *Adults who as children made disorganised attachments will react to bereavement by becoming depressed, helpless and potentially suicidal.* This will be shown by significant correlations between Disorganised Attachment scores and the above indicators of depression and helplessness.

Results

Table A.7.1 shows that, as predicted, people with disorganised attachments in childhood say that they would turn in on themselves when at the end of their tether. Although there was no correlation between Disorganised Attachment and the EoT Seek Help score, significant findings did emerge when the two questions about seeking help from family and friends were considered

Table A.7.1 Tests of Prediction 1

	Spearman's rho	Significance
Disorganised Attachment × End of Tether – Turn In	0.25	0.000**
Disorganised Attachment × End of Tether – Seek Help	0.02	N/S
Disorganised Attachment × End of tether – Seek Help from Family and Friends	−0.15	0.034*

** p. <0.01, * p. <0.05, N/S Not significant.

separately. This significant negative correlation suggests that people in this sample with Disorganised Attachments are less likely than others to seek help from their friends and family although they may seek help from doctors and others.

In Table A.7.2, confirming Prediction 2, the End of Tether – Turn In score turns out to be a highly significant predictor, at moderate correlations, of current Anxiety/Panic and Depression/Medication. It is also a predictor of agreement with the question about self-harm. It did not predict Alcohol Problems.

The End of Tether – Seek Help score was negatively associated with the question about self-harm. This indicates that people who say they would seek help at the end of their tether are less likely also to say that they would take an overdose or otherwise harm themselves.

The predictions of a negative association between EoT Seek Help and current scores of Anxiety/Panic, Depression and Alcohol Problems was not confirmed, neither was this the case if the calculation was limited to those seeking help from friends and/or family.

Supporting Prediction 3, we see, in Table A.7.3 that the Disorganised

Table A.7.2 Tests of Prediction 2

	Test	Significance
End of Tether (EoT) – Turn In score × Anxiety/Panic	Spearman rho 0.28	0.000**
EoT – Turn In score × Depression/Medication	Spearman rho 0.21	0.002**
End of Tether – Turn In score × Alcohol Problems	Spearman rho 0.21	N/S
End of Tether – Turn In score × At EoT would 'Take an overdose or otherwise harm yourself'	Mann Whitney z 2.6	0.008**
End of Tether – Seek Help score × Anxiety/Panic	Spearman rho 0.07	N/S
EoT – Seek Help score × Depression/Medication	Spearman rho 0.01	N/S
EoT – Seek Help score × Alcohol Problems	Spearman rho 0.01	N/S
End of Tether – Seek Help score × At EoT would 'Take an overdose or otherwise harm yourself'	Mann Whitney z −3.6	0.000**

** p. < 0.01, N/S Not significant.

Table A.7.3 Tests of Prediction 3

	Test	*Significance*
Disorganised Attachment × Anxiety/Panic	Spearman rho 0.28	0.000**
Disorganised Attachment × Depression/Medication	Spearman rho 0.10	0.071 N/S
Disorganised Attachment × Alcohol Problems	Spearman rho 0.23	0.001**
Disorganised Attachment × At End of Tether would 'Take an overdose or otherwise harm yourself'	Mann Whitney z 1.9	0.064 N/S

** p. < 0.01, N/S Not significant.

Attachment score is correlated at moderate levels, of high significance, with current Anxiety/Panic and Alcohol Problems and at low levels, of borderline significance, with Depression/Medication and agreement with the statement that, at the end of their tether, the respondents would take an overdose or otherwise harm themselves.

Path analysis accounting for measurement error

To answer the question whether or not the influence of Disorganised Attachment on the Anxiety/Panic score is explained by its influence on the Coping Turn In score, two path analyses were carried out using Lisrel 8.52 as in the analysis described on p. 321. The exogenous variable was the score of Disorganised Attachment and the endogenous variables Coping Turn In score and current Anxiety/Panic. The two path analyses comprise: (a) an indirect model in which the link is assumed to run in sequence from Disorganised Attachment to Coping Turn In to Anxiety/Panic; (b) a mixed indirect and direct model in which an additional link is included from Disorganised Attachment direct to Anxiety/Panic.

The results of these analyses are summarised in Figure A.7.1 (a) and (b). The manifest variables are shown by the rectangles and the latent variables by ellipses. Taking the fairly high levels of error variance into account, in model (b) the indirect effect of the latent variable of Disorganised Attachment on Coping Turn In is shown by a path coefficient of 0.76 (t = 2.15, p < 0.05, 2 tailed) and that of Childhood Coping Turn In on Anxiety/Panic by a highly significant path coefficient of 1.23 (t = 3.45, p < 0.001 2-tailed).

In the second model, the path coefficients between the three variables do not approach statistical significance. Neither do the differences between Chi-squared measures of the two models. This means that the indirect model A.4.1(b) is not a significantly poorer fit to the data than model A.4.1(a). Indeed the magnitude of the path correlations indicate that it is this indirect model which best represents the data and confirms the supposition that, because those who have experienced disorganised attachment in childhood are more likely to turn in on themselves, they are more likely to suffer anxiety

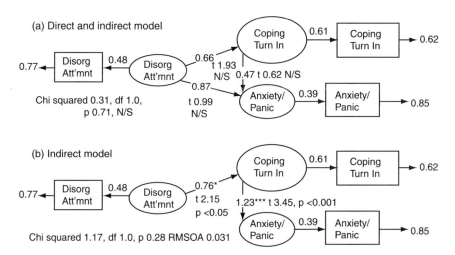

Figure A.7.1 Path diagrams with error correction linking Disorganised Attachment × Coping Turn In × Anxiety/Panic.

and a tendency to panic after bereavement. The same analyses using Depression/Medication as the exogenous variable, in place of Anxiety/Panic, gave similar results but at lower levels of significance.

Concomitants of the inclination to overdose or self-harm

Table A.7.4 shows that people who say that at the end of their tether they would take an overdose or otherwise harm themselves are significantly less likely to say that they would turn for help to family, friends, doctors or others and more likely to be 'filled with regret about something which you did or said, but cannot now put right'.

Disorganised attachments in Ward's control group

Within the full sample of 77 young women in Ward's comparison group there were 27 who obtained scores of four or more on the measure of Disorganised Attachment in childhood. In Table A.7.5 these are compared with the 28 in the age and sex matched psychiatric group who obtained similar scores. Only four members of Ward's 'Disorganised' control group replied 'No' to the question 'Do you have anyone in whom you can confide your inmost feelings?' This is a much lower proportion than that in the psychiatric 'Disorganised' group, nearly half of whom lacked a confidante. The 'Disorganised' controls also reported significantly lower EoT Turn In scores than the 'Disorganised' psychiatric group. Although 'Disorganised' controls reported slightly fewer marital disagreements and scored less on Aggressive/Assertiveness than the psychiatric group, these differences did not reach statistical significance.

Table A.7.4 Coping Strategies and Self-Reproaches in those tending to Self-Harm

IV/17 At End of Tether would you:	IV/17 At End of Tether would you (g) 'Take an overdose or otherwise harm yourself?'			
	Yes	No	NK	Fisher's Exact p.
(a) Seek help from friends	3 (13%)	67 (53%)	5 (46%)	0.005**
(b) Seek help from family	3 (13%)	59 (42%)	3 (18%)	0.001**
(c) Seek help from doctor	10 (44%)	85 (60%)	6 (35%)	0.000**
(d) Seek help from other	3 (13%)	38 (27%)	2 (12%)	0.001**
II/17 'Filled with regret'	17 (74%)	71 (50%)	7 (41%)	0.001**
Total	23	141	17	

** p. < 0.01, Percentages are proportion of totals in each column.

Table A.7.5 Comparison of those with high scores of Disorganised Attachment (4+) in psychiatric and non-psychiatric samples

	Psychiatric group	Ward's controls	Chi squared	Significance
N.	28	27		
Q3/6 Do you have anyone in whom you can confide your inmost thoughts and feelings? Yes	15 (54%)	23 (85%)	9.56	0.008**
End of Tether: Turn In (Mean score)	1.14	1.00	10.10	0.02*
Cope Aggressive/Assertive (Mean score)	1.73	1.52	15.80	0.07 N/S
Marital Disagreements (Mean score)	2.58	2.46	11.80	0.10 N/S

** p. < 0.01, * p. < 0.05, N/S Not significant.

Table A.7.6 Intercorrelation of Insecure Attachment Pattern scores

	Spearman Correlations		
	Anxious/Ambivalent	Avoidant	Disorganised
Anxious/Ambivalent	X	0.42**	0.51**
Avoidant		X	0.61**
Disorganised			X

** p. < 0.001

Overlap of attachment pattern scores

The figures in Table A.7.6 are Spearman correlation coefficients. There is a high correlation between the Disorganised Attachment score and the Avoidant Attachment score, a fairly high correlation between Disorganised Attachment and Anxious/Ambivalent Attachment and a moderate correlation between Anxious/Ambivalent and Avoidant Attachment scores. All correlations are highly significant.

Appendix 8: Separation from parents

In Table A.8.1 the Insecure Attachment score was obtained by summing the other three attachment scores. Unlike the Security of Attachment score used elsewhere in this study, it does not include the Separation score. Spearman correlations between all attachment scores and separations from mother are much higher than they are from father and that between separations from mother and the score of Disorganised Attachment is the highest of all.

Separations from father are correlated at a fairly low but mostly significant level with insecure attachments. Only the correlation with Anxious/ Ambivalent Attachments falls below statistically significant levels.

The Insecurity of Attachment and the Avoidant and Disorganised Attachment scores correlate at a moderate level with the combined Separations from either or both parents and the Anxious/Ambivalent score correlates with Separations at a lower level.

Age at separation and childhood vulnerability

In Table A.8.2 we can observe the influence of separations from mothers and fathers at different ages. Separations from parents are associated with increased Childhood Vulnerability in all age ranges with a slight tendency for children to suffer more from separation from mother during the early years of life and from separation from father during the teenage years. Only separations

Table A.8.1 Correlation between Separation scores and Attachment scores

Separations from	Mother	Father	Either/Both Parents
Anxious/Ambivalent Attachment score	0.22**	0.10 N/S	0.18**
Avoidant Attachment score	0.36**	0.27**	0.34**
Disorganised Attachment score	0.39**	0.29**	0.38**
Insecure Attachment score	0.38**	0.26**	0.36**

** p. < 0.01, N/S Not significant.

Table A.8.2. Separations and Childhood Vulnerability

| Separation from Mother | n. | *Overall Childhood Vulnerability* | | | |
		Low	Medium	High	p.
0–5 years	20	15%	20%	65%	0.009**
6–11 years	44	27%	16%	57%	0.001**
12–16 years	44	21%	23%	57%	0.001**
Separation from Father	*n.*	*Low*	*Medium*	*High*	*p.*
0–5 years	33	19%	33%	49%	0.025*
6–11 years	61	31%	26%	43%	N/S
12–16 years	61	21%	26%	53%	0.001**

** p. < 0.01, N/S Not significant.

from father during the so-called 'latency' period, aged 6 to 11, are not associated with a statistically significant increase in Childhood Vulnerability.

Although space will not permit all of the scores that make up Childhood Vulnerability to be shown here, each is significantly correlated with the Overall Separation score, the highest being Childhood Unhappiness.

Separations and relationships in adult life

Table A.8.3 shows the influence of the score of Separations from either or both parents on relationships in adult life. There is a low correlation between separation from parents in childhood and disagreements with the spouse in adult life which reaches the 0.05 level of significance.

Separations from parents are not significantly related to any of the measures of the relationship with the deceased person although there is a borderline trend (p. = 0.075) for people with more separations to report more disagreements with the person now deceased. This measure of disagreements, as we have seen (p. 46), is a less sensitive measure than the Marital Disagreements score.

Table A.8.4 shows that although none of the correlations is high, that between separations from either parent and the End of Tether – Turn In score reached a high level of significance. At the lower (p < 0.05) level there were significant correlations between separations from father and the Aggressive/Assertiveness score and between separations from mother and the Emotional Inhibition/Distrust score.

The combined separation score for both parents was associated with significantly positive answers to the choice at End of Tether to 'Take an overdose or otherwise harm yourself' (Mann Whitney test z.2.09 p. = 0.037*). This only reached the 0.05 level of significance and dropped below this when separation from each parent was considered separately.

Table A.8.3 Childhood Separations from Parents and Adult Relationships

	Test	*Significance*
Separation score × Marital Disagreement	Spearman rho 0.18	0.014*
Separation score × Dependent on Partner	Mann Whitney z 0.32	N/S
Separation score × Disagreements with Deceased Person	Spearman rho 0.18	N/S
Separation score × Dependent on Deceased Person	Mann Whitney z. 0.00	N/S

*p. < 0.05, N/S Not significant.

Table A.8.4 Separation from Parents in Childhood and Coping in Adult Life

Coping by	*Separations from*		
	Mother	*Father*	*Either/Both Parent*
Emotional Inhibition/Distrust	0.13*	0.05	0.11
Aggressive/Assertiveness	0.09	0.16*	0.15*
End of Tether – Seek Help	0.06	0.02	0.06
End of Tether – Turn Inward	0.25**	0.25**	0.22**

Figures are Spearman correlations. ** p. < 0.01, * p. < 0.05, N/S Not significant.

There were no significant correlations between any of the Separation scores and the EoT Seek Help score (see pp. 109–10 for a possible explanation for this finding). Correlations with the Symptoms and Distress scores are shown in Figure 8.1 (p. 132).

Separations in Ward's non-psychiatric sample

The full sample of 77 young women was included in Table A.8.5. As in the psychiatric sample the score of Separations from Mother and Father, both individually and together, are significantly correlated with Insecure Attachments. Separations from Mother are correlated with all three types of Insecure Attachment score, Separations from Father are correlated with all except Avoidant Attachments and are most highly associated with Disorganised Attachments.

Concomitants of low distress in the non-psychiatric sample despite a history of separations from parents

Of Ward's control group 32 scored two or more on the Parental Separation score. In Table A.8.6 they were divided into 16 who scored 4 or more on the Overall Distress score and 16 with lower scores. Comparable figures are also

Table A.8.5 Spearman correlation of Separation scores and Attachment scores in Ward's non-psychiatric sample

Attachments in childhood	*Separations from*		
	Mother	*Father*	*Either/Both Parents*
Anxious/Ambivalent Attachment score	0.21**	0.24*	0.24*
Avoidant Attachment score	0.27**	0.08 N/S	0.18 N/S
Disorganised Attachment score	0.27**	0.40**	0.40**
Insecure Attachment score	0.29**	0.34**	0.36**

** p. < 0.01, * p. < 0.05, N/S Not significant.

Table A.8.6 Concomitants of Distress in non-psychiatric sample who were Separated from their Parents, with additional data from unmatched psychiatric sample

		Non-Psychiatric			*Psychiatric*
	N.	Low (0–3) Distress 16	High (4+) Distress 16	Significance p.	94
III/7b Respondent Dependent on Spouse		5 (36%)	11 (69%)	0.074 N/S	52 (63%)
Mean Separation Scores		Mean	Mean		
EoT Turn In score		0.38	1.31	0.008**	1.10
Sum of Insecure Attachment scores		14.00	19.50	0.01**	17.43

Notes
All figures refer to respondents with Separation scores of 2+.
** p. < 0.01, N/S Not significant.

given from the 94 bereaved psychiatric patients with similar high separation scores (most of whom suffered high Overall Distress). Tests of the significance of differences between the psychiatric patients and the controls are not appropriate because the samples could not be matched.

Among those separated controls who expressed high distress, two-thirds reported that they had been dependent on their spouse. This is similar to the proportion in the unmatched, separated psychiatric group. By contrast only one-third of the separated controls with low distress were dependent on their spouse. This difference just misses statistical significance.

The End of Tether Turn In scores in the separated controls with low Overall Distress were about one-third of the level reported by the other two groups. The difference from the control group with high Overall Distress is highly significant. It seems reasonable to conclude that people whose experience of parental separation has not caused them to turn in on themselves at times of stress are better able to cope emotionally with bereavement.

The combined score of Insecure Attachment is significantly lower in the separated controls with low Overall Distress than in either the controls with high distress or the psychiatric group. It seems that those who have secure attachments in childhood and experience separations from parents often achieve autonomy in adult life and cope well with bereavements and other stresses.

Appendix 9: Trauma and bereavement

Since most of the people in the current study had experienced traumatic types of bereavement this only leaves a small number without trauma who can be compared with them. On the other hand, the Trauma score does allow us to examine the influence of degrees of trauma and is therefore a more satisfactory indicator than the simpler all-or-none measure of trauma.

Table A.9.1 shows that there was a small but significant correlation between the level of Trauma and the level of current Overall Distress. Here the Pearson correlation is used because Overall Distress is normally distributed. The only clinical diagnosis associated with Trauma at a statistically significant level is post-traumatic stress disorder.

As in previous sections the number of people with chronic or delayed grief was too small to justify statistical analysis although there was a trend for people with trauma to be diagnosed as suffering chronic grief. When the presence or absence of any trauma is taken as the criterion it is found that all of the 16 people diagnosed as having chronic grief had some degree of trauma (Fisher's Exact Test, two-sided, significant p. = 0.034*) by comparison with those who reported no indicators of trauma.

Table A.9.1 Trauma, Coping and Reaction

	Test	*Significance*
Trauma score × Overall Distress score	Pearson rho 0.17	0.035*
Trauma score × Clinical Anxiety	Kruskal Wallis Chi 4.84	N/S
Trauma score × Clinical Depression	Kruskal Wallis Chi 1.65	N/S
Trauma score × Clin. Psychosomatic Disorder	Kruskal Wallis Chi 1.64	N/S
Trauma score × Clinical Alcohol Problem	Kruskal Wallis Chi 1.26	N/S
Trauma score × Clinical PTSD	Kruskal Wallis Chi 12.75	0.013*
Trauma score × Emotional Inhibition/Distrust	Spearman rho −0.01	N/S
Trauma score × End of Tether − Turn In	Spearman rho 0.17	0.026*
Trauma score × Anxiety/Panic score	Spearman rho 0.01	N/S
Trauma score × Grief/Loneliness score	Spearman rho 0.24	0.004**

** p. < 0.01, * p. < 0.05, N/S Not significant.

The expectation that traumatic bereavements would be associated with higher scores of Emotional Inhibition/Distrust was not confirmed although there was a small but significant association between Trauma and the EoT Turn In score. The expected association with high Anxiety/Panic was not confirmed but the Trauma score correlated significantly with Grief/Loneliness, revealing an unexpected link with persisting grief.

Trauma and insecure attachments

To examine the interaction of insecure attachments, trauma and the various reactions to bereavement it is necessary to use multivariate methods of analysis. Table A.9.2 shows the results of a hierarchical regression in which the dependent variable was Overall Distress and the following independent variables were entered in turn: Insecurity of Attachment, Trauma score and Problematic Coping.

R squared for this combination of variables was 0.26 (i.e. together they account for 26 per cent of the variance in Overall Distress). Insecurity of Attachment was highly correlated with Overall Distress with a beta

Table A.9.2 Hierarchical regression – Insecurity of Attachment, Trauma, Coping and Overall Distress

Model Summary

Model	R	R Square	Adjusted R Square	Std. Error of the Estimate	Change Statistics				
					R Square Change	F Change	df1	df2	Sig. F Change
1	.472[a]	.223	.216	2.8255	.223	34.347	1	120	.000
2	.499[b]	.249	.236	2.8094	.026	4.126	1	119	.044
3	.512[c]	.262	.243	2.7759	.014	2.162	1	118	.144

1 Predictors: (Constant), Insecurity of Attachment
2 Predictors: (Constant), Insecurity of Attachment, Trauma Score
3 Predictors: (Constant), Insecurity of Attachment, Trauma Score, Problematic Coping

ANOVA[d]

Model		Sum of Squares	df	Mean Square	F	Sig.
1	Regression	274.214	1	274.214	34.347	.000[a]
	Residual	958.039	120	7.984		
	Total	1232.253	121			
2	Regression	306.316	2	153.158	19.684	.000[b]
	Residual	925.937	119	7.781		
	Total	1232.253	121			
3	Regression	322.977	3	107.659	13.971	.000[c]
	Residual	909.276	118	7.706		
	Total	1232.253	121			

1 Predictors: (Constant), Insecurity of Attachment
2 Predictors: (Constant), Insecurity of Attachment, Trauma Score
3 Predictors: (Constant), Insecurity of Attachment, Trauma Score, Problematic Coping
Dependent Variable: Reaction – Overall Distress

Coefficients[a]

Model		Unstandardised Coefficients			Standardised Coefficients	t	Sig.
		B		Std. Error	Beta		
1	(Constant)	6.363		.477		13.352	.000
	Insecurity of Attachment	.134		.023	.472	5.861	.000
2	(Constant)	5.619		.596		9.421	.000
	Insecurity of Attachment	.136		.023	.475	5.982	.000
	Trauma score	.447		.220	.161	2.031	.044
3	(Constant)	5.523		.597		9.251	.000
	Insecurity of Attachment	.119		.025	.416	4.687	.000
	Trauma score	.430		.219	.155	1.961	.052
	Problematic Coping	.156		.106	.131	1.470	.144

Dependent Variable: Reaction – Overall Distress

Excluded Variables

Model		Beta In	t	Sig.	Partial Correlation	Collinearity Statistics Tolerance
1	Problematic Coping	.147	1.641	.103	.149	.797
	Trauma Score	.167	2.100	.038	.190	.999
2	Trauma Score	.161	2.033	.044	.185	.997

1 Predictors in the Model: (Constant), Insecurity of Attachment
2 Predictors in the Model: (Constant), Insecurity of Attachment, Problematic Coping
Dependent Variable: Reaction – Overall Distress

coefficient of 0.47, which was unaffected by the addition of the Trauma score, although this score was significantly correlated with Overall Distress in its own right. This suggests that the influence of insecure attachment is not determined by its effect on vulnerability to trauma. When Problematic Coping is added to the equation the beta coefficients of the other two scores drop only slightly suggesting that the influence of trauma is not substantially mediated by its effect on coping.

These findings suggest that the influence of Trauma on Overall Distress is relatively independent of either Insecurity of Attachment or Coping. Its influence is additive rather than multiplicatory. This said, some influences did emerge when the influence of individual patterns of attachment were examined separately.

Anxious/ambivalent attachments, trauma and grief/ loneliness scores

We saw above that Trauma is significantly correlated with Grief/Loneliness and in Chapter 3 that Anxious/Ambivalent Attachment is also correlated with Grief/Loneliness. The question then arises whether these two influences

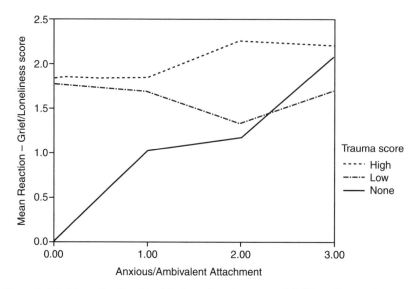

Figure A.9.1 Mean Anxious/Ambivalent Attachment × Grief/Loneliness × Trauma.

are linked. Does Anxious/Ambivalence act by making people more vulnerable to traumatic bereavement, or are they relatively independent of each other?

Figure A.9.1, shows that people with low scores of Anxious/Ambivalent Attachment only report high levels of Grief/Loneliness if they have moderate to high Trauma scores. Those with high Anxious/Ambivalence have high scores of Grief/Loneliness regardless of Trauma. This finding has been confirmed by hierarchical regression although space does not permit the inclusion of this data. It seems that among people who seek psychiatric help after bereavement both trauma and anxious/ambivalent attachments are associated with severe and lasting grief. Anxious/ambivalence does not act by increasing the influence of trauma.

Avoidant attachments, trauma and emotional inhibition

We saw in Chapter 6 that the Avoidant Attachment score predicts inability to express grief or affection in adult life, the best measure of which was the Emotional Inhibition/Distrust score. Other studies (see p. 33) lead us to expect that trauma will also be associated with the inhibition of affect. Figure A.9.2 shows that in the current study the level of trauma had little or no influence on the level of Inhibition/Distrust; this was more closely related to the level of Avoidant Attachment. This finding was confirmed by hierarchical regression, but again there is no space to give details here.

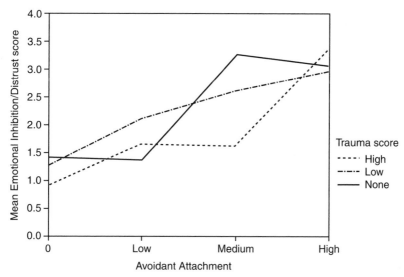

Figure A.9.2 Avoidant Attachment × Mean Emotional Inhibition/Distrust score × Trauma.

Disorganised attachments, trauma and emotions/symptoms

Figure A.9.3, which contrasts with the findings of Figure A.9.1, shows that at low levels of Disorganised Attachment the Trauma score has little influence on the level of Overall Distress. At higher levels, however, the two factors interact

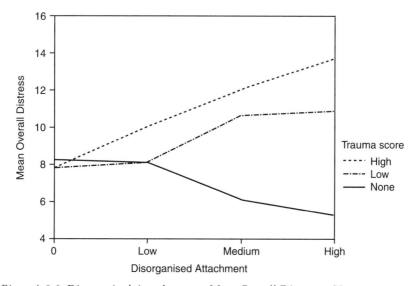

Figure A.9.3 Disorganised Attachment × Mean Overall Distress × Trauma.

so that the highest scores of Overall Distress are found in those who had Disorganised Attachments and Traumatic Bereavements. Very similar pictures emerged when Anxiety/Panic, Grief/Loneliness and Depression/Medication were charted against Disorganised Attachment at these levels of Trauma. This implies that in people seeking psychiatric help after bereavement the reaction to trauma is greatly affected by the level of Disorganised Attachment.

If, as we suppose, Disorganised Attachment leaves the individual with few coping strategies it may be that inability to cope with trauma is a result. By comparison people with reasonably good strategies for coping may be relatively better able to cope with traumatic circumstances attending bereavement.

To test this hypothesis a hierarchical regression was carried out in which the dependent variable was Anxiety/Panic. This was chosen because it was the Symptom/Distress score most closely associated with Disorganised Attachment (see p. 340). The independent variables entered in sequence were: Disorganised Attachment, Trauma score and End of Tether – Turn In score. Together these variables account for 25 per cent of the variance in Anxiety/Panic. The results are shown in Table A.9.3.

Table A.9.3 Hierarchical regression of Disorganised Attachment, Coping by Turning Inward, Trauma and Anxiety/Panic

Model Summary

Model	R	R Square	Adjusted R Square	Std. Error of the Estimate	Change Statistics				
					R Square Change	F Change	df1	df2	Sig. F Change
1	.393	.154	.147	2.9590	.154	21.530	1	118	.000
2	.430	.185	.171	2.9174	.031	4.392	1	117	.038
3	.499	.249	.230	2.8116	.064	9.967	1	116	.002

a Predictors: (Constant), Disorganised Attachment
b Predictors: (Constant), Disorganised Attachment, Trauma Score
c Predictors: (Constant), Disorganised Attachment, Trauma Score, Cope – EoT Turn Inward Score

ANOVA

Model		Sum of Squares	df	Mean Square	F	Sig.
1	Regression	188.513	1	188.513	21.530	.000
	Residual	1033.167	118	8.756		
	Total	1221.680	119			
2	Regression	225.890	2	112.945	13.270	.000
	Residual	995.790	117	8.511		
	Total	1221.680	119			
3	Regression	304.680	3	101.560	12.847	.000
	Residual	917.000	116	7.905		
	Total	1221.680	119			

a Predictors: (Constant), Disorganised Attachment
b Predictors: (Constant), Disorganised Attachment, Trauma Score
c Predictors: (Constant), Disorganised Attachment, Trauma Score, Cope – EoT Turn Inward Score
d Dependent Variable: Reaction – Anxiety/Panic

Coefficients

Model		Unstandardised Coefficients B	Std. Error	Standardised Coefficients Beta	t	Sig.
1	(Constant)	7.395	.387		19.108	.000
	Disorganised Attachment	.337	.073	.393	4.640	.000
2	(Constant)	6.580	.545		12.077	.000
	Disorganised Attachment	.343	.072	.400	4.792	.000
	Trauma Score	.484	.231	.175	2.096	.038
3	(Constant)	5.996	.557		10.769	.000
	Disorganised Attachment	.291	.071	.339	4.100	.000
	Trauma Score	.353	.226	.128	1.560	.122
	Cope – EOT Turn Inward Score	1.138	.360	.265	3.157	.002

a Dependent Variable: Reaction – Anxiety/Panic

Excluded Variables

Model		Beta In	t	Sig.	Partial Correlation	Collinearity Statistics Tolerance
1	Trauma Score	.175	2.096	.038	.190	.998
	Cope – EoT Turn Inward Score	.289	3.481	.001	.306	.951
2	Cope – EoT Turn Inward Score	.265	3.157	.002	.281	.919

a Predictors in the Model: (Constant), Disorganised Attachment
b Predictors in the Model: (Constant), Disorganised Attachment, Trauma Score
c Dependent Variable: Reaction – Anxiety/Panic

Initially the standardised beta coefficient of Disorganised Attachment and Anxiety/Panic is highly significant at 0.39. The addition of Trauma is accompanied by no appreciable change in the beta value attributable to Anxious/Ambivalence although Trauma is itself significantly associated with Anxiety/Panic (beta 0.18, p = 0.038). The effect of adding the Turn In score is to reduce the beta level of the influence on Anxiety/Panic of the other two variables so that Trauma drops below significance while Disorganised Attachment remains significant (beta 0.27, p = 0.002).

We can conclude from these findings that the interaction effect of Trauma and Disorganised Attachment on Anxiety/Panic is, to a large extent, mediated by a tendency to turn inward. If the Turn In score is, as we suppose, a measure of helplessness, it is a likely response to trauma in people who have experienced disorganised attachments in childhood.

Appendix 10: Gender differences

All figures refer to the 43 men and 138 women who sought psychiatric help after bereavement.

Men reported higher scores than women of Emotional Inhibition/Distrust. Other differences are not significant (Table A.10.1).

The gender difference in the Emotional Inhibition/Distrust scores is shown to result from men more often saying that they never cry and find it hard to show affection and grief (Table A.10.2).

Table A.10.1 Coping × Gender mean scores and significance

	Men	Women	Mann Whitney z	Significance
Emotional Inhibition/Distrust	2.60	1.88	−2.84	0.005**
Aggressiveness/Assertiveness	1.33	1.52	−1.00	N/S
End of Tether – Seek Help	1.58	1.73	−1.01	N/S
End of Tether – Turn In	0.88	0.94	−0.49	N/S
Overall Problematic Coping	3.23	2.61	−1.42	N/S

** p. < 0.01, N/S Not significant.

Table A.10.2 Gender × Numbers and percentages replying 'Yes' to questions on Emotional Inhibition/Distrust

	Men	Women	Chi Squared	Significance
IV/5 Finds it hard to trust other people	21 (49%)	67 (49%)	0.22	N/S
IV/19 Never cries	9 (21%)	7 (5%)	14.55	0.001**
IV/20 Wishes could cry more	19 (44%)	50 (36%)	1.14	N/S
IV/21 Finds it hard to show affection	26 (60%)	47 (34%)	9.50	0.009**
IV/23 Finds it hard to express sadness or grief	26 (60%)	51 (37%)	7.47	0.024*

** p. < 0.01, * p. < 0.05, N/S Not significant.

The only trend is for women to report slightly higher scores of Grief/Loneliness, but only at a borderline level of significance (Table A.10.3).

Personality disorders were diagnosed more frequently in men than in women. Women, on the other hand, had rather more diagnoses of anxiety states and psychosomatic disorders. Although twice as many women as men were diagnosed as having chronic grief the small numbers involved do not allow an adequate statistical test of this difference (Table A.10.4).

Table A.10.3 Gender × Symptoms/Distress – mean scores and significance

	Men	*Women*	*Mann Whitney z*	*Significance*
Anxiety/Panic	2.47	2.76	−1.11	N/S
Grief/Loneliness	1.77	2.01	−1.62	N/S
Depression/Medication	1.82	1.82	−0.21	N/S
Clinging	1.60	1.74	−0.78	N/S
Alcohol	0.56	0.43	−1.11	N/S
Overall Distress	**8.22**	**8.76**	**−1.09**	**N/S**

N/S Not significant.

Table A.10.4 Gender × Clinical Diagnosis – numbers, percentages and significance

	Men	*Women*	*Chi Squared*	*Significance*
Anxiety States	29 (67%)	107 (78%)	6.62	0.039*
Depression	27 (64%)	86 (63%)	0.17	N/S
Psychosomatic	9 (21%)	36 (26%)	6.77	0.034*
Personality Disorder	11 (26%)	6 (4%)	17.80	0.000**
Alcohol/Drug	19 (23%)	29 (15%)	1.82	N/S
Post-Traumatic Stress Disorder	3 (7%)	12 (9%)	0.17	N/S
Chronic Grief	3 (7%)	22 (16%)	2.95	N/S
Delayed Grief	5 (12%)	17 (12%)	0.98	N/S

** p. < 0.01, * p. < 0.05, N/S Not significant.

Appendix 11: Loss of a parent in adult life

The number of bereaved respondents losing a parent (31) is not large and differences would have to be large to reach statistical significance.

People who sought help after loss of a mother were more often unmarried, separated or divorced than those who sought help after the death of a father (Table A.11.1).

Comparison of parent loss with other loss

The mean age at referral of people losing a parent was 36.8 years. This compares with 43.6 years in those who suffered other bereavements (Pearson Rho 0.21, p. = 0.01). None of the insecure attachment patterns differentiates the two groups (Table A.11.2).

People who have lost a mother are more likely than others to say that they were unusually close to her (Table A.11.3). No other differences in parenting were reported.

The number of parent-bereaved who answered questions about relationship with the parent who died is too small for statistical analysis and not included here.

No significant differences. There is a trend, at borderline significance, for parent-bereaved to cling following bereavement (Table A.11.4).

Table A.11.1 Loss of Mother or Father × Marital Status of Bereaved Respondent

Marital Status	n.	Lost Mother 22	Lost Father 9
Never Married		7	1
Married		3	6
Cohabiting		3	1
Separated		5	1
Divorced		2	0
Widowed		0	0
Not Known		2	0

Table A.11.2 Loss of Mother or Father × mean score Attachment Pattern

	Mean Attachment Pattern scores		Mann Whitney	Significance
	Lost Mother	Lost Father	z.	
Anxious/Ambivalent Attachment	7.29	6.63	0.50	N/S
Avoidant Attachment	3.32	3.48	0.24	N/S
Disorganised Attachment	4.35	3.93	0.80	N/S
Insecurity of Attachment	16.29	15.77	0.41	N/S

N/S Not significant.

Table A.11.3 Loss of Mother × Unusual Closeness: mean scores and significance

		Mean scores		Mann Whitney	Significance
	n.	Lost Mother 22	Other Loss 96	z.	p.
Unusually Close to Mother		1.31	0.64	3.66	0.000**
Unusually Close to Father		0.55	0.50	0.25	N/S

** p. < 0.01 N/S Not significant.

Table A.11.4 Loss of Parents × Adult Situation: mean scores and significance

		Mean scores		Mann Whitney	Significance
	n.	Parent 31	Other 87	z.	p.
Marital Disagreements		2.18	1.67	0.73	N/S
Trauma score		1.29	1.61	1.23	N/S
Coping scores					
Emotional Inhibition/Distrust		1.99	1.84	0.55	N/S
Aggressive/Assertive		1.41	1.41	0.06	N/S
End of Tether – Seek Help		1.55	1.74	0.48	N/S
End of Tether – Turn In		1.01	0.89	0.73	N/S
Problematic Coping		2.85	2.40	0.98	N/S
Symptoms/Distress scores					
Anxiety/Panic		2.83	2.59	0.86	N/S
Depression/Medication		1.79	1.83	0.20	N/S
Grief/Loneliness		1.98	1.97	0.06	N/S
Clinging		1.87	1.51	1.87	0.062 N/S
Alcohol Problems		0.39	0.46	1.18	N/S
Overall Distress		8.86	8.35	0.67	N/S

N/S Not significant.

Table A.11.5 shows no significant differences.

Table A.11.5 Loss of Parent × Clinical Diagnosis: numbers, percentage and significance

Clinical diagnosis	Lost Parent	Lost Other	Chi squared	Exact significance
Anxiety State	23 (74%)	64 (74%)	0.86	N/S
Depression	19 (61%)	53 (61%)	0.45	N/S
Psychosomatic Disorder	5 (16%)	21 (24%)	1.67	N/S
Alcohol or Drug Problems	4 (13%)	15 (17%)	1.04	N/S
Personality Disorder	3 (10%)	5 (6%)	1.16	N/S
Post-Traumatic Stress Disorder	1 (3%)	10 (12%)	3.20	N/S
Chronic Grief	4 (13%)	17 (20%)	1.02	N/S
Delayed Grief	4 (13%)	13 (15%)	1.05	N/S

N/S Not significant.

Appendix 12: Loss of a child

Comparison of expected and actual numbers of bereavements by death of a child in normal and psychiatric samples

To obtain figures for the expected numbers of bereavements by deaths of children in the 151 people in our psychiatric sample (after excluding multiple bereavements), the *Bills of Mortality for England and Wales* were consulted. Table A.12.1 shows the distribution of deaths during the year 1992 (Office of Statistical Censuses and Surveys 1992). Of the total deaths in England and Wales 0.34 per cent were of girls during the first year of life (1933 × 100/557,313). Other proportions are calculated in a similar way.

If we assume an equivalent distribution of deaths in our sample of 151 bereaved patients, Table A.12.2 shows the numbers of deaths that we expect to find. This can be compared with the actual numbers in each category of age and sex.

Dividing the Actual by the Expected numbers of deaths, the ratios of actual to expected figures shown in Table A.12.3 is found. Thus, the actual number of people seeking help after the death of a child exceeds the expected number by a ratio of seven to one. We would expect 1.2 deaths to have occurred during the first year of life in our sample and 0.9 in later childhood; in fact 3 took place during the first year of life and 12 thereafter.

The group having the greatest discrepancy between actual and expected numbers are people losing a daughter aged 1 to 17 years. They show an 18-fold excess in the bereaved psychiatric patients. Deaths during the first year of

Table A.12.1 Deaths in England and Wales from Bills of Mortality for 1992

	Daughters	Sons	Both
A Deaths in first year of life	1,933 (0.34%)	2,606 (0.47%)	4,539 (0.81%)
B Deaths aged 1–19 years	1,232 (0.22%)	2,080 (0.37%)	3,312 (0.59%)
C Total Deaths all ages	271,732 (48.8%)	285,581 (51.2%)	557,313 (100%)

Table A.12.2 Actual and expected deaths of children by gender and age group

	Daughters		Sons		Both	
	Actual	Expected	Actual	Expected	Actual	Expected
Deaths in first year of life	1	0.51	2	0.71	3	1.22
Deaths aged 1–19	6	0.33	6	0.56	12	0.89
All child deaths	7	0.84	8	1.27	15	2.11
Total deaths all ages	122	74.7	29	77.3	151	151

Table A.12.3 Ratios of actual/expected deaths of children

	Daughters	Sons	Both
	Actual/Expected	Actual/Expected	Actual/Expected
Deaths in first year of life	2.0:1	2.8:1	2.5:1
Deaths aged 1–19	18.2:1	10.7:1	13.5:1
All child deaths	8.3:1	6.3:1	7.1:1
Deaths all ages	1.6:1	0.38:1	1:1

life are few and associated with only a twofold to threefold excess in the psychiatric patients.

When it is a child under 18 who has died it is reasonable to assume that they will have left a surviving parent. National figures for the deaths of people over the age of 18, however, do not permit comparison with the deaths of adult children in our sample since they give no indication whether or not there is a surviving parent.

Comparison of child bereaved with other bereaved people

Those who had lost children were significantly more likely than people who lost others to have been separated from their parents (particularly mothers) during childhood and report higher scores of Rejection/Violence by their mother (Table A.12.4). The latter differences were not so large as to sway the Attachment Pattern scores, which did not distinguish child loss from other losses. They also had significantly higher scores of Traumatic Bereavement. Other differences did not reach statistical significance.

Approximately a half of those seeking psychiatric help after the loss of a child reported separation from their own parents between the age of 6 to 11 years and the proportion from 12 to 16 years is not much lower (Table A.12.5). These are about double the frequency of parental separations in those suffering the loss of other relatives. The differences are statistically significant.

Table A.12.4 Child Loss × Attachment and Adult Life Variables: mean score and significance

	n.	*Mean scores*		*Mann Whitney*	*Significance*
		Child Loss 29	*Other Loss* 122	*z.*	*p.*
Attachment scores					
Anxious/Ambivalent Attachment		6.10	7.03	0.96	N/S
Avoidant Attachment		4.03	3.25	1.51	N/S
Disorganised Attachment		4.64	4.45	0.02	N/S
Overall Insecurity Att.		17.52	15.38	0.79	N/S
Parenting scores					
Separation from Mother		1.28	0.50	3.07	0.002**
Separation from Father		1.72	1.04	2.09	0.037*
Rejection/Violence					
By Mother		0.62	0.24	3.25	0.001**
By Father		0.83	0.52	1.14	N/S
Trauma score		2.07	1.45	2.61	0.009**
Coping scores					
Emotional Inhib./Distrust		1.67	2.00	1.31	N/S
Aggressive/Assertiveness		1.56	1.46	0.59	N/S
End of Tether – Seek Help		1.54	1.76	0.94	N/S
End of Tether – Turn In		0.90	0.92	0.07	N/S
Problematic Coping		2.59	2.62	0.08	N/S
Symptoms/Distress scores					
Anxiety/Panic		2.38	2.72	0.96	N/S
Depression/Medication		1.86	1.80	0.38	N/S
Grief/Loneliness		1.94	1.96	0.27	N/S
Clinging		1.43	1.73	1.18	N/S
Alcohol Problems		0.57	0.40	1.35	N/S
Overall Distress		8.22	8.59	0.64	N/S

** p. < 0.01, * p. < 0.05, N/S Not significant.

Table A.12.5 Child Loss × Separations from Parents: numbers, percentages and significance

Separated from	Child Loss	Other Loss	Exact significance
Mother aged 0–5 years	4 (14%)	8 (6.6%)	0.177 N/S
Mother aged 6–11 years	14 (48%)	19 (16%)	0.000**
Mother aged 12–16 years	11 (38%)	22 (18%)	0.022*
Father aged 0–5 years	9 (31%)	22 (18%)	0.103 N/S
Father aged 6–11 years	15 (52%)	33 (27%)	0.011*
Father aged 12–16 years	14 (48%)	35 (29%)	0.038*

** p. < 0.01, * p. < 0.05, N/S Not significant.

Appendix 13: Loss of a spouse or partner

Table A.13.1 compares the mean scores of those psychiatric patients who lost a partner with those of other bereaved patients. Although there were no significant differences between the attachment patterns reported by these two groups, people who lost a partner had significantly lower scores of separation from their father. Comparing these figures with those reported in Appendix 12 (p. 363) it is clear that it is not those seeking help after the loss of a partner but, rather, people who lose a child who have been most affected by separations from parents. The higher score of Rejection/Violence by father in those who have lost a partner just misses statistical significance.

There was a trend for the partner-bereaved to have lower scores of Marital Disagreement and Aggressiveness/Assertiveness and higher scores of End of Tether – Seek Help than the rest. These findings explain the fact that their Problematic Coping scores were also low. The partner-bereaved scored higher than the rest on Grief/Loneliness but there were no other significant differences between the groups in their Symptom/Distress scores and the Overall Distress scores were not significantly different.

Table A.13.2 shows that those who lost a partner were significantly more likely than others to report having been unusually close and mutually dependent on that partner. They were also marginally more likely to say that they were unusually close to their father in childhood.

Note that there is no need to show separate figures for relationship with the deceased in this section because the deceased person was the partner.

Table A.13.1 Partner Loss × Attachment and Adult Life Variables: mean score and significance

	Mean scores		Test	Significance
	Partner Loss n. 40	Other Loss 47		p.
Attachment Pattern			Mann Whitney	
Anxious/Ambivalent	6.86	7.15	0.22	N/S
Avoidant	3.68	3.13	0.31	N/S
Disorganised	4.35	3.94	0.91	N/S
Overall Insecurity	15.54	15.87	0.42	N/S
Separations from Mother	0.63	0.72	0.58	N/S
Separations from Father	0.70	1.30	Exact Test 1-tailed	0.027*
Rejection Violence by Mother	0.33	0.26	Mann Whitney z. 0.88	N/S
Rejection Violence by Father	0.68	0.57	Exact Test 1-tailed	0.110 N/S
Marital Disagreements	1.38	2.00	Exact Test 1-tailed	0.110 N/S
Mean Coping scores			Mann Whitney	
Emot. Inhib./Distrust	1.88	2.16	z. 2.75	N/S
Aggressive/Assertiveness	0.97	1.48	2.68	0.007**
End of Tether – Seek Help	2.05	1.47	2.37	0.018*
End of Tether – Turn In	0.77	0.92	0.98	N/S
Problematic Coping	1.57	3.10	2.39	0.007**
Symptoms/Distress				
Anxiety/Panic	2.73	2.71	0.04	N/S
Depression/Medication	1.90	1.86	0.14	N/S
Grief/Loneliness	2.23	1.79	2.23	0.006**
Clinging	1.81	1.68	0.56	N/S
Alcohol	0.59	0.47	0.03	N/S
Overall Distress	9.27	8.51	1.24	N/S

**p. < 0.01, * p. < 0.05, N/S Not significant.

Table A.13.2 Loss of Partner × Closeness to Parents and Partner: numbers, percentages and significance

	Lost Partner	Lost Other	Exact 1-tailed p.
I/24 Were you unusually close to your mother (Yes)	10 (29%)	32 (38%)	N/S 0.093
I/24 Were you unusually close to your father (Yes)	12 (35%)	18 (21%)	N/S
Unusually Close to Deceased Partner	10 (29%)	55 (85%)	0.011*
Dependent on Deceased Partner	27 (79%)	36 (55%)	0.015*
Partner Dependent on Respondent	24 (71%)	31 (48%)	0.024*

*p. < 0.05, N/S Not significant.

Appendix 14: Social isolation and support

Living alone × living with others

Figure A.14.1 shows the mean Grief/Loneliness scores in bereaved people of different age groups who lived alone versus those living with others. At all ages those living alone reported more Grief/Loneliness than those living with others. However, whereas Grief/Loneliness declines with age in those who live with others, there is a clear increase in Grief/Loneliness in those over the age of 50 who live alone.

In Table A.14.1 we see that those living alone are older and suffer greater Grief/Loneliness than those living with others. Contrary to expectation, living alone was not associated with lower Social Support scores than living with others. Neither overall level of insecure attachment nor any one particular pattern of insecure attachment distinguishes those living alone from those living with others.

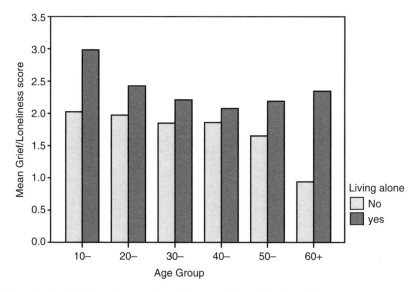

Figure A.14.1 Living Alone × Age Group × Mean Grief/Loneliness score.

Table A.14.1 Living Alone × Age, Attachment and Symptoms/Distress: means and significance

	n.	*Living Alone* 60	*With Others* 121	*Test*	*Significance*
Mean Age (years)		46.1	38.8	Pearson Rho 0.25	0.000**
Mean Social Support score		1.64	1.41	Mann Whitney z. 1.18	N/S
Mean Attachment scores					
Anxious/Ambivalent		7.83	6.66	z. 1.21	N/S
Avoidant Attachment		3.95	3.69	z. 0.27	N/S
Disorganised Attachment		4.98	4.23	z. 0.82	N/S
Insecure Attachment		18.36	16.26	z. 1.40	N/S
Mean Symptoms/Distress					
Anxiety/Panic		2.56	2.87	z. 1.40	N/S
Depression/ Medication		1.75	1.85	z. 0.66	N/S
Grief/Loneliness		2.24	1.81	z. 2.79	0.005**
Overall Distress		8.9	8.3	z. 0.93	N/S

**p. < 0.01, N/S Not significant.

Table A.14.2 confirms expectations that it is loneliness that is the significant problem in people who now live alone.

Table A.14.3 shows that the Social Support score, which reflects having a confidante and being willing/able to turn to friends and/or family when at the end of one's tether, is not correlated, at a significant level, with the age of the respondent.

Since age is normally distributed and no particular prediction was made about the direction of any correlation a Pearson correlation and two-tailed test was used in this calculation. Other variables were not normally distributed and were expected to be correlated in the direction shown consequently Spearman correlations and one-tailed tests were used.

These show that Social Support is negatively correlated, at significant levels, with Insecure Attachment and each of its constituent scores. The highest correlation is with Avoidant Attachment. This implies that people who were insecurely attached in childhood, particularly if their attachments were avoidant, have poorer social supports in adult life than others.

Higher scores of Social Support are associated with lower levels of Grief/ Loneliness and Overall Distress, also, at borderline levels of significance, with

Table A.14.2 Lives Alone × Questions re Grief and Loneliness: numbers, percentages and significance

Question	Lives Alone n. 61	With Others 121	Chi Squared 1-tailed	Significance
IV/14 Do you spend a lot of time pining or longing for someone or something that you have lost? (Yes)	45 (75%)	82 (68%)	1.2	N/S
IV/11 Are you very lonely?(Yes)	47 (78%)	54 (45%)	18.6	0.000**
IV/24 Are you filled with regret about something which you did or said but cannot now put right? (Yes)	34 (57%)	61 (50%)	2.6	N/S

**p. < 0.01, N/S Not significant.

Table A.14.3 Social Support correlated with Age, Attachment and Symptom/Distress scores

	Correlation	Significance
Age	Pearson rho 0.09	N/S
Attachment score	Spearman's rho	
Anxious/Ambivalent	−0.09	0.013*
Avoidant	−0.25	0.002**
Disorganised	−0.14	0.044*
Insecure Attachment	−0.27	0.001**
Symptoms/Distress		
Anxiety/Panic score	−0.14	0.047*
Depression/Medication	−0.12	0.076 N/S
Grief/Loneliness	−0.20	0.009**
Overall Distress	−0.20	0.009**

**p. < 0.01, *p. < 0.05, N/S Not Significant.

Anxiety/Panic and Depression/Medication. In Table A.14.4 we see that higher scores of Social Support are associated with less difficulty in trusting others.

Comparison of 29 bereaved psychiatric patients and 29 matched bereaved non-psychiatric

Of the bereaved psychiatric patients 16 (55%) answered 'Yes' to the question 'Do you have anyone in whom you can confide your inmost

Table A.14.4 Social Support × Adult Trust: mean scores and significance

	Yes	No	Mann Whitney z.	Significance
IV/5 'Do you find it hard to trust other people?'	71	62		
Mean Social Support score	1.10	1.18	4.1	0.000**

** p. < 0.01

Table A.14.5 Bereaved patients with and without children under aged 16 at home

		Child <16 yrs at home	None	Test	Significance
	n.	38	143		
Mean Age (years)		36	43	Pearson Rho 0.21	0.002**
Symptoms/Distress				Exact Test	
Anxiety/Panic		3.02	2.61		0.046*
Depression/Medication		1.72	1.84	Mann Whitney z. 0.83	N/S
Grief/Loneliness		2.07	1.92	z. 1.02	N/S
Overall Distress		9.31	8.46	z. 1.76	0.078 N/S

**p. < 0.01, *p. < 0.05, N/S Not significant.

thoughts and feelings?'(III/6) compared with 26 (90%) of the bereaved non-psychiatric controls (exact two-tailed test 0.039*). The other components of the Social Support score did not distinguish the two groups at significant levels.

Table A.14.5 shows that, as expected, those patients with children under 16 at home were younger than those without. There is a significant trend for people with children under 16 at home to report more Anxiety/Panic than those without.

Hierarchical regression analyses

A hierarchical regression was carried out with the Grief/Loneliness score as the dependent variable. This aimed to clarify the causal chain linking Avoidant Attachment to Grief/Loneliness. The variables were entered in the following order: Avoidant Attachment score, Gender, scores of Emotional Inhibition/Distrust, Aggressiveness/Assertiveness and Social Support. The results of this analysis are shown in Table A.14.6.

Table A.14.6 Predictors of Grief/Loneliness: hierarchical regression analyses

Coefficients		Unstandardised coefficients		Standardised coefficients	t	Sig.
Model		B	Std. Error	Beta		
1	(Constant)	1.753	0.117		15.009	0.000**
	Avoidant Attachment	6.034E-02	0.023	0.219	2.635	0.009**
2	(Constant)	1.389	0.361		3.852	0.000**
	Avoidant Attachment	6.355E-02	0.023	0.231	2.753	0.007**
	Sex	0.198	0.186	0.089	1.067	0.288
3	(Constant)	0.953	0.373		2.557	0.012*
	Avoidant Attachment	2.527E-02	0.025	0.092	1.004	0.317
	Sex	0.301	0.183	0.136	1.651	0.101
	Cope – Emotional Inhibition/ Distrust	0.197	0.060	0.304	3.285	0.001**
4	(Constant)	0.953	0.374		2.548	0.012*
	Avoidant Attachment	2.817E-02	0.027	0.102	1.028	0.306
	Sex	0.314	0.189	0.141	1.663	0.099
	Cope – Emotional Inhibition/ Distrust	0.198	0.060	0.305	3.282	0.001**
	Cope Aggressive/ Assertive Score	−2.291E-02	0.084	−0.025	0.272	0.786
5	(Constant)	1.089	0.415		2.627	0.010**
	Avoidant Attachment	2.604E-02	0.028	0.094	0.943	0.347
	Sex	0.304	0.189	0.137	1.604	0.111
	Cope – Emotional Inhibition/ Distrust	0.180	0.064	0.279	2.802	0.006**
	Cope Aggressive/ Assertive Score	−1.542E-02	0.085	−0.017	−0.181	0.856
	Social Support	−5.811E-02	0.076	−0.068	−0.767	0.445

Dependent Variable: Reaction – Grief/Loneliness score **$p < 0.01$, *$p < 0.05$

The Avoidant Attachment score is significantly related to Grief/Loneliness with a beta value of 0.219 when first entered. This is not influenced by the sex of the respondent but drops to 0.092 (not significant) when the score of Coping by Emotional Inhibition/Distrust is added. Emotional Inhibition/ Distrust then takes over as the strongest predictor of Grief/Loneliness and remains highly significant despite the subsequent addition of Cope – Aggressiveness/Assertiveness and Social Support neither of which contributes significantly to the equation.

Appendix 15: Other influences on the reaction to bereavement

Immigrants

Table A.15.1 shows the mean scores in the Immigrant and the Native groups along with numbers and percentages of replies to question II/4 concerning dangers in childhood. We see that those immigrants who sought psychiatric help after bereavement were significantly more likely than other bereaved psychiatric patients to have been separated from their parents in childhood. This contributes to their Insecurity of Attachment score that, along with the Anxious/Ambivalent Attachment score, is slightly higher in the immigrant group but only at borderline levels of significance. Despite this, the Childhood Vulnerability score was no higher in the immigrant group, nor were any of

Table A.15.1 Immigrant and Native Groups, Psychiatric Sample: mean scores and significance

	Immigrant n. *20*	*Native* *161*	*Test*	*Significance*
Age of Respondent (Mean)	44.9	40.8	'T' Test T 1.25	N/S
Attachment scores (Mean)			Mann Whitney	
Anxious/Ambivalent	8.18	6.91	z. 1.73	0.08 N/S
Avoidant	4.65	3.66	z. 1.57	N/S
Disorganised	5.27	4.38	z. 0.67	N/S
Separation (Mean)	3.60	1.99	z. 2.20	0.028*
Childhood Vulnerability	7.80	7.43	z. 0.66	N/S
Insecure Attachment	20.65	15.50	z. 1.88	0.060 N/S
Symptoms/Distress (Mean scores)				
Anxiety/Panic	3.00	2.66	z. 1.27	N/S
Grief/Loneliness	1.99	1.95	z. 0.09	N/S
Depression/Medication	1.90	1.81	z. 0.67	N/S
Overall Distress	8.85	8.61	z. 0.43	N/S
II/4 'Was your family subjected for a long time to serious danger or persecution?'				
(Yes) Number/Percentage	7 (33%)	13 (8%)	Exact Test	0.000**

** p. < 0.01,* p. < 0.05, N/S Not Significant.

the scores of current Symptoms and Distress. Immigrant families were more often than natives subjected to danger and/or persecution.

Illness and disability

Twenty respondents (11%) reported life-threatening illness before the age of 6 and 17 (9%) in later childhood. Taken together 33 (18%) reported such illness at some time before the age of 17, but only four (2.2%) reported illness during both time spans.

Table A.15.2 shows the mean Attachment scores of people reporting Childhood Illness in each age range. Because of the small numbers in the Child Illness groups Fisher's Exact Test (one-tailed) has been used throughout. As we may have expected, illness was often responsible for separations from parents and the mean Parental Separation score was significantly higher in those who reported childhood illness both aged 0–5 and 6–16.

All three Insecure Attachment scores were associated with illness aged between 0 and 5 although the Disorganised Attachment score just missed significance. The Avoidant Attachment score was the only one to be significantly associated with illness later in childhood. Six out of 17 people who had severe illnesses aged 6 to 16 were immigrants and this proportion was significantly higher than in non-immigrants (Fisher's Exact Test 0.005).

Table A.15.3 shows the mean Coping Symptoms/Distress and Adult Disability scores of people reporting Childhood Illness in each age range. Again Fisher's Exact Test has been used. No significant influence of childhood illness on Problematic Coping or on Symptoms/Distress score at either age period were found although there were trends suggesting an association between severe illness in both periods of childhood and the Depression/Medication score.

Severe childhood illness in the 6–16 age range was significantly correlated with the Disability score in adult life. Table A.15.4 shows correlation between the Adult Disability score and other relevant variables. As expected there is a highly significant correlation between older age and higher scores of Disability. Less expected is the modest but significant correlation between

Table A.15.2 Illnesses in Childhood × Age Group × Attachment Patterns (means and significance)

Mean scores	Illness aged 0–5	No illness	Exact sig.	Illness 6–16	No illness	Exact sig.
Parental Separation	3.5	2.0	0.019*	3.2	2.1	0.022*
Attachment Pattern						
Anxious/Ambivalent	9.0	6.8	0.018*	7.5	7.0	N/S
Avoidant	4.8	3.7	0.039*	5.2	3.6	0.024*
Disorganised	5.6	4.3	N/S	5.6	4.4	N/S

* p. < 0.05, N/S Not significant.

Table A.15.3 Illnesses in Childhood × Age Group × Coping, Distress and Adult Disability: means and significance

Mean scores	Illness aged 0–5	None	Exact sig.	Illness 6–16	None	Exact sig.
Problematic Coping	2.66	2.77	N/S	2.86	2.75	N/S
Symptoms/Distress						
Anxiety/Panic	2.46	2.72	N/S	2.49	2.72	N/S
Grief/Loneliness	1.94	1.96	N/S	1.95	1.96	N/S
Depression/Medication	1.66	1.86	0.154 N/S	1.54	1.34	0.064 N/S
Clinging	1.66	1.72	N/S	1.85	1.69	N/S
Alcohol	0.57	0.45	N/S	0.27	0.48	N/S
Overall Distress	8.26	8.68	N/S	8.10	8.69	N/S
Adult Disability	1.55	1.04	0.151 N/S	2.41	0.96	0.003**

** $p. < 0.01$, N/S Not significant.

Table A.15.4 Disability score × Other Variables: correlations and significance

	Spearman Rho	Significance
Age of Respondent	0.23	0.002**
Living Alone	0.19	0.015*
Social Support	0.07	N/S
Attachment score		
Anxious/Ambivalent	−0.01	N/S
Avoidant	0.15	0.043*
Disorganised	0.17	0.022*
Insecure Attachment	0.09	N/S
Problematic Coping	−0.02	N/S
Overall Distress	0.00	N/S

** $p. < 0.01$,* $p. < 0.05$, N/S Not significant.

Disability score and living alone. There was virtually no correlation between Disability score and Social Support.

In testing the significance of the correlations between Disability and Attachment scores a two-tailed test was applied because I had been unable to predict whether any correlation, positive or negative, would be found between the variables. In the event both Avoidant Attachment and Disorganised Attachment were significantly correlated with Adult Disability although the level of correlation was not high. The Disability score does not correlate with Coping scores or Overall Distress scores.

Appendix 16: Attachments in non-bereaved psychiatric patients

Psychiatric patients

Table A.16.1 shows the numbers and percentages of bereaved and non-bereaved psychiatric patients on relevant categorical data and tests the significance of any differences.

Non-bereaved respondents were more often males than bereaved. Bereaved were more often diagnosed as suffering anxiety states, depression and PTSD, all at borderline levels of significance. Bereaved were no more or less suicidally inclined than other psychiatric patients as evidenced by their assertion that at the end of their tether they might take an overdose or otherwise harm themselves.

Table A.16.2 shows the mean scores and significance of any differences between the non-bereaved and bereaved psychiatric patients on each of the main variables. The non-bereaved were slightly younger than the bereaved respondents. No significant differences were found between non-bereaved and bereaved patients on social support or attachment scores. There was a trend

Table A.16.1 Non-Bereaved × Bereaved Psychiatric Patients compared: numbers, percentages and significance

	n.	Non-Bereaved Psychiatric 97	Bereaved Psychiatric 181	Test	Significance
Gender Male		40 (41%)	43 (24%)	Chi Sq. 9.2	0.002**
Living Alone		26 (27%)	80 (33%)	Exact 2-tailed	N/S
Clinical Diagnosis					
Anxiety State		61 (63%)	136 (75%)		0.048*
Depression		47 (49%)	113 (62%)		0.058 N/S
Psychosomatic Dis.		22 (23%)	45 (25%)		N/S
Personality Dis.		9 (9.3%)	17 (9.4%)		N/S
PTSD		3 (3.1%)	15 (8.3%)		0.054 N/S
IV/17g End of Tether – Overdose or harm self		14 (16.5%)	23 (14%)		N/S

** p. < 0.01, * p. < 0.05, N/S Not significant.

Table A.16.2 Non-Bereaved × Bereaved Psychiatric Patients compared: mean scores and significance of differences

	Non-Bereaved Psychiatric	Bereaved Psychiatric	Test	Significance
Age (Mean)	37 years	41 years	T Test 2.51	0.012*
Social Support	1.61	1.47	0.99	N/S
Attachment (Mean scores)			MannWhitney	0.094
Anxious/Ambivalent	6.07	7.07	z. 1.67	N/S
Avoidant	3.85	3.46	z. 0.96	N/S
Disorganised	2.97	3.47	z. 1.12	N/S
Insecurity of Attachment	10.50	12.16	z. 0.32	N/S
Marital Disagreements	1.90	2.09	z. 0.63	N/S
Coping scores				
Emot. Inhibition/Distrust	1.94	2.06	z. 0.62	N/S
Aggressive/Assertiveness	1.34	1.47	z. 1.14	N/S
End of Tether – Seek Help	1.92	1.70	z. 1.70	0.089 N/S
End of Tether – Turn In	0.99	0.93	z. 0.57	N/S
Symptoms/Distress scores				
Anxiety/Panic	2.63	2.69	z. 0.40	N/S
Depression/Medication	1.54	1.81	z. 2.23	0.026*
Grief/Loneliness	1.52	1.96	z. 3.28	0.001**
Clinging	1.64	1.71	z. 0.39	N/S
Alcohol	0.71	0.46	z. 1.49	N/S
Overall Distress	8.05	8.63	z. 0.85	N/S

** p. < 0.01,* p. < 0.05, N/S Not significant.

for bereaved controls to have higher Anxious/Ambivalent Attachment scores than non-bereaved. There were no significant differences between the two groups on scores of Coping. There was a trend for non-bereaved patients to say that they would seek help when at the end of their tether.

As expected, the Grief/Loneliness score was significantly higher in the bereaved than the non-bereaved patients. The Depression/Medication score was also higher in that group though at a lesser degree of significance. There was a trend for Alcohol Problems to be more frequent in the non-bereaved but not significantly so. Other scores were similar in the two groups.

Non-psychiatric matched samples of young women

Table A.16.3 compares the mean scores in Ward's non-psychiatric control group of 26 non-bereaved women with 26 bereaved women matched by age ± 5 years. There are no significant differences between the groups on measures of marital state. The only difference on measures of Coping to approach significance is the trend for bereaved controls to report that they would be less likely than non-bereaved to seek help if they came to the end of their tether.

Table A.16.3 Age-matched groups of non-bereaved and bereaved non-psychiatric young women compared: mean scores and significance of differences

	n.	Non-B'd Non-Psych 26	Bereaved Non-Psych 26	T Test t	Significance p.
Marital Disagreements		2.69	1.86	0.61	N/S
Marital Dysfunction		3.87	2.57	1.09	N/S
Adult Coping					
Emotional Inhibition/Distrust		1.95	2.23	−0.94	N/S
Aggressive/Assertive		1.30	1.46	−0.80	N/S
End of Tether – Seek Help		2.37	1.94	1.79	0.08 N/S
– Turn In		0.48	0.69	−1.13	N/S
Symptoms/Distress					
Anxiety/Panic		1.48	1.54	−0.21	N/S
Depression/Medication		0.45	0.46	−0.05	N/S
Grief/Loneliness		0.63	0.94	−1.48	0.14 N/S
Clinging		0.93	1.31	−1.71	0.09 N/S
Overall Distress		3.95	4.57	−0.72	N/S

N/S Not significant.

All current Symptom/Distress scores except the Alcohol Problem score are higher in the bereaved controls than the non-bereaved although none of the differences reaches statistical significance.

Psychiatric samples v. controls, bereaved and non-bereaved

Table A.16.4 shows the Spearman correlations with key variables in the non-bereaved and bereaved respondents in psychiatric and control groups together with the significance of any differences. Note that it was not possible to match all four of these comparison groups.

Looking first at the differences between bereaved and non-bereaved psychiatric patients which are shown in the first two columns, the correlation between the Insecure Attachment score and the Current Overall Distress score in the bereaved group was high (0.43), almost the same as the correlation in the non-bereaved group (0.46). This suggests that reported insecurity of attachment in childhood influences current levels of overall distress to a high degree in both groups of psychiatric patients.

Although non-bereaved patients reported just as many marital disagreements as the bereaved their marital problems were less likely to be attributable to insecure attachments or to correlate with current overall distress. Other factors, such as the influence of the mental illness itself, may explain the marital problems in this non-bereaved group.

The Anxious/Ambivalent Attachment score correlated with the current

Table A.16.4 Spearman correlations with key variables in unmatched non-bereaved v. bereaved respondents in psychiatric and control groups

	n.	Psychiatric		Non-psychiatric	
		Non-B'd 97	Ber'd 181	Non-B'd 40	Ber'd 35
Overall Parenting					
× Overall Distress		0.23*	0.39**	0.32*	0.48**
Childhood Vulnerability					
× Overall Distress		0.40**	0.44**	0.60**	0.46**
Insecure Attachment					
× Overall Distress		0.46**	0.43**	0.51**	0.51**
× Marital Disharmony		0.00 N/S	0.34**	0.43**	0.50**
Marital Disharmony					
× Overall Distress		0.00 N/S	0.28**	0.38**	0.43**
Anxious/Ambivalent					
× Clinging		0.16 N/S	0.31**	0.44**	0.28 N/S
× Anxiety/Panic		0.30**	0.33**	0.36**	0.43**
× Grief/Loneliness		0.30**	0.24**	0.21 N/S	0.30**
× Marital Disagreements		0.03 N/S	0.27**	0.27 N/S	0.54**
Marital Disagreements × Clinging		0.03 N/S	0.20**	0.22 N/S	0.21 N/S
× Grief/Loneliness		0.00 N/S	0.18**	0.12 N/S	0.18 N/S
Avoidant Att. × Inhibition/Distrust		0.41**	0.45**	0.47**	0.23 N/S
× Aggression/Assertion		0.43**	0.39**	0.18 N/S	0.14 N/S
× Hard to Express Grief		0.39**	0.30**	0.39**	0.41**
Cope Aggression × Hard to Express Grief		0.20*	0.07 N/S	0.21 N/S	0.12 N/S
Disorganised Attachment × EoT Turn In		0.44**	0.24**	0.29*	0.36*
× EoT Overdose (IV/17g)	∃	p. 0.46 N/S	p. 0.03*	None	None
× Anxiety/Panic		0.17 N/S	0.25**	0.27*	0.44**
× Depression/Medication		0.13 N/S	0.07 N/S	0.34*	0.24 N/S
× Alcohol Problems		0.15 N/S	0.21**	0.43**	0.31*
× Grief/Loneliness		0.35**	0.14*	0.19 N/S	0.57**
× Overall Distress		0.28**	0.35**	0.43**	0.39**
× Very Lonely (IV/11)	∃	p. 0.03*	p. 0.05*	p. 0.36 N/S	p. 0.00**
× Living Alone (III/2)	∃	p. 0.01**	p. 0.29 N/S	p. 0.05*	p. 0.02*
End of Tether Turn In × Anxiety/Panic		0.37**	0.28**	0.35*	0.23 N/S
× Depression/Medication		0.30**	0.21**	0.51**	0.14 N/S

** $p < 0.01$, * $p > 0.05$, N/S Not significant, ∃ = Fisher's Exact Test giving exact p. value.

Grief/Loneliness and Anxiety/Panic scores to a similar degree in both non-bereaved and bereaved groups. This implies that it is not only after bereavement by death that anxious/ambivalence can contribute to severe and lasting grief/loneliness and that similar degrees of anxiety are present in both groups.

Although the correlation between the Anxious/Ambivalent Attachment score and the Clinging score does not reach statistical significance in the non-bereaved psychiatric patients, the trend is in the expected direction.

All of the correlations between Avoidant Attachments and later variables in the non-bereaved patients resembled those in the bereaved patients. Thus the Avoidant Attachment score correlated with scores of adult coping by Emotional Inhibition/Distrust (0.41) and Aggression/Assertion (0.43), also with positive replies to the question 'Do you find it hard to express feelings of sadness and grief?' This suggests that Avoidant Attachment patterns persist into adult life in both groups of psychiatric patients.

In the non-bereaved, as in the bereaved psychiatric patients, the Disorganised Attachment score correlated highly with the End of Tether Turn In score and this correlated with both Current Anxiety/Panic and Depression/Medication scores. Although in the non-bereaved patients the correlations between Disorganised Attachment score and current Anxiety/Panic or Alcohol score did not reach statistical significance, the trends were in the expected direction.

The non-bereaved patients are just as likely as the bereaved to say that at the end of their tether they might overdose or harm themselves, but in the non-bereaved group this reply was not associated with Disorganised Attachment.

Disorganised Attachments did correlate with Overall Distress in the non-bereaved, as in the bereaved patients, and this was largely attributable to a significant correlation with Grief/Loneliness, particularly to positive responses to the question 'Are you very lonely?' Looking more closely at this finding we find that in these non-bereaved patients the Disorganised Attachment score is not only associated with our principle indicator of social support (EoT Turn In), but is also associated with living alone. This suggests that it is the interaction of a history of disorganised attachment and social isolation that accounts for much of the loneliness and distress in these psychiatric patients.

Ward's non-bereaved young women are shown in the third and fourth columns of Table A.16.4. Despite the small size of the sample and the younger mean age of Ward's control group, most of the correlations are very similar to those reported by the psychiatric patients. Whereas the non-bereaved patients differed from the bereaved in respect of the correlates of marital problems and suicidal ideation, as described above, differences were rarely found between bereaved and non-bereaved controls. This supports the notion that the marital problems in the non-bereaved psychiatric patients are often a consequence of the effect of the mental illness on the marriage. There were no members of the control group who were motivated to overdose.

While it comes as no surprise to find that bereaved members of the control group complained of more Grief/Loneliness than the non-bereaved, it is worth noting that they also complained of much more loneliness, thereby differing from the non-bereaved controls.

The samples shown in Table A.16.4 were not matched differences between the controls and the psychiatric samples may well reflect the age and sex differences. To remedy this 26 non-bereaved psychiatric patients were matched by age and sex with 26 of the non-bereaved control group. Results of this comparison are shown in Table A.16.5.

The small size of the samples means that Fisher's Exact Test was used and only large differences are likely to be significant. Even so most of the Symptom/Distress scores are about twice as high in the non-bereaved psychiatric as in the non-bereaved control group and only the Alcohol Problems score failed to reach significance. Among the Coping scores only Emotional Inhibition/Distrust fails to reach significance with higher scores of Aggressive/Assertiveness and EoT Turn In in the psychiatric group along with lower EoT Seek Help scores. The Avoidant Attachment score and the Disorganised Attachment score were both higher in the psychiatric than the control groups but these differences did not quite reach statistical significance. The mean social support score was significantly higher in the non-bereaved controls than non-bereaved psychiatric patients implying that the controls are better supported. The numbers living alone in both groups is small and no significant differences are found.

Table A.16.5 Spearman correlations with key variables in non-bereaved, matched psychiatric and non-psychiatric respondents

		Mean scores		*Exact test*
	n.	*Psychiatric* 26	*Non-Psychiatric* 26	*Significance p.*
Symptoms/Distress				
Anxiety/Panic		2.42	1.46	0.02*
Grief/Loneliness		1.47	0.77	0.02*
Depression/Medication		1.32	0.62	0.00**
Clinging		1.85	0.96	0.00**
Alcohol Problems		0.91	0.62	0.21 N/S
Overall Distress		7.97	4.27	0.00**
Coping				
Emotional Inhibition/Distrust		1.90	2.00	0.48 N/S
Aggressive/Assertiveness		1.94	1.23	0.00**
End of Tether: Seek Help		2.00	2.38	0.04*
End of Tether: Turn In		1.26	0.54	0.00*
Childhood Attachment scores				
Anxious/Ambivalent		5.98	7.50	0.19 N/S
Avoidant Attachment		5.46	4.23	0.09 N/S
Disorganised Attachment		3.96	2.38	0.06 N/S
Separations from Parents		1.88	1.31	0.20 N/S
Social Support		1.77	2.31	0.00**
Living alone		n. 10	n. 7	
		38.5%	26.9%	N/S

** p. < 0.01, * p. > 05, N/S Not significant.

The correlations within the 40 non-bereaved women in Ward's control group are shown in the third column of Table A.16.4. They indicate that the various insecure attachment patterns are correlated with most of the same variables from adult life as those found both in the bereaved controls and the bereaved and non-bereaved psychiatric patients. This implies that whatever the explanation for these correlations, they are found consistently in all four of the life situations studied here.

There is a high correlation between the EoT Turn In score and current Depression/Medication in the non-bereaved but not the bereaved controls. It seems that in these young women turning in on oneself is less likely to reflect or give rise to depression after bereavement than it is in normal life. It can perhaps be seen as a part of normal grieving.

Appendix 17: Disorders of attachment

Table A.17.1 shows the correlations between the Dysfunction score and the other scores which contribute to the Disorders of Attachment (described on pp. 310 and 226). A high score on each of these variables is associated with a significantly raised level of psychological dysfunction. The correlations are highest with the measures of Current Clinging and Anxiety/Panic. These are the main indicators of Separation Anxiety Disorder in adult life.

Table A.17.2 shows the numbers and percentages of bereaved and non-bereaved psychiatric patients who met the criteria for Separation Anxiety

Table A.17.1 Spearman correlations between Dysfunction score and selected variables with significance of differences

	Rho
Symptoms/Distress	
Clinging	0.54**
Anxiety/Panic	0.53**
Very Lonely (IV/11)	0.24**
Coping:	
Emotional Inhibition/Distrust	0.27**
Aggressive/Assertiveness	0.25**

** p. < 0.01

Table A.17.2 Numbers and percentages of bereaved and non-bereaved psychiatric patients who met criteria for Attachment Disorders

	Bereaved n. 181	*Non-Bereaved* 97	*Exact significance*
Separation Anxiety Disorder	43 (24%)	24 (25%)	0.46 N/S
Avoidant Attachment Disorder	25 (14%)	14 (14%)	0.51 N/S

N/S Not significant.

Disorder and Avoidant Attachment Disorder (described on pp. 233 and 237). These disorders were equally common in both bereaved and non-bereaved psychiatric samples.

Table A.17.3 shows that both types of attachment disorder more often caused women to seek for psychiatric help than men, particularly after bereavement.

Only two members (5.7%) of Ward's non-psychiatric control group met criteria for Separation Anxiety Disorder and one (3%) for Avoidant Disorder. These compared with 11 (31%) and 6 (18%) of the age and gender matched psychiatric patients. Although the small numbers make statistical comparison of the Avoidant Disorder group inappropriate Chi-squared test shows the difference in incidence of Separation Anxiety Disorder to be significantly higher in the psychiatric patients (Chi squared 4.03, 1 d.f., p. 0.028).

Given that these attachment disorders are found with similar incidence in both bereaved and non-bereaved psychiatric patients the figures shown in Table A.17.4 are based on the combination of both samples. This shows that each attachment disorder is significantly correlated with the type of

Table A.17.3 Ratio of males to females among bereaved and non-bereaved psychiatric patients who met criteria for Attachment Disorders

	Bereaved	*Non-bereaved*	*Both psychiatric samples*
Separation Anxiety Disorder	7/36	8/16	15/52
Avoidant Attachment Disorder	5/20	6/8	11/28

Table A.17.4 Attachment Disorders × Childhood Attachments, Age, Year of Birth and Marital Disagreements: mean scores and significance of differences (full sample n = 278)

	Mean scores		*Spearman Rho/p.*
	Separation Anxiety Disorder	*None*	
Anxious Ambivalent Attachment	11.1	7.4	0.25**
Age (Years)	37.8	40.2	−0.07 N/S
Year of Birth (Mean)	1953	1950	0.09 N/S
	Avoidant Disorder	*None*	
Avoidant Attachment	4.9	2.6	0.30**
Age (Years)	34.7	40.7	−0.19*
Year of Birth (Mean)	1956	1950	0.21**
Marital Disagreements	3.2	2.0	0.11*

** p. < 0.01, * p. < 0.05, N/S Not significant.

attachment pattern from which it is expected to derive. Although these correlations are highly significant they are only of moderate size implying that the attachment pattern may not be the sole cause of the disorder.

Avoidant Attachment Disorder is more highly correlated with year of birth than with age. This suggests that it has become more common as the years go by. It is also associated with some increase in marital disagreements. Among those with Avoidant Attachment Disorder, 72 per cent (28/37) answered 'Yes' to question IV/24 'Are you filled with regret for something which you did or said but cannot now put right?' This compares with only 45 per cent (107/239) of the other psychiatric patients (Exact Test p. = 0.008). It seems that people with Avoidant Attachment Disorder are filled with regrets.

Appendix 18.1: Prevention, therapies and outcome

As described on p. 299, 45 bereaved psychiatric patients were followed up.

In Table A.18.1 the mean scores on each of the Coping and Symptoms/Distress measures are shown as recorded at the time of initial contact and on follow-up. On follow-up respondents are now significantly more likely to seek help (as indicated by an increase in the End of Tether: Seek Help score). At a borderline level of significance they may be slightly more Aggressive/Assertive. Significant symptomatic improvement on follow-up is limited to the Depression/Medication score. At borderline levels of significance Alcohol Problem and Overall Distress scores also improve.

Table A.18.1 Comparison of initial and follow-up assessments of Coping and Symptoms/Distress: mean scores and significance of differences

	n.	*Mean scores*		*Exact test*	*Significance*
		Initial 45	*Follow-up* 45	*z.*	*p.*
Coping					
Emotional Inhibition/Distrust		2.00	1.94	0.52	N/S
Aggressive/Assertiveness		1.22	1.43	1.72	0.15 N/S
End of Tether – Seek Help		1.66	2.00	2.3	0.007**
End of Tether – Turn In		0.81	0.76	0.64	N/S
Symptoms/Distress					
Anxiety/Panic		2.48	2.35	0.47	N/S
Depression/Medication		1.62	1.30	1.91	0.03*
Grief/Loneliness		1.88	1.78	0.71	N/S
Clinging		1.40	1.51	0.80	N/S
Alcohol Problems		0.56	0.37	1.48	0.08 N/S
Overall Distress		7.94	7.10	1.40	0.08 N/S

** $p. < 0.01$, * $p. < 0.05$, N/S Not significant.

Change scores

Change scores were obtained by subtracting the score on follow-up from the initial score. Positive scores imply that the score is lower on follow-up (if a symptom this is now improved). Among 16 bereaved patients who received an antidepressant drug, the mean improvement in the Depression/Medication score was 0.23. On the other hand the mean improvement among those 19 who did not receive an antidepressant was 0.60.

Although those who did not take antidepressants improved over twice as much as those who did, the small numbers involved mean that the overall finding does not reach statistical significance (Exact 2-tailed p. = 0.192).

Table A.18.2 shows the correlation between Childhood Attachment scores and the scores of Change in Symptoms/Distress. It indicates that although the majority of correlations were in a positive direction (indicating that high scores on this attachment pattern were associated with improvement), none of the Attachment scores influence improvement or deterioration in any of the scores of Symptom/Distress to a statistically significant extent.

Table A.18.3 shows the correlations between change in selected Coping scores

Table A.18.2 Spearman correlations between Attachment scores and change in Symptoms/Distress on follow-up

Change in Symptoms/Distress	Anxious/ Ambivalent	Avoidant Attachment	Disorganised Attachment	Insecure Attachment
Anxiety/Panic	−0.01	0.18	0.21	0.16
Depression/Medication	−0.06	−0.17	−0.05	−0.13
Grief/Loneliness	0.10	−0.05	0.10	0.08
Clinging	0.12	0.08	0.12	0.17
Alcohol Problems	0.06	0.04	0.12	0.17
Overall Distress	0.03	−0.01	0.18	0.08

None of these correlations reach statistical significance.

Table A.18.3 Spearman correlations between change in Coping scores and change in Symptoms/Distress with tests of significance

Change in Symptoms/Distress	Change in Emotional Inhibition/Distrust		Change in EoT: Seek Help	
	rho	p.	rho	p.
Anxiety/Panic	0.36	0.008**	−0.06	N/S
Depression/Medication	0.28	0.03*	−0.35	0.01**
Grief/Loneliness	0.41	0.002**	−0.06	N/S
Clinging	−0.08	N/S	−0.13	N/S
Alcohol Problems	0.03	N/S	−0.08	N/S
Overall Distress	0.40	0.003**	−0.16	N/S

** p. < 0.01, * p. < 0.05, N/S Not Significant.

and change in the Symptoms/Distress scores. It indicates that a decrease in the Emotional Inhibition/Distrust score on follow-up is associated with a significant fall in Grief/Loneliness, Anxiety/Panic, Depression/Medication and Overall Symptoms/Distress.

It also indicates that an increase in the End of Tether Seek Help score is associated with significant improvement in the score of Grief/Loneliness.

Appendix 18.2: Organisations concerned with attachment and loss

Association for Death Education and Counselling
342 North Main Street
Hartford CT 06117–2507
USA
Tel: (860) 506 7503
Fax: (860) 506 7550
Email: info@adec.org
Internet: www.adec.org

Centre for Attachment-based Psychoanalytic Psychotherapy
LVS Resource Centre
356 Holloway Road
London N7 6PA
Tel: 020 7794 4306
Fax: 01435 866216
Email: capp@dial.pipex.com

Compassionate Friends (for parents losing a child)
Internet: www.compassionatefriends.org/

Cruse Bereavement Care
126 Sheen Road
Richmond
Surrey TW9 1UR
Tel: 020 8939 9530
Fax: 020 8940 7638
Email: info@crusebereavementcare.org.uk
Internet: www.crusebereavementcare.org.uk

Cruse Youth Involvement Project
Internet: www.rd4u.org.uk

International Attachment Network
1 Fairbridge Road
London N19 3EW
Tel/fax: 020 7281 4441
Email: iattachnet@yahoo.co.uk
Internet: www.attachmentnetwork.org

References

Aber, J.L., Slade, A., Berger, B., Bresgi, B. and Kaplan, M. (1985) The parent development interview, unpublished manuscript, Barnard College, Columbia University.

Adam, K.S. (1994) Suicidal behaviour and attachment: a developmental model, in M.B. Sperling and W.H. Berman (eds) *Attachment in Adults: Clinical and Developmental Perspectives*, New York: Guilford Press, pp. 275–98.

Adam, K.S., Sheldon-Keller, A.E. and West, M. (1996) Attachment organisation and history of suicidal behavior in clinical adolescents, *Journal of Consulting and Clinical Psychology* 64: 264–272.

Ainsworth, M.D.S. (1963) The development of mother–infant interaction among the Ganda, in B.M. Foss (ed.) *Determinants of Infant Behaviour*, Vol. 2, London: Methuen, pp. 67–104.

Ainsworth, M.D.S. (1991) Attachments and other affectional bonds across the life cycle, in C.M. Parkes, J. Stevenson-Hinde and P. Marris (eds). *Attachment across the Life Cycle*, London: Routledge, pp. 33–51.

Ainsworth, M.D.S. and Eichberg, C. (1991) Effects on infant–mother attachment of mother's unresolved loss of an attachment figure, or other traumatic experience, in C.M. Parkes, J. Stevenson-Hinde and P. Marris (eds) *Attachment across the Life Cycle*, London: Routledge, pp. 160–86.

Ainsworth, M.D.S., Blehar, M.C., Waters, E. and Wall, S. (1978) *Patterns of Attachment: A Psychological Study of the Strange Situation*, Hillsdale, NJ, Lawrence Erlbaum Associates Inc.

Allen, J.P., Hauser, S.T. and Borman-Spurrell, E. (1996) Attachment theory as a framework for understanding sequelae of severe adolescent psychopathology: a 11-year follow-up study, *Journal of Consulting and Clinical Psychology* 64: 254–263.

Ambrose, J.A. (1961) The development of the smiling response in early infancy, in B.M. Foss (ed.) *Determinants of Infant Behaviour*, Vol. 1, London: Methuen.

American Psychiatric Association (APA) (1994) *Diagnostic and Statistical Manual of Mental Disorders*, 4th edn, Washington, DC: American Psychiatric Association.

Archer, J. (1999) *The Nature of Grief: The Evolution and Psychology of Reactions to Loss*, London: Routledge.

Arvay, M.J. (2001) Shattered beliefs: reconstituting the self of the trauma counselor, in Robert Neimeyer (ed.) *Meaning Reconstruction and the Experience of Loss*, Washington DC: American Psychological Association Press, pp. 215–216.

Azhar, M.Z. and Varma, S.L. (1995) Religious psychotherapy as management of bereavement, *Acta Psychiatrica Scandinavica* 91: 233–235.

Barone, L. (2003) Developmental protective and risk factors in borderline personality disorder: a study using the Adult Attachment Interview, *Attachment and Human Development* 5: 64–77.

Bartholomew, K. and Horowitz, L.M. (1991) Attachment styles among young adults: a test of a four-category model, *Journal of Personality and Social Psychology* 61: 226–244.

Bartholomew, K. and Perlman, D. (eds) (1994) *Advances in Personal Relationships*, Vol. 5: *Attachment Processes in Adulthood*, London: Jessica Kingsley Publishers.

Bateson, G., Jackson, D.D., Haley, J. and Weakland, J.H. (1956) Toward a theory of schizophrenia, *Behavioural Science* 1: 251–264.

Bauer, J. and Bonanno, G. (2001) Doing and being well (for the most part): adaptive patterns of narrative and self-evaluation during bereavement, *Journal of Personality* 69: 798–816.

Beck, A.T. (1967) *Depression: Clinical, Experimental and Theoretical Aspects*, New York: Hoeber.

Beck, J. (1995) *Cognitive Therapy: Basics and Beyond*, New York: Guilford Press.

Belsky, J. (1996) Parent, infant and social-contextual antecedents of father–son attachment security, *Developmental Psychology* 32: 905–913.

Belsky, J., Rovine, M. and Taylor, D.G. (1984) The Pennsylvania Infant and Family Development Project: III. The origins of individual differences in infant–mother attachment: maternal and infant contributions, *Child Development* 55: 718–728.

Benoit, D. and Parker, K. (1993) Stability and transmission of attachment across three generations, manuscript for publication.

Billings, A.G. and Moos, R.H. (1981) The role of social responses and coping resources in attenuating the stress of life events, *Journal of Behavioral Medicine* 4: 139–157.

Birtchnell, J. (1975) Psychiatric breakdown following recent parent death, *British Journal of Medical Psychology* 10: 699–713.

Bowlby, J. (1944) Forty four juvenile thieves: their characters and home life, *International Journal of Psychoanalysis* 25: 19–52, 107–127.

Bowlby, J. (1953) *Child Care and the Growth of Love*, London: Pelican.

Bowlby, J. (1958) The nature of the child's tie to its mother, *International Journal of Psychoanalysis* 39: 350–373.

Bowlby, J. (1960) Separation anxiety, *International Journal of Psychoanalysis* 41: 2, 9.

Bowlby, J. (1969) *Attachment and Loss*, Vol. 1: *Attachment*, London: Hogarth Press.

Bowlby, J. (1973a) *Attachment and Loss*, Vol. II: *Separation: Anxiety and Anger*, London: Hogarth Press.

Bowlby, J. (1973b) Self-reliance and some conditions that promote it, in R.G. Gosling (ed.) *Support, Innovation and Autonomy*, London: Tavistock, pp. 23–48.

Bowlby, J. (1980) *Attachment and Loss*, Vol. III: *Loss: Sadness and Depression*, London: Hogarth Press.

Bowlby, J. (1988) *A Secure Base: Clinical Applications of Attachment Theory*, London: Routledge.

Bowlby, J. (1990) *Charles Darwin: A Biography*, London: Hutchinson.

Bowlby, J. (1991) Postscript, in C.M. Parkes, J. Stevenson-Hinde and P. Marris (eds) *Attachment across the Life Cycle*, London: Routledge, pp. 293–297.

Bowlby, J. and Parkes, C.M. (1970) Separation and loss within the family, in E.J. Anthony (ed.) *The Child in his Family*, New York: Wiley.

Brennan, K.A. and Shaver, P.R. (1995) Dimensions of adult attachment, affect regulation, and romantic relationship functioning, *Personality and Social Psychology Bulletin* 21: 267–283.

Brennan, K.A. and Shaver, P.R. (1998) Attachment styles and personality disorders: their connections to each other and to parental divorce, parental death, and perceptions of parental caregiving, *Journal of Personality* 66: 835–878.

Brennan, K.A., Clark, C.L. and Shaver, P.R. (1998) Self-report measurement of adult attachment: an integrative overview, in J.A. Simpson and W.S. Rholes (eds) *Attachment Theory and Close Relationships*, New York: Guildford Press.

Brennan, K.A., Shaver, P.R. and Tobey, A.E. (1991) Attachment styles, gender and parental problem drinking, *Journal of Social and Personal Relationships* 8: 451–466.

Breuer, J. and Freud, S. (1893) On the psychical mechanisms of hysterical phenomena: a preliminary communication, Standard Edition of *The Complete Psychological Works of Sigmund Freud*, Vol. 2, London: Hogarth Press.

Brom, D., Kleber, R.J. and Defares, P. (1989) Brief psychotherapy for post-traumatic stress disorders: a controlled outcome study, *Journal of Consulting and Clinical Psychology* 57: 607–612.

Brown, D. (1958) Sex-role development in a changing culture, *Psychological Bulletin* 54: 232–242.

Brown, G.W. and Harris, T. (1978) *Social Origins of Depression: A Study of Psychiatric Disorder in Women*, London: Tavistock.

Bunch, J., Barraclough, B.M., Nelson, B. *et al.* (1971) Suicide following death of parents, *Social Psychiatry* 6: 193–199.

Byng-Hall, J. (1991) The application of attachment theory to understanding and treatment in family therapy, in C.M. Parkes, J. Stevenson-Hinde and P. Marris (eds) *Attachment across the Life Cycle*, London: Routledge, pp. 199–215.

Carlson, E. (1998) A prospective longitudinal study of Attachment Disorganisation/ Disorientation, *Child Development* 69: 1107–1128.

Carlson, V., Cicchetti, D., Barnett, D. and Braunwald, K. (1989) Disorganised/ Disoriented Attachment relationships in maltreated infants, *Developmental Psychology* 25: 525–531.

Cicchetti, D., Toth, S.L. and Rogosch, T.A. (1999) Efficacy of Toddler–Parent Psychotherapy (TPP) to increase attachment security in offspring of depressed mothers, *Attachment and Human Development* 1: 34–66.

Cleiren, M.P.H.D. (1991) *Adaptation after Bereavement*, Leiden: DSWO.

Collick, E. (1986) *Through Grief*, London: Darton, Longman and Todd.

Collins, N.L. and Read, S.J. (1990) Adult attachment, working models, and relationship quality in dating couples, *Journal of Personality and Social Psychology* 58: 644–663.

Cornwell, J.B., Nurcombe, B. *et al.* (1977) Family response to loss of a child by sudden infant death syndrome, *Medical Journal of Australia* 126: 656–658.

Cox, M.J., Owen, M.T., Henderson, V.K. and Margand, N.A. (1992) Predictions of infant-father and infant-mother attachment. *Developmental Psychology* 28: 474–483.

Crittenden, P.M. and Clausen, A.H. (2000) *The Organization of Attachment Relationships*. Cambridge University Press, Cambridge.

Crowell, J.A., Treboux, D. and Waters, E. (2000) The Adult Attachment Interview and the Relationship Questionnaire: relations to reports of mothers and partners, *Personal Relationships* 6: 1–18.

Cruse Bereavement Care (2004) *Cruse Annual Report*, Richmond: Cruse Bereavement Care.

Darwin, C. (1872) *The Expression of the Emotions in Man and Animals*, London: Murray.

Deutsch, H. (1937) Absence of grief, *Psychoanalytical Quarterly* 6: 12.

Dobson, K. (1989) A meta-analysis of the efficacy of cognitive therapy for depression, *Journal of Consulting and Clinical Psychology* 57: 414–419.

Doka, K. (ed.) (1989) *Disenfranchised Grief*, Lexington, MA: Lexington.

Douglas, J.D. (1990) Patterns of change following parental death in mid-life adults, *Omega* 22, 2: 123–138.

Dozier, M. and Kobak, R.R. (1992) Psychophysiology in Attachment Interviews: converging evidence for deactivating strategies, *Child Development* 63: 1473–1480.

Dozier, M., Cue, K. and Barnett, L. (1994) Clinicians as caregivers: role of attachment organisation in treatment, *Journal of Consulting and Clinical Psychology* 62: 793–800.

Dozier, M., Stovall, K.C. and Albus, K.E. (1999) Attachment and psychopathology in adults, in J. Cassidy and P.R. Shaver (eds) *Handbook of Attachment: Theory, Research and Clinical Applications*, New York: Guilford Press, pp. 497–519.

Dyregrov, A. (1990) Parental reactions to the loss of an infant child: a review, *Scandinavian Journal of Psychology* 31: 266–280.

Easterbrooks, M.A. and Goldberg, W.A. (1984) Toddler development in the family: impact of father involvement and parenting characteristics, *Developmental Psychology* 20: 504–514.

Egeland, B. and Sroufe, L.A. (1981) Attachment and early maltreatment, *Child Development* 52: 44–52.

Elicker, J., Engelund, M. and Sroufe, L.A. (1992) Predicting peer competence and peer relationships in childhood from early parent–child relationships, in R. Parke and G. Ladd (eds) *Family–Peer Relations: Models of Linkage*, Hillsdale, NJ: Lawrence Erlbaum Associates Inc, pp. 77–106.

Elkin, I., Shea, M., Watkins, J. *et al.* (1989) NIMH treatment of depression collaborative research program: general effectiveness of treatment, *Archives of General Psychiatry* 46: 971–982.

el-Guebaly, N., West, M., Maticka-Tyndale, E. and Pool, M. (1993) Attachment among adult children of alcoholics, *Addiction* 88: 1405–1411.

Erikson, E.H. (1950) *Childhood and Society*. New York: Norton.

Erickson, M., Sroufe, L.A. and Egeland, B. (1985) The relationship between quality of attachment and behavior problems in pre-school in a high risk sample, in I. Bretherton and E. Waters (eds) *Growing Points of Attachment Theory and Research*, Monographs of the Society for Research in Child Development 50, 1–2, serial Number 209, 66–104.

Fahlberg, V. (1990) *Residential Treatment: A Tapestry of Many Therapies*, Indianapolis: Perspective Press.

Faschingbauer, T.R., De Vaul, R.A. and Zisook, S. (1977) Development of the Texas Inventory of Grief, *American Journal of Psychiatry* 134: 696–698.

Feeney, J.A. (1991) The attachment perspective on adult romantic relationships, unpublished doctoral dissertation, Queensland University.

Feeney, J.A. (1999) Adult romantic attachment and couple relationships, in J. Cassidy and P. Shaver (eds) *Handbook of Attachment: Theory, Research, and Clinical Applications*, New York: Guilford Press, pp. 355–377.

Feeney, J.A. and Noller, P. (1990) Attachment style as a predictor of romantic adult relationships, *Journal of Personality and Social Psychology* 58: 281–291.

Feeney, J.A., Noller, P. and Patty, J. (1993) Adolescents' interaction with the opposite sex: influence of attachment style and gender, *Journal of Adolescence* 16: 169–186.

Fish, W.C. (1986) Differences in grief intensity in bereaved parents, in T.A. Rando (ed.) *Parental Loss of a Child*, Champaign, IL: Research Press, pp. 415–428.

Fleming, S. and Robinson, P. (2001) Grief and cognitive-behavioral therapy: the reconstruction of meaning, in M.S. Stroebe, R.O. Hansson, W. Stroebe and H. Schut (eds) *Handbook of Bereavement Research: Consequences, Coping and Care*, Washington, DC: American Psychological Association, pp. 647–669.

Fonagy, P., Steele, H. and Steele, M. (1991) Maternal representations of attachment during pregnancy predict the organisation of infant–mother attachment at one year of age, *Child Development* 62: 891–905.

Fonagy, P. H., Leigh, T., Steele, M., Steele, H., Kennedy, R., Mattoon, G., Target, M. and Gerber, A. (1996) The relation of attachment status, psychiatric classification and response to psychotherapy, *Journal of Consulting and Clinical Psychology* 64: 22–31.

Fonagy, P., Target, M., Steele, M., Steele, H., Leigh, T., Levinson, A. and Kennedy, R. (1997) Morality, disruptive behavior, borderline personality disorder, crime and their relationship to security of attachment, in L. Atkinson and K. Zucker (eds) *Attachment and Psychopathology*, New York: Guilford Press, pp. 223–274.

Fox, N.A., Kimmerly, N.L. and Schafer, W.D. (1991) Attachment to mother/ attachment to father: a meta-analysis, *Child Development* 62: 210–225.

Freud, S. (1914) On narcissism: an introduction, *Collected Papers*, Vol. 4, London: Hogarth Press, pp. 30–59.

Freud, S. (1917) Mourning and melancholia, *The Standard Edition of the Complete Psychological Works of Sigmund Freud*, under the general editorship of James Strachey, in collaboration with Anna Freud, assisted by Alix Strachey and Alan Tyson, London: Hogarth Press, 1953– Vol. 14, pp. 239–258.

Fried, M. (1962) Grieving for a lost home, in L.J. Duhl (ed.) *The Environment of the Metropolis*, New York: Basic Books.

Frodi, A., Dernevik, M., Sepa, A., Philipson, J. and Bragesjo, M. (2001) Current attachment representations of incarcerated offenders varying in degree of psychopathy, *Attachment and Human Development* 3, 3: 269–283.

Fulton, R. and Owen, G. (1977) *Adjustment to Loss through Death: A Sociological Analysis*, Minnesota: University of Minnesota, Center for Death Education and Research.

George, C. and Solomon, J. (1989) Internal working models of caregiving and security of attachment at aged six, *Infant Mental Health Journal* 10: 222–237.

George, C. and Solomon, J. (1996) Representational models of relationships: links between caregiving and attachment, *Infant Mental Health Journal* 17: 198–216.

Gerlsma, C. and Lutejin, F. (2000) Attachment style in the context of clinical and health psychology: a proposal for the assessment of valence, incongruence, and accessibility of attachment representations in various working models, *British Journal of Medical Psychology* 73, 1: 15–34.

Goodall, J. van L. (1971) *In the Shadow of Man*, London: Collins.

Grand, S. (2004) 'I'm sorry, has your brain broken?', *Guardian: Life* 7, 29 January.

Greenberg, M.T. (1999) Attachment and psychopathology in childhood, in J. Cassidy and P. Shaver (eds) *Handbook of Attachment: Theory, Research, and Clinical Applications*, New York: Guilford Press, pp. 369–496.

Griffin, D.W. and Bartholomew, K. (1994) The metaphysics of measurement: the case of adult attachment, in K. Bartholomew and D. Perlman (eds) *Advances in Personal Relationships*, Vol. 5: *Attachment Processes in Adulthood*, London: Jessica Kingsley Publishers, pp. 17–52.

Grossmann, K.E. and Grossmann, K. (1991) Attachment quality as an organiser of emotional and behavioral responses in a longitudinal perspective, in C.M. Parkes, J. Stevenson-Hinde and P. Marris (eds) *Attachment Across the Life Cycle*, London: Routledge pp. 93–114.

Gunning, M., Conroy, S., Valoriani, V. *et al.* (2004) Measurement of mother–infant interactions and the home environment in a European setting: preliminary results from a cross-cultural study, *British Journal of Psychiatry* 184: s38–s46.

Hall, M. and Irwin, M. (2001) Physiological indices of functioning in bereavement, in M.S. Stroebe, R.O. Hansson, W. Stroebe and H. Schut (eds) *Handbook of Bereavement Research: Consequences, Coping and Care*, Washington, DC: American Psychological Association, pp. 473–492.

Harris, T. and Bifulco, A. (1991) Loss of a parent in childhood, attachment style and depression in adulthood, in C.M. Parkes, J. Stevenson-Hinde and P. Marris (eds) *Attachment across the Life Cycle*, London: Tavistock/Routledge, pp. 234–267.

Harris, T., Brown, G.W. and Bifulco, A. (1986) Loss of parent in childhood and adult psychiatric disorder: the role of adequate parental care, *Psychological Medicine* 16: 641–659.

Hart, J.T. (1971) The inverse care law, *Lancet* 1: 405–412.

Hazan, C.G. and Shaver, P. (1987) Romantic love conceptualised as an attachment process, *Journal of Personality and Social Psychology* 52: 511–524.

Hazan, C.G. and Shaver, P. (1990) Love and work: an attachment theoretical perspective, *Journal of Personality and Social Psychology* 59: 270–280.

Hazan, C. and Zeifman, D. (1994) Sex and the psychological tether, in K. Bartholomew and D. Perlman (eds) *Advances in Personal Relationships*, Vol. 5: *Attachment Processes in Adulthood*, Jessica Kingsley London: Publishers, pp. 151–77.

Hertsgaard, L., Gunnar, M., Erickson, M.F. and Nachmias, M. (1995) Adrenocortical responses to the strange situation in infants with disorganised/disoriented attachment relationships, *Child Development* 66: 1100–1106.

Hickie, I., Parker, G., Wilhelm, K. and Tennant, C. (1990a) Perceived interpersonal risk factors of non-endogenous depression, *Psychological Medicine* 21: 399–412.

Hickie, I., Wilhelm, K. and Parker, G. (1990b) Perceived dysfunctional intimate relationships: a specific association with non-melancholic depressive type, *Journal of Affective Disorders* 19: 99–107.

Hobson, P. and Patrick, M. (1998) Objectivity in psychhoanalytic judgement, *British Journal of Psychiatry* 173: 172–177.

Hodgkinson, P.E. and Stewart, M. (1991) *Coping with Catastrophe: A Handbook of Disaster Management*, London: Routledge.

Holmes, J. (1993) *John Bowlby and Attachment Theory*, London: Routledge.

Holmes, J. (2001) *The Search for the Secure Base: Attachment Theory and Psychotherapy*, Hove, UK: Brunner-Routledge.

Hopkins, J. (1991) Failure of the holding relationship: some effects of physical rejection on the child's attachment and inner experience, in C. M. Parkes, J. Stevenson-Hinde and P. Marris, (eds) *Attachment across the Life Cycle*, London: Routledge.

Horowitz, M.J. (1986) *Stress Response Syndromes*, Northvale, NJ: Aronson.

Horowitz, M.J., Wilner, N. and Alvarez, W. (1979) Impact of event scale: a measure of subjective stress, *Psychosomatic Medicine* 41: 209–218.

Horowitz, M.J., Krupnick, J., Kaltreidwer, N. *et al.* (1981) Initial psychological response to parental death, *Archives of General Psychiatry* 137, 10: 1157–1162.

Howe, D. and Fearnley, S. (1999) Disorders of attachment and attachment therapy, *Adoption and Fostering* 23, 2: 19–30.

Hughes, P., Turton, P., Hopper, E., Slyter, H. and Evans, C.D.H. (2002) Assessment of guidelines for good practice in psycho-social care of mothers after stillbirth, *Lancet* 9327: 114–118.

Ivarsson, T., Larsson, B. and Gillberg, C. (1998) A 2–4 year follow-up of depressive symptoms, suicidal ideation, and suicide attempts among adolescent psychiatric in-patients, *European Child and Adolescent Psychiatry* 7, 2: 96–104.

Jacobs, S. (1993) *Pathologic Grief: Maladaptation to Loss*, Washington, DC: American Psychiatric Press.

Jacobs, S. (1999) *Traumatic Grief: Diagnosis, Treatment and Prevention*, New York: Taylor and Francis.

Janoff-Bulman, R. (1992) *Shattered Assumptions: Towards a New Psychology of Trauma*, New York: Free Press.

Kaufman, I. C. and Rosenblum, L. A. (1969) Effects of separation from mother on infant monkeys, *Annals of the New York Academy of Science* 159, 3: 681–695.

Kehoe, P., Hoffman, J.H., Austin-LaFrance, R.J. *et al.* (1995) Neonatal isolation enhances hippocampal dentate response to tetanization in freely moving juvenile male rats, *Experimental Neurology* 136: 89–97.

Kirkpatrick, L.A. (1999) Attachment and religious representations and behavior, in J. Cassidy and P.R. Shaver (eds) *Handbook of Attachment: Theory, Research and Clinical Applications*, New York: Guilford Press, pp. 803–822.

Kirkpatrick, L.A. and Shaver, P.R. (1990) Attachment theory and religion: childhood attachments, religious beliefs and conversion, *Journal for the Scientific Study of Religions* 29: 305–334.

Kissane, D. and Bloch, S. (2002) *Family Focused Grief Therapy: A Model of Family-Centred Care during Palliative Care and Bereavement*, Maidenhead: Open University Press.

Kobak, R. (1994) Interview with Robert Karen, in R. Kobak *Becoming Attached: Unfolding the Mystery of the Infant–Mother Bond and its Influence on Later Life*, New York: Warner pp. 388–389.

Klass, D. (1988) *Parental Grief: Solace and Resolution*, New York: Springer.

Klass, D., Silverman, P.R. and Nickman, S. (eds) (1996) *Continuing Bonds: New Understandings of Grief*, London: Taylor and Francis.

Knoj, H.J. and Keller, D. (2002) Mourning parents: considering safeguards and their relation to health, *Death Studies* 26, 7: 545–566.

Lakatos, K., Toth, I., Nemoda, Z., Ney, K., Sasvari-Szekely, M. and Gervai, M. (2000) Dopamine D4 Receptor (DRD4) gene polymorphism is associated with attachment disorganisation: interaction of the exon III 48 bp repeat and the −521 C/T promotor polymorphisms, *Molecular Psychiatry* 7: 27–31.

Larose, S. and Boivin, M. (1997) Structural relations among attachment working models of parents, general and specific support expectations and personal adjustment in late adolescence, *Journal of Social and Personal Relationships* 14: 579–601.

Lazarus, R. and Folkman, S. (1984) *Stress, Appraisal and Coping*, New York: Springer.

LeDoux, J.E. (1996) *The Emotional Brain: The Mysterious Underpinnings of Emotional Life*, New York: Simon and Schuster.

Lewis, M., Feiring, C., McGuffog, C. and Jaskir, J. (1984) Predicting psychopathology in six-year-olds from early social relations, *Child Development* 55: 123–136.

Lieberman, A.F. Weston, D.R. and Pawl, J.H. (1991) Preventative intervention and outcome with anxiously attached dyads, *Child Development* 62: 199–209.

Liebowitz, M. (1983) *The Chemistry of Love*, New York: Berkley Books.

Lindemann, E. (1944) The symptomatology and management of acute grief, *American Journal of Psychiatry* 101: 141.

Liotti, G. (1991) Insecure attachment and agoraphobia, in C.M. Parkes, J. Stevenson-Hinde and P. Marris (eds) *Attachment Across the Life Cycle*, London: Routledge, pp. 216–233.

Liotti, G. (1992) Disorganised/disoriented attachment in the aetiology of the dissociative disorders, *Dissociation* 1964: 196–204.

Littlefield, C.H. and Rushton, J.P. (1986) When a child dies: the sociobiology of bereavement, *Journal of Personality and Social Psychology* 51: 797–802.

Lorenz, K. (1952) *King Solomon's Ring*, London: Methuen.

Lorenz, K. (1963) *On Aggression*, London: Methuen, p. 186.

McCallum M. and Piper W.E. (1990) A controlled study of effectiveness and patient suitability for short-term group psychotherapy, *International Journal of Group Psychotherapy* 40: 431–452.

McCallum, M., Piper, W.E. and Morin, H. (1993) Affect and outcome in short-term group therapy for loss, *Nursing Research* 47: 2–10.

McFarland, D. (1981) *The Oxford Companion to Animal Behavior*, Oxford: Oxford University Press, pp. 303–305.

Main, M. (1977) Analysis of a peculiar form of reunion behavior seen in some day-care children: its history and sequelae in children who are home-reared, in R. Webb (ed.) *Social Development in Childhood: Day-Care Programs and Research*, Baltimore, MD: Johns Hopkins University Press.

Main, M. and Cassidy, J. (1988) Categories of response to reunion with the parent at aged 6: predictable from infant attachment classifications and stable over a one-month period, *Developmental Psychology* 24: 415–426.

Main, M. and Goldwyn, R. (1984) *Adult Attachment Scoring and Classificatory System*, Berkeley: University of California.

Main, M. and Hesse, E. (1990) Parents' unresolved traumatic experiences are related to infant disorganised attachment status: is frightened and/or frightening parental behavior the linking mechanism?, in M. Greenberg, D. Cicchetti and M. Cummings (eds) *Attachment in the Preschool Years*, Chicago: University of Chicago Press, pp. 121–60.

Main, M. and Solomon, J. (1990) Procedures for identifying infants as disorganised/disoriented during the Ainsworth Strange Situation, in M. T. Greenberg, D. Cicchetti and E. M. Cummings (eds) *Attachment in the Preschool Years*, Chicago: University of Chicago Press, pp. 121–160.

Main, M. and Weston, D.R. (1982) Avoidance of the attachment figure in infancy: descriptions and interpretations, in C.M. Parkes and J. Stevenson-Hinde (eds) *The Place of Attachment in Human Behavior*, New York: Basic Books, pp. 31–59.

Main, M., Kaplan, N. and Cassidy, J. (1985) Security in infancy, childhood and adulthood: a move to the level of representation, in I. Bretherton and E. Waters (eds) *Growing Points of Attachment Theory and Research*, Monographs of the Society for Research in Child Development 50 (1–2, serial no. 209), 66–104.

Manassis, K., Owens, M., Adam, K.S., West, M. and Sheldon-Keller, A.E. (1999) Assessing attachment: convergent validity of the adult attachment interview and the parental bonding instrument, *Australia and New Zealand Journal of Psychiatry* 33, 4: 1440–1614.

Marmar C.R., Horowitz M.J., Weiss, D.S., Wilner, N.R., and Kaltreider, N.B. (1988) A controlled trial of brief psycotherapy and mutual-help group treatment of conjugal bereavement, *American Journal of Psychiatry* 145: 203–209.

Marris, P. (1974) *Loss and Change*, London: Routledge and Kegan Paul.

Martin, J.L. and Dean, L. (1993) Bereavement following death from AIDS: unique problems, reactions and special needs, in M.S. Stroebe, W. Stroebe and R.O. Hansson (eds) *Handbook of Bereavement*, Cambridge: Cambridge University Press, pp. 317–30.

Mawson, D., Marks, I.M., Ramm, L. and Stern, R.S. (1981) Guided mourning for morbid grief: a controlled study, *British Journal of Psychiatry* 138: 185–193.

Melzack, R. and Wall, P.D. (1965) Pain mechanisms, *Science* 150: 971–979.

Mikulincer, M., Florian, V. and Weller (1993) Attachment styles, coping strategies, and post-traumatic psychological distress: the impact of Gulf War in Israel, *Journal of Personality and Social Psychology* 64: 817–826.

Miles, M.S. (1985) Emotional symptoms and physical health in bereaved parents, *Nursing Research* 34, 2: 76–81.

Mireault, G., Bearor, K. and Thomas, T. (2002) Adult romantic attachment among women who experienced childhood maternal loss, *Omega* 44, 1: 97–104.

Moffat, E. (2000) The emotional relationship between people and companion animals (encompassing attachment, anthropomorphism and decentering), *Journal of the Society for Companion Animal Studies* 22, 3: 4–5.

Moorey, S. (1996) When bad things happen to rational people: cognitive therapy in adverse life circumstances, in P. Slakovskis (ed.) *Frontiers of Cognitive Therapy*, New York: Guilford Press, pp. 450–469.

Moss, M.S. and Moss, S.Z. (1997) Middle-aged children's bereavement after the death of an elderly parent, in J.D. Morgan (ed.) *Readings in Thanatology*, Amityville, NY: Baywood, pp. 347–356.

Moss, M.S., Resch, N. and Moss, S.Z. (1997) The role of gender in the responses of middle-aged children to parental death, *Omega* 35: 43–65.

Moss, M.S., Moss, S.Z. and Hansson, R.O. (2001) Bereavement and old age, in M.S. Stroebe, R.O. Hansson, W. Stroebe and H. Schut (eds) *Handbook of Bereavement Research: Consequences, Coping and Care*, Washington, DC: American Psychological Association Press, pp. 241–260.

Muncie, W. (1948) *Psychobiology and Psychiatry*, 2nd edn, St Louis: Mosby.

Munoz, L. (1980) Exile as bereavement: socio-psychological manifestations of Chilean immigrants in Britain, *British Journal of Medical Psychology* 53: 227–232.

Neimeyer, R. (ed.) (2001) *Meaning Reconstruction and the Experience of Loss*, Washington, DC: American Psychological Association Press.

Nixon, J. and Pearn, J. (1977) Emotional sequelae of parents and sibs following the drowning or near drowning of a child, *Australian and New Zealand Journal of Psychiatry* 11: 265–268.

Noelen-Hoeksma, S. and Larson, J. (1999) *Coping with Loss*, Mahwah, NJ: Lawrence Erlbaum Associates Inc.

Norris, F.H. and Murrell, S.A. (1990) Social support, life events and stress as modifiers of adjustment to bereavement by older adults, *Psychology and Aging* 5: 429–436.

O'Connor, T.G. and Croft, C.M. (2001) A twin study of attachment in pre-school children, *Child Development* 72: 1501–1511.

Office of Statistical Censuses and Surveys (1992) *Bills of Mortality for England and Wales*, London: HMSO.

Oltjenbruns, K.A. (1999) Developmental context of childhood: grief and regrief phenomena, in M.S. Stroebe, R.O. Hansson, W. Stroebe and H. Schut (eds) *Handbook of Bereavement Research: Consequences, Coping and Care*, Washington, DC: American Psychological Association Press, pp. 169–218.

Owen, G., Fulton, R. and Markusen, E. (1982) Death at a distance: a study of family survivors, *Omega* 13: 191–226.

Parker, G. (1994) Parental bonding and depressive disorders, in M.B. Sperling, and W.H. Berman (eds) *Attachment in Adults: Clinical and Developmental Perspectives*, New York: Guilford Press.

Parker, G., Tupling, H. and Brown, L.B. (1979) A parental bonding instrument, *British Journal of Medical Psychology* 52: 1–10.

Patrick, M., Hobson, R.P., Castle, D., Howard, R. and Maughan, B. (1994) Personality disorder and the mental representation of early social experience, *Development and Psycho-Pathology* 6: 375–388.

Parkes, C.M. (1964a) Recent bereavement as a cause of mental illness, *British Journal of Psychiatry* 110: 198–204.

Parkes, C.M. (1964b) The effects of bereavement on physical and mental health. A study of the case records of widows, *British Medical Journal* 2: 274.

Parkes, C.M. (1971) Psychosocial transitions: a field for study, *Social Science and Medicine* 5: 101–115.

Parkes, C.M. (1972) Components of the reaction loss of a limb, spouse or home, *Journal of Psychosomatic Research* 16: 343–349.

Parkes, C.M. (1976) The psychological reaction to loss of a limb: the first year after amputation, in J.G. Howells (ed.) *Modern Perspectives in the Psychiatric Aspects of Surgery*, New York: Brunner Mazel, pp. 515–33.

Parkes, C.M. (1981) Evaluation of a bereavement service, *Journal of Preventive Psychiatry* 1: 179–188.

Parkes, C.M. (1991) Attachment, bonding and psychiatric problems after bereavement in adult life, in C.M. Parkes, J. Stevenson-Hinde and P. Marris (eds) *Attachment Across the Life Cycle*, London: Tavistock/Routledge, pp. 268–92.

Parkes, C.M. (1993) Psychiatric problems following bereavement by murder or manslaughter, *British Journal of Psychiatry* 162: 49–54.

Parkes, C.M. (1995) Guidelines for conducting ethical bereavement research, *Death Studies* 19: 171–181.

Parkes, C.M. (1996) *Bereavement: Studies of Grief in Adult Life*, 3rd edn, London: Routledge.

Parkes, C.M. and Brown, R.J. (1972) Health after bereavement: a controlled study of young Boston widows and widowers, *Psychosomatic Medicine* 34: 449–461.

Parkes, C.M. and Markus, A. (eds) (1998) *Coping with Loss: Helping Patients and their Families*, London: BMJ Books.

Parkes, C.M. and Weiss, R.S. (1983) *Recovery from Bereavement*, New York: Basic Books.

Parkes, C.M., Benjamin, B. and Fitzgerald, R.G. (1969) Broken heart: a statistical study of increased mortality among widowers, *British Medical Journal* 1: 740.

Pascal, B. (c.1655) *Pensees IV, 277.*

Pasternak, R.E., Reynolds, C.F., Schlernizauer, M. *et al.* (1991) Nor-Triptyline therapy of bereavement-related depression in later life, *Journal of Clinical Psychiatry* 52: 307–310.

Pastor, D.L. (1981) The quality of mother–infant attachment and its relationship to toddlers sociability with peers, *Developmental Psychology* 17: 326–335.

Paykel, E.S. (1974) Life stress and psychiatric disorder, in B.S. Dohrenwendt and B.P. Dohrenwendt (eds) *Stressful Life Events: Their Nature and Effects*, New York: Wiley.

Peppers, L.G. and Knapp, R.J. (1990) *Motherhood and Mourning: Perinatal Death*, New York: Praeger.

Perlin, S. and Schmidt, A. (1975) Psychiatry, in S. Perlin *A Handbook for the Study of Suicide*, Oxford: Oxford University Press.

Pistole, M.C. (1994) Adult attachment styles: some thoughts on closeness–distance struggles, *Family Process* 33: 147–160.

Pitt, B. (1974) *Psycho-Geriatrics: An Introduction to the Psychiatry of Old Age*, Edinburgh: Churchill Livingstone.

Price, J. (1967) The dominance hierarchy and the evolution of mental illness, *Lancet* 2: 243.

Prigerson, H.G., Frank, E., and Kasl, S.V. (1995a) Complicated grief and bereavement-related depression as distinct disorders: preliminary evaluation in elderly bereaved spouses, *American Journal of Psychiatry* 152, 1: 22–30.

Prigerson, H.G., Masiejewski, P.K. and Newsom, I. (1995b) The Inventory of Complicated Grief: a scale to measure maladaptive symptoms of loss, *Psychiatry Research* 59: 65–79.

Prigerson, H.G., Bierhals, A.J. and Kasl, S.V. (1996) Complicated grief as a distinct disorder from bereavement-related depression and anxiety: a replication study, *American Journal of Psychiatry* 153: 84–86.

Radke-Yarrow, M., McCann, K., de Mulder, E., Belmont, B., Martinez, P. and Richardson, D.T. (1995) Attachment in the context of high-risk conditions, *Development and Psychopathology* 7: 247–265.

Rando, T.A. (1986) *Loss and Anticipatory Grief*, Lexington, MA: Lexington Books.

Rando, T.A. (2002) The 'curse' of too good a childhood, in J. Kauffman (ed.) *Loss of the Assumptive World*, London: Brunner-Routledge, pp. 171–92.

Range, L.M., Kovac, S.H. and Marion, M.S. (2000) Does writing about the bereavement lessen grief following sudden, unintentional death?, *Death Studies* 24: 115–134.

Raphael, B. (1977) Preventive intervention with the recently bereaved, *Archives of General Psychiatry* 34: 1450–1454.

Reynolds, C.F., Miller, M.D. and Pasternak, R.E. (1999) Treatment of bereavement-related major depressive episodes in later life: a controlled study of acute and continuation treatment with nortriptyline and interpersonal psychotherapy, *American Journal of Psychiatry* 156, 2: 202–208.

Reynolds, J.J. (2004) Stillbirth: to hold or not to hold, *Omega* 48, 1: 85–88.

Ricciutti, A.E. (1992) Child–mother Attachment: a twin study, unpublished doctoral dissertation, University of Virginia.

Robertson, J. and Bowlby, J. (1952) Responses of young children to separation from their mothers, *Courier of the International Children's Centre, Paris* 2: 131–140.

Robertson, J. and Robertson, J. (1967–73) *Young Children in Brief Separation*, film series, Ipswich: Concord Films.

Rodning, C. Beckwith, L. and Howard, J. (1991) Quality of attachment and home environments in children pre-natally exposed to PCP and cocaine, *Development and Psychopathology* 3: 351–366.

Rosenblatt, P.C., Walsh, R.P. and Jackson, D.A. (1976) *Grief and Mourning in Cross-Cultural Perspective*, Washington, DC: HRAF Press.

Rosenstein, D. and Horowitz, H.A. (1996) Adolescents attachment and psycho-pathology, *Journal of Consulting and Clinical Psychology* 64: 244–253.

Rutter, M. (1972) *Maternal Deprivation Reassessed*, Harmondsworth: Penguin.

Sanders, C.M., Mauger, P.A. and Strong, P.A. (1991) *A Manual for the Grief Experience Inventory*, Palo Alto, CA: Consulting Psychologists Press.

Scarf, M. (1973) Goodall and the chimpanzees at Yale, *New York Times Magazine* 18 February.

Scharlach, A.E. and Fredriksen, K.I. (1993) Reactions to the death of a parent during midlife, *Omega* 27, 4: 307–320.

Scheper-Hughes, N. (1992) *Death Without Weeping: The Violence of Everyday Life in Brazil*, Berkeley, CA: University of California Press.

Schuengel, C. and van Ijsendoorn, M.H. (2001) Attachment in mental health institutions: a critical review of assumptions, clinical implications and research strategies, *Attachment and Human Development* 3, 3: 304–323.

Schuengel, C., van Ijsendoorn, M.H. and Bakermans-Kranenberg, M.J. (1999) Frightening maternal behavior linking unresolved loss and disorganised infant attachment attachment, *Journal of Consulting and Clinical Psychology* 67, 1: 54–63.

Schut, H., de Keijser, J., van den Bout, J. and Stroebe, M.S. (1997a) Cross-modality grief therapy: description and assessment of a new program, *Journal of Clinical Psychology* 52, 3: 357–365.

Schut, H.A.W., Stroebe, M.S., van den Bout, J. and de Keijser, J. (1997b) Intervention for the bereaved: gender differences in the efficacy of two counseling programs, *British Journal of Clinical Psychology* 36: 63–72.

Schut, H., Stroebe, M.S., van den Bout, J. and Terheggen, M. (2001) The efficacy of bereavement interventions: determining who benefits, in M.S. Stroebe, R.O. Hansson, W. Stroebe and H. Schut (eds) *Handbook of Bereavement Research: Consequences, Coping and Care*, Washington, DC: American Psychological Association Press, pp. 705–737.

Senchak, M. and Leonard, K. (1992) Attachment style and marital adjustment among newlywed couples, *Journal of Social and Personal Relationships* 9: 51–64.

Seligman, M.E.P. (1975) *Helplessness*, San Francisco: Freeman.

Shaver, P.R. and Mikulincer, M. (2002) Attachment-related psychodynamics, *Attachment and Human Development* 4, 2: 133–161.

Shaver, P. R., Belsky, J. and Brennan, K. A. (2000). The Adult Attachment Interview and self reports of romantic attachment: associations across domains and methods, *Personal Relationships* 7: 25–43.

Sikkema, K.J., Hansen, N.B., Kochman, A., Tate, D.C. and Defranciesco, W. (2004) Outcomes from a randomised controlled trial of a group intervention for HIV positive men and women coping with AIDS-related loss and bereavement, *Death Studies* 28, 3: 187–210.

Silverman, G.K., Johnson, J.G., Prigerson, H.G. (2001) Preliminary explorations of the effects of prior trauma and loss on risk for psychiatric disorders in recently widowed people, *Israel Journal of Psychiatry and Related Sciences* 38: 202–215.

Simpson, J.A. and Rholes, W.S. (1994) Stress and secure base relationships in adulthood, in K. Bartholomew and D. Perlman (eds) *Advances in Personal Relationships, Vol. 5: Attachment Processes in Adulthood*, London: Jessica Kingsley Publishers, pp. 181–204.

Simpson, J.A., Rholes, W.S. and Nelligan, J.S. (1992) Support-seeking and support-giving within couples in an anxiety-provoking situation: the integration of three behavioral systems, in R.J. Sternberg and M. Barnes (eds) *The Psychology of Love*, New Haven, CT: Yale University Press, pp. 434–46.

Sireling, L., Cohen, D. and Marks, I. (1988) Guided mourning for morbid grief: a controlled replication, *Behavior Therapy* 19: 121–132.

Spangler, G. and Grossmann, K.E. (1993) Biobehavioral organization in securely and insecurely attached infants, *Child Development* 64: 1439–1450.

Sperling, M.B. and Berman, W.H. (eds) (1994) *Attachment in Adults: Clinical and Developmental Perspectives*, New York: Guilford Press.

Sroufe, L.A. (1983) Infant–caregiver attachment and patterns of adaptation in pre-school: the roots of maladaptation and competence, in M. Perlmutter (ed.) *The Minnesota Symposia on Child Psychology: Vol. 16. Development and Policy Concerning Children with Special Needs*. Hillsdale, NJ: Lawrence Erlbaum Associates Inc, pp. 41–83.

Sroufe, L.A. and Waters, E. (1977) Heart rate as a convergent measure in clinical and developmental research, *Merrill-Palmer Quarterly* 23: 3–27.

Steele, H. and Steele, M. (1994) Intergenerational patterns of attachment, *Attachment Advances in Personal Relationships* 5: 93–120.

Steele, H., Steele, M. and Fonagy, P. (1996) Associations among attachment classifications of mothers, fathers and their infants, *Child Development* 67: 541–555.

Stewart, M.F. (1999) *Companion Animal Death: A Practical and Comprehensive Guide for Veterinary Practice*, Oxford: Butterworth/Heinemann.

Stroebe, M.S. and Schut, H. (2001a) Models of coping with bereavement: a review, in M. S. Stroebe, W. Stroebe and R.O. Hansson (eds) *Handbook of Bereavement*, Cambridge: Cambridge University Press, pp. 375–404.

Stroebe, W. and Schut, H. (2001b) Risk factors in coping with bereavement: a methodological and empirical review, in M.S. Stroebe, W. Stroebe and R.O. Hansson (eds) *Handbook of Bereavement*, Cambridge: Cambridge University Press, pp. 349–372.

Stroebe, M. and Stroebe, W. (1983) Who suffers more? Sex differences in health risks of the widowed, *Psychological Bulletin* 93: 297–301.

Stroebe, M.S. and Stroebe, W. (1993) Determinants of adjustment to bereavement in younger widows and widowers, in M.S. Stroebe, W. Stroebe and R.O. Hansson (eds) *Handbook of Bereavement* Cambridge: Cambridge University Press, pp. 208–226.

Stroebe, M.S., Hansson, R.O., Stroebe, W. and Schut, H. (eds) (2001) *Handbook of Bereavement Research: Consequences, Coping and Care*, Washington, DC: American Psychological Association Press.

Struhsaker, T. T. (1967) Auditory communication among vervet monkeys, in S. A. Altmann (ed.) *Social Communication among Primates*, Chicago: University of Chicago Press.

Tarnow, J.D. (1987) Pediatric and adolescent patients in rehabilitation, in D. W.

Krueger (ed.) *Emotional Rehabilitation of Physical Trauma and Disability*, New York: Spectrum.

Tatelbaum, J. (1997) *The Courage to Grieve*, London: Random House.

Theut, S.K., Jordan, L., Ross, L.A. and Deutsch, S.I. (1991) Caregiver's anticipatory grief in dementia, *International Journal of Ageing and Human Development* 33, 2: 113–118.

Umberson, D. and Chen, M.D. (1994) Effects of a parent's death on adult children: relationship salience and reaction to loss, *American Sociology Review* 59: 152–168.

Vachon, M.L.S., Roger, J., Lyall, W.A., Lancee, W.J., Sheldon, A.R. and Freeman, S.J. (1982) Predictors and correlates of adaptation to conjugal bereavement, *American Journal of Psychiatry* 139: 998–1002.

Vanderwerker, L.C., Jacobs, S.C., Parkes, C.M. and Prigerson, H.G. (2006) Childhood separation anxiety as a risk for complicated grief in later life, *Journal of Nervous and Mental Diseases*, in press.

Van Ijzendoorn, M. H. and Bakermans-Kranenburg, M. J. (1996) Attachment representations in mothers, fathers, adolescents, and clinical groups: a meta-analytic search for normative data, *Journal of Consulting and Clinical Psychology* 64, 1: 8–21.

Van Ijzendoorn, M.H., Kranenburg, M.J., Zwart-Woudstra, H.A. and van Busschbach, A.M. (1991) Parental attachment and children's socio-economical development: some findings in the validity of the adult Attachment Interview in the Netherlands, *International Journal of Behavioral Development* 14: 375–394.

Van Ijzendoorn, M.H., Feldbrugge, J.T.T.M., Derks, F.C.H., de Ruiter, C., Verhagen, M.F.M., Philipse, M.W.G., van der Staak, C.P.F. and Riksen-Walraven, J.M.A. (1997) Attachment representations of personality disordered criminal offenders, *American Journal of Orthopsychiatry* 67: 449–459.

Van Tilburg, M.A., Vingerhoets, A.J. and Van Heck, G.L. (1996) Homesickness: a review of the literature, *Psychological Medicine* 26, 5: 899–912.

Warner, J., Metcalfe, C. and King, M. (2001) Evaluating the use of benzo-diazepines following recent bereavement, *British Journal of Psychiatry* 178: 36–41.

Warren, S.L., Huston, L., Egeland, B. and Sroufe, L.A. (1997) Child and adolescent anxiety disorders and early attachment, *Journal of the American Academy of Child and Adolescent Psychiatry* 36: 637–644.

Wartner, U.G., Grossmann, K., Fremmer-Bombik, E. and Suess, G. (1994) Attachment patterns at aged six in south Germany: predictability from infancy and implications for preschool behavior, *Child Development* 65: 1014–1027.

Waskowic, T.D. and Chartier, B.M. (2003) Attachment and the experience of grief following the loss of a spouse, *Omega* 47, 1: 77–91.

Waters, E., Merrick, S., Treboux, D., Crowell J. and Albersheim, L. (2005) Attachment security in infancy and early adulthood: a twenty-year longitudinal study, *Child Development* 71: 684–689.

Weekes, C. (1984) *Self-Help With Your Nerves*, New York: Angus and Robertson.

Weinfeld, N.S., Whaley, G.J.L. and Egeland, B. (2004) Continuity, discontinuity and coherence in attachment from infancy to late adolescence: sequelae of organization and disorganization, *Attachment and Human Development* 6, 1: 73–97.

Welch, M. (1988) *Holding Time*, New York: Simon and Schuster.

Wilkinson, S.R. (2003) *Coping and Complaining: Attachment and the Language of Dis-ease*, London: Brunner-Routledge.

Woods, T. (2000) Unpublished lecture to Society for Companion Animal Studies.

World Guide (2000) *World Guide 1999–2000: A View from the South*, Oxford: New Internationalist.

Wortman, C.B. and Silver, R.C. (1989) The myths of coping with loss, *Journal of Consulting and Clinical Psychology* 57: 349–357.

Yüksel, S. and Olgun-Özpolat, T. (2004) Psychological problems associated with traumatic loss in Turkey, *Bereavement Care* 23, 1: 5–7.

Zimmermann, P. and Grossmann, K. (1996) *Transgenerational aspects of stability in attachment quality between parents and their adolescent children*, paper presented at International Society for the Study of Behavioral Development, Quebec, Canada.

Zisook, S., Shuchter, S.R., Pedrelli, P., Sable, J. and Deauciuc, S.C. (2001) Buproprion sustained release for bereavement: results of an open trial, *Journal of Clinical Psychiatry* 62, 4: 227–230.

Index